GLOBAL
POLITICS

AGGIE HIRST

DIEGO DE MERICH

JOE HOOVER

ROBERTO ROCCU

GLOBAL POLITICS

MYTHS AND MYSTERIES

1ST EDITION

OXFORD
UNIVERSITY PRESS

Great Clarendon Street, Oxford, OX2 6DP,
United Kingdom

Oxford University Press is a department of the University of Oxford.
It furthers the University's objective of excellence in research, scholarship,
and education by publishing worldwide. Oxford is a registered trade mark of
Oxford University Press in the UK and in certain other countries

Published in the United States of America by Oxford University Press
198 Madison Avenue, New York, NY 10016, United States of America

British Library Cataloguing in Publication Data
Data available

Library of Congress Control Number: 2022943696

ISBN 978–0–19–882082–6

Printed in the UK by
Bell & Bain Ltd., Glasgow

ACKNOWLEDGEMENTS

Creating a new textbook, in a discipline as pluralistic and existentially anxious as International Relations (IR), requires a great deal of effort on the part of many people. From the outset, we approached this project as a group endeavour involving many engaging discussions, the sharing and revising of multiple draft chapters, and a conscious effort to link themes and concepts across the volume. As colleagues and friends, we learned from one another, poked, prodded, and suggested when needed, and delighted in the many instances where new examples or interpretations helped to illuminate an idea in ways we hadn't anticipated. What has emerged—we hope—after several years of working in this mode is a shared voice that reflects our common pedagogical style, while retaining features of our individual research interests across political and IR theory, critical war studies, Deweyan pragmatism, care ethics, and critical IPE.

The impetus for this book came from an undergraduate module developed by Aggie and Joe while at City, University of London, along with Amin Samman, whom we wish to thank for his contributions at this early stage. For the long journey from the book's inception to print, our many thanks go to the editors and production team at OUP. Thank you to Sarah Iles, to whom the project was originally pitched and who assisted us in securing the contract with OUP, and to Katie Staal, whose patience, efficiency, and thoughtful interventions have kept the project on course to fruition. Thank you to our many reviewers whose comments and incisive feedback we engaged with carefully to improve the text. We hope that the end result is a book that you would be happy to use in your classes and seminars. We would also like to thank Sophie Crowe at QMUL for producing the ancillary and online materials for the book. Sophie's help was made possible by the European & International Studies Research Fund at King's College London.

In taking a new approach to the classical IR theory textbook, we realised how indebted we are to the inspiring teachers who were instrumental in shaping our own passion for making sense of the world around us, and for sharing that passion with our own students. Aggie wishes to thank Stephen Rigby, without whose encouragement—and fiendishly difficult final year module—she would likely never have gained the confidence to undertake a PhD and pursue an academic career, and also Tom Houseman for the leap of faith of our first teaching experience. Diego is forever grateful to the kind and brilliant Henry Thomas, whose UWC *Adriatic* classes in English Literature and World Cultures were like a 'big bang' that invited his students' curiosity about art, music, culture, and the social world to expand like the cosmos. Joe wishes to thank Claudia Mills, whose classes made political and ethical philosophy a living and vital endeavour, and Kim Hutchings, Chris Brown, and Kirsten Ainley, whose example illustrates the power and importance of bringing political theory into conversation with international and global politics. Roberto is grateful to his late aunt Elena Roccu, Latin high school teacher, for instilling a healthy scepticism of 'flavour-of-the-month' approaches to literature and much more, for never hiding the many frustrations—but also countless rewards—of teaching, and for the serendipitous ripples that long after her passing still bring so much joy to his life.

While this project was developed through the early stages of our academic careers, we have now accrued a combined forty years of teaching experience, and so our biggest thanks go to our many students. It is because of them that we seek to constantly better our own teaching practices—to make the words of ancient, modern, and contemporary scholars alike come alive in classrooms and lecture halls; to help demonstrate how the concepts and lines of inquiry of our discipline are, in fact, deeply pertinent to their daily lives. For each of us, the roles of educator and facilitator of thoughtful debate are integral to being an academic. We are grateful for all of the 'aha' moments which appeared on the faces of our students—a delight for any teacher!—and we hope that this volume provides you, the reader, with such moments too.

While theory is often criticised by students for being too abstract or complicated, we hope to demonstrate in these pages that it is very much a lived and ongoing practical activity of reflection and revision, engagement and contestation. In our understanding, *theory is a verb*; something you can constantly interrogate, expand upon, and *do*, rather than simply read and apply. We hope that this volume will prove a useful guide as you set out on your adventures in making sense of the complicated and colourful political landscapes you inhabit, from the local to the global.

Aggie, Diego, Joe, and Roberto

BRIEF CONTENTS

DETAILED CONTENTS

ABOUT THE AUTHORS

Dr Aggie Hirst is Reader in International Relations Theory and Methods at King's College London. Situated in international political theory and critical military studies, her research focuses on play, games, and violence.

Dr Diego de Merich is Senior Lecturer in Politics and International Relations at Queen Mary University of London. His research focuses on care ethics, human affect and empathy, on equalities mainstreaming in public policy, and on the ethics of international development.

Dr Joe Hoover is Senior Lecturer in Political Theory at Queen Mary University of London. His work examines questions of global ethics drawing on philosophical pragmatism and agonistic political theory.

Dr Roberto Roccu is Reader in International Political Economy at King's College London. His research focuses on different dimensions of the impact of globalisation and neoliberal restructuring on the Middle East and North Africa.

GUIDE TO THE ONLINE RESOURCES

 www.oup.com/he/hirst1e

This textbook is accompanied by many helpful additional resources for both students and lecturers, providing opportunities to consolidate understanding and further develop skills of critical analysis, and applying IR theory to practice.

STUDENT RESOURCES

Extended IR case studies encourage you to apply theories to current and evolving global events

Further reading lists provide annotated suggestions of further reading recommendations to guide you through your reading

Web links to journal articles, blogs, and video content to deepen your understanding of key topics and explore your research interests

Interactive flashcards of key terms and concepts from the book, so you can check your understanding of IR terminology

LECTURER RESOURCES

These resources are password-protected, but access is available to anyone using the book in their teaching. Please contact your local sales representative.

Customisable **PowerPoint® slides**, arranged by chapter, for use in lectures or as hand-outs to support efficient, effective teaching preparation

A **Question bank** of seminar activity and essay questions encourages critical reflection on core issues and themes within each chapter

INTRODUCTION
MYTH-MAKING

1

1.1 OUR INTUITIVE UNDERSTANDINGS OF GLOBAL POLITICS

We all know things about global politics before we study it at university. And we all know things about global politics before we learn about theories that try to make sense of global events and relationships. In your everyday lives, you experience global politics as a matter of course. From a climate or anti-racism protest in your neighbourhood to global crises like the Russian invasion of Ukraine and the Covid-19 pandemic, global politics is all around us. You will likely have seen news reports about political actors, for example scandals involving politicians or activists protesting police violence. And you might have heard about campaigns around issues like LGBTQIA+ equality or global finance involving institutions such as the United Nations or the World Bank. You may follow global political events in news programmes or social media, and have debated with friends and family the merits of humanitarian intervention or a universal basic income. You might also be aware of deeper structural processes and habits of thought that are political in character, for instance norms about gender or ethics. These arrangements and dynamics shape how we think and talk about global politics, and even how we act politically.

The things we already know about global politics are often latent and unarticulated, picked up as we go about our everyday lives. For example, a person might support a particular political party because their family has always done so rather than because they have really thought about it. We also consciously learn by hearing, reading, and repeating ideas about global politics that circulate around us. For instance, the person might one day decide to stop supporting a political party because they have learned more about its principles and record. Beginning our study of global politics with an exploration of the knowledge we already have is important for two reasons. First, learning to think critically about our intuitive understanding **empowers** us by alerting us to assumptions or gaps in it. Second, critical thinking shows us that our intuitive understanding of global politics may rely on myths. Such myths may seem to solve the messy, confusing, and mysterious puzzles of global politics. But they may also rely upon assumptions and stories that obscure as much as they reveal.

So, we all already know something about global politics. But these intuitive understandings are not neutral. We have all internalised **narratives** about what global politics is and how to explain the events we observe, but those narratives are shaped by **power relations**. Power relations influence who gets to tell the stories that make up global politics, and the kinds of stories that are told. They thus reflect **privileged** experiences of global politics, a privilege that is strengthened as these stories get told and retold, ultimately coming to function as truths. However, when looked at more closely, some of the most seemingly obvious or natural truths turn out to be based on myths.

For example, you may have heard statements from politicians or historical figures such as 'might makes right' or 'men should be the head of the household because they are physically stronger than women'. You may have argued with a family member or friend about a claim such as 'imperialism is a thing of the past', 'capitalism is the only viable economic system', or 'we are ethically responsible to people inside the borders of our state but not those outside'. Each of these statements confidently expresses a specific conventional wisdom used to determine and justify political beliefs and actions. And each of the statements has been made by a particular individual or group, and they will have particular (although not always conscious) reasons for advocating them. Statements like this can become deeply ingrained, and influence people's ideas and identities as common-sense norms. For example, they might lead people to believe that there is no place for ethics in global politics, that people of different genders are fundamentally unequal, or that we have no obligation to assist people seeking refuge from conflicts occurring outside our region. However, they often amount more to myths than factually grounded statements.

As this suggests, our intuitive understanding often rests on inherited truths, for example about human nature, the necessity of authority and hierarchy, or the impossibility of social or economic change. Like the narratives and principles that give shape to our intuitive understandings, these truths are the products of conventional thinking. Such inherited wisdom tends to express the interests and inequalities of our world, but it often lacks critical and reflective thinking. We believe that critical thinking is extremely important if we are to understand and try to improve the world around us. Because of this belief, this book starts from our intuitive understanding of global politics, and our desire to further develop that understanding by studying at university. Its aim is to help you develop skills to refine your understanding, to make it more reflective and critical, and to empower you to become an active participant in the study of global politics.

One way of improving our intuitive understandings of global politics is examining the narratives, principles, and apparent truths that underpin them. We will speak about this underpinning as the *myths* about global politics that shape our experiences and understandings. These myths make sense of global politics—its puzzles, problems, and paradoxes—but they also disempower us because they rest on convention, established power relations, and particular interests that should be questioned. Yet even as we seek to challenge the myths we inherit, and the ways of thinking that are uncritical of these myths, we also recognise that myths can be valuable. Myths can provide us with ways of understanding the world, giving us a common language to discuss global politics, and directing us towards possibilities for acting politically. Consequently, our goal is not to do away with myth but rather to help you *recognise* and *see beyond* these myths, and to bring to light their effects on our understandings of global politics.

As a first step, it is important to recognise that our intuitive understandings are likely to be limited in some way. While we may have thought hard about some of our beliefs, others we may have accepted just because they seem obvious or normal. We believe it is important to question our intuitive assumptions and, if necessary, revise them. Because of this, throughout this book you'll be invited to undertake a series of 'Reflective Activities' as you read. These activities ask you to think about and take a view on the subject matter discussed. They are not tests, there are no 'correct' answers, and you are not expected to stick with your original intuitive responses. Rather, the aim is for you to draw out your existing ideas and beliefs, and actively reflect upon them, through a process of *critical thinking*. Having done some critical thinking about your existing views in these activities, you may decide to stick with them or to change them. Here is the first one:

REFLECTIVE ACTIVITY 1.1

Take a pause and consider this statement:

> *'Politics can never truly be "ethical" because power always corrupts those who wield it.'*

Do you agree or disagree? And why do you take this view? Consider whether your view has been influenced by particular people or ideas, and think about how you came to hold it. Do you think these are good reasons to hold your view? Make a note of your answers.

Through critical reflection of this kind, we become more aware of our assumptions and spot gaps in our reasoning. While considering this statement, you may have thought that your view is based on solid arguments or reasoning, and therefore you stand by it. Or you may have reflected that you're not quite sure why you hold the view you hold—it's just an assumption you have. You might equally have thought that your views are not based on sufficiently solid arguments after all, and that you need to take more time to consider and research the issues to decide where you stand. The point here is not that there is a correct answer—indeed philosophers have argued about this point for centuries—but to realise that if we put existing views under the microscope and ask the question 'why do I think what I think?', our understanding and knowledge will improve. This is precisely the point of studying at university.

A second step in improving our intuitive understanding, and overcoming limiting myths about global politics, is to adopt a similar critical orientation towards the **academic disciplines** and theories we use to study global politics. We think it is vital that students, from the start of their time at university, think critically about the theories and traditions of thought used to study global politics. This is because academic fields are also shaped by myths, though these are often more comprehensive than popular myths. In fact, many popular myths about global politics are informed by academic theories and traditions, and vice versa.

So, just like our intuitive understanding, academic disciplines have their myths. Like all myths, they can be useful sometimes. In the field of **International Relations** (IR) different theoretical perspectives, for example, are built on myths. For instance, realists think human beings are naturally prone to competition and violence, while Liberalism is based on a uto-pian faith in progress. These myths provide convenient shorthands, but we do not want them to become unquestioned ideas that determine what and how students think about global politics. We think it is better to see these myths as emerging out of a wider and longer academic conversation about global politics. As a student you are already a part of that conversation. Even before you start your studies you will have picked up snippets of it, and throughout your university experience you will be surrounded by it. We want you to move from listening to that conversation to *contributing* to it.

Our focus in this book is to help you learn to engage in this ongoing conversation by thinking theoretically. Our aim is to help you improve your understanding of global politics by *empowering* you to think theoretically and critically in a way that debunks myths (both those in your own thinking and those in academic debates) by challenging and resisting the power of conventional wisdom. It also encourages you to engage in theorising, contribut-ing to the ongoing work of answering questions and making better stories to improve our understanding of the complexities of global politics. And, finally, we also hope the book will help you see a broader horizon of possibilities within which to *act politically*.

This approach to theory and theorising is different to most introductory texts and mod-ules. The standard introduction to theory in IR presents students with a catalogue of exist-ing theoretical approaches. This often involves beginning with the 'traditional' IR theories, including **Liberalism**, **Realism**, and **Constructivism**. From there, such an introduction pre-sents the 'critical' IR theories, like **Marxism**, **Feminism**, **Postcolonial/Decolonial Theory**, and **Poststructuralism**. In this conventional approach, students are invited to read about and discuss each of these established '-isms' in turn, and to ultimately choose between them in order to claim: 'I am a realist' or 'I am a feminist', and so on. Having spent a combined forty years teaching theory, we believe this approach is limited for three main reasons.

First, this approach presents theory as a ready-made object to be accepted or rejected rather than a series of ongoing conversations and contestations. This has the effect of posi-tioning students 'outside' the debates and implying the thinking has already been done by the academic theorists whose views students are compelled to adopt. Second, this approach implicitly tells students to leave their existing ideas, and their motivations for doing a degree in the field, at the door. By channelling theory conversations through the existing '-isms', the space for thinking and theorising is narrowed in advance, and students are implicitly positioned as user-consumers, rather than creators, of theoretical knowledge. This has the effect of delimiting in advance the topics and ideas up for debate. Third, this approach decouples theory from the real world from which it emerges. For example, feminist theory is often taught in IR abstracted from the global social movements or activism in which it was generated. And Liberalism is frequently presented in IR without sufficient exploration of its role in the maintenance of empire. Such abstraction often leaves students with the impression that theory is separate from the real world, as though disconnected from their more empirical modules. This can make theory appear an optional, and sometimes inconvenient, 'add-on' to their studies.

Against this standard approach, we believe theory is not a spectator sport but rather an active process of *doing critical thinking*. In other words, we believe theory is a *verb*. This means we seek to show students that they are already part of theoretical conversations. Theorising is not, as the standard approach implies, an activity done only by academic experts or long-dead philosophers. Nor is it disconnected from the concrete political world. Rather, theorising is for *everyone*! And it happens whenever we think about or study the political world, and our place within it. And as our societies grapple with rectifying the exclusions suffered by people of colour, queer and trans people, disabled people, women, and other marginalised groups in processes of knowledge production, it is all the more important that everyone takes part in debates about big questions. Affirming your place in, and potential contribution to, these ongoing conversations, will encourage your interest in global politics, improve your understanding, and further develop your ability to think critically and independently. And, if we may be more hopeful still, by encouraging you to be an active participant in theorising, we hope to empower you to act politically too.

In Section 1.2 we discuss the idea of 'mysteries' as a series of enduring puzzles about global politics, and 'myths' as a collection of narratives, principles, and truths that function as convenient, but not always robust, solutions to these puzzles. In order to clearly show what we mean by this, we will set out the specific myths and mysteries examined in the book. Having laid this groundwork, we demonstrate that global politics happens all around us—for example, when we use money, travel to another country, or deal with state authorities. Introducing the idea of '*everyday global politics*', we show that studying the political world is deeply connected to the everyday lives we each live. From there, the chapter explores what we mean by *thinking theoretically*, why we think students should be encouraged to theorise from the start of their studies, and why the myths upon which our intuitive understandings of politics are based are a good place to start this theorising. In addition, we discuss how this book will prepare you to study the theories and traditions of thought that shape the academic study of global politics.

1.2 MYTHS AND MYSTERIES

The global political landscape is littered with puzzles that have kept academics—including philosophers, political scientists and theorists, and economists—contemplating and arguing for centuries. Some believe politics is governed by laws similar to those found in nature, while others think political relationships and events follow no such fixed patterns. Some argue that change is possible and desirable, while others suggest humans are doomed to make the same mistakes over and over again. Some believe that elites hold all the power, while others argue it is ordinary people who can alter the course of things. One way of thinking about these puzzles is as '*mysteries*'. In this book, we are interested in addressing a series of these enduring mysteries about global politics in order to consider both what you currently think about them, and to exercise critical thinking to see whether your views change.

If a mystery is a puzzle, a '*myth*' is a story or narrative used to resolve that puzzle. Importantly, it is not the only possible solution to the puzzle. And often it rests on assumptions rather than solid reasoning. It may seem strange that we have given myths such a prominent role in a textbook about global politics. Our intuitive understanding of myths may bring to mind fantastical stories or ancient tales. We might think that myths are entertaining diversions found in animated films, fantasy literature, or urban legends. We may reflect that myth sounds unserious, premodern, and prescientific, a concept out of place in a book about the academic study of global politics. Myths might appear as mere stories told to serve a political end, an idea as old as Plato's *Republic* (see Chapter 2) but still very much with us today. For example, the nostalgic promise made by former US President Donald Trump to 'Make America Great Again' mobilised national myths deeply rooted in US political culture and values.

In this book we are using the idea of myth as a widely held solution to a specific mystery about global politics. While a particular myth is not the only possible solution, it is a powerful one that can make it look as though the mystery is resolved. In other words, 'political myths are . . . understood by most modern theorists as either a powerful paradigmatic narrative or a deeply engrained commonly held belief' (Bliesemann de Guevara, 2016, 1). The function of these myths is to organise the world for us and make it more easily intelligible—they underpin our common-sense understanding of the world. But myths should not be accepted without question. Rather, they simplify, distort, and produce our understanding. And they make it possible for us to accept as natural things we might otherwise resist.

Myths have this function for our intuitive understanding of global politics, but they are also a feature of the academic study of global politics, and its theorisation. As IR professor Cynthia Weber writes:

> The myth function in IR theory is the transformation of what is particular, cultural, and ideological . . . into what *appears* to be universal, natural, and purely empirical. It is naturalizing meanings—making them into common sense—that are the products of cultural practice. Put another way, the myth function in IR theory is making a 'fact' out of an interpretation (2020, 6–7).

Focusing on the function of myth in our understanding of global politics reveals that in both our everyday and academic understandings of global politics we are not simply encountering an objective reality as detached observers. Rather, it shows that what we see, how we see, and how we talk about that seeing are influenced by the histories, cultures, and politics we are born into. Identifying the myths that shape our understanding of global politics, and finding a language to speak about them, enables us to understand global politics, and our place in it, with greater insight.

At the start of this chapter, we discussed myths in terms of narratives, principles, and truths that we have learned unconsciously. As Weber notes, the philosopher Roland Barthes (2000) describes myths as a structure of meaning, lying beneath and informing the things we say explicitly. This unspoken quality is both what gives myths their power and makes them difficult to identify and interrogate. As narratives, political myths tell stories about how political life functions, who the protagonists and antagonists are, what the central conflicts are, and how these stories should resolve. Throughout the chapters that follow we will encounter many such stories. In addition, these stories include ideas and claims about how things should be: mythical stories guide our actions. Finally, the stories and actions myths narrate rest on unexamined (and often unarticulated) 'truths' about the world and human nature.

To illustrate this idea, we can think about the practice of humanitarian intervention, particularly as it developed in the 1990s and 2000s. As an explicit policy, humanitarian intervention is based on the principle that the norm of non-intervention, which prevents one sovereign state from interfering in the affairs of another, should be disregarded when the government of a sovereign state is violating the rights of its people. Yet the application of that principle, especially by powerful Western states, is shaped by myths about the legitimacy and beneficence of those states. As Anne Orford (1999) highlights, the emergence of military humanitarian intervention at the end of the 20th century drew on a narrative in which powerful Western states played the role of 'heroes' called in to save the poor and unfortunate victims of 'illiberal' or 'failed' states. This narrative justified the principle that liberal Western states had a special obligation to do something (a 'responsibility to protect'), both because of their capacity to act and their unique legitimacy in the post-Cold War international system. Both the saviour narrative of humanitarian intervention and the principle that 'something must be done', were underpinned by the 'truth' that wealthy liberal states embodied the best possible political and economic arrangements. This gave their actions legitimacy and obscured their often direct and harmful role in perpetuating humanitarian crises and rights violations.

Myth-making of this sort is rarely achieved by the intentional actions of a discrete group of people. Myths are not conspiracies. Rather, as Halvard Leira and Benjamin de Carvalho argue, 'myths and myth-making are an inescapable part of the life of human collectives, and related to the need for cognitive consistency and understanding. Old myths might be discarded, but there is every reason to believe that what replaces them is in some way or another yet another myth' (2018, 223). To illustrate this, think about your own use of social media in which you select links, words, images, or videos to represent yourself online. The images you post, for example, are not simply documenting your reality, they are selected for what they say about you, where you fit in socially, the values you hold, and things you do—but to communicate in this way you have to be aware of, and mobilise, existing stories. All of us engage in myth-making some of the time, often without realising it.

Myth renders that which is historical, cultural, and political into something natural and obvious, into our common sense. And while some myths are particularly dangerous and damaging, demystification is not about eliminating myths. Rather, it is about seeing how myths function and how they obscure, simplify, and narrow our experience and understanding. Therefore, myths can function both ideologically—naturalising and depoliticising that which is contingent and political—but also constructively—legitimising and enabling communication and collective action, which can be necessary and positive. Myths are part of how we make sense of the world, so the goal is not to distinguish simply between myths as lies and demystification as truth, but rather to recognise that myths are a part of our understanding of global politics, seeking to understand their function, and enabling ourselves to critique and challenge the myths, while recognising that the process of myth-making does not stop.

Weber elaborates on this point, speaking specifically about the myths of IR theory:

> By disrupting the *apparent truth* of IR myths, opportunities arise for new theories of IR to be written. Yet these, too, will be myths. So why bother interrogating the myth function in IR theory if we will never escape it? The answer to this question is in the question itself. *Because we will never escape the myth function in IR theory, we had better interrogate it.* We had better prepare ourselves to be the best critical readers of IR myths we possibly can be. Otherwise, we will just be repeating cherished stories of IR myths without grasping what makes these stories *appear* to be true, without appreciating what makes them function. We will be circulating a particular way of making sense of the world without knowing how to make sense of that sense. That would make us look pretty naïve (2020, 8).

What is suggested here is that reading, interrogating, and making (better) myths is central to taking part in the ongoing conversations that try to make sense of global politics. As Weber notes, theories rely on myth to become conventional wisdom, to function as ideology, to relieve us of the need to do the work of critical inquiry. And while we think it is vital to constantly resist the naturalising of myth by way of critical inquiry, we cannot interrogate everything all at once—we will live with some myths, we will reject others, and we will make new myths. Therefore, we think it is essential to move from accepting myths to becoming critical myth explorers. Equally, we believe it is vital not simply to understand established theories but to learn to theorise. We thus challenge the myth that theory is only for those with special training or aptitude. Theorising is something we all already do and something we can all benefit from learning to do better.

1.2.1 MYTHS AND MYSTERIES IN THIS BOOK

So, what myths and mysteries will we explore in this book? **Chapter 2: Politics** explores the mystery of what politics is, and where politics operates at the global level. It examines and challenges the myth that only powerful elites engage in politics, showing instead that politics is at work all the time in our everyday lives and experience. In doing so, it shows that *becoming political*, understood as learning to think critically about the political world, is itself a political act. This is because it alters our everyday understanding of the world around us and thereby opens up new possibilities for action.

From there, **Chapter 3: Power** explores the mystery of how power works in global politics, and contests the myth that power is simply a coercive force that elite actors use to promote their interests. Against this myth, the chapter shows that power is 'productive' in the sense that it *produces things* like knowledge, social norms, and even identity. Understood in this way, the chapter seeks to uncover some of the subtle ways power influences our lives and, crucially, how an awareness of *power relations* can open up possibilities for resistance and change in global politics.

Developing these ideas about power relations, **Chapter 4: Ethics** examines the mystery of why people often claim that ethics has no place in global politics. Against the myth that ethics and politics are antithetical, the chapter shows that ethics is more than a series of rules of laws that govern our behaviour, and that thinking theoretically about the relationship between ethics and politics is a truly global endeavour.

Having explored the relationship between politics and ethics, **Chapter 5: Violence** deals with the mystery of why, despite the rise of institutions and legal systems designed to prevent it, violence remains so pervasive in global politics. To do this, it challenges the myth that violence is only physical in character and questions the assumption that violence carried out by states is legitimate while nonstate violence is illegitimate. It also explores whether and how we can work towards non-violence in global politics. Against a fatalistic view that infers that because it is ubiquitous we should be resigned to the inevitability of violence, the chapter shows that we all have the power to reduce violence in global politics.

Chapter 6: Law focuses on the mystery of how law has come to function as a fundamental form of authority in global politics. It reveals the flaws in the myth that international law provides a form of moral authority justifying the rules, institutions, and enforcement mechanisms that will civilise global politics and make it more peaceful and just. At the same time, it demonstrates the limitations of the myth that international law is an impossibility, as global politics is dominated by the struggle for survival between states and their conflicting self-interest.

Chapter 7: Money examines the mystery of the origins and function of money in global politics. It challenges the myth that money developed in a politically neutral way as the most functional mode of exchange, showing instead that the power and violence of empire—including conquest and enslavement—were central to the emergence and functioning of money. It also explores some possible futures of money, such as cryptocurrencies and local currencies, and the challenges these might pose to the historically strong link between money and state power.

Building on this analysis, **Chapter 8: Empire** explores the mystery of why people claim that imperialism is a thing of the past, why some people are nostalgic about empires, and why the field of IR has conventionally sidelined issues of imperialism and racism. The purpose of the chapter is to contest the myth that imperialism has come to an end, showing instead that many of the imperial attitudes, racialised power hierarchies, and material inequalities that structured the era of empires remain in place today. In light of this, it invites you to consider whether and how IR might take account of its imperial origins, and the ways in which academia more generally could work in promotion of decolonisation and anti-racism.

Chapter 9: Capitalism addresses the mystery of why many people claim that capitalism is the only viable economic system. The chapter contests the myth that capitalism operates as a system of free enterprise independent of state involvement, and shows that, rather than operating in a separate economic sphere, capitalism is a deeply political system with far-reaching effects on the international system today. In doing so, it invites you to think about why it is so difficult to imagine a world beyond capitalism—both as an economic but also as a political system—and to nevertheless try to do precisely this.

Having explored these political dimensions of capitalism, **Chapter 10: The State** explores the mystery of why the state is treated in IR as the most—or in some theories the only—important actor in global politics. To do this, it challenges the myth that the state is the locus of power in global politics. It does so by interrogating the idea that state was founded by a social contract, and the claim that the global politics as we know it today can be explained by the twin pillars of 'sovereignty' and 'anarchy'. These IR building blocks have led us to think that the locus of all power in global politics lies almost naturally and exclusively with the state. Against this, the chapter shows that states are shaped and maintained by a myriad power relations which operate beyond the remit of state authority.

Finally, in **Chapter 11: Conclusion: Making Change**, we explore the mystery of where we might go from here. Having explored a series of myths as a vehicle to develop critical thinking and theorising skills, how can we work to make meaningful change in the political world around us? We believe that learning to think theoretically can open up new pathways for political action. Accordingly, we challenge the myth that theory is politically ineffectual or abstract. On the contrary, we show that how we *think* is intimately connected to how we *act*. If we want to act differently, in other words, learning to think differently can show us how and where we might usefully intervene in concrete ways.

1.3 EVERYDAY EXPERIENCE

Our everyday understanding of the world—and, within that, of global politics—is not dissimilar to how we come to speak our native language (or languages, for some of us). We may not necessarily be aware of the intricacies of grammar and syntax, or of the mechanisms enabling us to assemble individual words into sentences, and then individual sentences into a coherent speech or paragraph. And yet we express ourselves in ways that are comprehensible to others who speaks our language. We should, however, resist the temptation to think that there is no value in digging deeper into the underlying rules and mechanisms we have absorbed without much reflection. Approaching global politics from the perspective of *existing* conversations about it enables us to identify an important difference with language. The variety of viewpoints on, for example, what power means and how it is exerted in global politics is much wider than the variety of viewpoints on the uses of the present tense or subjunctive mood in English. There is an inherent element of contestation when it comes to political topics that makes it even more important to reflect upon our intuitive knowledge and the myths that form part of it.

One of the major consequences of this invitation to start from looking at what we already know about global politics, and perhaps one element that sets this book apart from many other introductions to the field, is that we will regularly refer to our *everyday experiences*. For example, we may look at border controls to make sense of how global politics shape our ability to move across different territories, or we might consider our grocery list to understand the reach of global value chains in contemporary capitalism and how they might be affected by war, economic sanctions, or new trade deals. This link to everyday experiences reminds us that politics does not happen in a distant sphere of activity and decision-making but rather all around us and all the time. Furthermore, by uncovering the connections between our everyday experiences—like shopping, studying at university, or working in a job—and more explicitly political activities like activism or voting, we begin to understand that the so-called 'non-political' world is much smaller than we might have supposed.

Realising that global politics happens in all these areas allows us to expand the ways we can act politically, beyond things like political campaigns or government work. As Benedict Kerkvliet (2009) explored in his analysis of peasant politics in Vietnam, a more thoughtful understanding of everyday experience yields a better understanding of everyday politics. This in turn helps us to identify the most useful or effective methods for everyday *resistance*. And it is this resistance—against leaders, regimes, institutions, processes, or social structures which we deem to be unjust—which shows that we have identified, considered, and if necessary moved beyond our intuitive understanding.

There are two main reasons that motivate this approach. First, we are all affected by, and part of, global politics, often in rather intimate ways. For instance, restrictions on travel imposed during the Covid-19 pandemic made it difficult for many of us to see loved ones for extended periods of time. While clearly affecting the private sphere of our lives (see Chapter 2 for more on this), this limitation on mobility was shaped by global politics, for example through uneven access to vaccines and differential travel permissions. For many who hold Western passports, it was a glimpse into the lived experience of many people who are denied the possibility of travelling by punitive visa regimes that are often **racialised**. That global politics affects us all is acknowledged by an increasing number of books which introduce the discipline of International Relations, but we situate this at the heart of our approach.

Second, our relationship with global politics cuts both ways. We are not merely passive spectators of global transformations—whether technological, political, economic, or cultural. Rather, we are active participants in global politics, even if we do not attend G20 meetings or contribute to the drafting of international trade agreements. Here our attention to everyday experience can enable us to see not only how global politics constrains our ability to act in certain ways (while enabling others' actions and behaviours) but also how our everyday actions may reproduce or resist global power relations. Such resistance takes place, for example, in the countless protests in many countries of the Global South against the austerity policies mandated by international financial institutions such as the International Monetary Fund. It also takes place in the feminist organisations that fought to insert a reference to 'gender-based violence' in the international Arms Trade Treaty (Enloe, 2014). There are even more subtle forms of everyday resistance, famously characterised by James Scott (1985) as 'weapons of the weak', including apparently innocent acts such as gossiping, wilful stupidity, and dragging your feet while at work. Insofar as they seek to halt or at least slow down the concrete effects of power relations, these everyday actions are themselves political and hence worthy of our attention.

REFLECTIVE ACTIVITY 1.2

Take a moment here to consider the connections we just described—between everyday experience, everyday politics, and everyday resistance—in order to respond to the following prompts:

1. *Experience: Think of any activity that you engaged in today (something you purchased, something you ate, some place you went to), and as many details as you can remember about that activity. (Consider where it was purchased, what were the ingredients used, what mode of transport you used to get there.)*

2. *Politics: For each of the details about this activity, try to think of some politically significant connection to that detail (e.g. the item purchased was made in a country with notoriously poor labour laws or low pay, the loaf of bread you purchased is smaller and more expensive than usual due to grain shortages caused by an international war, you took a taxi because there was no public transport option).*

3. ***Resistance:*** *If, in outlining the political significance of the details of your experience, you find yourself troubled by the realisations you arrive at, consider what forms of resistance you might engage in as a response (e.g. you will purchase locally made items or begin to campaign for corporate labour reform; you will eat less bread or purchase local ingredients to make your own; you will only vote for candidates who advocate for better public transport in the upcoming elections).*

If it is easier, you can organise your thoughts in a simple table with three columns. By thinking through the experience, the politics and the potential for resistance—for anything that you do—you are already engaging in the very nuts and bolts of theorising about global politics!

This book is not the first to argue that we should consider everyday experiences when discussing global politics. In fact, scholars of IR and global politics have in the past couple of decades devoted some attention to the everyday. According to Matt Davies (2016), however, this 'turn' to the everyday has lacked theoretical depth, often recreating unhelpful oppositions between the sphere of action of global institutions and processes, and the sphere where the effects of these actions are felt, reproduced, resisted, and challenged. Mindful of this risk, we follow Henri Lefebvre (2005) in seeking to go beyond considering the everyday, and our everyday life, simply as the raw material upon which we build our understanding of the world. Rather, we see everyday experience as woven through our thinking about global politics. We hope that the process of critical reflection encouraged by this book will affect how each of you will think about your everyday experiences of politics and resistance.

While only a tiny portion of the world's population earns a living from working as IR theorists, absolutely everyone can learn how to think theoretically. Antonio Gramsci (whom you will meet again in Chapter 3) (see photo 1.1) went even further, arguing that '[e]veryone is a philosopher, though in his [*sic*] own way and unconsciously, since even in the slightest manifestation of any intellectual activity whatever, in "language", there is contained a specific conception of the world, one then moves on to the second level, which is that of awareness and criticism' (1971, 323).

This quote enables us to develop two essential points. First, our intuitive understanding of global politics (what Gramsci calls 'a specific conception of the world') is not entirely—or even mainly—a product of our own making. Rather, it is profoundly shaped by the environment we grow up in. Society influences in rather dramatic ways how we come to understand the world we live in. Second, our ambition should be to move away from merely taking 'part in a conception of the world mechanically imposed by the external environment', as Gramsci (1971, 323) puts it, but instead to move to the next level, 'that of awareness and criticism'. This means, for instance, acknowledging that hierarchies in wealth, power, and status have a key role in shaping specific narratives about what matters in global politics, why, and how.

If we are willing to reflectively connect the dots linking our everyday experiences to global power relations, we might then find it easier to do the same when looking at issues usually associated with the relationships between states at the international level. For instance, one of the most common narratives in contemporary global politics revolves around how the rise of China poses a threat to the international system. This claim captures important dynamics, for instance related to how China's increased economic activism abroad,

Photo 1.1 **Italian writer, political philosopher, Marxist thinker, and linguist Antonio Gramsci.**

© World History Archive / Alamy Stock Photo

exemplified by the Belt and Road Initiative (BRI), threatens established interests in many regions of the planet (see photo 1.2).

At the same time, this claim obfuscates other equally important elements, one of which is that these established interests are not necessarily the interests of local populations but may be oriented towards benefitting a narrow constituency, not necessarily located within the territory under consideration. For example, much has been made of China's growing investment in African countries, but this investment is displacing investment directed by the US and European states, not necessarily undermining national and local interests. Additionally, using the language of threats when framing China's rise also implies a normative judgement about the desirability of the existing international system, irrespective of the very skewed distribution of its benefits and costs, which we discuss at length in many of the chapters that follow.

The next step in our critical thinking might be to highlight how, in this narrative, the stability of the international system is little more than a proxy for the preservation and reproduction of existing institutions, practices, as well as concepts and theories that disproportionately serve specific interests. Crucially, pointing this out does not mean taking 'China's side', for critical thinking is most effective when deployed throughout. As part of our critical reflection we would also reflect upon the BRI's consequences in terms of environmental degradation, increased indebtedness of other countries involved, and the

Photo 1.2 **A map of China's Belt and Road Initiative. A global infrastructure development strategy adopted by the Chinese government to invest in nearly 70 countries and international organisations.**

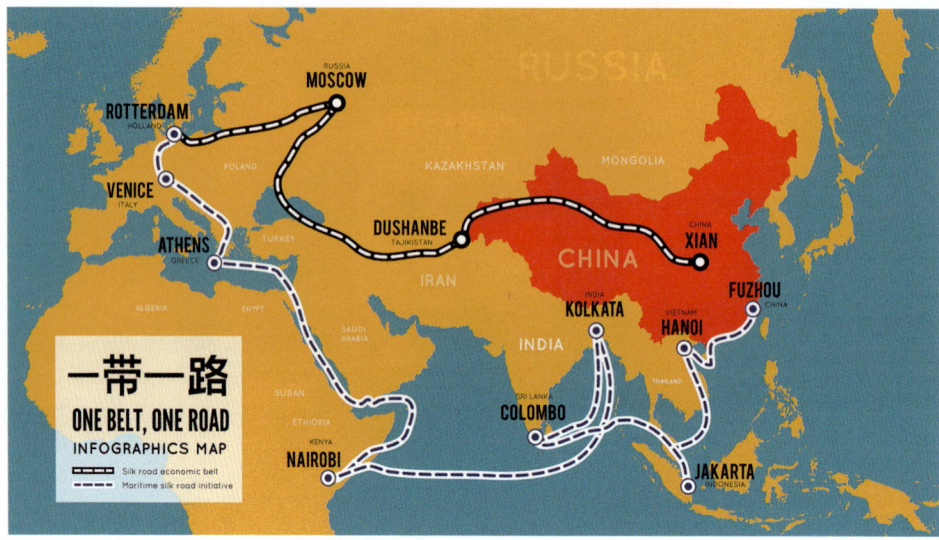

© My Portfolio / Shutterstock.com

wider political implications of China as a global power with explicitly non-democratic institutions and an authoritarian governing ideology. The deconstruction of these narratives, whether mundane or tied to the high politics of diplomatic gatherings, is best accomplished through the identification, critical assessment, and demystification of key myths that organise, at times in contradictory form, our everyday understanding of global politics.

1.4 FROM THEORY TO THEORISING

Thinking critically is a demanding and time-consuming endeavour. One of our goals, as theorists, is to understand how theories are formed, how they function, and how and for whom they are useful. This is related to, but different from, learning about the existing theories used in the study of global politics. As noted in Section 1.1, many IR textbooks are organised around the question: what are the major theories of international politics? In this approach, theories are presented chronologically, providing the history of 'IR as a discipline' through the lens of a series of debates between different traditions of thought. While not dismissing the question of which theories have been most influential, nor seeking to replace a deep-dive approach into established theories during the course of a degree, this book invites you to begin your examination of theory from a different starting point. This approach provides you with tools for thinking theoretically that you may take with you as you undertake your degree, critically evaluate established theories, engage with other academic disciplines, and reflect on the politics of your everyday lives.

1.4.1 KEY QUESTIONS

In this book, we seek to answer three important questions about theory and learning to theorise. The first is: what is theory? Instead of presenting you with theories as ready-made objects to be learned and applied, we hope to introduce you to theory not as an identity to be chosen and announced but rather as a *mode of thinking* about global politics. This is why we start from what we already know, often without even being aware that we know it. Our everyday experience provides us with an intuitive understanding of global politics, one that is primarily implicit, and often unsystematic, or even contradictory. Taking this as our starting point enables us to present theories not as something detached from everyday experiences and practices but rather as a way of making sense of them.

Additionally, the use of the plural (e.g. 'experiences', 'practices') highlights the fact that the everyday experiences of a Syrian refugee, for example, attending university on a scholarship or bursary, is most likely very different from that of a Canadian exchange student whose parents have paid for their year abroad. In other words, it makes us sensitive to how our specific position in the social world—in terms of wealth, status, and geographical location—shapes, but in no way determines, how we experience global politics and how we then theorise about it. This is often presented as the impact of **positionality** on how we think theoretically. While we direct you to Chapter 2 for more on different types of theories and ways of theorising, we can already tell you that we present theory as an attempt at developing a systematic account of how different forces, actors, and processes relate to one another, while simultaneously also addressing questions pertaining to the desirability and sustainability of those resulting arrangements.

The second question that we seek to address is: how should I engage with theory? Many introductory textbooks, in addition to providing a list of IR theories, also further provide a series of dates and historical events to remember. In so doing, it is suggested that these specific events shaped IR as a discipline (or, as many would have it, as a sub-discipline of Political Science). This list typically includes: The **Peace of Westphalia** of 1648; the two World Wars book-ending 'the twenty years' crisis'; the 1989 fall of the Berlin Wall, with the ensuing disintegration of the Soviet bloc; and 9/11 ushering in the 'War on Terror'. This depiction of a discipline as 'set-piece' debates, punctuated by specific events, introduces IR through a rather narrow lens. Students are simply asked to learn the exchanges of past or current participants in those debates, or to study the different positions taken in the conversation. Much less attention is devoted to what we are talking about, and why that conversation is important in the first place.

In our experience as teachers, we have found that this often has an unwelcome effect on students, who are taking a course in IR or global politics because of an interest in what they see happening in the world around them, much more than because of their passion for the differences between Classical Realism, Neorealism, and Neoclassical Realism. Encouraging students to engage with these traditions without first making explicit why and how these conversations matter can dampen the motivation of even the most enthusiastic students. This is where we believe that relating these often quite abstract theories to everyday experiences and practices provides an ideal vantage point from which to engage in two important and complementary exercises (in response to the 'how should I engage with theory' question).

On the one hand, this approach enables us to show how each of us is already involved in these conversations, even if we do not express this engagement in academic terms. In so doing, it also shows how we can master the academic tools that can help us identify the importance of the things that we are arguing about, understand the different conversations that have already occurred and the different positions within them, and get more involved in those conversations. On the other hand, we hope that through this process you will feel more confident contributing not only to these conversations about global politics but also to global politics as a set of practices through your own conscious deliberations and actions. In this respect, we are very much guided by the critical pedagogical approach developed by John Dewey (1916), bell hooks (1994), and Paulo Freire (1996), which emphasise that learners are not passive recipients but rather co-producers of their educational experience as well as of active agents of the world they inhabit.

Finally, the third question orienting this book is: how do I theorise? Perhaps surprisingly, the answer to this question is in fact the most straightforward. Whenever you are thinking critically, you are already engaged in the process of theorising. This may not result in an '-ism', but that is not necessarily a bad thing. Rather, our task in this respect will be two-fold. First, we will need to identify the key ideas and narratives that shape the way we talk about global politics. Second, we will also encourage you to develop a critical relationship to these ideas and narratives, for instance asking questions about their origins (where do they come from?), their explanatory power (how do they help us understand specific political phenomena?), their accuracy (does the historical and empirical record support such ideas and narratives?), their silences or omissions (what or who do they leave out?), and the effect these ideas and narratives may have on how we act in the world (how do they shape the way we 'do' global politics?). If you are able to ask these questions and to develop your own answers to them, you will not only be taking part in and contributing to conversations about global politics but you will have engaged in the process of theorising. Should you find this approach helpful, you will be able to take it with you throughout your studies and use it to help you to act politically in a reflective and critical way.

1.5 **TERMINOLOGY**

This introduction was intended to guide your engagement with the text and to explain our approach to the study of global politics. In this final section we will briefly address some important points regarding terminology. You may have noticed that we have already used the terms global politics, world politics, international politics, and International Relations to refer to our subject matter. We are using International Relations/IR (in capital letters) whenever we refer to the academic field most commonly associated with the study of global politics. At the same time we take a broad understanding of this field, one that is not only influenced by political science but also most notably by political theory, philosophy, sociology, and political economy. We will at times speak of global politics, at times of international politics, and at times also of world politics. While each of these terms entails a slightly different emphasis, you can take these terms as synonyms unless we explicitly advise you not to.

In addition, as we highlighted in Section 1.2, the structure of this book is different to other introductory texts. We think it is vital to start with the stuff that makes up global politics—the things we care about, argue over, and want to see change or stay the same. So again, we have chosen to take an approach that does not follow convention. We do not focus on founding moments of IR, such as the peace of Westphalia or formalisation of the discipline after the First World War, nor we do start with traditions of thought or established '-isms'. Finally, we do not begin with contemporary 'issues'. Rather, we introduce a series of important puzzles—*mysteries*—about global politics, and put under the microscope some of the conventional solutions—*myths*—we rely upon to solve them. Because we already know something about at least some of these myths and mysteries, we can use this familiarity to reflect upon our intuitive understanding and thereby involve you in the rewarding work of theorising. The mysteries we focus on sit at the heart of global politics. Engaging with them critically will enable you to look at your degree programme, and the wider academic discipline, in a similarly critical manner.

So, to summarise: our intention is to introduce you to global politics and to thinking critically about global politics in an empowering way. We start with your intuitive understandings, challenge popular and academic myths, and encourage you to participate in the ongoing conversations through which we think theoretically about global politics. The book is structured around the concepts, practices, and institutions that we know, care about, and argue over in order to prepare you to understand and to join us in the academic study of global politics as self-motivated, critical participants. The discontinuity between our approach and that of other introductory texts is intentional, and any discomfort that this generates, we hope, will in the end prove enlivening and empowering.

 Access the online resources at www.oup.com/he/hirst1e for case studies to help contextualise your understanding of key concepts, further reading recommendations to guide you through your reading, and a library of web links to journal articles, blogs, and video content to help you take your learning further.

POLITICS

2

READERS' GUIDE

Chapter 2: Politics explores the mystery of what politics is, and where politics operates at the global level. It examines and challenges the myth that only powerful elites engage in politics, or that we are only acting politically when we vote, showing instead that politics is at work all the time in our everyday experience. In doing so, it shows that *becoming political*, understood as learning to think critically and theoretically about the political world, is itself a political act. This is because it alters our everyday understanding of the world around us and thereby opens up new possibilities for action.

2.1 INTRODUCTION

Politics depends on myths, on the stories we tell to explain why the world is the way it is (see Section 1.3). For example, Thomas Hobbes (1996), writing in 1651, tells us that we must submit to the power of the state, lest we risk descending into a savage war of all against all. Today, nearly four hundred years later, this story is repeated. In his presidential inauguration speech in 2017, Donald Trump invoked an image of 'American carnage', from which he would save the country. Trump is hardly alone in mobilising this myth; it is favoured by authoritarian leaders around the world. And we are still making myths, such as in the 1980s, when the end of the Cold War gave rise to a story about the 'End of History'. This myth, most famously associated with Francis Fukuyama (1989), claimed ideological conflict was over, resolved in favour of liberal capitalism. This meant there was no point arguing about the economy anymore, capitalism was the best system—and if it was not the best system, it was the only possible system. Recent history, unwilling to simply end, has shown that liberal capitalism's victory is not so complete or final.

The myths we tell about politics have us in their grip; even when we might want to reject them, we have to unmake them. Contemporary movements for racial justice illustrate this, as **race** is a construct, a myth, retold again and again, as the 'civilising mission' that justified European colonialism (Kipling, 1899), and as the 'clash of civilisations' that structures ethno-nationalist politics today (Huntington, 1993). Similar myth-making works to justify patriarchy and uphold traditional gender roles and identities, which contemporary movements for gender justice are still struggling against. All these myths are tied together by the idea that there is a 'natural' order to the world, and by extension a correct way of arranging our political lives, reflecting deep truths about society and people. This idea is an old and powerful political myth, famously expressed by the Greek philosopher Plato (1991), who we will discuss in Section 2.3.2, as a 'noble lie' rulers should tell to convince people of the justness of their place in society. But politics is not only about maintaining and justifying order, it is also a creative and collective activity. Thinking about politics more carefully, thinking theoretically and critically, will help us understand this paradox, and help us to think beyond simplifying myths that obscure our understanding and limit the possibilities of politics.

In this chapter we will consider the meaning of politics and the mystery of where politics operates at the global level. Reflecting our distinctive approach to theorising global politics (outlined in Chapter 1), the meaning of politics is first explored through our everyday uses and understandings, which we organise around ideas of coercion, authority, and legitimacy. It examines and challenges the myth that only powerful elites engage in politics, showing instead that politics is at work all the time in our everyday lives and experience. We then move from the everyday to the theoretical, examining how influential thinkers define politics. We also discuss what it means to think theoretically about politics. The chapter ends with a consideration of how thinking critically and theoretically about politics is itself a political act that alters our everyday understanding of the world around us and opens up new possibilities for action, challenging the myth that there is a natural way of organising politics by drawing on the philosopher Hannah Arendt (2005) to examine politics as a form of collective world-making, which she suggests is in a way quite 'miraculous'—and we encourage you to become political, to become a little bit miraculous.

2.2 POLITICS AND THE EVERYDAY

Politics is all around us. This pervasiveness is more than the endless reporting of the decisions, mistakes, or scandals of politicians and governments. Politics emerges from our relationships with one another. Yet not every social relationship is political. For many, the most obvious political relationships we have are with government institutions, such as a local council or the national government. What is less obvious is what makes our relationships with these institutions political. There is no uncontroversial definition of politics and we will not pretend to offer one. Instead, this chapter will help you understand politics in its complexity. All social relations have power dynamics (see Section 3.1) and politics addresses this aspect of our relationships. To begin, we focus on everyday experiences where we are subjected to the power of others, both individuals and institutions. We then consider how the concept of authority can make coercion legitimate through political institutions such as courts or elections. This, then, leads to a consideration of whether politics only happens within **nation-states**—meaning there is a categorical difference between domestic and global politics; we contend politics transcends state borders, even as the nation-state system gives contemporary global politics a distinctive form (see Section 10.1). Finally, we examine the different ways our social relationships are political. While this section ends with lingering questions, this chapter will help you begin to answer them.

2.2.1 COERCION AND AUTHORITY

We all know what it feels like to be **coerced**, to be forced to do something we would not otherwise choose to do (see Section 3.2). Perhaps you have been denied entry at a bar or club. Maybe parents or other family members made you to do things you would not have chosen for yourself. Your experience of coercion might be more extreme: perhaps you have been a victim of crime or violent conflict, or maybe you have been detained by the police or at an international border. Coercion can also be subtler, such as experiencing street harassment (e.g. 'catcalling') or being asked 'where are you *really* from?' by someone from a dominant ethnic group. In such moments, the actions of others may force you to alter your behaviour, such as what you wear, or discuss things you would rather not, such as justifying your identity to those who presume you don't 'belong'. If you have been coerced, you have probably wondered why this happened or whether it was justified.

We know there are individuals, institutions, and rules we are expected to follow. All of us, at some point, must do as we are told, so some coercion is justified. Teachers tell you what to read and penalise you when you fail to follow instructions. Churches, mosques, and temples are places where we learn how to behave in accordance with long standing traditions and are warned of the consequences of not respecting them. The law tells us what we must do and what we must not do, applying punishments if we break the law, by taking away our freedom or our money, for example. Even our interactions with friends, workmates, and strangers follow unspoken rules, and failing to do so can risk being ostracised. The individuals, institutions, and rules we are expected to obey hold **authority** over us. And authorities are all around us; authority is held by individuals with special social status, institutions regulating our actions, and **norms** influencing how we understand our world.

We also know it's not absolute. Authority says 'Do as I say!'. But, in turn, authority must answer the question 'why?'. The everyday experience of questioning authority is a starting point for developing a critical understanding of politics. Authority requires **legitimacy** if it is more than force or violence (see Sections 4.1 and 5.2). A teacher who is unconcerned with the learning of his pupils and lacks the necessary expertise to guide them is a petty tyrant demanding obedience. A police officer with no concern for the law or the safety of her community is only a bully. A political leader not acting out of a sincere concern for the common good of their constituency is little more than a con artist. Legitimacy justifies authority and transforms force into warranted coercion, which edifies, protects, or empowers (see Sections 4.6 and 6.2.3). Politics emerges, then, when we pursue the 'solution to the problem of order which chooses conciliation rather than violence and coercion', as British political theorist Bernard Crick argued (2005, 15). We engage in politics when we regulate our social interaction through common rules that give concern to the shared consequences of those interactions and aim at the common good.

2.2.2 LEGITIMATE AUTHORITY AND THE COMMON GOOD

Most of us know something about how to hold authority to account, to ask 'why?' of those with power over us. You might ask your professors why your curriculum is based mainly on the work of white men, or you might ask your university administrators why student facilities and services are not improving when tuition fees are rising. You might demand to know why the police in your community apply 'stop and search' policies in a discriminatory manner. We might collectively ask politicians why they pursue economic policies that benefit wealthy individuals or corporations. Challenging the legitimacy of authority does not guarantee we get the response we want, but it involves us in politics. Politics, on one level, is about managing relationships in which differences in power lead to the potential for conflict, coercion, and violence. But on another level, we also engage in politics to challenge and remake existing relationships, which involves renegotiating and redistributing social status and power. As Crick (2005, 15) notes, we attempt to do this without resorting to the use of force or violence, but that does not mean force and violence are absent from politics (see Section 5.3); rather it means politics attempts to give order to our social actions, while also providing a means of questioning and changing that order. Absolute authority and pure violence spell the end of politics.

We can engage in politics because authorities must abide by some standards in order to have legitimacy. Those standards must be addressed to those who are subject to coercive power, giving reasons to accept coercion. The authority of a teacher does not rest on her possession of an advanced degree; rather it comes from her dedication to her students' learning. The authority of a border agent checking our passport does not come from his personal feelings about our character but his faithful execution of the law. The authority of a political leader is not found in their charisma, it comes from their commitment to pursuing the common good for the whole community. Legitimacy is acquired when authority serves a common rather than a personal end.

Legitimate authority, then, creates a space in which those individuals involved in an activity are given reasons for why they should accept the power authorities have over them. The professor asks her students to listen attentively while she speaks in order to learn the material presented. This reason creates a relationship between the professor and the students, which can be questioned and challenged based on the shared goal of learning. This example can help us analyse the account of politics given thus far. First, there is a political quality to the relationship between a professor and a student because there is an imbalance of power. The professor has an institutional status granting them authority, along with more knowledge and wider experience of the subject they are teaching, which means the professor can force students to do things they otherwise wouldn't choose to do. Second, there is a political quality to learning, which means the authority of the professor is contingent and the inequalities between student and professor are justified because they are necessary to the common goal of learning. This means the legitimacy of the unequal relationship between professor and student depends on the professor's commitment to their student's learning.

Thus far, the discussion has focused on everyday experiences of coercion, authority, and legitimacy. It would not be surprising if you were beginning to wonder: 'When do we get to politics proper?' That is a fair question. Yet to start thinking about politics in terms of specific governmental institutions, recent foreign policy decisions, or even contrasting political ideologies risks narrowing our focus prematurely. To put it rather philosophically, determining the scope of 'politics proper' is itself a political act. Further, focusing on what we normally think of as politics tends to distance us from some important political questions. Some of us may be directly involved in party politics, others in various forms of activism, but a great many of us are not so engaged—or at least not yet. Politics, however, is bigger and wider than these obvious forms of engagement, and everyone is involved in political life. Therefore, before we consider 'politics proper', it is important to consider the variety of everyday political experiences we all have.

REFLECTIVE ACTIVITY 2.1

Using the ideas discussed so far, what political experiences can you identify in your everyday life?

While we often use the word 'politics' without too much thought, it is actually quite difficult to define. Try to define politics based on your own everyday understandings and experiences.

What makes political authority distinctive?

How is it different than other kinds of authority? For example, educational or spiritual authority?

2.2.3 YOUR MANY EVERYDAY EXPERIENCES OF POLITICS

To adapt a line from Leon Trotsky, the Russian revolutionary, even if you are not interested in politics, politics is interested in you. All of us are affected by politics, as we unavoidably have relationships with political actors and institutions, and those relationships impact on our lives. When the government raises tuition fees (such as in the UK in 2012) or adopts new legislation related to health care (such as in the US in 2010 and again in 2017), those decisions alter our expectations and possible actions. When a state fragments and civil war breaks out (such as in Syria in 2011), or supranational institutions change in fundamental ways (such as when the UK left the EU in 2021) it has consequences, both immediate and indirect, which affect us. The consequences of politics can also be deeply personal, affecting intimate aspects of our lives, such as legislation in more than a dozen European countries restricting religious attire, perhaps most famously in France where laws banning religious attire in schools (2004) and outlawing face coverings in public (2010), seen by many to target Muslim women, or the 2018 referendum in Ireland legalising abortion. Politics is about human relationships and the authority that shapes them. For example, from 2020, the Covid-19 pandemic brought home the intimate and global reach of politics with great force and clarity, as the pandemic led to lockdowns that limited personal freedoms, and access to essential items was restricted, from everyday essentials like toilet paper to life-saving medical equipment and vaccines.

Many of us experience politics primarily in the context of a nation-state. Most of us are **citizens** of, or recognised residents in, at least one country. This means there is a community in which we have certain privileges and responsibilities. Further, it means there are different rules governing our interactions when we leave our 'home' countries. Within the borders of our countries we have political encounters each day. For example, the law determines many of our actions. If you jump a barrier at the train station, then you may be ticketed or detained for failing to pay a fare. A century ago, homosexual relationships were against the law in nearly all countries—and still are in several countries, including Nigeria, Iran, and Indonesia. We may also encounter politics when we interact with public institutions, like schools, universities, hospitals, or government offices. When we pay taxes, we fund public services. When we vote, we participate in the act of governing. You might also engage in politics directly by canvassing for a political party, volunteering with a charity, or joining a demonstration.

However, politics is not limited to the nation-state. Beyond the border of our own countries many of us travel internationally, belong to multiple communities, and have important relationships that cross borders. The idea our political identity is linked to a single national community, associated with a specific piece of territory, is relatively new on the scale of human history, and doesn't reflect the experiences of everyone today. Many of us are migrants, thinking of multiple countries as our home. Also, European imperialism created connections between people that don't fit neatly into national borders. The Windrush Scandal in the UK illustrates this point (Serhan, 2018). For several years UK government policy created a 'hostile environment' for migrants in order to reduce the number of people moving to the UK from abroad. As part of this policy, individuals who legally moved to the UK from the Caribbean were targeted for deportation despite having legal rights of residence. Our lives are also connected in impersonal ways through the global economy, which is more integrated than ever. Our everyday experience makes it obvious politics does not only take place solely within nation-states. When we cross international borders, buy goods manufactured in countries around the globe, or when violent conflicts take place in multiple states, we are still wrestling with the question of how we relate to one another and who has authority in those relationships.

While an everyday sense of politics can help us to start thinking about politics more deeply and carefully, it can also be confusing. Defining politics is difficult, even though we all have some sense of what it is and how it affects us. Part of the difficulty is that while we can sketch an outline of politics from our everyday experiences, filling in the details leads to uncertainty and disagreement, as we all have different personal experiences which are limited by our particular perspective. How do we make sense of our diverse experiences? How can we put the general idea of politics being about coercion and authority in our social relationships to work in a way that helps us understand contemporary events? And, vitally, can we do this without relying on the myth there is a natural order that should shape our political lives? We can begin to address these problems by thinking about politics theoretically in abstract and general terms.

2.2.4 GLOBAL POLITICS OR INTERNATIONAL RELATIONS: WHAT'S IN A NAME?

If this is your first textbook on global politics, then you are likely find the fact that we start with politics unexceptional. Our choice to focus on politics in this context, however, is unconventional. You will find many books and courses on global (or international) politics that make limited reference to politics as a distinctive or central concept. You may find this strange; we certainly do. But to understand why this omission is unexceptional, we need to diverge briefly to discuss the politics of academic disciplines.

Often political relationships and activities occurring across national borders are referred to as international relations, and the academic discipline studying them is referred to as International Relations. There are two important reasons for this you need to understand. One has to do with the particularities of history. In the United Kingdom, International Relations developed as a separate discipline, related to but distinct from Politics. While in North America, International Relations developed as a subfield within Political Science. Throughout the 20th century the language of 'international relations' and the idea of International Relations as a distinctive area of study was dominant in English-speaking universities. You will notice we describe the subject of this book as global politics, which we see as part of the more general discipline of Politics. These small differences in terminology reflect substantive differences in understanding our topic and field of study, which takes us to the second reason for attending to these differences in terminology and disciplinary definitions.

There is a long-standing presumption politics within the nation-state is importantly different from politics outside of, or between, nation-states. In political theory, Crick (2005, 14) suggests that 'genuine politics remains an ideal in international relations' because where this is no government possessing effective **sovereignty** there can be no politics (see Section 10.3). Similarly, Martin Wight (1960, 48), an International Relations scholar, traces the difference between domestic and international politics to their being two different political experiences, with domestic politics concerned with 'normal relationships' and the pursuit of the 'good life' within a national community, while International Relations is about 'survival' in which extreme events, like wars, are normal. Both thinkers presume international relations are **anarchic** and lack the necessarily order and legitimate authority for proper political relationships to develop, especially the pursuit of a common good (see Section 10.3). Therefore, scholars adopting this view believe International Relations requires its own categories, as the relationships it is concerned with are different from political relationships within the nation-state. While we reject this premise, even if one accepts it, we would argue it is still necessary to understand what International Relations is not, if one hopes to know the subject fully. Too often the disjuncture between international relations and domestic politics is simply assumed, without attending to how one's understanding of politics can justify or undermine the disjuncture. So, we think whatever view you take, it is vital to understand politics.

Without wanting to pre-empt discussions to come, it is important to say something about why we reject the disjunction between domestic politics and international relations in favour of 'global politics'. First, even if we accept the validity of a stark distinction between domestic and international made at an earlier time, much has changed since Crick and Wight were writing in the 1960s. Of particular importance has been the increase in cross-border interaction in economics, politics, and social life, which we commonly summarise as **globalisation** (see Sections 7.3 and 9.1). Today, nation-states are less self-contained and borders more porous, making hard and fast distinctions between domestic and international tenuous. Further, the divide between the nation-state, as a site of legitimate order enabling the pursuit of the common good, and the international system, based on principles of anarchy and the pursuit of self-preservation between states, rests on the claim there is a lack of political order at the international level, as there is no world state or universal sovereign.

This claim is empirically contestable. For example, the political world Crick and Wight describe was actually an **imperial** order (see Chapter 8), in which European states exercised authority though coercion and violence over the majority of the world—even as there was a more anarchic form of order between the European colonial powers. As the anticolonial thinker Frantz Fanon (2001) draws out (see photo 2.1), the history and legacy of colonial domination results from the exercise of illegitimate colonial authority over the colonised, such that authority is not contained domestically within the nation-state but extended globally by colonising states (and former colonisers today, as we explore in Section 8.2).

Photo 2.1 **Franz Fanon, psychoanalyst and social philosopher.**

© Everett Collection Historical / Alamy Stock Photo

Therefore, the pursuit of the common good that Wight believes make domestic politics distinctive is, according to Fanon, actually only possible by the exploitation of lands and people outside the nation-state. Colonial authority is only one kind of authority that crosses national borders, with others, such as economic and legal authorities, giving further reasons to be sceptical of the conventional account of national sovereignty as the only form of political authority in global politics.

Finally, the strong division between domestic politics and international relations maintains its plausibility by drawing from a limited range of experiences. Global politics involves more than the traditional focus on wars and diplomacy between sovereign states. Feminist scholar Cynthia Enloe (2014) demonstrates the inadequacy of the conventional distinction between domestic and international in her classic study *Bananas, Beaches and Bases*, originally published in 1990, which reveals the diverse and all too often ignored experiences of women in global politics—focusing on diplomat's wives, domestic staff, and sex workers, who play vital but unappreciated roles in global politics. With these thoughts in mind we now shift back to thinking about politics—and our everyday experience of it—knowing that global politics is very much about politics and requires more nuanced consideration than the traditional distinction between domestic politics and international relations allows.

REFLECTIVE ACTIVITY 2.2

Can you list some of the political relationships that affect you in your everyday life?

As you answer this question think about how these relationships shape you, as well as whether or not you are able to influence those experiences yourself. Share your answers with a classmate.

How are your experiences similar and different?

As you think about these relationships, also think about who has authority within those relationships, as well as how we decide how these relationships should be organised.

2.3 THEORISING POLITICS

A theory of politics helps us to order our messy everyday experiences, allowing us to see politics differently—and hopefully more clearly. More will be said in Sections 2.3.3 and 2.3.4 about what theory is and how to think theoretically, but first we examine two influential theories of politics. We start with Harold Lasswell, who defined politics in terms of the competition for social resources. Then we will look at Plato (see photo 2.2), the ancient Greek philosopher, who understands politics as the art of pursuing the common good for the community as a whole. Both thinkers give us an abstract account of politics, separated from everyday experience in important ways. Therefore, as you read, consider how and why they do this. In addition, think about whether their theories of politics make sense to you in terms of your own experience.

2.3.1 LASSWELL'S THEORY OF POLITICS

Harold Lasswell, a 20th-century US political scientist, famously defined politics as the determination of who gets what, when, and how (Lasswell, 1936). What Lasswell means by this is that politics is fundamentally about who has influence in our social relationships and how that influence is used to decide who gets the social goods we all value. To break this down, first, we have to identify which goods have social value. This can involve material goods, like food or shelter, statuses such as citizenship or appointed office, and immaterial goods, such as legal recognition or social esteem. Then we must look at who has the power to distribute the goods we value, along with how they are distributed. There is then a question about whether the distribution of goods is legitimate according to established rules. Lasswell is not giving an account of his experience of politics but rather an abstract account using general ideas and relationships to inform our understanding of politics. Usually our everyday experience of politics is discussed in terms such as what the president or prime minister did, or the specific problems affecting local communities, and even when we are thinking about big events like a war or financial crisis, we tend to think of the specific event. A theoretical account of politics tries to explain the general relationships within governments that account for specific policy decisions, to connect local events to wider processes with general causes, and to understand why events like wars and financial crises keep happening.

Lasswell (1936, 25), for example, looks at deference, income, and safety as three social goods distributed politically—though he doesn't think this list is exhaustive. He then considers the different ways these goods are distributed, based on skill, class, and personality. For example, in our contemporary world, deference is generally thought to be distributed on the basis of skill rather than class. A real life example of this could include how members of parliament in the United Kingdom are elected based on their skill as representatives and law-makers—at least ideally. Government offices command deference, and in democratic societies this deference is justified when elected officials execute their work skilfully. Government office could be distributed in other ways: appointment by divine authority, as monarchs once were, or by chance, such as by the drawing of lots in ancient Athens. Lasswell gives us a starting point for thinking theoretically about politics in terms of general goods distributed according to general standards.

If we stop here, however, the theory we have is quite limited, as it only provides a way of making classifications of the goods and standards that structure our social relationships. A theory of politics usually aspires to give some explanation of political behaviours and events. Moving beyond classification, Lasswell (1936, 233–235) suggests power determines why the distribution of goods operates as it does, and that the power of the economic and political elite is most important in determining who gets what, when, and how. This central idea of Lasswell's theory touches on a common suspicion many of us may have, namely that the rich and privileged are able to manipulate social relationships to their own benefit. In place of this intuition, however, Lasswell gives us a theory to explain why and how the elite manipulate social relationships in their favour. Further, this explanation does not rely on the personal vices of specific elites, or particular moments of social conflict in which scarce goods need to be distributed; instead it gives us an account of politics as such.

REFLECTIVE ACTIVITY 2.3

An explanatory theory, despite being abstract, can help us understand politics in more detail, which may initially seem contradictory. We can apply Lasswell's theory to understand our everyday experience better. Take income as an example: the money we make from our wages, or the profit we make from an investment, is a *social* good, the distribution of which is determined by political authorities.

How is the income or profit you earn dependent upon social relationships?

You might want to object here, thinking, '*I* earned my income, surely it belongs to *me!*' As we will see in Section 2.3.3, it is not quite so straightforward.

How can Lasswell help us understand income as a good distributed according to political power? We can earn income by working for someone else, if they pay us a wage, or through an investment of time, effort, or money, which pays off more than we originally paid out. In either case, we are interacting with other people, as economic activity involves the transfer of resources, energy, and time (see Sections 7.2 and 9.2). Therefore, income and profit are social goods and their distribution is determined by the social rules governing those transfers. So, Lasswell helps us see income is a social good that is distributed unequally. He can also help us figure out how income is distributed and why it is distributed unequally.

Most of us have been taught income is distributed based on skill, such that one's intelligence, training, or craftsmanship leads to financial rewards. Yet we also know this explanation is not entirely accurate. Class is a huge determinant of income distribution, as people born into wealthy families tend to become wealthy adults, while people born into poor families rarely become wealthy individuals. Political recognition is likewise an important factor in the distribution of income. For example, global income inequality between nations is related to the history of colonialism in which European states dominated and exploited much of the world. Colonial domination was based on a refusal to recognise the legitimacy of non-European governments and societies, justifying the violent extraction of wealth from the colonised. We can also look at gender and its relation to income. Women, on average, are paid less than men—even for the same work. Partly this is due to crude discrimination, in which women are sometimes still wrongly seen as less capable than men. It is also due to the different circumstances women and men face, as household duties and childcare even now tend to fall disproportionately on women, affecting their engagement in the workplace. Lasswell gives us a theory of politics that abstracts from the detail of any specific experience, but it allows us to understand our everyday experience of earning income in new ways by helping us to see the structures and dynamics of our social interactions.

Something seems to be missing, however, in Lasswell's account of politics. Surely politics is more than the exercise of power, as important as this is to politics. As we discussed in Section 2.2.2, politics is also about the legitimacy of the authorities that determine our social relationships, and legitimacy is based in some notion of the common good. It is important to note Lasswell (1936, 3) does not think a theory of politics involves giving an account of how social goods *should* be distributed; rather he sought to *describe* how influence was achieved and maintained in politics. As we see in Section 2.3.2, an **explanatory theory** like Lasswell's avoids addressing questions a **normative theory** takes to be central. Explanatory theory eschews normative questions for many reasons, but two are particularly influential. First, some political scientists believe questions about right and wrong cannot be answered scientifically, so should be left to personal conviction and political activism. Second, some explanatory theories aim to describe the truth of political life, setting out natural and unavoidable features of our interactions and the behaviour of individuals. This way of understanding politics can contribute to the myth of a natural order when theorists appeal to ideas such as the inherent selfishness of individuals or the naturalness of ethnic or racial identities. It is important to note this danger, as thinking theoretically about politics on its own does not dispel myths.

2.3.2 PLATO'S THEORY OF POLITICS

Lasswell's theory of politics does not address whether the distribution of goods or the political relationships determining their distribution is legitimate. Therefore, he doesn't help us judge whether the political world we live in is good or bad, nor does he help us determine what a good political order should be (see Section 4.1). In contrast to explanatory theory, normative theory is concerned with how political life *should* be organised. This approach has deep historical roots, as we can see in Plato's account of politics.

Photo 2.2   **An 18th-century engraving of a bust of the Greek philosopher Plato.**

Plato is among the most famous ancient philosophers and *The Republic* (1991), his major political work, was written around 380 BCE. For Plato, politics is fundamentally about living well together, and he advances one of history's most influential accounts of how a political community *should* be organised. In contrast to Lasswell, Plato focuses on what makes for good social relationships to show how authority can be made legitimate. A good political community, which for Plato was a city-state, must be organised harmoniously so each member of the community is fulfilling their distinctive role, leading both to individual and collective fulfilment. He thinks this commitment to the common good is necessary because politics is unavoidable, as human beings are not self-sufficient and depend upon each other to live. Therefore, since we must live together, living well as an individual requires taking the common good into account.

According to Plato, a harmonious city-state should balance different classes of people, each doing their part within the collective. Plato thinks the majority of people are driven by their appetites, and thus should be concerned with fulfilling the needs of the city by growing food and creating the goods needed by the city's inhabitants. The city, however, also requires protection and guidance, leading Plato to identify a class of guardians to serve the common good (Plato, 1991, 52). The guardians are further distinguished into two classes. First, there are 'auxiliaries', individuals driven by 'spirit' and defined by their fortitude and vigour (Plato, 1991, 120). Plato suggests the auxiliaries serve as the warriors protecting the city and executing its laws. The laws of the city, however, are determined by the guardians, who are those rare individuals driven primarily by 'reason' (Plato, 1991, 183). These guardians are defined by their intellect and capacity for dispassionate reasoning; therefore they are the most capable of ruling. The best political order, then, is one in which the mass of people, driven by their appetites, follow the wisdom of philosopher kings able to determine what is good for the whole community without being swayed by their own self-interests. These benevolent rulers should be served by the auxiliaries, who possess the strength and discipline to ensure that a just order is maintained.

Plato's ideas have proved controversial. The British philosopher Karl Popper branded him an enemy of individual freedom (2002). While Plato argues his guardians are driven by reason and therefore able to act in the best interests of society, his ideal city-state is constructed on the assumption there are natural rulers and followers (Plato, 1991, 92). This sort of hierarchical thinking is commonly rejected today, and may give us reason to be sceptical of Plato's views, but his philosophy has been enormously influential. Without suggesting we should agree with Plato, there are two important ideas we can take from *The Republic*.

First, Plato helps us see conventional social relationships are subject to critique. For example, he challenged many customs in his own time, such as including women in the guardian class, as both auxiliaries and rulers, going against convention in ancient Athens. He also thought family life would impede the work of the guardians, encouraging them to be partial and biased, so he suggested the children of the guardian class should be raised communally. Further, we can in turn critique Plato's idea of natural hierarchy based on contemporary ideas of human equality, even as hierarchical thinking was unremarkable in Plato's context. Theories about politics give us a perspective from which to criticise conventional social arrangements—and to suggest alternatives. There is a second important idea we can take from Plato. When we think theoretically about politics, we are concerned not only with knowing and describing how our social relationships operate; we are also passionately concerned with their legitimacy. We find ourselves asking: are these good social relationships? Once we begin to ask if our social relationships are legitimate, we also open up a new question about political action: what changes would make our social relationships legitimate? The desire to improve our social relationships depends upon an account of the common good. Plato gives us one of the oldest and most influential accounts of this and, in doing so, helps us see what is at stake when we think theoretically about politics. Thinking theoretically involves thinking generally about the relationships and processes of political life as well as making critical evaluations of existing arrangements and judgements about how politics could be improved.

You may have critical questions about Plato's account of justice, as it relies on the idea that each individual has an essential nature, and that these drives can be put into a true and proper order, in which reason is served by spirit to control appetite. Plato's account of justice gives rise to the question, 'why would the majority—who he thinks are natural followers, incapable of governing—accept their place within his system?'. Historically, we know that they did not, as Plato's *Republic* was written as an alternative to the democratic government of ancient Athens. Plato was aware of this problem for his account of justice, so part of his programme of reform included what he called a 'noble lie', which provided a myth to explain why some people were born to rule and others to serve. This admission of the need for dishonesty shows us how normative theories, like explanatory ones, can perpetuate harmful myths. Normative theory often appeals to timeless and rational ideals about human beings to both criticise convention and provide alternative political orders. These ideals, which may seem obvious and natural to some, are experienced by others as merely conventional, a political order held in place by force rather than justice.

REFLECTIVE ACTIVITY 2.4

The idea of the common good is at the centre of politics, yet despite thousands of years of consideration, there is no definitive answer and we still ask ourselves this question today.

What is the common good?

Try to answer this question with reference to your own town or city, to your nation-state, or to the international order that exist between states. Whichever way we frame the question of justice, what Plato helps us to see is that politics is always a matter of both what is and what ought to be.

2.3.3 THEORY AND POLITICAL CRITIQUE

Thinking of explanatory and normative theories as inherently linked allows us to ask additional questions. As outlined in Section 2.3.2, moving from an everyday to a theoretical understanding of politics allows us to abstract from the specific to the general. In doing so, we can gain insight into how politics works as we consider the actors, relationships, and causes at play. This insight, then, can upset our conventional ways of acting as existing political arrangements are revealed to be problematic. And, in understanding politics more deeply and becoming critical of the conventional arrangement of politics, we create space to think about how we could change politics for the better. For example, the issue of wealth and income inequality returned to prominence after the 2008 financial crisis, with much of the discussion presuming inequality is bad. But how do we know income and wealth inequality is bad? This question cannot be answered without thinking theoretically. Any answer depends, first, upon a knowledge of the extent and causes of income inequality, but it adds an additional normative premise that at some point too much inequality is intolerable. Our reasons for this vary: because too much inequality can lead to social instability, or because the poorest lack the resources to live a dignified life, or because economic equality has intrinsic value. These normative reasons for our judgements are central to understanding politics, as we will see throughout this book.

Yet it is problematic to presume our reasoned judgements can be justified if they are based on ideals drawn from myths about the essential nature of society and individuals. This problem can be addressed by bringing explanatory and normative theories together to achieve political change—rather than accepting the given order as inevitable or appealing to a timeless political order divorced from experience. If our normative judgements give us cause to think the current political order is illegitimate, then this creates an imperative for change. We can see this in Karl Marx's (2000, 85–94) argument about the **exploitation** of workers (see photo 2.3), and their broader **alienation**. Marx (2000, 93), in his *Economic and Philosophical Manuscripts*, argues economic inequality is rooted in this relationship of exploitation. This does not mean the owner is intentionally trying to harm the worker but that the owner generates profit by paying their workers less than the value of their labour (see Section 9.2.1).

For example, a company making mobile phones must bring together the materials for the phones, the tools for assembling them, and the people who do the actual labour. Each

Photo 2.3 **Karl Marx held that workers in a capitalist society are exploited as they are forced to sell their labour power to capitalists for less than the full value of the commodities they produce with their labour.**

element going into the phone has a price the owner of the company must pay. Yet the actual phone has a value higher than the cost of materials and labour, from which, according to Marx, the owner makes her profit. Value has been added somewhere. Marx claims it has been added by the worker, as the owner does not pay the workers for the full value of their work (Marx, 2000, 273–292). After identifying the exploitative nature of wage-labour as a key source of inequality, Marx goes on to argue exploiting the labour of workers in this way is unjust. Workers are alienated from their labour because they are working for someone else and they are forced to sell their time and energy. Marx thinks the worker, who must earn a wage to survive, is essentially forced to trade portions of their life to the owner—it is because of this coercion socialists sometime use the term 'wage slavery'. Marx thinks exploitation limits the workers' freedom and fails to respect their fundamental humanity. In light of this, he argues existing relationships of capitalist economic production must be altered to address this injustice. The descriptive and normative elements of politics are brought together in Marx's account, resulting in a normative call to action, inspired by an analysis of existing social relations, seeking to improve conditions through political change rather than an appeal to a just natural order. Theories explicitly bringing these elements together are called **critical theories**.

In looking at contrasting theories of politics we have drawn out a number of different things a theory of politics does:

- Develops a general account of political actors and relationships
- Exposes conventional political arrangements to critical scrutiny
- Highlights the need to consider the legitimacy of existing political arrangements
- Provides opportunity for normative judgements that inspire political action

What needs further consideration, however, is how we go about thinking theoretically. It is one thing to read a theory of politics; it is more challenging to think theoretically yourself.

2.3.4 THINKING THEORETICALLY ABOUT POLITICS

You will have noticed that in examining different theories of politics we have moved away from the everyday experiences we started with, as we have abstracted from specific experiences to think about politics in general. We have begun to think theoretically. As outlined in Chapter 1, our goal in this book is to help you understand how to theorise politics, particularly global politics. It is not a book that will teach you the different theories of global politics, nor will it give you lots of facts about global politics. Our goal is to help you learn how to theorise.

Theory is built upon everyday experiences and ideas we can all understand. In fact, each of us already makes use of an implicit set of concepts, relationships, and judgements to make sense of the world. Attending to the sources of this everyday understanding helps us see how theoretical concepts already shape our perceptions. Additionally, approaching theory in a reflective and critical way is itself political, as the ready-made theories we use to understand the political world are inherited tools for thinking, which we should continually criticise and improve. Each of us already knows quite a lot about theory. Further, each of us has the capacity to think critically about the concepts we have inherited. Therefore, being a student of politics involves developing your own ability to think theoretically about politics, to actively theorise, even as a student just beginning to study global politics.

REFLECTIVE ACTIVITY 2.5

To explore what it means to theorise, stop for moment and consider the everyday experiences of politics discussed already as well as your own that you reflected on earlier. The examples we have given you are easily understandable. Your own examples may come readily to mind. You already know quite a lot about politics! So, ask yourself:

Why do you think the things you think about politics?

If the question seems strange, pause for a moment and read it again slowly. We see immediately it is not a 'normal' question as the language itself is difficult: 'think the things you think'. This is what some people might disparage as a philosophical question, suggesting it is intentionally baffling or of little practical consequence. Philosophical questions address how we think and why we believe the things we do (we will use the language of theory rather than philosophy, but the point is the same). These questions are intended to be disruptive and can make us uncomfortable because we have to reflect on our own thoughts and experiences. Give it a go, try to reflect on why you think about politics in the way that you do.

Undoubtedly part of your answer to the question in Reflective Activity 2.5 is deeply personal, having to do with your particular relationships, education, and political experiences. Another part of your answer, however, is likely to be a bit more mysterious. We all have ideas we picked up from somewhere, but most of us do not have a very good idea of where exactly we got the ideas we have. A key task in thinking theoretically is to identify the ideas we use to understand the world, while also developing a critical relationship to those ideas, asking questions about where they come from, whether they are accurate, and considering what effect they may have on how we act in the world. While theory is unavoidably abstract, it is also deeply personal as it reveals something about why we think what we think about politics. Theory is also deeply practical, even if the process of theorising can feel frustratingly divorced from practical questions, because how we understand the world determines what kind of political action we believe is necessary and possible.

Becoming aware of how theoretical ideas shape our thinking, and learning how to theorise, helps us become more self-aware. In our everyday experience of politics there is much that seems mysterious and that we take for granted. For example, whether we agree with the ideas or not, most of us will have heard claims such as:

- War is inevitable
- Politics is about power rather than ethics
- Capitalism is the only viable economic system
- Nation-states should be sovereign

These sorts of claims are usually offered without much thought of how we know them; they are presented as if they are natural and obvious. When we dig deeper into our everyday ideas about politics, it is common to find ideas that are more like myths than careful explanations or precise concepts. As discussed in Chapter 1, these political 'myths' are stories we tell ourselves to make sense of the world. For example, the claim people are naturally violent comes readily to our lips when we are pushed to explain violent conflicts, but this depends upon ideas about human nature, which are more myth than science. And we appeal to imagined continuities of people and land when we assert the necessity of national identities, but again this is an appeal to an origin myth not an historical fact. Or, as we saw in Section 2.2.4, when someone says global politics is only about survival and competition, they are appealing to a myth about the eternal nature of national sovereignty rather than global political history.

Our everyday understanding of politics is rife with mystery, with events that do not make sense, with obscure forces that shape our choices, and with ideas we have picked up, which in turn dictate our actions. Received ideas—political myths—are brought in to explain what is beyond our everyday understanding—mysteries. However, such an approach to thinking about global politics is deficient; it relies upon simple ideas to alleviate our confusion rather than enlightening us. The contemporary world of global politics is complex and often confusing. There is a general sense our traditional ideas are inadequate to explain what is happening around us. One example of this is the popularity of conspiracy theories to explain events, such as the belief that the terrorist attacks in New York City on September 11, 2001 were faked by the United States government, or the long-running idea there is a mysterious cabal coordinating global events, given new expression in the QAnon conspiracy closely associated with former President Trump (see photo 2.4).

Photo 2.4 **QAnon followers believe an unfounded theory that former President Trump was waging a secret war against elite Satan-worshiping paedophiles in government, business, and the media.**

© Sean Rayford / Getty Images

These ideas express the confusing nature of the world we live in and the inadequacy of received wisdom. While we don't endorse conspiracy theories, we also don't want to discount the impulse that gives rise to these false and misleading views. The impulse to look behind our everyday experience, to abstract from the immediate, to question received wisdom is the beginning of theory. Further, it's understandable our impulse to try to understand global politics is often impaired, as we live in a complex and confusing world where clarity and depth are rarely valued or displayed in our everyday discussions of politics. Our goal in the book is to nurture and refine that theoretical impulse, to help you begin to theorise for yourself, critically and carefully, in a way that improves your understanding of the world and your capacity to act politically.

REFLECTIVE ACTIVITY 2.6

Before we move to the next section, consider the following question:

Lasswell and Plato give us very different theories of politics. Can you identify some key theoretical ideas that each thinker employs? How would you evaluate their ideas?

Consider, for example, Lasswell's idea of influence, or Plato's appeal to the common good. These are ideas central to how they understand politics. Are they convincing? Why or why not? What aspects of Lasswell or Plato's ideas do you find insightful? Which do you think are wrong?

2.4 POLITICS AND THE PUBLIC

As we have discussed, there is a connection between the common good and legitimacy. Here we explain how this connection is central to politics, which clarifies the social relationships and authorities that are distinctly political. We can have many different types of relationships: with other people, with animals, with objects, and with physical spaces. It might be tempting to think politics is just about relationships between people. This is not quite right, however, even though human relationships are clearly very important to politics. There are some relationships between people not generally considered political, such as friendship, while there are relationships to animals, objects, and spaces we would consider political, such as the maintenance of national borders, which mark out political spaces and control the movement of objects and animals as well as humans. Politics, then, is not defined by a single type of relationship.

The same issue arises when we think about authority. Not all agents of authority are political. Authorities in the arts, such as esteemed performers or critics, are not granted political power based on their artistic skills or extensive knowledge of art. Similarly, religious or business leaders may have authority, but it does not grant them political positions or powers—although there are times when power in other spheres may be used politically. The defining characteristic of politics must therefore lie somewhere else. Lasswell and Plato both provide hints. Lasswell looks at the distribution of socially valuable goods, while Plato considers the common good of the city-state. They are both concerned with a special kind of social interaction; they are both concerned with public relationships.

2.4.1 WHAT IS THE PUBLIC?

We have already been talking about the 'public', but it's one of those tricky ideas we use in an intuitive way without thinking too much about its exact meaning. As we'll see, it's an important and complex idea. At its most basic level the public is what is shared by all people within a group. A public school is open to all pupils. Public knowledge is available to everyone. A public service is paid for by, and provided to, the whole community. The public can also refer to a group of people as a whole. Individuals and subgroups are also part of the public. Again, most of us have an everyday understanding of this, but as we try to pin down its meaning we see it is rather complex. Lasswell's theory addresses the public because he is concerned with the distribution of goods that are valuable to everyone, and the resulting distribution affects everyone. Plato's theory addresses the public because he is concerned with the best arrangement of the common life of the city-state in an effort to achieve a good life for the community as a whole. As a theoretical concept, the public is not only complex but also contested. Its basic meaning can be clear enough, but determining what should or should not be included in the public realm, or what is in the public interest, are not questions with a single and final answer; rather they are questions we debate and argue over. However, the fact the public is a complex and contested idea should not prevent us from using it to develop a more robust understanding of politics.

To return to our consideration of which social relationships are political, we can begin with the premise politics is concerned with the public aspects of our social relationships. This does not mean politics is only about the relationships involved in the work of governments or the activity of citizens. The home, for example, is a political space, as the social arrangement of the intimate aspects of our lives has wider effects and vice versa. The historical exclusion of women from political life was a consequence of the unequal power granted to men in patriarchal relationships, and it had the effect of further limiting the power of women to challenge their exclusion. Thus, more egalitarian gender relations have significant political consequences, which in turn alter interpersonal relationships. If a nuclear family model (i.e. two parents and children) predominates in society, this has effects on how the care of children is organised, with each family responsible for the welfare of their children and requiring individual access to goods like doctors, schools, and recreation facilities. Other family models would have different political effects. As we saw in Section 2.3.2, Plato suggested the care of children should be a communal, with children having multiple parental figures in the community and their needs met collectively.

Additionally, thinking of politics as concerned with the public aspects of our social relationships does not mean politics only takes place within defined political communities, as social relationships involving numerous communities have effects on multiple publics, such as when manufacturing processes stretch across the globe. For example, a new manufacturing centre financed by foreign investment may disrupt the local economy in an impoverished area of Bangladesh. This investment creates new opportunities for some workers, but is also likely to create new conflicts within that community and generate new local public concerns, such as when women are drawn into the formal economy, which can lead to new competition with male workers and create tensions within families. However, because the investment has come from abroad, the local community is now linked to, and in many ways dependent upon, activities originating and controlled from elsewhere. Also, an extended

supply chain for consumer goods, where they are made in multiple countries but destined for sale in another, makes global transportation routes highly valuable, increasing the number of parties interested in the regulation of ocean trade routes. Today, the South China Sea is a nexus for many political disputes for this reason. Finally, moving the manufacture of goods away from the communities in which they are purchased and used also alters the economies of consuming countries. For example, in the United States the loss of manufacturing industries has impoverished communities where jobs were eliminated and never replaced, and altered the balance of power within the national economy as the focus shifted to service industries.

Thinking of politics as concerned with the public aspects of our social relationships specifies the scope of politics without restricting its domain. The scope of politics is the public aspect of our social relationships, and especially the role and legitimacy of coercion in those relationships. The domain in which our social relationships become political, however, is far more open. This is an important point to understand. Often, we presume politics is limited to what politicians do in established institutions of government, or we think of politics in terms of national elections or relationships between states. This conventional understanding is insufficient. As we have seen, political relationships emerge wherever we have social relationships with public effects. That is a rather general and abstract idea, but as we discussed, this helps us develop a critical understanding of our everyday experience. Understanding the public in this way helps us appreciate how political relationships and institutions are constantly evolving, yet politics remains a concept that speaks to a distinctive aspect of our lives (Dewey, 2012). In the chapters that follow we focus on the international and global dimensions of politics, but this does not mean we are only concerned with interactions between states and their representatives; we are concerned with all those political relationships that cross over, or entirely ignore, national borders.

2.4.2 SHELDON WOLIN: *POLITICS* AND *THE POLITICAL*

In Section 2.2.1 we considered how coercion is linked to legitimacy, and thus our everyday sense of politics includes the capacity to ask 'why' when we are confronted with coercive authority. Yet, in defining politics as the public aspect of our existing social relationships, we risk losing sight of the critical aspect of politics. Throughout our discussion, we have looked at the relationship between political order and political action, but more needs to be said about political action. Sheldon Wolin (1994), an American political theorist, helps us understand this by contrasting *politics* and *the political*. For Wolin, *politics* refers to the political order, or the existing institutional arrangements for the management of our social relationships, including the form political community takes, the allocation of protections and privileges provided by the government, as well as the distribution of goods and services (Wolin, 1994, 22). *Politics* refers to the political order we find in place at any given moment, and the work of *politics* is the maintenance and manipulation of that order. By contrast, for Wolin, *the political* refers to political action, or those moments when diverse people come together to act collectively in a way that disrupts the given *politics* to pursue the common good (Wolin, 1994, 23). Wolin thinks *the political* is momentary and episodic. This means it upsets the operation of *politics*, as the expected way of conducting our social relationships.

Photo 2.5 **Protesters in Cairo's Tahrir Square, Egypt, November 2011.**

© Hang Dinh / Shutterstock.com

The political involves challenging normal social relationships and political authority, as individuals work collaboratively to change existing institutions and ways of interacting.

Looking at a real-world example can clarify how *politics* and *the political* interact. In 2011, as the Arab Spring spread across the Middle East and North Africa, protestors in Egypt gathered in Tahrir Square (see photo 2.5) to challenge the government of Hosni Mubarak.

The protest grew, and the Egyptian public forced the president's resignation, and in the process fundamentally altered Egyptian politics (Hoover, 2011). In Wolin's terms, *politics* (the continued autocratic rule of Mubarak) was challenged by *the political* (expressed through the protests across the country calling for his resignation). This distinction helps us see there are two distinct logics at work when we try to understand politics. Politics, on the one hand, structures our social relationships and exerts power over our actions. On the other hand, politics is the activity of altering the social order through collective action. We need to be aware of these different logics to understand the political world around us. In addition, we need to pay attention to how the way we study politics affects what aspects of the political world we see. Throughout this book we keep both logics of politics in view and approach the study of politics in a critical way that undermines the myth of a natural order in political life. This also means we are concerned both with what is happening in global politics and how it could be altered.

Wolin's distinction between *politics* and *the political* enables a critical understanding of politics, as it shows us both the explanatory and the normative elements of theory are in flux, subject to change but also prone to reification. A central challenge in studying politics is to ensure we do not mistake the political order that is for either the best or only possible world. The things we value, the social conditions we assume are normal, the ways of interacting we see as appropriate, all of these are strongly influenced by *politics* and can be altered by *the political*. Therefore, the study of politics is both deeply personal and uniquely concerned with our ability to act freely. As we study politics, we begin to understand the social order better, while also learning how to judge the values that give legitimacy to political authorities. We should begin to appreciate the importance of politics as a distinctly human endeavour: understanding politics gives us the capacity to choose to act differently as political subjects, to act freely rather than merely responding to the existing political order. The abstract and seemingly impersonal theoretical ideas of *politics* and *the political* are actually deeply personal and can help us understand our own experiences differently.

REFLECTIVE ACTIVITY 2.7

Reflecting on your own political experiences answer the following questions:

*How do the ideas of **politics** and **the political** help you understand political experience?*

Along with these ideas, also think about how ideas of coercion, authority, and legitimacy change how you think about your own experiences.

What are some of the things that are valued in contemporary society? How might their value stem from unequal social relations?

Also, consider how the relationship between values and power might change how you think about your own experiences.

2.5 BECOMING POLITICAL

In considering Wolin's distinction between *politics* and *the political*, we've emphasised the importance of political action. But how does politics lead to a distinctive kind of action? In our everyday experience, politics is often thought of as something to avoid. Some still consider it impolite to talk about politics with family or friends. Others only engage in politics antagonistically, disparaging those they disagree with or complaining about the failings of the government. It has even been suggested we live in a post-political age, where people do not care about politics beyond wanting the government to be run efficiently. We suspect these attitudes are familiar to many readers. They push against our contention that we are all unavoidably affected by politics and should be politically engaged. How, then, does a theoretical understanding of politics help us overcome apathy and disinterest? To help us with this question we turn to the work of Hannah Arendt (see photo 2.6), a 20th-century German philosopher whose main works were written after the Second World War while she was living in the US.

In her book, *The Promise of Politics* (2005), Arendt claims politics is unavoidable because individuals are all different; the human condition, she suggests, is one of plurality. Each of us is unique because we have the capacity for free thought and action. Yet we must live

Photo 2.6 **Hannah Arendt in 1949. Arendt was a political philosopher, author, and Holocaust survivor.**

© dpa picture alliance / Alamy Stock Photo

together. Therefore, if our lives together are to be concerned with more than survival, we will have to come to some agreement about the values and standards that will shape our social relationships; we will have to engage in politics. Unlike Plato, Arendt doesn't suggest there is a natural order that is best for society. Instead, she focuses on how we find agreement on such matters. Because human beings are unique, it's inevitable we will disagree. One way to cope with disagreement is for some individuals to exercise power over others. Plato advocates this explicitly when he argues the philosopher kings should determine what is best for the city-state. For Arendt, an order based on the power of the strongest or the intellect of the wisest cannot be legitimate because it takes away the equal freedom of individuals. She believes people are, and should remain, free.

REFLECTIVE ACTIVITY 2.8

To help you understand what Arendt means here, ask yourself the following questions:

Are my actions freely chosen? If so, what justifiable limits can there be on my freedom?

You might start by thinking about the decisions you've made today, but then consider larger life decisions you've made, or overtly political decisions. See if you can distinguish between actions that were more or less free, then think about what limits your freedom in order to reflect on which limits might be legitimate, and which might be illegitimate.

Can we act freely? While this may seem like another 'philosophical' question, it's of great practical importance as most of us think we are free and behave accordingly. We know there are times when our freedom is constrained, but few people understand themselves as lacking the freedom to make their own choices or think their own thoughts. Freedom, for Arendt, is something we all possess—it is the source of plurality, as each of us experiences the world differently and reacts according to our unique will. A political order based on domination denies human freedom, so another solution to the problem of disagreement is needed. For Arendt, the central question of political legitimacy is: how can we exercise our freedom in concert with others without violence and domination?

On some level, the answer has to be political authority is only legitimate if it preserves freedom and plurality. There are many ways of responding to this dilemma. Here we're interested in Arendt's answer because of her emphasis on our inevitable entanglement in politics and the need for political action. For Arendt, we must recognise the distinctiveness of politics before we can understand how authority can be made legitimate. Politics involves all of us acting collectively. Therefore, the distinctive task of politics is the creation of a common world among diverse individuals. The collective creativity expressed through political action gives diverse individuals a common space in which further collective action is possible. For example, Arendt saw declarations as key moments in which political communities are established; the US Declaration of Independence was a favourite reference.

Political declarations are real-world examples of collective political action, which Arendt thinks create the common world necessary to sustain political life. A declaration, like other political acts, is at the most basic level an exercise of our judgement. It is not simply an exclamation of our desires; it's a reflective judgement about what our shared world should look like. The Declaration of Independence, for example, claimed legitimate government must be based on the consent of those subject to it. It was more than a demand the authors be given what they wanted, as it set out new terms of legitimacy and redefined the political community. Yet this judgement was lacking, as there were many individuals excluded from its concern, whose freedom it did not recognise. A central exception to the Declaration's inalienable rights was the recognition withheld from enslaved people and women, as both groups were considered less than fully human. This exclusion, however, does not discredit Arendt's ideas about political action. Rather, it shows us political action is ongoing.

A less famous declaration was made by the abolitionist and women's rights advocate, Sojourner Truth (see photo 2.7), who declared 'Ain't I a woman?' in a speech in 1851.

While no verbatim transcript of Truth's speech exists, what is known is that her speech declared her equality both with men and with white people (Truth, 2015). As a formerly enslaved woman of African descent, Truth was doubly excluded from the Declaration, but in her counter-declaration she corrected that exclusion through the force of her judgement. In declaring her equality, Truth was using the public space created by the Declaration to appeal

Photo 2.7 **Sojourner Truth, 1870. Truth became a well-known anti-slavery speaker, and delivered the speech 'Ain't I a woman?' at the Women's Convention in Akron, Ohio in 1851.**

© Alpha Historica / Alamy Stock Photo

to others to recognise her freedom and equality. This does not mean Truth's freedom was dependent upon the recognition of others but that correcting her exclusion from politics required getting others to accept her judgement. A similar example can be seen in the Black Lives Matter movement today (see photo 2.8), as the demand for recognition at the heart of the movement is about getting other members of the political community to change their judgement.

The movement is not claiming Black lives do not matter until they are recognised, but that those lives need to be treated equally within the political sphere. This is why the response 'all lives matter' is fundamentally mistaken. The underlying moral value motivating the Black Lives Matter movement is exactly that all lives matter, and the political problem they're confronting is that in practice all lives are not valued equally, even with formal legal equality. It's the everyday failure to value and protect all lives equally that makes the demand for the political recognition of the value of Black lives necessary.

Arendt helps us to see the world we live in is a political world, created by the actions of others taken in the past, based on their judgements. We are unavoidably involved in

Photo 2.8 **Black Lives Matter protesters in London, 2016.**

© Janine Wiedel Photolibrary / Alamy Stock Photo

politics. Further, Arendt insists each of us has the freedom to act, to continue the political activity of making judgements and engaging in collective action. When we make judgements based on our experiences and draw general conclusions, these judgements then form the basis for our actions. These judgements expressed through our actions can be accepted, rejected, or contested by others in an ongoing process. A consequence of Arendt's argument is each of us is already engaged in politics, and the important question is whether we are exercising our freedom.

The common social world created by politics is based on many value judgements made in the past, leading to general rules derived from those specific experiences—these are what Arendt calls prejudices. While we need these past judgements as guides for how to behave, we must also remember they can and should be challenged. The work of making our common world is always ongoing, which is why Arendt sees political action as an expression of human freedom. Legitimate political authority, then, is authority based on consensus within the political community that leaves space for future political creativity.

One of the important things Arendt shows us is that thinking theoretically is a kind of politics. When we theorise, we are trying to extract general ideas or principles from specific experiences in order to come to a clearer understanding of politics—and ideally this understanding should be one we can share with others. In this sense, theorising is a public conversation about how our social relationships function as well as how we think they should function. Further, these different aspects of our public conversation are not separate; rather they reflect the complex nature of politics. As we have discussed in this section, politics is about order and stability as well as creativity and change. Not only do the concepts involved in the study of politics directly impact each of us but we also all take a position on these concepts; we make judgements. For example, we might think the nation-state is natural or war is always bad, without understanding the concepts deeply or examining our own judgements. Arendt helps us see what is at stake in our political judgements and how we might go about improving them.

REFLECTIVE ACTIVITY 2.9

Becoming political, then, involves becoming aware of the contingency of the existing political order and our own capacity to change that order. To start, try this exercise:

Describe and analyse an experience in which you realised you were a 'political subject'. Reflect on how this felt and what it revealed to you about politics.

As you reflect on your own experiences try to use the ideas we have looked at thus far.

2.6 **CONCLUSION**

We started with a broad definition of politics in order to specify some of the key ideas that lie behind our everyday sense of what politics is all about, but the aim of this book is not to offer a narrow definition of politics. Rather, in the following chapters we consider some of the key ideas vital to understanding global politics, which empower you to think critically about the theories of global politics you learn as part of your degree. In later chapters, we look at fundamental ideas—power, law, and money—and important historical developments shaping how we think about politics—empire, capitalism, and the nation-state. As we introduce these concepts, we encourage you to put these ideas to work and analyse them yourself, thinking about whether you agree or disagree with them. Learning to think theoretically and critically will prepare you to approach your further study of politics in a more informed and active way.

Access the online resources at www.oup.com/he/hirst1e for case studies to help contextualise your understanding of key concepts, further reading recommendations to guide you through your reading, and a library of web links to journal articles, blogs, and video content to help you take your learning further.

POWER

3

READERS' GUIDE

Chapter 3: Power explores the mystery of how power works in global politics, and contests the myth that power is simply a coercive force that elite actors use to promote their interests. To do this the chapter examines, first, the 'three faces of power' debate that helps us understand how power works at both obvious and hidden levels. From there, it introduces the idea of *power relations*, and shows how they influence the political world around us as well as our opinions and values. Against the myth that power is a coercive force used by elites, the chapter shows that power is 'productive' in the sense that it *produces things* like knowledge, social norms, and even identity. Understood in this way, the chapter seeks to uncover some of the subtle ways power influences our lives and, crucially, how an awareness of power relations can open up possibilities for resistance and change in global politics.

3.1 INTRODUCTION: WHAT IS POWER, AND WHY STUDY IT?

As political subjects, just as we have all experienced coercion and authority in some form or another (as discussed in Chapter 2), we all already know quite a bit about how power works in global politics. It is clear that some actors in the global arena have more power than others.

Politicians wield significant decision-making power, while transnational corporations exercise power through material wealth, and states use the threat of military power to advance their interests. We can all think of times when power was exercised over us, perhaps by a government official, a family member, or a complete stranger. Similarly, we can all identify moments when we felt powerless to act in accordance with our preferences, when circumstances, protocol, or fear prevented us from doing or saying something. And many of us have heard the claim that power is the driving force of global politics, that actors like states seek power in order to survive in the international system. Yet, despite our familiarity with these kinds of power relations, power is not something we can easily see, grasp, or define. What we perceive most often are the effects of power rather than power itself.

Power sits right at the heart of the study of global politics. A good way to illustrate its importance is political scientist Colin Hay's suggestion that power is to the political as the economy is to economics, or as time is to history (2002, 168–169). That is, power is the fundamental **object of study** in the field of global politics. However despite, or perhaps because of, its importance, power is one of the most hotly debated concepts in the discipline. For some scholars, power is similar to force or coercion, and can be used by states, groups, or individuals to promote their interests. Others view power as a structure rather than an instrument, a sort of invisible web or network which constrains and directs actors' behaviour. Still others suggest it plays a key role in shaping our ideas, values, and beliefs, even influencing our individual and collective identities. Power can also be understood as a force which underpins **resistance** and change in global politics; when people are empowered they can confront and alter existing political arrangements.

The purpose of this chapter is to explore the mystery of how power works in global politics, and to challenge some common myths about who has power, and what can be done with it. Our main aim is to contest the myth that power is simply a coercive force that elite actors use to promote their interests. This is important because this myth makes it seem as though ordinary people have no access to, and so can do nothing about, the operation of power in global politics. Against this myth, the chapter shows that power is 'productive' in the sense that it *produces things* like knowledge, **social norms**, and values. What this means, we suggest, is that all of us wield, and are affected by, relations of power. By looking at power in this light, we will uncover some of the ways it influences our lives in the subtlest of manners. We will see that many features of the political world which appear natural or inevitable are actually the product of '**power relations**', which are political in character. Most importantly, the chapter challenges this myth in order to show that by unearthing these power relations we can open up possibilities for resistance and change in global politics.

In order to do this, we will explore two approaches to the study of power in global politics. First, we will examine a descriptive mode of study which seeks to *understand* power. Second, we will turn to a normative approach which seeks to *critique* it. The former aims to help us explain how power works, while the latter is concerned with evaluating and changing contemporary power relations and their material effects (see Chapter 2). By exploring these different styles of analysis, the chapter raises several key questions underpinning the study of global politics:

- Should we conceptualise power so that it is easily measurable, even if this means we leave important elements out, or would it be better to have a more nuanced understanding even if this means power becomes very difficult to measure?

- Should we view power as something which can be acquired and used by actors such as states, institutions, or individuals, or is it better understood as a relationship between them?

- Do we want to focus on the power brokering of elites operating within and between nation-states, or are we concerned with everyday power relations which subjugate people on the basis of ethnicity, gender, class, sexuality, citizenship status, religion, and so forth?

- Most fundamentally, perhaps, is the idea to make value-free observations about power, or should we try to change existing power relations?

REFLECTIVE ACTIVITY 3.1

It might be difficult to decide what you think about these questions at this stage. But take a moment to consider them and make a note of your preliminary answers as we will return to them later.

Which do you think is the best approach in each bullet point above, and why? What are the benefits and drawbacks of each option, in your view?

Your answers to these questions will likely be reflected in the theoretical approaches that you choose to use as you progress through your studies. Discuss your answers with a fellow student or friend.

Before we proceed, it is worth pausing to ask a question. Why have we decided to explore power at this early stage in the book? Why not begin with something more concrete like the state or the historical founding of the current global order? After all, this is what most introductory texts do. And it might make life simpler as these ideas, unlike power, are relatively easy to understand. The reason is that in our view, power comes *before*, and not *from*, key actors or institutions like the state or international organisations. In other words, far from being the *source* of power, these actors and institutions are *shaped and maintained* by power relations. If we were to begin with the state or the founding of the state system, we would be presenting these as the foundational building blocks from which to study global politics. This would have the effect of presenting them as natural or inevitable, which would discourage questions about their origins and effects, and hide the power relations that underpin them.

This is also the reason we do not begin our analysis with specific framings of power derived from established theories of International Relations (IR), such as the Realist notion of the 'balance of power' or IR professor and former US Assistant Secretary of Defense for International Security Affairs Joseph Nye's framing of 'hard' power (force, coercion), 'soft' power (persuasion, diplomacy), and 'smart' power (a combination of both) (Nye, 2011). To begin with these would mean going along with common assumptions about power in global politics which in our view are not justified. For example, the Classical Realist view that state behaviour is driven by the pursuit of power because human beings are by nature self-interested and prone to conflict is often presented as self-evidently true in global politics. We certainly see plenty of examples of self-interested activity on the part of states, such as when one invades another. Yet this pessimistic view of human nature has never been convincingly proven.

Other theories, like Liberalism for example, suggest that states can be motivated by concerns other than self-interested power politics because human beings have the capacity to cooperate and act for common interests. The rise of international institutions and development of aid and humanitarian intervention programmes suggest that states can and do act for reasons other than increasing their power. What this shows is that if we were to simply begin from established views of the role of power in governing state behaviour, we would be going along with assumptions rather than building on solid ground. Far better, we believe, is an approach which calls into question the power relations which generate and sustain these political and theoretical constructs.

Rather than taking anything for granted, then, we want to critically explore the concept of power. Key to a critical engagement with global politics is learning to seek out, analyse, and challenge many kinds of power relations, including those which found and maintain the key institutions of the current global order and IR's theoretical traditions. As struggles such as the civil rights/anti-racist, decolonial, feminist, and LGBTQIA+ movements show, established power relations can be changed if they are identified, denaturalised, and challenged. But for this to be possible, we must understand how power relations work and be able to critique them.

3.2 UNDERSTANDING POWER

Many explorations of power in global politics begin with what political theorist Steven Lukes calls the 'three faces of power' debate, which occurred during the mid to late 20th century. While this approach has its limitations, it provides a good way to begin our exploration of what power is, who has it, and how it works. Borrowing Hay's (2002) useful framing of decision-making, agenda-setting, and preference-shaping power, we will evaluate each of these 'faces of power' in turn.

3.2.1 THE FIRST FACE OF POWER: DECISION-MAKING

The first face—'decision-making power'—is likely to be closest to our existing understanding of power. According to political scientist Robert Dahl, this kind of power is at work when *person A gets person B to do something that B would not otherwise do, and which is not in B's interests* (1952). In other words, one person has power over another person when the former can make the latter change their behaviour so that they do something they would not have done otherwise, and which is not good from their perspective. In this framing, power is similar to coercion; power is something that can be used to change someone's actions or fate. It is, then, a question of one actor dominating another actor. Whether through force, the threat of force, or some other capability, power is exercised when person A impacts on person B's ability to freely choose their own path. We might call this 'power over', or, as IR scholar Felix Berenskoetter (2007) suggests, the power to win conflicts.

In broad terms, this corresponds to Nye's notion of 'hard' power, understood as a resource or capability that can be obtained and used by states. Such hard power can take the form of military, but also economic, dominance, and can be used to compel or coerce targets either by its use or the threat of its use. This is also similar to how Realists in IR view power, though there is some variation in this tradition as to whether power is measurable (such as through a metric like population or military capabilities), relational (understood

Photo 3.1 **An Extinction Rebellion protester being arrested in London, 2019. This is an example of the 'first face' of power—power *over* another person.**

© Karl Nesh / Shutterstock.com

as the ability to influence actors), and whether it is a means to an end or an end in itself (Schmidt, 2005, 527).

An example of this first face of power is the US-led coalition's removal of Saddam Hussein's regime from power in Iraq in 2003, and the banning of Ba'ath Party members from higher offices in the new government. Actor A, the US-led coalition, changed the behaviour of actor B, the Ba'athist regime, in a manner contrary to B's interests. Similarly, as you can see in photo 3.1, if a police officer arrests someone participating in an Extinction Rebellion (XR) or Black Lives Matter (BLM) protest, the officer has exercised power over that person by preventing them from continuing to participate in the event, which is against their wishes. Understood in this way, power is something an actor has or possesses, an instrument or capability which can be used to change others' actions.

REFLECTIVE ACTIVITY 3.2

Take a pause here to think of other examples of this kind of power, both in your personal experience and the sphere of global politics. Then consider these questions:

Where have you seen this 'hard' form of power in your everyday life?

What effect did this have on the people involved?

What do you make of this definition of power? Is it convincing? What is left out of this framing?

While this framing accords with popular understandings of power, scholars like Peter Bachrach and Morton Baratz have argued that it is limited. Critics of Dahl's approach have suggested that it assumes that power is only present if person A's interests *conflict with* person B's interests. If there is no conflict, then no force has been applied to change B's behaviour, and so power is absent from the situation. Accordingly, this kind of power is relatively easy to measure. All we need to do to see the workings of power is identify which actors change the behaviour of other actors and catalogue this. But what if power isn't only at work in circumstances where conflict is present? And what if power affects actors in subtler ways which prevent conflict from happening? In addition, critics have also shown that Dahl's view presupposes that actors can be sure of what is and what is not in their interests. After all, if there is any ambiguity about whether B's preferred action is in fact in their interest, we cannot be sure that A has successfully altered B's behaviour in a way that is contrary to B's interest. What happens, though, if the alteration turns out in fact to be in B's interest? These questions led to the conceptualisation of a second face of power.

3.2.2 THE SECOND FACE OF POWER: AGENDA-SETTING

Key limitations of the first face of power were pointed out by Bachrach and Baratz in their 1962 article 'Two Faces of Power'. While they accepted that decision-making is an important dimension of how power works, they argued that a second type of power—'**agenda-setting power**'—is also at play in the political sphere. Specifically, they claimed that the situation is more complicated than just looking at whether A successfully changes B's behaviour by exerting observable force. In particular, they argued that this focus on *overt* decision-making fails to acknowledge the *covert* uses of power that go on before and behind the taking of decisions. What they mean becomes clear when we consider how the decisions we take are frequently limited in advance by placing particular issues on, or preventing them from getting onto, the political agenda. This happens in several ways.

First, it is possible to put something new on the agenda. The idea of universal basic income, for example, has recently been gaining traction in many parts of the world as a possible way of dealing with the decreasing disposable income of consumers caused by stagnating wages and the broader ongoing fallout from the 2008 global financial crisis. Similarly, the 2016 Brexit referendum—in which the UK decided to leave the European Union (see photo 3.2)—was possible only because the possibility of a referendum was successfully placed on the agenda, something which had previously not been achieved despite significant anti-EU sentiment in right-wing political parties in the UK.

A good deal of attention is currently being paid by activists, NGOs, and parties across the political spectrum to the question of how issues can successfully be placed on the agenda of public and political debate, as this is a complex and difficult thing to achieve. Many commentators, such as *The Atlantic*'s Jay David Bolter, have suggested that social media sites like Facebook, Twitter, and Instagram are increasingly important for getting issues onto the political agenda.

Second, it is possible to prevent issues from getting onto the agenda, or from receiving much attention in discussions if they do. If we return to the example of the 2003 invasion of

Photo 3.2 **The 2016 Brexit referendum happened because politicians managed to get the idea of the UK's withdrawal from the EU onto the political agenda.**

© Anthony Collins / Alamy Stock Photo

Iraq, agenda-setting power was exercised by US spokespersons at the UN Security Council when they sidelined options such as economic/diplomatic sanctions, and instead pushed for the interventionist policy of 'regime change' by emphasising the threat posed by weapons of mass destruction. What the Iraq example shows here is that *before* the overt use of US military power to remove the Ba'ath Party from office took place, covert power had *already* been exercised in setting the agenda so that the invasion appeared to many as the best course of action. In other words, behind the first face of power, the second face had already been operating.

Finally, it is possible to remove issues from the agenda. For example, former US President Donald Trump orchestrated the removal of terms like 'climate change' and 'global warming' from government websites and academic researchers were put under pressure not to include such terms in funding bids. While global attention to environmental issues had risen in the years before Trump's time in office, his drive to remove these terms from sites of public and academic debate meant that the perceived significance of climate change issues was reduced, taking attention and resources away from them. It remains to be seen what action will be taken by Joe Biden's presidential administration to correct this, but it is likely that this has negatively impacted the global response to the climate emergency at least in the short term.

REFLECTIVE ACTIVITY 3.3

Take a pause to reflect on these questions:

Do you agree that social media platforms are important for getting issues onto the political agenda? Why or why not?

Which actors have been successful recently in preventing issues from making it onto the international agenda?

What other examples of removing issues from the political agenda come to mind?

As these examples suggest, while the first face deals with the open, transparent exercise of power, the second face explores more secretive and less visible forms of power. While this gives us a more nuanced understanding of how power works, it means that it is no longer possible to see and measure power so easily. Unlike decision-making activities which lead directly to changes in behaviour, agenda-setting power is at work behind the scenes, influencing not just the decisions that are taken but whether an issue even makes it into the arena of debate at all. Importantly, while the first face of power stipulates that power is only at work when conflict arises, the second face suggests that it can be present when conflict is not visible. This is because putting things on, or taking things off, the agenda means that particular conflicts will never arise. This is a commonplace tactic of political parties the world over when it comes to issues likely to cause them electoral problems.

One of the most interesting points raised by Bachrach and Baratz is that there is a serious cost to focusing just on decision-making, and not agenda-setting, power. If we do this, they argue, we simply accept whatever agenda we are presented with, ignoring the question of who decides what is and is not included, and failing to ask whose interests it serves. This would be a serious problem for students and scholars of global politics, whose key concern is a deep exploration of power and its consequences.

REFLECTIVE ACTIVITY 3.4

Consider the following questions, and share your ideas with a friend or classmate:

Why do we need to look at 'agenda-setting' power in addition to 'decision-making' power in the study of global politics?

Is this as far as we need to go in order to understand how power works in global politics? What, if anything, is left out?

While many scholars agreed that the second face of power was an improvement on the first, some, such as Steven Lukes, argued that it too suffered from important limitations.

Specifically, observing the way that social forces and norms impact upon people's beliefs, values, and opinions, the question arose of whether power relations might run even deeper than political agenda-setting. What if power influences not just the political agenda but also our individual and collective political views? Accordingly, a third face of power was identified, explored in Section 3.2.3.

3.2.3 THE THIRD FACE OF POWER: PREFERENCE-SHAPING

The third face of power—'preference-shaping power'—was conceptualised by Lukes in 1974. Lukes' most important contribution to the debate was to show that in addition to decision-making and agenda-setting, power operates in a further, and even less visible, way (2005). Whereas in the first two faces power operates *outside* the actors involved in the formal and informal corridors of power, the third face of power is active *within* the thoughts and preferences of people. Power, Lukes argues, shapes not only the political agenda but also our individual and collective ideas, values, and interests. Drawing on the ideas of the Marxist revolutionary Antonio Gramsci (see Chapter 1 and photo 1.1), Lukes shows that we do not identify and pursue our political preferences outside of power relations. Instead, the social and political context in which we are situated has a significant impact on how we decide what our interests are. This means that our political opinions do not spring just from us as individuals. Instead, they are formed in light of ideas about right and wrong in our society. These ideas are, for Lukes, influenced by the workings of power.

This is a very disorientating thought, so let's pause for a second. What seems to be suggested here is that our ideas and beliefs are not simply our own. Lukes' argument implies that power influences us at the level of our conscious and unconscious minds as we decide what our political preferences are. This seems to threaten the idea of free will and individual autonomy. But surely this is something many of us have thought of before. When it comes to our political preferences, many of us develop values similar to those of our families and communities. Others break with these background values, and develop different preferences through meeting new people, reading, travel, and political engagement. The point is that whatever our political views, we are always influenced by the world around us, taking on and rejecting ideas as we encounter them. In this sense, our preferences have always been shaped by the power relations of society.

It is also the case that actors in the international arena take steps to deliberately influence public preferences. To illustrate this, we can turn again to the example of the invasion of Iraq. Between the 9/11 attacks in 2001, and the invasion of Iraq in March 2003, advocates of the 'regime change' policy in both the US and UK went to significant lengths to shape public preferences to support the invasion. Arguments about the importance of liberating the Iraqi people, the threat posed by the then president of Iraq, Saddam Hussein, to the stability of the Middle East, and the dangers posed by weapons of mass destruction and a possible allegiance with Al-Qaeda dominated the broadcast and print media. Pro-invasion rhetoric was also widespread outside these explicitly political sectors, for example in video-games, WWE wrestling, and the food industry (as shown in the changing of 'French fries' to 'freedom fries' in three Congressional cafeterias and more widely in the US). These measure and others like them, contributed to shaping people's preferences in support of the invasion without them realising it.

The third face of power thus addresses the complex question of how our ideas about what is good, and what is in our interests, are formed. To get at this problem, Lukes' account of the third face of power draws on Gramsci's idea of 'false consciousness'. False consciousness refers to the idea that people are encouraged by the ruling classes to adopt preferences which ultimately do not benefit them. In this account, people are unable to identify their real interests because they are misled by powerful groups into adopting ideas which are really in the latter's interests. This happens through the promotion of social norms, myths, and ideals which people internalise as their own.

One way to illustrate this is to look at why many people vote for policies and parties which do not serve their material interests. For example, many US citizens whose economic interests would be better promoted by a Democratic government than a Republican one nevertheless vote Republican. For many Republican voters, programmes like Medicaid and Medicare would mean access to potentially life-saving medical treatment, and yet they reject state-funded healthcare. Similarly, in the 2016 US election many women and people of colour deemed it in their interests to vote for Trump (see photo 3.3) despite his evident sexism and racism. Why might this happen?

Photo 3.3 **Despite a public record of sexism and racism, women and people of colour contributed to Donald Trump's US Presidential election win in 2016 by voting for him. Can you explain their reasons for doing this?**

© Philip Scalia / Alamy Stock Photo

REFLECTIVE ACTIVITY 3.5

Take a moment to consider the following questions:

What does Lukes mean by 'preference-shaping power'? Can you think of any examples of your preferences being influenced by this kind of power?

Why do people sometimes vote in ways which seem to be contrary to their material interests? What might we do about this?

When it comes to voting, we draw upon family and community traditions, ideas circulating in the media, long-standing patriotic narratives, and a host of other factors to help us decide what to do. What appears to be the right thing, or just plain common sense, may actually be strongly influenced by far-reaching power relations which shape our judgements and preferences in ways we do not see or realise. While it may appear to us as though we are making free choices, according to Lukes power has already affected the formation of our ideas, beliefs, and values. We cannot, therefore, simply assume that what *appears* to us to be in our interest really *is* in our interest. Instead, we have to pause and ask ourselves why we view particular things as in our interests. This involves the rather complicated exercise of considering not just *what* we think but also *why* we think what we think. Sometimes powerful political traditions and myths win out over more concrete considerations.

Many accounts of power in global politics stop here. We already have a fairly complex picture of how power works, and we have covered several well-known analyses. If we think critically, however, there is a further puzzle to address. Given that power has the capacity to shape our preferences in ways we cannot see, how do we decide which of our preferences are 'true', in the sense of coming from us and reflecting our real interests, and which are 'false', in the sense of being influenced by power relations? Neither Lukes, nor Gramsci before him, managed to solve this problem. The idea of false consciousness cannot help us here—it cannot offer a way of deciding which interests have, and which have not, been influenced by powerful groups' agendas. Moreover, its claim that people cannot tell when they are being duped by those in power has patronising implications. We can, however, push our analysis further by exploring the idea of 'power relations' which influence not just our preferences but who we are as people. To do this, we will explore a different way of studying power, one which is concerned not just with *understanding* existing global power relations but also *challenging* and *changing* them.

3.3 CRITIQUING POWER

Political theorist Clarissa Rile Hayward (1998) argues that we should 'de-face' power. The three faces debate compels us, she suggests, to view power as something that the powerful acquire and wield at the expense of the powerless. Instead, she argues, power should be viewed as a 'network of social boundaries that constrain and enable action for all actors'

(1998: 2). There are two key points here. First, we should stop thinking of power as something actors have or use. Power is not a possession or a capability. Instead, we should view it as a network of social norms and principles which affect our actions. Second, we should drop the idea that some actors have power and others lack it. Instead, all actors are situated within the network of power, which means that all actors' behaviour is influenced by power relations and in turn influences power relations. What this suggests is that we should stop trying to decide which of our preferences are, and which are not, affected by power and see instead that *all of them* are in some way or another.

REFLECTIVE ACTIVITY 3.6

Pause here to reflect and consider these questions:

Does the idea that all our preferences have been shaped through power relations sound convincing to you? What would the consequences of this be?

Can you think of any preferences or values you hold which have not been shaped by power relations?

3.3.1 GLOBAL POWER RELATIONS

Hayward's alternative framing draws on the work of philosopher and social theorist Michel Foucault (see photo 3.4). Foucault's analysis of power has had a far-reaching impact across the social sciences and beyond—he was in fact the most cited author across the humanities in the first decade of the 21st century. Indeed, some have suggested, against Hayward's claim that we should de-face power, that Foucault's analysis should be considered the fourth face of power (Digester, 1992).

For Foucault, power runs even deeper than for Lukes, influencing not just our political interests but also *who we are as people*. In this framing, the effects produced by power relations are not only to be found at the level of our concrete preferences, as Lukes has it. Instead, according to Foucault, they are incorporated into, and help to produce, our very *identities* (Foucault, 1980; 2003) This is because from the moment we are born, we are placed inside social, political, and moral codes. Rather than simply having an influence on our preferences, these codes—or 'power relations'—play a big part in forming *who we become*.

Take, for example, the issue of gender. We all have gendered expectations placed on us. Men, for instance, experience pressure to be assertive, decisive, and to perform leadership roles in employment and family environments. In contrast, women are often encouraged to please others and perform caretaking roles at work and at home. People who are transgender (an umbrella term to describe people whose gender is not the same as, or does not sit comfortably with, the sex they were assigned at birth), or nonbinary (an umbrella term for people whose gender identity doesn't sit comfortably with binary understandings or 'man' or 'woman'), have a range of pressures placed upon them, including dealing with misgendering and transphobic discrimination. While we may think that prevailing gender norms are simply 'natural', or based on biological sex differences, a Foucauldian analysis argues that they develop through power relations. Far from spontaneously or naturally occurring, this approach suggests these hierarchical relationships developed in ways which benefit

Photo 3.4 **Michel Foucault. Foucault believed that power relations affect and help shape our identities, and his ideas have influenced a wide range of academic fields.**

© INTERFOTO / Alamy Stock Photo

some at the expense of others. We must ask ourselves, consequently, where these power relations come from rather than simply accepting them.

According to Foucault, then, our patterns of thought, common-sense assumptions, and even our most deeply held beliefs all develop through the prism of power relations. This might sound highly counter-intuitive. Even scary. The idea that our thoughts, beliefs, and sense of self are deeply interwoven with power relations is certainly unsettling. To make sense of these ideas, the next sections of this chapter examine how power relations are deeply embedded in our political lives and identities. They do this by exploring how power relations work at three interrelated levels. First, we explore the relationship between power and knowledge, specifically the idea that what we know is not neutral but rather *political*. Second, we will turn to the question of how power affects social norms and values through the operation of powerful **narratives** known as '**discourses**'. And finally, we will address the ways in which power impacts our individual and collective identities, through a process called '**subjectification**'.

Key to understanding power relations at all these levels is the idea that power is not *repressive* but rather *productive*. The three faces debate treats power as though it constrains, restricts, or supresses our actions—in this sense it is seen as a negative force. Against this, Foucault argues that we should not think of power as the same as repression or prohibition.

It is not, for him, a command, like 'Thou shalt not . . .' (1980, 140). Instead, to better understand how power works, we should view it as 'productive'. By productive, he does not mean good or useful but rather that it *produces effects,* rather than simply constraining or directing things that already exist. Power is productive, according to Foucault, because it produces all kinds of things, such as what we think of as right and wrong, what we find pleasurable and unpleasant, and what we know about the world. Indeed, he goes as far as to say that power relations influence society's most fundamental truths. In his words, 'truth isn't outside power or lacking in power . . . Truth is a thing of this world' (2003, 316). Each society, he argues, has its own 'regime of truth':

> 'Truth' is to be understood as a system of ordered procedures for the production, regulation, distributions, circulation, and operation of statements. 'Truth' is linked in a circular relation with systems of power that produce and sustain it, and to effects of power which it induces and which extend it—a 'regime' of truth (2003, 317).

In this view, what we think of as 'truth' isn't simply neutral or objective but rather mediated through power relations. Foucault describes this as the '**power/knowledge nexus**'.

3.3.2 POWER/KNOWLEDGE

According to Foucault, the knowledge we have about the world isn't value-free but rather reflects all sorts of power relations. An excellent example of this is provided by visual story-teller and IR professor David Campbell (2013, 224–225). In schools and universities across the world, the Mercator world map is used to teach geography and related topics (see Figure 3.1). This is the world map you will likely be used to seeing. While we tend to think of a map as simply a factual representation of the world, Campbell shows that the Mercator map is actually a product of power relations. Drawn in the 16th century, the Mercator map was used for charting shipping courses for the imperial European powers. Because it had this purpose, the map was drawn with Europe at the centre, and it significantly distorted the relative size and location of the rest of the world's continents. Despite the development of more accurate alternatives such as the Gall-Peters Projection map (see Figure 3.2), the Mercator is still widely used. Many have suggested that this reflects ongoing colonial attitudes and devalues the Global South by representing it as small and peripheral.

REFLECTIVE ACTIVITY 3.7

To further explore this point, follow this link to a clip of the TV series 'The West Wing': https://youtu.be/eLqC3FNNOaI (we are grateful to Dr Chris Rossdale of the University of Bristol for this exercise)

Watch this with a classmate or friend and answer the following question:

What should CJ and Josh have done following the presentation by the Organization of Cartographers for Social Equality?

Figure 3.1 **The Mercator World Map, created by Flemish cartographer Gerardus Mercator in 1569 to facilitate navigation. It places the Global North on the top and the Global South on the bottom, and distorts the relative size of these areas, but is nevertheless still widely used today.**

© Daniel R. Strebe, 16 December 2011

The central point here is that an apparently politically neutral artefact—a map—is actually shot through with power relations. Through the Mercator map, Europe is able to present itself as larger and more geographically central than it really is, inflating its apparent importance relative to other areas. This is because the map was made by Europeans, reflecting their interests and ideas about themselves and the rest of the world. Importantly, the Mercator map is not used just in Europe but globally. This means that people outside Europe will also be using a map which positions Europe as the core and them as peripheral.

Figure 3.2 **The Gall-Peters Projection Map, originally the idea of Scottish clergyman James Gall in 1885 and reintroduced by German historian Arno Peters in 1973, was intended to correct the distortions of the Mercator map. It has since been criticised for its own distortions and limitations.**

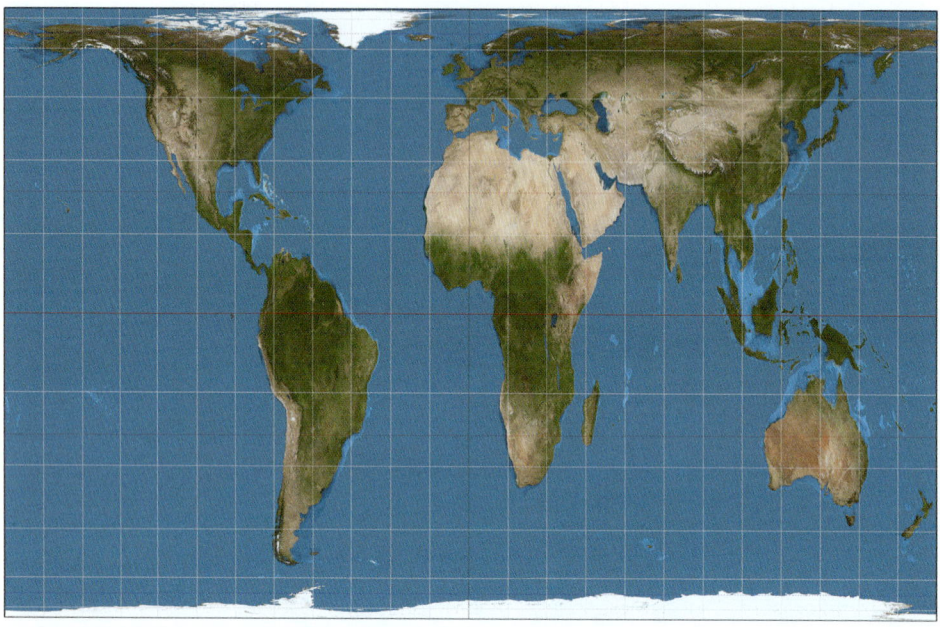

© Daniel R. Strebe, 15 August 2011

REFLECTIVE ACTIVITY 3.8

Look at Figure 3.1 The Mercator World Map.

What consequences might the continuing use of the Mercator map have for people outside Europe?

Can you think of other forms of representation which have this kind of effect?

Foucault therefore uses the idea of the power/knowledge nexus to show that knowledge is produced not *outside of*, but rather *within*, power relations. How, where, and by whom knowledge gets produced makes it *political*. Because we cannot stand outside of the political and social world we study, we cannot help but produce knowledge which reflects our political and social context. What we 'know', then, is not simply **objective** but rather bound up with the workings of power relations.

We should pause here again. Surely truth is simply a reflection of facts? Surely facts, especially those grounded in science or maths, are not affected by power relations? Foucault's aim is not to challenge the validity of science or maths in a wholesale manner but rather to show that the knowledge we generate in all fields of study is bound up with power relations. Who gets to produce knowledge, the language in which it is produced, who is educated sufficiently to engage with it, how and by whom it is funded, how it is transmitted, and the questions guiding the production of knowledge mean that it is never politically neutral. Importantly, however, it is not just academic knowledge that is formed in and through power relations. The social norms and values upon which society is based are also, Foucault argues, produced in this way.

3.3.3 SOCIAL NORMS AND DISCOURSE

In addition to exploring the ways in which knowledge is produced through the play of power relations, Foucault demonstrates that the social norms of society are also influenced by them. Social norms include things like our collective moral and legal codes, our shared ideas of right and wrong, our cultural and religious affinities, and the practices that govern our everyday interactions with one another. In this sense, they are similar to the myths that this book is interested in challenging. Far from being natural or spontaneously occurring, according to Foucault these social norms are produced and reproduced in light of power relations. He uses the idea of 'discourse' to illustrate this point.

A discourse is a collection of narratives or accounts about something, such as a historical event or political struggle. Discourses of various kinds circulate as people describe and interpret these things. When a particular discourse becomes dominant, it becomes the standard or common-sense understanding. A dominant discourse emerges when a debate is apparently resolved so that a specific conventional wisdom is established. For example, a powerful discourse has become established which tells us that the Second World War was a 'good' war fought by the Allies in the name of freedom and democracy. This discourse tells us that there were 'good guys' and 'bad guys' in the conflict, and that great leaders like Churchill, Roosevelt, and Truman led the good guys to victory. The discourse emerged and is perpetuated in many ways, such as the way 20th century history is taught in schools in North America and Europe, and the way we commemorate key events like D-Day and VE/VJ Day. This discourse also contributes to ways the Allies' use of atomic weapons has traditionally been presented as justified, despite the huge civilian death toll and widespread destruction.

The point here is not whether or not the discourse is correct, in the sense of whether the Second World War really was a 'good war' but rather that the prevailing discourse is a powerful one and that people are under some pressure to accept it. Anglo-American school children who submit assignments critical of Allied activities, such as the use of atomic weapons on Hiroshima and Nagasaki or the bombing of Dresden, might be reprimanded by their teacher or given a bad grade. Anti-militarist activists who campaign for global disarmament are often told that the Axis powers in the Second World War (Germany, Italy, and Japan) would have won if the Allies had not used robust military force. Similarly, as we will explore in Chapter 8, there has been a strong public backlash against journalists and academics who have recently criticised Churchill's imperialism and racism. Such challenges serve to discipline people to adopt the dominant discourse by telling them that to believe otherwise is wrong in some sense—they might be told that they are unpatriotic, naive, or ungrateful to the service members who fought and lost their lives. This disciplinary power makes it quite difficult, and sometimes risky, to challenge a dominant discourse.

Discourses, however, are not only to be found in historical topics or events. In fact, discourses about contemporary political issues and struggles are all around us. For instance, in recent years migrants and refugees have been subject to discourses which frame them in negative ways. Right-wing political parties in the UK, for example, have promoted the idea that immigrants are 'stealing' jobs from British people, and that Europe is under siege from 'swarms' of refugees and migrants. Former President Trump (see photo 3.3) made similar claims about Mexicans and other groups in the USA. While this kind of discourse is not new, anti-immigrant sentiment has been increasing in many parts of the world in recent years. Importantly, as these anti-immigrant discourses become more prevalent, there have been corresponding real-world effects, many of them catastrophic. For instance, 24,152 people have died or gone missing trying to cross the Mediterranean Sea to enter Europe between 2014 and 2022, yet legal restrictions have been placed on NGOs' rescue vessels which prevent them from operating, and some European states like Italy have closed their ports to them. Many commentators have argued that through these discourses, migrants like those you can see in Photo 3.5 have been dehumanised to such a degree that European leaders and populations are indifferent to their deaths.

Discourses, then, are comprised of powerful narratives which influence our understanding of past and present events, relationships, and issues. In order for discourses of this kind to influence social norms in this way they must also, according to Foucault, have effects on us as individuals.

Photo 3.5 **Greece, 2015. Refugees and migrants approach the Greek shore crossing the five-mile distance from Turkey, fleeing conflict in Syria. Anti-migrant rhetoric from right-wing political parties across Europe frames a negative discourse around displaced people.**

© ZUMA Press, Inc. / Alamy Stock Photo

REFLECTIVE ACTIVITY 3.9

Take a moment to reflect on the ideas from Section 3.3.3. Then consider these questions:

What other discourses—understood as powerful stories that come to function as common-sense truths—can you identify?

Why is it so difficult to challenge dominant discourses?

3.3.4 PRODUCING IDENTITY

In addition to producing knowledge and social norms, Foucault argues that discourses and power relations contribute to producing our individual and collective identities. Rather than being the person you are today from the moment of your birth, you will have become that person over time and in relation to your experiences. Certain tendencies and behaviours will have been nurtured while others will have been discouraged. This process of identity production will occur in relation to dominant social norms, the things society considers good and bad, polite or rude, attractive or unattractive, and so forth. This process is known as 'subjectification'. Think back to the discussion in Chapter 2 of becoming a 'political subject' in order to grasp the meaning of this term.

Processes of subjectification—in other words, *becoming who we are as subjects*—begin at the very earliest stages of our lives. When babies are born, they are often dressed in clothes of a particular colour. In the West today, this is often gendered: pink for a girl and blue for a boy. Indeed, this gender coding often begins before the baby is born, such as the colours used in decorations and cakes at 'gender-reveal' parties. As a child grows, they are given toys—often things like cars, spaceships, and action figures for boys, and dolls, tea sets, and jewellery-making kits for girls. When boys injure themselves, they are often told not to cry, that they are acting like a girl if they do. Girls are frequently praised for looking pretty and being sweet or obedient rather than for their practical or intellectual achievements. Parents often have higher expectations of boys' capacities and strength, and leave them to work out how to do a task for longer, while they offer help to girls of the same age sooner. Children are thus presented with gendered objects and activities which steer them towards certain behaviours and away from others. These directions are then internalised as the 'correct' way of doing things.

Importantly, these processes of identity formation—or subjectification—are social and political, not reflections of our innate nature or abilities. As we can see when we look at different cultural expectations for girls' and boys' behaviour, there is no universally accepted archetype. For example, in some cultures, boys are dressed in trousers or shorts, with garments like dresses or skirts being considered for girls only. In other cultures, it might be standard practice for boys to wear tunics similar to those worn by girls. Similarly, while blue and pink have been used in the Western world for clothes and toys for boys and girls respectively, this has been the case only since the 20th century, and elsewhere in the world these colour codings do not apply.

This variety suggests that these processes of subjectification are not natural or inevitable but rather a consequence of the power relations which predominate in a given time and place. However, we frequently hear justifications of gender inequalities based on supposedly 'natural' biological or psychological differences. For example, it is sometimes claimed that men should be the head of the household as they are physically stronger, or that women are not suited to participate in political life as they are led by their emotions rather than reason. These justifications are highly dubious as they ignore the role that power relations play in these configurations. As IR professor Cynthia Enloe argues,

> Too often gender incurious commentators attribute women's roles in international affairs to tradition, cultural preferences, and timeless norms, as if each of these existed outside the realms where power is wielded, as if they were beyond the reach of decisions and efforts to enforce those decisions. What sacrifices a woman should make as a mother, what priorities a woman as a wife should embrace, what sexualized approaches in public a woman should find innocent or flattering, what victim identity a refugee woman should adopt, what boundaries in friendships with other women a woman should police, what dutiful daughter model a girl should admire— in reality, all of these are shaped by the exercise of power by people who believe that their own local and international interests depend on women and girls internalizing these feminized expectations. If women internalize these expectations, they will not see the politics behind them (2014, 11).

The examples given by Enloe show that the prevailing gender norms in a given society are not natural but rather *constructed* through power relations. As many feminist theorists have shown, the key question we need to ask ourselves is: who benefits from these gender norms and hierarchies?

Another issue relating to subjectification is that for some people, these processes are easier because the expectations placed upon them fit with their existing inclinations and habits, but for others this is not the case. Consider the experience of a child growing up under colonial rule in the British Empire. Novelist and scholar Ngũgĩ wa Thiong'o, who you can see in photo 3.6, argues that being forced to speak English in colonial schools has a profound effect on children. Following the declaration of a state of emergency in Kenya in 1952, he explains, schools were placed under the District Education Board, which was chaired by Englishmen. English consequently became the formal language of education. A child caught speaking another language, such as Gĩkũyũ, received three to five whips with a cane on bare skin, or was made to carry a plate saying 'I am stupid' or 'I am a donkey'. In other cases, children were issued fines which their families could not afford to pay, while others were made to inform on one another by being instructed to pass a tell-tale button to classmates heard speaking languages other than English (1986, 11).

Thiong'o's argument shows us that processes of subjectification are shot through with power relations. In his words, the 'physical violence of the battlefield was followed by the psychological violence of the classroom . . . The bullet was the means of the physical subjugation. Language was the means of the spiritual subjugation' (1986, 9). This is because, Thiong'o argues, as well as being a means of communication, language is also a carrier of culture. It functions as a 'collective memory bank' through which knowledge, history, and identity are transmitted and preserved.

For Thiong'o and other postcolonial theorists, the aim of colonialism was to control and exploit the material wealth of the colonised. However, physical means alone were

Photo 3.6 **Ngũgĩ wa Thiong'o. Thiong'o argues that enforcing language on colonised people functions as a form of power to control identity and culture, and that this should be resisted by colonising our minds.**

Sueddeutsche Zeitung Photo / Alamy Stock Photo

insufficient to realise this aim. He explains: '[The] most important area of domination was the mental universe of the colonised, the control, through culture, of how people perceived themselves and their relationship to the world . . . To control a people's culture is to control their tools of self-definition in relationship to others' (1986,16). Seen in this way, forcing children to speak English can be read as a process of subjectification imposed by the English in order to realise their colonial project. In order to decolonise, Thiong'o concludes, we must not only dismantle the colonial and imperial power relations that structure the political world but also those that have worked their way inside us, by decolonising our minds (see Chapter 8).

REFLECTIVE ACTIVITY 3.10

Pause here to consider these questions:

In light of Enloe's commentary, how do the gender expectations placed on you as a political subject differ from what people experience in a different part of the world?

Why might colonial rulers force children to speak English? What effects might this have?

What do you make of the global dominance of the English language today, for instance in the academic field of International Relations?

3.4 **WHY DOES POWER MATTER FOR GLOBAL POLITICS?**

This chapter has made the case that the common assumptions that power is simply coercion, and only political or economic elites have power, are myths that come apart under critical examination. Rather, each of us exercises power, and each of us is affected by power, because we are situated within the global web of power relations. The chapter has argued that moving through the three faces of power debate, and arriving at a Foucauldian understanding of power of as productive of ideas, norms, and even identity, can help us gain insight into the mystery of power and its effects. The final sections of this chapter turn to the question of why this matters, both for the study of global politics and in our everyday lives, by turning first to the power relations at work in International Relations theory, and in practices of resistance in the political world.

3.4.1 **POWER IN IR THEORY**

We have posed the question of how to study power in global politics. More specifically, we are faced with the decision of whether to use an approach which seeks to *understand* and *effectively wield* power, or a critical approach in which power relations are *challenged* and *changed*. The former corresponds broadly to 'traditional' theories in International Relations—namely Realism, Liberalism, and mainstream Constructivism. For example, Nye (2011) argues that the US promotes its global dominance by means of 'hard', 'soft', and 'smart' power. By hard power, he means force and the threat of force. By soft power, he refers to diplomatic and persuasive power. And by smart power, he means a combination of the two. This framing offers theoretical and analytical concepts designed to help us understand how the US's power works and how its power can be used to its advantage.

In contrast, 'critical' International Relations theories, including Marxism, Feminism, Postcolonial and Decolonial Theory, Queer Theory, Critical Constructivism, and Poststructuralism, are committed to changing something about contemporary global power relations. Marxian theories, for instance, argue that the US plays a leading role in the perpetuation of an unjust economic order—neoliberal capitalism. Rather than simply observing how neoliberal capitalism works and how powerful states can best promote their interests within it, Marxists seek to challenge the inequalities and injustices it produces for members of different socio-economic classes. Similarly, Feminist theories argue that global power relations are gendered in ways that significantly disadvantage women, girls, and gender nonconforming people, for instance in terms of political representation, domestic labour, and violence. Queer Theory argues that global politics is governed by heteronormative power relations which disadvantage people in queer relationships, for example by prosecuting people for having homosexual sex and forbidding gay marriage. And Postcolonial and Decolonial Theories are concerned with what sociologist Aníbal Quijano (2000) calls 'the coloniality of power', which explores the power relations at work in empire, Eurocentrism, and globalisation. While each has a different marginalised group in mind, all critical IR theories share a commitment to trying to change something about the existing power relations in global politics.

REFLECTIVE ACTIVITY 3.11

Take a break here and reflect on these questions.

*What are the pros and cons of a 'traditional' approach which seeks to **understand** power? Is it enough to grasp the ways power works, or should we take further steps and evaluate power?*

*Does a 'critical' approach which seeks to **challenge and change** existing power relations offer a good alternative? What sorts of critical challenges and areas for change can you identify?*

Discuss you answers with a classmate or friend.

What unites these various critical approaches to the study of power is that there is no 'outside' of power relations. We are always within the network of power, whether we are talking about the production of knowledge, social norms, or our individual and collective identities. This is just as true for those who appear to have more power as for those who seem to have less. Importantly, however, this is not a bad thing. To be always inside the network of power is *not* to be powerless. Nor does it mean we have surrendered our capacity to act or exercise freedom. On the contrary, it means that all of us, even those who appear to have very little power, are actually already participating in power relations, even if we are not aware of it. This is because where there are relations of power there are also relations of resistance.

3.4.2 POWER RELATIONS AND YOU

If power relations are everywhere—in our knowledge, our social norms, and even our identities—this means it is not something wielded by dominant individuals and groups. Instead, we *all* participate in the workings of power. Because of this we are all involved in 'the political', as discussed in Chapter 2, whether or not we are aware of it. The implication of this is that we cannot escape power relations. Whether we like it or not, our individual and collective actions have an impact on the world around us. This realisation is an important step in beginning to critically reflect about global politics because it means that the ways we think and act have political consequences.

REFLECTIVE ACTIVITY 3.12

Pause here to think about these questions:

What power relations are you currently participating in?

At university? At home? At work? In the street? As a consumer? As a citizen or resident of a particular state? As a member of a particular religious, social, ethnic, gender, or class group?

Are you helping to reproduce or resist prevailing power relations?

Consider the question of the power relations at work in the university. Lecturers and tutors have the power to choose the content and create reading lists of modules, hold lectures and classes, set and grade assignments, penalise students for plagiarism, and write books like this one. Is this a justified arrangement in your view? We might want to go a step further and ask about the power relations of the chapter you are currently reading. What if we had arranged the sections differently, or left out one or more of the approaches we've covered? Even here in our discussion of power, we are exercising power by presenting the Foucauldian framing as more convincing that other approaches. What impact might this have made on your understanding of power in global politics? Would you be thinking differently if we'd made the case for sticking with the first, second, or third face of power? As is always the case, we have left some things out for reasons of space constraints. We have also prioritised the things we think are most important in the study of power in global politics. Our decisions, and those of your lecturers and tutors, about what authors and ideas to discuss will influence how and what you learn. That makes this chapter, and this book as a whole, part of the power/knowledge nexus. And this is true of any other book we or other academics might write.

REFLECTIVE ACTIVITY 3.13

Before we end this chapter, there are some important questions remaining. Take a moment to consider these points:

What kinds of power relations are at work in this chapter?

What kinds of sources have we drawn upon? Do we see an equal number of references to male and female authors? What about authors with European or Western-sounding names as compared with those from other parts of the world? What kinds of power relations might this reflect?

One thing you will likely quickly notice when you reflect on the power relations that affect you is that you can identify not just one, such as class, gender, ethnicity, sexual orientation, disability, and so on, but rather several of these all at once. A person might, for example, be a **cisgender** woman, disabled, white, and working class. Or a person might be a **trans** man of colour, with no disability, from a middle-class background. And so on. Belonging to these various groups brings with it certain privileges and certain barriers. This means that a person can be privileged in some aspects of their background, and disadvantaged in others, depending on how their society values and devalues these traits.

The term used to describe these multiple interrelating power relations is '**intersectionality**'. Intersectionality was coined by Law professor Kimberlé Crenshaw in 1989 in her study of Black women's experience of the US legal system. In this study, she documented how Black women are doubly discriminated against, and fall outside established categories, on the basis of *both* their sex/gender *and* race. This means, she argued, that we cannot disentangle or choose between the power relations at work in terms of sex/gender and those at work in processes of racialisation. Instead we have to think of them as interwoven and inseparable—in other words, intersectional. If we are to challenge inequality, we must take these intersectional experiences into account or we risk reproducing discrimination of one kind even as we try to remedy another kind. Crenshaw's insights apply far beyond the realm of courts and law; indeed they are at work all the time in our everyday lives as well as our academic theories and practices. One key example of this is the challenge that Black and postcolonial feminists have brought to Western feminist theories which fail to examine issues of racism and colonialism. bell hooks, for example, published the poignantly titled 'Ain't I a Woman: Black Women and Feminism' (1981), in which she argued that Black women were left out of struggles for women's suffrage in much of the Western world, and in many cases experienced racism from white feminists, but were *also* marginalised in Black men's struggle for the vote. This left them doubly excluded and facing a double bind, either to ally themselves with white feminists who had excluded them or to support Black men's suffrage which reinforced the patriarchal order. What this shows is that even movements which seek to challenge injustice, like Feminism, can reproduce other forms of injustice, like racism.

These arguments about intersectionality are directly relevant to global politics. For example, as sociology professor Patricia Hill Collins (1998) argues, while traditional 'family values' are often seen as benign and remote from global politics, they actually play a significant role in the formation of national identity. Focusing on the case of the US, Collins traces a series of 'naturalised hierarchies' which work to normalise particular power relations, specifically male headship of the family and deferent female domestic labour. Far from natural, she argues, these power relations are maintained through actual or implicit force. In addition to these gendered effects, she shows, these hierarchies devalue nontraditional families and nonheterosexual couples, who are subject to disapproval or disciplinary power. Furthermore, it privileges a white ideal type which impacts negatively on people of colour.

REFLECTIVE ACTIVITY 3.14

We've covered some complex concepts and ideas, so pause here to think about the following questions:

What is intersectionality?

What intersectional power relations are you affected by?

Discuss your answers with a friend or classmate.

Now that we have a developed a nuanced understanding of power relations and their intersectional manifestations, we can begin to consider how we might go about challenging them.

3.4.3 POWER AND RESISTANCE

As well as implicating us in political life, if power relations are everywhere we cannot find a neutral or apolitical space from which to conduct our studies. Some have argued that this fundamentally undermines academic study—if we cannot be value-free, we cannot tell the truth about history or society or politics. However, there is another way to look at the situation. If we are always situated within power relations then just as they impact upon us, we in turn impact upon them. This means that if we change our behaviour we can help to change current power relations.

Consider for a moment how social movements like anti-racist, decolonial, feminist, or LG-BTQIA+ groups gain traction. They are effective to the degree that they identify, draw attention to, and challenge particular power relations. This often requires a long and difficult process of changing dominant social norms, such as white supremacism, sexism and misogyny, homophobia, and transphobia. This can be done in a number of ways, such as lobbying, protesting, and various forms of direct action like occupations and sit-ins. Other tactics can involve the destruction of property, like pulling down statues of colonial figures or damaging aeroplanes or tanks to be sold to states involved in conflict. Sometimes violence is renounced by social movements, such as Mahatma Gandhi in India or Martin Luther King in the US. Other resistance movements use violence, such as Nelson Mandela's African National Congress in the struggle against Apartheid in South Africa and the Black Panthers in the US.

Engaging in acts of resistance can be dangerous, especially for people of colour, people without citizenship, and gay, queer, and trans people (see photo 3.7).

If we consider the BLM movement (see also photo 2.8), it is clear that in addition to already facing often lethal police violence, Black activists are at risk of retaliatory violence for taking part in protests. What this shows is that dominant groups often resist change, sometimes using violent means. As IR scholar Chris Rossdale (2019) explains, such a

Photo 3.7 **Claim Our Space Now, an intersectional Black Queer Immigrant led community action organisation, protest violence towards Black trans people at the KJB Rally Freedom during Pride celebrations in New York in 2020.**

© Kevin RC Wilson / Alamy Stock Photo

backlash can occur when the established order is challenged: 'Apparently solid political orders are shaken by the recognition that they are predicated on a compliance and obedience that can be withdrawn, often spectacularly'. It is not only states that engage in this kind of retaliation—often members of the public do so too. For example, if a man walks in a way coded as feminine, he may experience street harassment or physical violence. If a woman dresses in a masculine way, she may be mocked, intimidated, or attacked. People who are transgender, or reject binary gender identities, are especially at risk of being assaulted and even killed as they go about their everyday lives.

And yet by taking these risks and resisting conventional gender roles, people have challenged dominant discourses and social norms and many societies have become less intolerant of gender nonconformity as a result. Returning to the examples of discourses surrounding refugees and migrants, it is clear that they are very powerful, but it is also clear that they too can be changed. One way of doing so is by challenging the ideas and assumptions on which they are based, for instance by showing that far from 'stealing jobs', European economies depend on migrant labour across a range of sectors (Maxmen, 2018). Another way is to take **direct action** to tackle the real-world consequences of these discourses, such as the rescue operations of groups like Médecins Sans Frontières, Save the Children, Proactiva Open Arms, Sea Eye, Alarm Phone, and Watch the Med.

What these examples show is that ordinary people have more power than we might assume to resist and change current political arrangements. By deciding whether to support or challenge specific power relations, we add weight to the climate of opinion, and further the production and reproduction of knowledge, social norms, and political subjects. This might be through a highly visible act of protest, like dropping a banner calling for action on climate change from a government building, or a small act like calling out a friend or family member for a sexist or racist joke. In this way, power is closely connected to resistance. As IR scholars Jenny Edkins and Veronique Pin-Fat argue,

> relations of power entail resistance . . . If resistance and power go hand in hand, then there is no possibility of a grand refusal of overcoming power relations . . . [But] pessimism is not justified, for just as relations of power can form a dense web that seems to solidify into institutions like the state and sediments into forms of domination, so points of resistance can come together to lead to revolution . . . [or] shifting cleavages and regroupings (2004, 5).

What this means is that where power relations are found—which, as this chapter has shown, is everywhere—so too will relations of resistance be found.

Such resistance can be organised in a social movement, but equally it might take the form of what James C. Scott (1989) calls '**everyday resistance**'. In contrast to organised and highly visible resistance, everyday resistance involves small, often unnoticed acts undertaken by ordinary people. Giving the examples of resistance enacted by peasants and enslaved people, Scott includes things like poaching, foot-dragging, false compliance, squatting on land, nonpayment of taxes, and desertion from conscripted military service. Such acts might not at first seem political, but Scott argues that they may in fact involve resistance to existing power relations, even if the actors involved don't think of their behaviour in this way. Indeed, as Scott argues, these everyday forms of resistance are often the only option available to groups who would face strong reprisals if they openly declared a struggle against police or armed forces. For example, people involved in a riot might be motivated by a sense of anger and injustice about socio-economic deprivation, rather than self-consciously intending to challenge power relations. And yet their actions, and the feelings that motivate them, might have an impact on power relations, such as drawing attention to the poverty experienced by marginalised groups or racist surveillance and policing practices.

REFLECTIVE ACTIVITY 3.15

Take a pause here to consider the following questions:

What kinds of resistance activities are you involved in? Are these organised or everyday forms of resistance?

Is the lens of 'everyday resistance' useful in understanding how people challenge power relations?

3.5 CONCLUSION

This chapter has explored the mystery of how power works in global politics, and challenged some common myths about who has power, and what can be done with it. The chapter contested the myth that power is simply a coercive force that elite actors use to promote their interests. This is important because this myth makes it seem as though ordinary people have no access to, and so can do nothing to change, the operation of power in global politics. Against this myth, the chapter has shown that power is 'productive' in the sense that it produces things like knowledge, social norms, and values. What this means, we have suggested, is that all of us wield, and are affected by, relations of power. The chapter has argued that if we look at power in this way, we can uncover some of the ways it influences our lives in the subtlest of ways. What this means is that many features of the political world that appear natural or inevitable are actually the product of power relations which are political in character. Finally, and importantly, the chapter has challenged this myth in order to show that by unearthing these power relations we can open up possibilities for resistance and change in global politics.

Having explored both a descriptive approach which seeks to *understand* power, and a normative approach which aims to *challenge* and *change* power relations, we can now return to questions posed at the beginning of the chapter in order to compare our original answers with our current ones:

- Should we conceptualise power so that it is easily measurable even if this means we leave important elements out, or would it be better to have a more sophisticated understanding even if this means power becomes very difficult to measure?

- Should we view power as something which can be acquired and used by actors, or is it better understood as a relationship between them?

- Do we want to focus on the power brokering of elites operating within and between nation-states, or are we concerned with everyday power relations which subjugate people on the basis of race, gender, class, sexuality, citizenship status, religion, and so forth?

- Should we make value-free observations about power, or should we try to change existing power relations?

REFLECTIVE ACTIVITY 3.16

Using your knowledge of the three faces of power debate and Foucault's idea of power relations, consider the questions above again.

Refer back to your answers from the beginning of the chapter. Have they changed? Why or why not?

Discuss and compare your answers with a friend or classmate.

Learning to identify how and where power relations are operating is an empowering skill which sits at the heart of the study of the political world. The reflective exercises set throughout this chapter, and the book as a whole, have been designed to get you to think critically about the ideas and arguments explored. The aim is to encourage you to use your critical capacities to reflect upon, rather than just accept, the information you are presented with. This kind of **reflexivity** should be exercised both in our academic studies and in regard to our own ideas and assumptions because by doing this we can identify and challenge the hidden power relations at work in every sphere of our lives. With this in mind, we can move on to Chapter 4 which explores the possibility of ethics in global politics.

 Access the online resources at www.oup.com/he/hirst1e for case studies to help contextualise your understanding of key concepts, further reading recommendations to guide you through your reading, and a library of web links to journal articles, blogs, and video content to help you take your learning further.

ETHICS

4

READERS' GUIDE

Chapter 4: Ethics examines the mystery of why people often claim that ethics have no place in global politics. With the rise of the modern state system, a persistent myth took root, and flourished—a myth which suggests that power politics can (and indeed should) be conducted without consideration for morality. Against the long-standing suspicion that ethics and politics are antithetical to one another, this chapter shows that ethics are more than simply a series of rules or laws that govern our behaviour, and that thinking theoretically about the relationship between ethics and politics is a perennial, and truly global, endeavour.

4.1 INTRODUCTION: 'RIGHT VS WRONG' IN (GLOBAL) POLITICS

In Chapter 2, Section 2.3.1, we were introduced to Harold Laswell's description of politics as the ongoing determination as to 'who gets what, when, and how'. The implied or missing question in this formulation—*why*—is equally important to any thorough investigation of politics. Insofar as political issues revolve around notions of the common good or around myriad social goods that we have reason to value, it is impossible to understand them without some reference to the ethical justifications which deem them to be of value in the first place. On the most intuitive of levels, we understand ethics and morality as relating to right vs wrong. We are introduced to this notion from an early age in our closest relationships and through praise or admonishment for our actions and behaviour.

Yet in a contemporary political world which is rife with examples of bribery of public officials, crises in healthcare or social care, nepotism, questionable lobbying practices, and complicated corporate tax avoidance schemes, it is easy to understand why many would see the relationship between politics and morality as tenuous at best, impossible at worst. Furthermore, given that power sits at the heart of the study of global politics (as we discussed in Chapter 3), it is also entirely possible that power itself has the effect of warping individuals' understandings of right and wrong. The most well-known version of this idea is the historian (and politician) Lord Acton's belief that: 'Power tends to corrupt, and absolute power corrupts absolutely. Great men are almost always bad men' (1887).

Here, however, a distinction between *morality* and *ethics* might be helpful. For many ethical theorists, morality relates to principles, values, or norms which are understood to apply universally to all human beings at all times. It relates to the values and norms which we often associate with the cultures, religions, or broader systems of belief into which we have been socialised. Morals can be deeply held convictions which are informed by these broader systems of belief. Ethics, instead, relate to the principles, values, and norms that we might associate with particular roles, contexts, or social groupings. Put simply, it is the distinction between arguing that it is always wrong to kill (morality) or that there might be certain contexts or conditions—such as war, medical treatment, or punishment for a crime—under which killing or letting a person die might be justifiable (ethics). On the one hand, this distinction helps to highlight the fact that politics is a specific realm of human endeavour and relationship which therefore must also have its own set of rules, norms, or principles of behaviour. On the other hand, it is difficult to see how broader moral understandings of right and wrong are not already embedded within specific political cultures, eras, practices, and ethics (and vice versa). Consider the fact that certain faiths forbid the consumption of pork or of alcohol (their consumption is morally wrong). In ancient times, the lack of refrigeration for food meant that pork was a natural carrier of pathogens. The ethical requirement of the Semitic peoples of the Levant—not to spread disease and possible death through the sale and consumption of pork—then became a moral interdiction of the faith itself. Similarly, the religious requirement to abstain from alcohol has manifested itself in liquor licensing laws, minimum age requirements, bar opening hours, or fixed minimum prices—justified on ethical grounds (for public order or public health), not explicitly on moral or religious values of right and wrong. Any interrogation of the relationship between politics and ethics, therefore, must take this tension (between morality and ethics) into account.

It is also the case that ethical judgements themselves—the *why* question described above—never occur within a vacuum. They are made within contexts which are already deeply political, and therefore imbued with differential power relations, protections, and privileges. A morally questionable act is often justified on strictly legal grounds, for example, to the obvious benefit of those with more material power in that society. A telling example is the distinction between tax evasion and tax avoidance. Few would argue a moral difference between the two—as both lead to a marked decrease in the State revenue necessary for realising plans relating to the common good—and yet only one is proscribed by law (evasion). Avoidance, instead, through the use of shell corporations and complicated accounting schemes, has resulted in the *legal* squirrelling away of trillions of dollars in tax havens such as Switzerland, the Cayman Islands, Delaware, or the Channel Islands. By 2015, it was estimated that 55% of the foreign profits of US firms alone—almost $130 billion—was held in such havens, and that foreign wealth held in Switzerland (often by individuals) had reached $2.3 trillion (Zucman, 2015, 4).

More recently, as the Covid-19 pandemic tore through the lives and livelihoods of communities across the globe, relative differences in power—and the ethical questions which they revealed—were put into sharp relief. National governments, after decades of privatisation or austerity within the healthcare sector, scrambled to build temporary hospitals, to shut borders, to implement costly quarantine or virus-testing regimes, and to set out guidelines for who should receive emergency care in the face of an acute shortage of ventilators or emergency care spaces. Citizens were instructed to work from home, except for those deemed 'essential' (often mostly low-paid workers)—who continued to venture out to care for the sick, to work on production lines, building sites, or public transport, or to deliver goods and services to those sheltering at home—despite the clear and present danger to them. Internationally, ethical debates around 'vaccine nationalism' (rushing to vaccinate one's own population first) or 'vaccine diplomacy' (the leveraging of geopolitical competition to limit or provide doses to other countries) took centre stage in 2021. The massive rise in public spending (through borrowing), used to offset both the equally large rise in unemployment and the woefully inadequate initial responses to the pandemic by some governments, is a matter which will occupy political and ethical debates for generations to come. Moments of crisis—and the political responses which they engender—are also always moments of significant ethical importance. They reveal the moral priorities or principles used by a community in order to explain practical or power-political decisions.

Insofar as ethical questions often arise in politics, only when we are alerted to an action we deem to be wrong, is it easy to understand why many believe that politics and ethics pertain to two different spheres of human behaviour. In this chapter we will explore the origin of this myth in order to argue the opposite. Equally problematic is the myth that ethics can be reduced to a series of rules or laws which, when simply applied properly, will always achieve an ethical outcome. This myth is based on a European tradition of both law as the source of all legitimate political authority and of ethics as a purely rational, individualistic undertaking, often focused on rights. Contemporary psychology studies into moral development have highlighted instead various sources for our moral judgements, many based on sentiment or emotion and on the relationships or contexts in which we find ourselves. Related to this idea of multiple sources or methods for arriving at ethical judgements lies a third myth. Insofar as the international system of states found its origin in these same European traditions, and was foisted upon the world through colonialism and imperialism, it is no wonder that so much academic theorising on the link between politics and ethics would lead one to think that this is a mostly Western undertaking. Nothing could be further from the truth. Traditions such as Confucianism, Ubuntu, or Sumak Kawsay point to myriad communities which, across time and space, have always grappled with the *why* question in politics in order to better organise their social affairs.

In a world marked by political problems which cannot be neatly contained within national, cultural, or religious borders—climate change, war, migration, pandemic preparedness and response, or international aid and development to name a few—the exploration of these myths should also help to move any discussion of ethics and politics beyond the simple binary of right and wrong. Here we might view ethics as an **imaginary** for both political present and future. At its most basic, ethics is presented as a code which provides rules to pre- and proscribe our political behaviour. It also allows for a thoughtful and necessary built-in critique of our many political actions (by forcing us to ask if a particular decision is good or right and by what standards). Finally, in light of what we determine to be good or right, ethics compels us to ask what we think requires changing in the world around us in order that it better express this sense of good or right. It reflects, in Kenan Malik's (2014) framing, humanity's ongoing quest for a 'moral compass' with which to orientate ourselves on an ever-changing political map.

REFLECTIVE ACTIVITY 4.1

Just as with the example of tax avoidance and tax evasion above, can you think of other examples in the contemporary world which reflect the tension between morality and ethics in relation to politics?

Make a list of the significant political decisions taken during the Covid-19 pandemic which affected you personally. What do those decisions reveal to you about the ethical considerations which informed those decisions?

4.2 POLITICS VS ETHICS: THE MYTH OF *THE PRINCE*

> . . . So as a prince is forced to know how to act like a beast, he must learn from the fox and the lion; because the lion is defenceless against traps and a fox is defenceless against wolves. Therefore one must be a fox in order to recognise traps, and a lion to frighten off wolves—*The Prince* [Chapter XVIII].

Insofar as politics is centrally concerned with power—the struggle to grasp, to consolidate, to maintain, and to wield it—Machiavelli's *The Prince* has served as the ultimate guidebook for leaders and students of politics for over five hundred years. The reason this oft-quoted passage so shook the Renaissance world is that it seemed to suggest that the moral foundations upon which European polities had built themselves—Christian piety, acceptance of the supremacy of God in the ordering of the affairs of man, and the promise of glory only in the life hereafter—might not be the proper basis for the establishment of well-run kingdoms and principalities. In plain, logical, and simple prose, Machiavelli (see photo 4.1) sought to outline for the young prince the myriad ways in which principalities can be established, and to highlight the acumen required in maintaining power once it is acquired.

What so offended the moral sensibilities of the time was the claim that lofty ideals (justice, temperance, kindness, or even benevolence in the Christian sense) often led to *bad* government and failed or ruined principalities. In the medieval Christian ordering of the cosmos, a *Rota Fortunae* (wheel of fortune) spun and determined the fate of great men. Machiavelli

Photo 4.1 **Niccolò Machiavelli: Italian writer, historian, politician, and philosopher.**

© GL Archive / Alamy Stock Photo

instead suggested that in order to give proper value to human freedom (and the ability of princes to *decide*), the prince must be endowed with certain *virtù* (virtues) which would allow him to preserve and protect the state from those moments when *fortuna* sweeps through the plains like a raging river, intent on destruction. A capable prince was meant to 'act like a beast'. As a lion he might use brute force, intimidation, and fear to vanquish the wolves, and as a fox he might use diplomacy or cunning statecraft in order to avoid the traps and to keep potential usurpers at bay. Each of these skills he understood to be intrinsically linked with the pursuit of the national interest and realpolitik. Therefore, to be a *good* ruler meant being in possession of skill, forcefulness, cunning, bravery, and ruthlessness when necessary. Machiavelli tells us that 'men should either be caressed or crushed' (Machiavelli, 1532 [2019], 9), but that minor damage will only lead them to seek revenge. As such, he argues that if injury must be inflicted upon an enemy, it should be done in such a way that a ruler need not fear that enemy's vengeance.

This world of power struggles and treachery around every corner forms the backdrop of the political life that Machiavelli paints. The most important parts of the text focus on how a prince should conduct himself in his dealings with enemies, allies, and subjects. It is here that we find his principal *ethical* arguments against both classical and Christian virtues. Where the ancients suggested the need to banish fear and uphold love, Machiavelli famously argued the opposite: 'My view is that it is desirable to be both loved and feared; but it is difficult to achieve both and, if one of them has to be lacking, *it is much safer to be feared than loved*' (57). It is no wonder that statements such as this, peppered throughout the text, led Christian and humanist scholars alike to decry his 'evil' teachings or to see them as little more than an instruction manual for tyrants. This view of Machiavelli as immoral or amoral gets at the heart of the distinction between ethics, morality, and politics.

The Christian understanding of *gloria* (the good or ultimate aim of life) was arrived at only in heaven and only by conducting oneself according to the virtues of piety, charity, benevolence, forgiveness of enemies, mercy, sacrifice, love of God, and a belief in the afterlife and ultimate glory. Machiavelli, without ever dismissing this worldview, instead articulated a more earthly *gloria,* namely the long-term and successful preservation of the state. His use of the same language and grammar of the dominant morality of the time (*fortuna, virtù, gloria*), in order to articulate a different ethical understanding of 'the good', is what made his arguments so compelling. As philosopher Isaiah Berlin has argued, the originality of Machiavelli—indeed the true reason that this text so scandalised his contemporaries—is in a basic truth that it revealed to us about ethics and morality:

> . . . Machiavelli's cardinal achievement [. . .] stems from his de facto recognition that ends equally ultimate, equally sacred, may contradict each other, that entire systems of value may come into collision without possibility of rational arbitration, and that not merely in exceptional circumstances, as a result of abnormality or accident or error [. . .] but (this was surely new) as part of the normal human condition (Berlin, 1980, 74–75).

The mistake, then, would be to understand ethics as necessarily linked to morality. In the realm of politics, Machiavelli makes clear that those 'ultimate and sacred ends' which were deemed to be good by the moral standards of his time, were in most cases obstacles to the establishment of a stable political community. In an Italy beset by centuries of internecine conflict, insurrection, foreign invasion, and maladministration, Machiavelli pointed to the possibility of stability, peace, order, and good government—political ends which he saw as equally important to the human condition. To dismiss *The Prince* as an immoral text, then, misses the central arguments about *the good* which it advocates, regardless of whether or not we agree with Machiavelli's specific conclusions. Rather than view man as he ought to be (as some idealised Christian notion of man), Machiavelli suggests that an honest survey of the history of kingdoms and their rulers gives us a much better understanding as to how man actually was. The very fact that he articulated a specific understanding of 'the good' in political terms, speaks to the *ethics* of Machiavelli's politics. Yet this myth of the incommensurability of ethics/morality and politics has persisted. It has also given rise to many realist understandings of the state, human nature, and national interest in IR literature.

REFLECTIVE ACTIVITY 4.2

To what extent do you agree with this Machiavellian understanding of politics and of human nature? Does the preservation and 'gloria' of the state trump all other ethical or moral considerations? Why or why not?

In the same way that critics of Machiavelli might conflate ethics and morality, so too IR theorists such as Hans Morgenthau seem to conflate European/Christian morality with 'universal ethics.' In his 'The Twilight of International Morality' (1948), Morgenthau suggests that the focus of international ethics, until the Second World War, had been to extend the peacetime aim of the protection of human life even to the conduct of war. Ethics as a 'restraint' on the unfettered practice of power is the focus of his thesis, then, as he explores the ways in which the changing nature of warfare has weakened this restraint. Whereas in the past a small handful of aristocrats wielded power—thus making the use of targeted assassinations useful in the capturing of an enemy's territories—contemporary warfare is far more indiscriminate. The now 'total' nature of war, combined with a) the 'substitution of democratic for aristocratic responsibility in foreign affairs', and b) 'the substitution of nationalistic standards of action for universal ones', has led to a deterioration of the moral restraints once placed upon all states (Morgenthau, 1948, 88).

Put in simpler terms, with the deterioration of the moral code which held together the 'brotherhood' of European nations, Morgenthau suggests that the universal dictum of 'thou shalt not kill' has been replaced with a narrower rule, commanding individuals to kill, under certain conditions, the enemies of the nation. This change in moral landscape came about, he suggests, for three principal reasons. First, the modern nation-state is able to exert moral authority over its citizens in a way which previous generations' rulers were not able to. The 'faces' of power we explored in Section 3.2 had been consolidated to the state and the various tools of public opinion could now be marshalled in order to compel individuals to act in those same state interests. Secondly, this loyalty to the nation combined with technological advances has meant that an individual citizen is able to destroy the lives of hundreds of thousands of people with the dropping of a single bomb. Given the enormous moral weight and consequence of these first two reasons, he finally suggests that it is now much less likely for individuals to be loyal to some supranational ethical standard if it contradicts the moral demands of the nation. Like actors in some Greek tragedy, he suggests that the nationalistic masses, when meeting in the international arena, now meet 'under an empty sky from which the gods have departed', where the influence of supranational ethics is 'rather like the feeble rays, barely visible above the horizon of consciousness, of a sun which has already set' (Morgenthau, 1948, 99).

In many ways Morgenthau paints a bleaker picture than Machiavelli. At least for the latter, the morality of cut-throat politics could still exist in the same world as Christian morals, even if the latter was not always sufficient in achieving the glory of the state. Morgenthau's grim assessment instead suggests an extremely narrow understanding of ethics and morality in the pursuit of politics, as little more than a 'restraining force' on the actions of political players. This is a view which came to underpin the realist tradition in IR theory. Morgenthau is suggesting that the fragmentation of an aristocratic international society into states (concerned only with self-preservation) has made international ethics an impossibility. He uses the term morality and ethics interchangeably. By suggesting that the state is now the central moral and political authority in international politics—enforced through democratic and technological control—he describes an international ethical (dis)order in which national 'ethics' aspire to universalism. In his words, there are now 'as many ethical codes claiming universality as there are politically active nations' (96). In effect, for Morgenthau, ethics no longer guides the politics of many nations. Rather, each national ethical code seeks to impose itself on the international stage, claiming to provide a framework which other nations should adopt.

Whether or not we subscribe to Machiavelli's view of human nature and the ethical imperatives of a 'good' ruler—or to Morgenthau's view of the international fragmentation of morality—far from being divorced from politics, ethics and ethical justifications lie at the very heart of political life. It may also be worth noting that Morgenthau's essay was published in the same year (1948) which saw the adoption of the Universal Declaration of Human Rights by the United Nations, a document which asserts the rights of every individual to life, liberty, privacy, free speech, freedom from torture, social security, health, and education, to name a few. The most translated document of all time, it suggested an international ethics that was aspirational (rather than simply restraining), and it has been incorporated into myriad national and international legal instruments, treaties, economic agreements, and national constitutions the world over. It is the clearest indication that, in our drive to order the political and social world around us, ethical concerns are never far behind. In making sense of this moral landscape, it is helpful to now examine the key ethical traditions which have underscored the development of politics in modern times.

4.3 ENLIGHTENMENT TRADITIONS: THE MYTH OF THE LAW

In his reinterpretation of *gloria* for the purposes of good political conduct, Machiavelli played an integral part in the eventual decoupling of Christian morality from political ethics in modern Europe. The origin of political authority would eventually no longer be seen to be derived from God (i.e. divine right) but rather from foundational laws (a social contract), arrived at by members of that political community. Three key traditions of European Enlightenment thought form the basis of much of the ethical and moral thinking we see at play in our contemporary articulations of *the good* in political decision-making. Deontology, Utilitarianism, and Contractualism represent three distinct modes of ethical reasoning which rose to prominence in the 17th and 18th centuries. In various articulations they share a commitment to rules and to some notion of justice at their core. They are rationalist theories insofar as the basis for their claims can be arrived at by any moral theorist in possession of her faculties for reason, logic, and (in the case of Utilitarianism especially) through an empirical approach which considers the outcome of a particular act as the only way to judge its good or rightness.

Deontology (or deontological ethics) is most closely associated with the German philosopher Immanuel Kant (see photo 4.2). As Alasdair MacIntyre claimed, 'Kant stands alone at one of the great dividing points in the history of ethics' (MacIntyre, 2010, 183). Where divine dictum previously imparted the rules which governed our decisions and behaviours, Kant suggested that we could arrive at those same conclusions, laws, and norms through the act of pure practical reason alone. Acting rationally, therefore, was the equivalent to acting morally, when this was done for the purpose of arriving at those deeper moral truths. To act rightly but for the wrong reasons was immoral according to Kant because it represented a failure to ground one's actions in pure practical reason. In his 1785 *Groundwork of the Metaphysics of Morals*, Kant outlines for us one of his most important

Photo 4.2 **German philosopher Immanuel Kant, who equated practical reason with morality.**

© Science History Images / Alamy Stock Photo

contributions to this discussion—the *categorical imperative*. Such a moral imperative is considered absolute and unconditional; justified as an end in itself, following such a rule *is* an expression of 'the good'. Standard examples might include that it is always wrong to kill or to lie or to steal. A categorical imperative is distinguished from a hypothetical one, where the latter is simply an action taken in order to attain some specific outcome (normally for personal interest). Kant describes the categorical imperative in varying ways throughout the text, but two are particularly significant to this mode of moral reasoning. First, an individual must act only according to a maxim that she can *will* to become a universal law. You could see this as a built-in critique to the ethical decisions we take, by asking: *Can I understand this action that I am taking to be one which I would expect everyone to take, because it does not privilege my interests over everybody else's?* If so, then it is in accordance with a categorical imperative.

In a second articulation, Kant argues that in all of our actions, we must treat other individuals as 'ends-in-themselves' and never merely as a means to an end. This speaks to what Kant sees as the distinctiveness of human beings as rational and moral agents in the world, and sets deontological reasoning apart from consequentialist formulations of 'good' or 'right' actions (see below). In other words, for deontologists the consequences of a particular action have no ethical bearing on whether or not that action is good or right. What matters is the moral correctness of the act itself and not the outcome that this act will have.

One version of a standard critique of Deontology might be the following: *Imagine that you are living in a military dictatorship and that you are hiding a political dissident in your house. If the police were to knock at your door and to ask you if there was anyone else staying at your home, what should your response be?* A strict deontological response might be that lying is always wrong and that telling the truth should be a universal law. Further, telling the truth would be consistent with not treating the police officer as a 'means to an end' (i.e. lying in order to avoid the search and capture of the dissident or one's own arrest). Yet if telling the truth leads to your and the dissident's arrest, how can this be considered an ethical act?

Unlike deontological ethics, Utilitarianism (the most common variant of *consequentialism*) is concerned with moral principles only insofar as the *outcome* of the application of those principles is a good one. For utilitarians, the right or good action to take is the one which will 'maximise utility' (i.e. an act which satisfies as many of the informed preferences of the individuals within a given situation as possible). The principle of the maximization of utility requires an impartial assessment of various acts in order to determine if the outcome will be good compared to other acts. If an act has the consequence of being beneficial to most people, then it is considered morally right. This specific articulation of consequentialist thinking (with its focus on specific acts) is called *act Utilitarianism*. By contrast, if we were to determine a set of rules which pre- or proscribe our behaviour because they have been determined to lead to a maximization of utility, this is called *rule Utilitarianism*. One of the more common illustrations of the distinction between these two modes is the difference between a yield sign and a stop sign. If a yield sign is placed at a particular intersection, we might assume that act Utilitarianism applies (here each driver is left to decide whether stopping or proceeding through the intersection will lead to the best outcome). The stop sign instead commands a driver to stop at that particular intersection, likely because it was determined that this rule would lead to the fewest car accidents (i.e. maximising utility).

Perhaps the best articulated contemporary utilitarian argument is Peter Singer's (2009) account as to why we are morally responsible for eliminating world poverty. Singer poses his own moral mental exercise, roughly paraphrased as follows:

> You are walking to work and, en route, you pass a pond in which a little child is playing. While the water would not be more than knee-deep for you, you notice that the toddler is now flailing a bit and appears to be struggling, unable to stand up or to crawl out of the water. His parents or guardian don't seem to be present. You could easily step into the pond and rescue the child, but you would ruin your brand-new shoes and be late for work. What do you do? (Singer, 2009, 3).

If the response to Singer's dilemma seems morally obvious to you (of course you would save the child!), then why he asks are you not attempting to save the lives of the tens of thousands of children who are dying daily due to poverty, when you could do so with an inconsequential portion of your monthly income? Although the scale and proximity of the problem is different, the moral reasoning is the same. In the pond example, you determined that the cost of your shoes being ruined was not of greater value than the life of a child. If you were to put aside roughly 10% of your monthly salary, he argues, it would simply mean money you would not be able to spend on a new pair of shoes or some 'extra'. To a child in need, instead, it might well mean the difference between nourishment and starvation. If this 10% contribution were multiplied by millions of individuals making exactly the same calculation, then more than enough money would be raised to eliminate world poverty entirely. This is a classic consequentialist argument for the maximization of utility (in this case millions of lives saved). Further, it is easy to see how this argument could be extended from act-consequentialism (the child in the pond) to rule-consequentialism, if the 10% contribution were widely or universally adopted by all individuals. Although Singer does not suggest the adoption of a law which mandates 10% of personal earnings to be directed towards this cause, it is easy to see how the ethical dilemma of child poverty has been reduced to an easily understandable rule here. One might ask if 8% could be sufficient instead. Or, if it turns out that 15% is actually required, would providing only 10% now be considered *un*ethical? The simplification of these big ethical questions to straightforward rules and laws gives a slightly skewed understanding of the relationship between politics and ethics.

REFLECTIVE ACTIVITY 4.3

*Give an example of a **categorical imperative** which you might wish to see in the society around you? Now try to think of a situation in which following that categorical imperative would lead to a bad or harmful outcome.*

*Alternatively, think back to your experience of the Covid-19 pandemic. Of the political decisions taken (which you described in Reflective Activity 4.1), which ones appear to have been informed by a **utilitarian** or **consequentialist** logic?*

The link between rule Utilitarianism and Contractualism is fairly straightforward, then, as both modes of moral reasoning are concerned with an ideal ethical outcome, and both require a set of rules or laws in order to arrive at that outcome. As a central tradition in Enlightenment ethical reasoning, Contractualism sought to identify and explore the moral origins of political authority. Why, when in a state of nature we were ultimately free to do as we pleased, would we ever agree to join society and see those liberties curtailed? For social contract theorists such as Thomas Hobbes and John Locke the answer to this varied. For Hobbes, the reason was to gain protection from the brute force of others; for Locke, it was for the benefits which arise from association in law-abiding society. More recently, philosopher John Rawls returned to the theoretical trappings of the social contract in order to determine how, if given a choice, we might create an 'ideal' society which balanced individual liberties and equality (through the distribution of social goods). His *Theory of Justice* (1971) drew upon the social contract tradition in setting out a hypothetical place, 'the original position', within which individuals—unaware of the attributes, abilities, advantages, or disadvantages which they would face in a real world—would rationally choose the principles likeliest to lead to the most *just* (read: fair) society. From behind this 'veil of ignorance', Rawls suggests that the participants would most likely adopt a strategy which advantaged the least well off in any resulting society. His theory of distributive justice was articulated in the form of two basic principles (Rawls, 1971, 266):

1. Each person is to have an equal right to the most extensive total system of equal basic liberties compatible with a similar system of liberty for all.

2. Social and economic inequalities are to be arranged so that they are both:

    a. To the greatest benefit of the least advantaged [. . .] and

    b. Attached to offices and positions open to all under conditions of fair equality of opportunity.

The greatest equal liberty principle, the difference principle, and the equality of opportunity principle are considered to make this the most comprehensive political theory of justice to date and served to entrench a liberal, individualistic notion of 'justice as fairness' in subsequent political and ethical debates around global distributive justice.

Perhaps a more interesting variant of Contractualist ethical theory—developed directly in relation to international development—was the one articulated by a student of Rawls, Martha Nussbaum (see photo 4.3). Rather than focus on the distribution of social goods and liberties, Nussbaum is concerned with the distribution and fostering of *basic capabilities* for every individual in a society, capabilities which she sees as integral to the flourishing of an individual's life. So central are these ten capabilities that she suggests their absence would make for a life not worthy of human dignity. Nussbaum's ten capabilities (2011, 33–34) are:

1. Life
2. Bodily health
3. Bodily integrity
4. Senses, imagination, thought
5. Emotions
6. Practical reason
7. Affiliation
8. Other species
9. Play
10. Control over one's environment

Most of these capabilities are self-explanatory. She goes on to suggest that *practical reason* (the ability to 'form a conception of the good and to engage in critical reflection about the planning of one's life') and *affiliation* (to 'live with and toward others') are 'architectonic', pervading and informing the other eight (39). Without them, the other eight would not be fully seen to be commensurate with a life of dignity. The capabilities include not just elements of reason/rationality but also refer to the importance of emotions and to the various senses necessary to imagine a life worth living. Capability number 10 is an interesting one, as Nussbaum defines 'one's environment' in both political and material terms. The ability to take part in political decisions makes sense to our discussion of political ethics. More

Photo 4.3 **Martha Nussbaum: American philosopher who outlines a framework for ethical politics and human flourishing in her ten central capabilities.**

Martha Nussbaum: © Robin Holland / Wikipedia

particular to her liberal understanding of justice, instead, is the fact that capability 10 also includes the right to hold property on an equal standing with others within that society.

Nussbaum's careful and methodical elaboration of these ten capabilities fits with her underlying goal to see them incorporated into every national constitution in the world. It provides an ethical/moral floor, as she sees it, below which individuals must no longer fall. It is easy to understand, however, why critics would take issue with what almost amounts to a tick-box exercise in ethics. In fact, this speaks to a broader critique of all Enlightenment traditions—that they have limited the scope of our ethical imagination, casting us simply as rational, autonomous, utility-maximizing individuals. Whether applying a categorical imperative which is inadequate to a particular context; or reducing our understanding of the good to some empirical calculation of maximum pleasure, or limiting the central value of our ethical debate to justice-as-fairness, this myth of the law (as 'instruction manual') can be critiqued on a number of levels, as the following sections will demonstrate.

REFLECTIVE ACTIVITY 4.4

Place yourself for a moment behind Rawls's 'veil of ignorance'. Do you agree that 'fairness' would be the central value that you and every individual in the 'original position' would opt for in any society you designed? Or would other values be more important? Discuss.

Consider Martha Nussbaum's ten central capabilities. Create your own list of central capabilities and then consider what problems might arise in applying them, as she suggests, to every constitution of every country in the world. If this goal were achieved, do you think we would have achieved a truly 'ethical' global politics? Why or why not?

4.4 MORAL DEVELOPMENT: *IN A DIFFERENT VOICE*

In reducing the scope of our understanding of justice to 'fairness' and ethics to a determination of the best balance between liberty and equality, other ethical values (harmony, benevolence, care, compassion) are overlooked in a political world conditioned by law and justice. If we are to dispel the myth that ethics in politics only exist if they are codified into some legal framework, another important question arises. We might all agree that ethics are important to the guiding of our political behaviour in pursuit of the good life. Yet if we do not need God or the law in order to behave ethically, where does this impulse come from and how do individuals become ethical/moral agents in the first place? In a 20th century marked by an earnest desire to understand the individual psychological drivers of our behaviour, moral theorists turned to child developmental psychologists for the answer to this question. Lawrence Kohlberg, an American psychologist, began research into this question while still a graduate student at the University of Chicago in 1958. Over subsequent decades, informed by a longitudinal study he and colleagues conducted (of 58 working- and middle-class boys in the US), he developed a theory of moral development which consisted of six stages.

Moral reasoning, he argued, was the foundational basis for ethical behaviour. In *The Philosophy of Moral Development* (1981), he outlined the stages of moral reasoning as follows:

1. Pre-conventional Morality
    a. Stage One (obedience and punishment)
    b. Stage Two (self-interest driven)
2. Conventional Morality
    a. Stage Three (behaving according to social standards)
    b. Stage Four (social order obedience driven)
3. Post-conventional Morality
    a. Stage Five (social contract driven)
    b. Stage Six (universal ethical principles driven)

At the first level of moral reasoning (pre-conventional), respondents first follow rules if it helps to avoid punishment and then learn that they can do certain things in order to gain other things that they might want. At this level, stages one and two, a child has not internalised societal conventions and much of the moral reasoning is self-directed ('what's in it for me?'). At the second level of reasoning (conventional), an individual already tends to judge the morality of specific actions by comparing them to societal norms. Stage three includes 'the golden rule' and the desire to be considered a 'good child' by behaving in accordance with social standards. By stage four there is a further understanding that it is important to uphold these social norms and laws because they are necessary to the proper functioning of that society. Finally, at the third level (post-conventional), subjects already display a highly abstract level of moral reasoning. At stage five, laws are understood to form the basis of a social contract and, at stage six, moral reasoning is based on abstract universal ethical principles. At this final stage, laws are only understood to be valid if they are grounded in principles of justice (i.e. laws making up the social contract can be broken if they are seen to be unjust according to these abstract principles).

A number of observations can be made about these stages and how they are arrived at. Kohlberg suggested that the stages themselves could not be skipped (even if, once arriving at a higher stage of reasoning, a respondent reverted to a lower stage on occasion). Individuals progress through these stages through a combination of increasing psychological competence and through the resolution of conflicting social-value claims. When confronted with a moral dilemma involving competing value claims, a respondent takes a decision which Kohlberg refers to as a 'justice operation'. One of these possible justice operations, he refers to as 'reversibility' (where a respondent can see the same moral decision being taken even if the roles of the actors within that dilemma were reversed). The most famous of the moral dilemmas which Kohlberg posed to his respondents is known as the '*Heinz dilemma*'. In this scenario, Heinz has a terminally ill wife who requires a particular drug which the local chemist discovered and sells. Heinz is unable to secure more than half the funds required for the purchase of this drug, but the chemist refuses to sell it for less. In desperation, Heinz breaks into the chemist's shop and steals the drug. Was he right or wrong to do so?

REFLECTIVE ACTIVITY 4.5

Take a moment to respond to the 'Heinz dilemma' above. What ethical reasons would you give for your answer? Compare your reasons to the explanations given below.

Responses to the Heinz dilemma could then be mapped onto the six stages of moral development, ranging from stage one (Heinz should not steal the drug because he will be punished, which means he is a bad person) to stage six (Heinz should steal the drug because a human life has more value than private property). While this is a useful framing for the different modes and forms of moral reasoning and ethical behaviour that an individual might take, a few important criticisms should immediately be noted. For starters, Kohlberg's stages appear to determine a priori that the highest form or level of moral reasoning matches a Kantian deontological approach described in Section 4.3. In a similar vein, in this psychological worldview, justice appears to be the foundation for all 'good' moral reasoning ('justice operations', social contracts, etc.). Kohlberg's theory, in other words, takes the ethical traditions we explored above as the basis for a universal morality and then places respondents on a scale according to how well or badly their moral reasoning matches those same traditions. His original study involved only boys and specifically only American boys (making claims to universal applicability somewhat tenuous).

More significant, however, was the fact that when these same methods and stages were tested on both male and female respondents, the boys appeared to advance to stage six (on average) three years sooner than girls did. Take a moment to consider the implication of this. In a determination of the ability of individuals to develop into psychologically sound, socially conscious moral agents, Kohlberg's framework implied that boys were more advanced than girls in their ability to develop into ethical actors. These were boys and girls who came from similar geographical, class, and educational backgrounds. This empirical anomaly, then, caused Harvard psychologist Carol Gilligan (see photo 4.4) to question the very framework used by Kohlberg. In her seminal work *In a Different Voice* (1982), she explored the possibility of a similar three-part model of an 'ethic of care' which was central to the moral development of (primarily) girls. At the pre-conventional stage, she found, a girl's morality is self-and-others-directed and her ethical behaviour revolves around what she believes is best for her to do in a given situation. At the conventional stage, care and concern for concrete others becomes the guiding focus of her ethical behaviour. Finally, at the post-conventional stage, care expands beyond personal relationships, and judgements of care and concern are extended to various interpersonal relationships, more broadly.

To arrive at her parallel model of moral development in girls, Gilligan revisits the Heinz dilemma and the responses given by two respondents, Jake, and Amy. By stating that Heinz *should* steal the drug (because a human life is more valuable than property), Jake demonstrates the moral maturity required of stage six of Kohlberg's model. By contrast, Amy seems unsure as to what should be done, arguing on the one hand that it is wrong to steal, but on the other hand that it doesn't seem right for the chemist to withhold a drug if it leads to the death of Heinz's wife. By Kohlberg's definitions, Amy's responses are considered

Photo 4.4 **Carol Gilligan: American psychologist whose work with children led to a new understanding of ethical reasoning.**

Carol Gilligan: © Deror avi / Ravit / Wikipedia

a failure of logic and an inability to arrive at a clear ethical decision by that logic. Instead for Gilligan, Amy's responses are as clear and significant as Jake's; they do not focus on individual rational decisions but rather on the maintenance of the *relationships* within this moral dilemma:

> . . . Seeing in the dilemma not as a math problem with humans but a narrative of relationships that extends over time, Amy envisions the wife's continuing need for her husband and the husband's continuing concern for his wife and seeks to respond to the druggist's need in a way that would sustain rather than sever connection. Just as she ties the wife's survival to the preservation of relationships, so she considers the value of the wife's life in a context of relationships . . . (Gilligan, 1982, 28).

By Amy's reasoning, Heinz should not steal the drug because it would send him to prison, which in turn would prevent him from caring for a wife who needs him. In equal measure, the chemist should not be withholding the drug because it would be wrong for him to let Heinz's wife die as this in turn would hurt Heinz.

Gilligan's recentring of the foundations of moral reasoning in the *relationships* within which the moral agent finds herself—rather than in individual rational decisions or applications of a principle of justice—marked a watershed in the development of Western moral and ethical theory. She outlines for us the existence of two clearly distinct moral voices or modes of ethical reasoning, justice and care, arguing that *care* is as plausible a basis for our moral agency in the world as *justice* is. In subsequent texts and in her responses to critics, Gilligan also insists that this is a *different* moral voice rather than a strictly female or feminine one. As a fully elaborated theory of moral development, her different voice has expanded the ethical imaginary by which we might organise the world in pursuit of the good. Just as throughout the Enlightenment we have developed a political world framed around justice and the application of ethical principles, it is equally possible for us to imagine a world built upon care and the fostering and maintenance of good relationships.

While a number of prominent political theorists have taken Gilligan's ground-breaking findings and applied them to politics, Joan Tronto's theories are perhaps most germane to our discussion here. In *Caring Democracy* (2013), she builds upon her previous work on the topic to argue that care and caring practices should be understood as a central value around which to organise all other political activities in a society. Whereas within a justice framing of *equality,* individuals are understood as rights-bearers under the law, under this care framing, democratic citizens are equal in being care-receivers. In this formulation, 'citizens' needs for care and their interdependent reliance on others to help them to meet their caring needs become the basis for equality' (Tronto, 2013, 29). Linking back to Laswell's distributive definition of politics (Section 2.3.1), here *care* becomes the central social good in the determination as to who gets what, when, and how. Because care lies at the centre of our human lives, she argues, it does not make sense that our democratic political lives should instead be so focused on economics or material goods (where GDP is the primary measure of a society's well-being and where different claims to 'group rights' are pitted one against the other). Reframing politics and policy to focus on the maintenance of good relationships of care in a society might mean small changes (e.g. changing opening hours of various shops or services to fit with the schedules of carers in that society) or even big ones (requiring by law that both parents take paid parental leave when a child is born). Regardless, the political repercussions of taking this different voice seriously cannot be understated.

REFLECTIVE ACTIVITY 4.6

Consider relationships of care in your own life (where you are a caregiver or care-receiver). What sorts of political decisions or policies would you wish to see enacted in order for those relationships to be supported?

Now choose a well-known or contentious political issue (e.g. military intervention, the death penalty, abortion, universal basic income). How would a care ethics response to this issue differ from a justice ethics response?

Photo 4.5 **What relationships of care do you have in your life?**

© iStock / Delmaine Donson

So, where Nussbaum argues affiliation and practical reason to be 'architectonic' building blocks for a just society, Tronto suggests that affiliation is already a given and that practical reason should be aimed at addressing the caring needs of individuals within already existing relationships. In essence, what Carol Gilligan's theories helped to do was to recognise that the framing of different ethical and moral imaginaries may well require different voices through which to imagine and narrate these different ethical worlds. In contrast to the voice of justice—with its grammar of individual rationality, utility maximization, or the invocation of particular rights—an ethic of care intimates at a different moral foundation for political endeavour. It has also opened the way for a much more meaningful discussion of *other* distinct moral voices and ethical grammars, to which our survey of ethical myths and mysteries now turns.

4.5 ETHICAL VOICES: THE MYTH OF THE WEST

In Section 3.2, we were introduced to the different *faces* of power—decision-making, agenda-setting, and preference-shaping—which, combined, put our understanding of power right at the heart of global politics. Thanks to the work of Gilligan described in Section 4.3, we might see ethics as different *voices* through which we articulate our understandings of the good. We can think of voices as being able to express different stresses or inflections (timbre, tone, accent), different grammatical structures (language or dialect), all in order to better tell a narrative about the political world we envision. On an intuitive level this distinction between voices already makes sense to many of us when we think of the ability of some languages to operate better in some contexts than in others. In Europe, English has been a language of business and commerce, French of diplomacy, and German of philosophy and letters. We might think of Xhosa or Spanish as musical with their predominance of clicks or of vowels, or the languages of the Coast Salish peoples as better able to convey entire oral histories spanning millennia.

What an understanding of ethics as different voices also helps us to remedy is a third and final pervasive myth in our examination here. As Munyaradzi Murove has argued, for centuries African ethics have tended to be trivialized or outright ignored in most mainstream ethical discourses, leading to the accusation or mistaken belief that 'there are no ethics in Africa' (Murove, 2012, 36). The principal European ethical traditions outlined above developed in parallel with the state and then international states system, and so it might be easy to overlook the countless ethical and moral traditions which existed long before Enlightenment philosophers began thinking about social contracts, categorical imperatives, or the maximization of utility. The discussions of Confucianism, Ubuntu, and Sumak Kawsay in Sections 4.5.1, 4.5.2, and 4.5.3 are meant to highlight the polyphony of ethical voices and traditions which have, since time immemorial, sustained political communities across the globe. In making a case for 'the good' or in resolving the many ethical and political dilemmas which now confront us, a conversation between these many voices is critical. What these three distinct ethical traditions appear to hold in common with an ethic of care is their emphasis on relationships between people. This is most notable in the cases of Confucianism and Ubuntu.

4.5.1 CONFUCIANISM

Originating in China and spreading across much of East Asia, Confucianism had a deep influence on ethical ways of thinking about the promotion of moral order, stressing the centrality of the family (filial piety) in particular and relationships between people in general. Confucian ethics (based mostly on the writings of Confucius—see photo 4.6—and of Mencius) are seen to revolve around four key principles—*jen* (humanism), relating to feelings of warmth between people; *i*—faithfulness, loyalty, or justice; *li*—propriety or respect for social forms and decorum; and *chin*—wisdom (seen as a collective pursuit and achievement).

In a Confucian worldview, 'society is acknowledged to be a large family in which there is no contract, and which depends on family relationships' (Wada, 2014, 352). So, whereas in a contractual society, ethical principles are upheld by the idea and practice of individual rights, in a Confucian model, it is *jen* which provides the core to the ethical framework, incorporating ideas and practices around reciprocity, strong family relations, benevolence and loyalty.

We can see the parallels between this Confucian worldview and the emphasis placed by care ethics on relationships and reciprocity. While under a Contractualist ethics, reciprocity would be limited to an equal treatment of rights-bearers under the law (or a noninfringement upon others' rights), in both care and Confucian understandings reciprocity is more flexible (across space and across time). This is captured by various Chinese proverbs, such as 'an earlier generation plants trees under whose shade later generations find shelter and rest', or 'while you drink the water, you must not forget those who dug the well for you' (Wada,

Photo 4.6 **A painting of Chinese philosopher Confucius (551–479 BC), who was highly influential in promoting moral order centred around the family.**

© IanDagnall Computing / Alamy Stock Photo

2014, 354). In Enlightenment rationalist thinking, the individual is central to the political and social world (as a rational moral agent). In most Confucian ethics, the family is instead seen as the cornerstone of ethical life as it is then practised in broader society.

In determining how to apply this moral reasoning, Wada draws parallels between a care ethics idea of concentric circles of care with the Confucian idea of 'loving with gradation'. In Confucian thought, while it is understandable to have more care for a family member than for a distant stranger, it is still the case that this family relationship of ethical behaviour is meant to serve as the guide for how to treat that distant stranger, should the need arise. And so, while this may not at first glance appear as applicable to the alleviation of world poverty (in the way that Singer's utilitarian framing might offer), it does appear to suggest that an ethical amelioration of poverty should focus not simply on the material want, but on the relationship formed by such interactions. Equally, the proverbs above (where ethical considerations span across generations) might help to make better sense of long-term political issues, such as global heating, infrastructure investment, public debt, or pandemic preparedness.

In an attempt to apply Confucian ethics to global politics, the literary scholar Ming Dong Gu (2016) focuses on the interrelated Confucian values of *ren* (benevolence) and *shu* (tolerance). In seeking to find a new universal basis for a global ethic, he suggests that the substantive ethical value of benevolence towards all or towards humanity is best applied in practice through tolerance. Tolerance, in this framing, is the equivalent of a Kantian categorical imperative. Far from being imperatives of pure reason, however, he suggests that they are only made possible within the context of practices of reciprocal relations. In opposition to Western liberal framings, for Ming 'the Confucian Way of tolerance is based on a model of perfect virtue, which recognises each person's humanity and differences and constitutes a moral principle that coordinates and guides human relationships' (Ming, 2016, 799).

In order to make this principle applicable, he devises a 'pyramid of ethical practice' founded in applied 'tolerance', comprised of five rules. They are outlined in inverse order of importance and applicability, where 5 is the most important but least readily applicable and 1 the most applicable but least important (Ming, 2016, 800–801):

1. The Golden Rule: Do not do to others what you do not want yourself
2. The Silver Rule: Recommend to others what you want for yourself
3. The Platinum Rule: Help others realise what is good in what they desire
4. The Iron Rule: Repay kindness with kindness and repay injury with justice
5. The Jade Rule: A civilized person seeks harmony but not conformity. If another person does not follow you, try to win him over by your exemplary cultivated virtue.

Ming sets these five rules within a pyramid in order to highlight the interrelated nature of each ethical rule or step. As he notes, when taken together, 'they pay due respect to the liberal and democratic conception of the individual as a discrete, free, self-determining agent and the Confucian concept of an individual as an interdependent person, embedded in negotiative patterns of relations and nurtured by mutually beneficial actions' (Ming, 2016, 801).

The idea of applying Confucian ethics to global politics is also more than simply an interesting academic exercise. Much has been made in recent years of the rise of China as a global economic and political superpower to rival the United States in the coming decades. With President Xi Jinping (see photo 4.7), there has also been a marked emphasis on the importance of grounding Chinese political discourse in classical Chinese philosophy. As foreign policy scholars have noted, 'in almost every major foreign policy speech, [President Xi] has never failed to borrow from classical Chinese (including Confucian) ideas' (Zhang, 2015, 198).

In a conference marking the 2,565th anniversary of the birth of Confucius in 2014, President Xi delivered the keynote address. In it, he argues not only that the Chinese nation has always been peace-loving but that 'our love for peace is also deeply rooted in Confucianism' (Xi, 2014). In the speech, he decries the fact that 'many women and children are still struggling desperately in the shadows of war and poverty' and that the 'international community should join hands and make concerted efforts to preserve world peace'. Most notably, he goes on to make specific reference to classical Chinese precepts, such as 'associating with the benevolent and befriending neighbours is a precious virtue of the state', and 'within the four seas, all men are brothers', and 'a warlike state dies inevitably, no matter how big it is'. And while it might be easy to see this last invocation as simply a direct reference to the

Photo 4.7 **Leader of the Chinese Communist Party and President of China, Xi Jinping, has incorporated classical Chinese and Confucian ideas in his public pronouncements on good government.**

© Reynaldo Chaib Paganelli / Alamy Stock Photo

United States, it would be worth considering how (or if) the Chinese president squares these ideas with his own more recent failure to condemn Russia's brutal invasion of Ukraine in 2022, or his own country's militarisation of the South China Sea, mass internment of ethnic Uyghurs in Xinjiang, or repression of political dissidence in Hong Kong. In this sense, perhaps we return not to Confucius, as Xi would suggest, but to Machiavelli, where realpolitik trumps lofty moral ideals.

REFLECTIVE ACTIVITY 4.7

Given how closely President Xi has linked Chinese foreign policy to Confucian teachings, how should China be responding to any number of contemporary global problems?

To answer this question, choose a major global/political issue or event from recent years—e.g. Russia's invasion of Ukraine, the Covid-19 pandemic, the climate crisis, the recapture of Afghanistan by the Taliban, or the Palestinian-Israeli conflict.

Next, using specific Confucian concepts described in Section 4.5.1:

- *indicate what an ethical response from China should be according to Confucian thinking; and*
- *suggest what it might mean if China does not follow the ethical response that you have outlined.*

4.5.2 **UBUNTU**

Picking up this same thread of interdependent persons embedded in various patterns of relations, **Ubuntu** as an ethical approach is best captured by the Zulu saying *Umuntu ngomuntu ngabantu* or 'a person is a person because of other persons' (Murove, 2012, 37). This philosophical tradition is one shared by speakers of various Bantu languages and dialects, stretching across sub-Saharan and Southern Africa. The term itself means 'humanity' and so, in its most basic sense, Ubuntu is a humanist tradition, focusing on 'being' or 'existence' as a primary (relational) concept. It is not sufficient to understand personhood as relating to a specific constellation of physical and psychological factors. Rather, personhood only exists in relation to the community within which it finds itself. This focus on the 'substance and nature' of *being* falls broadly into four categories or concepts, often given in both their singular and plural variants:

- *Muntu/Bantu*—'being' with intelligence (notably human beings actually living, already dead, and not yet born)
- *Kintu/Bintu*—'being' not necessarily with intelligence (notably minerals, plants, and animals)
- *Hantu/Hantu*—a localized 'being' (i.e. a being within time and space)
- *Kuntu/Kuntu*—a modal 'being' (relating to how something *is* or *could be*)

Since the central concept here is 'humanity', the structure of much of the ethical enquiry within the literature is about locating 'Ubuntu' within the 'muntu/bantu' (or 'humanity within the person/people').

In this specific category, the two complementary expressions of Ubuntu are intelligence (*ubwenge*) and heart (*umutima*). Intelligence is understood in two ways—as practical intelligence (i.e. learned), typified by calculative rationality (slyness, cunning, sometimes deceit), and habitual intelligence, typified by 'comprehensive' rationality, described as 'the wisdom of life, the knowledge of relationships, of situations in life in which one is placed by the play of actual circumstances' (Ntibagirirwa, 2017, 126). In other words, comprehensive knowledge and rationality do not exist or develop within individual bantu but as a result of being part of a collective of beings. The second central aspect by which a person or community can be judged to have Ubuntu is 'heart', and relates to the capacity to be able to love and to relate to and with others. From this broad notion of love, different Bantu tribes placed emphasis on benevolence, empathy, generosity or liberality, or care or sensitivity to the needs of others. Ntibagirirwa goes on to distinguish these two core principles (intelligence and heart) by arguing that the dimension of loving takes priority over intelligence/knowledge. Love guides or commands *all* forms of knowing. Love is described as the 'cement that ties and strengthens relationships between members of the family, the tribe, the clan, and the community in general [. . .] and Ubuntu is assessed in terms of what a person can be and do for other people to enhance their life' (Ntibagirirwa, 2017, 126).

Perhaps for the simplicity of these two principles (or the ordering of their importance), Murove suggests that colonial scholarship viewed Ubuntu as either a primitive or infantile mode of moral reasoning, marked by the setting up of unhelpful relationships of dependency. As a mode of moral reasoning which existed long before colonial settlers, he suggests that it was almost taken for granted by the Bantu-speaking peoples, but then grew in parallel with colonial politics and incursions. For many, these principles marked the only reminder of humanity within an oppressive experience (colonialism) which was altogether dehumanizing. Equally important to the politics of contemporary Southern Africa, Ubuntu scholarship has once again been taken up as a means by which to explore national and cultural identity in the region. Murove's work has sought to describe business relations in the context of Ubuntu, so as to suggest that human beings are not solely self-interested and that business ethics inspired by this humanist ethic would be human-centred rather than purely profit-centred. In terms of a worldview inspired by Ubuntu, it is the fundamental reality of 'relatedness' and 'interrelatedness' which defines this ethic, and which likens it to a South American indigenous ethic which has also risen to prominence in recent years.

4.5.3 SUMAK KAWSAY/*BUEN VIVIR*

Sumak Kawsay originated within the Andean communities of South America. In more recent years, it has served as an ethical rallying cry for indigenous communities seeking to challenge the linear, economic growth-centric development programmes which for decades have been foisted upon various countries of the region. Most evident in the elections of Evo Morales in Bolivia (see photo 4.8) and Rafael Correa in Ecuador, many of the core principles of Sumak Kawsay were incorporated into the countries' new constitutions and policy programmes. Most scholars will highlight the fact that no literal translation seems adequate for this Quechua concept. Indigenous peoples argue that even the most common Spanish equivalent (*buen vivir*) is a pale metaphor for the Indigenous concept, where 'Sumak is that which is full of plenitude, is sublime, excellent, magnificent, beautiful, and superior, whereas Kawsay is life, to exist in a dynamic, changing, and active manner . . . [a] . . . life of fullness' (Villalba, 2013, 1430). *Buen vivir* has been deployed in Ecuador and Bolivia as a post-colonial, post-development project of social renewal in these countries. Contemporary international development programmes are seen to have imposed a Western conception of progress on these communities (focusing on GDP and economic growth over all else). The Sumak Kawsay paradigm instead constitutes something more than simply an ethical approach to the social world, to politics, or to economics. It represents a different ontology or way of comprehending the world itself. Where a modern (read: Western) ontology reflects a dualistic understanding, separating nature from man and society, an indigenous one instead stresses relationality and the interconnection of these elements of life. This is a cosmocentric rather than anthropocentric ontology. In other words, this indigenous ethic sees humans, other species, the natural world, and the wider universe as integral parts of the same whole. Similarly, while modern narratives contain a teleological understanding of time (i.e. that time and all things move forward towards some ultimate purpose or endpoint), Andean worldviews do not understand a beginning or end to time.

Common to most versions of Sumak Kawsay (and to many other indigenous world views in the Americas) are the central values of community, nature, consensus democracy, living well, and work as happiness. Community (the *Ayllu*) is not understood as a human social structure but rather as a unit of life comprising all forms of existence. The relationality described above means that these units of life (communities) live together with the *Pacha Mama* (Mother Earth), rather than separate from her. In terms of voice and representation,

Photo 4.8 **Bolivia's first indigenous president (2006–2019), Evo Morales, helped to incorporate the principles of Sumac Kawsay into the country's new constitution in 2009.**

Evo Morales: © EneasMx / Wikipedia

Indigenous self-government is consensus-based and therefore different to Western versions of individual representation or majoritarian decision-making. 'Living well' is understood in contrast to 'living better' (which is viewed as more associated with capitalism, consumerism, or competition). To live well is to live by the values of solidarity, reciprocity, and harmony. Finally, work is seen as integral to Sumak Kawsay. Linked to the land or to the flourishing of the Ayllu in some way; work is meant to be satisfying from childhood to old age and is seen as a form of existential learning (where ancestral knowledge is immanent to the Ayllu). While the rights of the Pacha Mama have been affirmed in their new constitutions, oil and mineral extraction in Bolivia and Ecuador still points to a disconnect between newly adopted traditional principles and the political or economic practices of the wider capitalist states system. The clash between equally valid, strongly held moral standpoints—just as we saw in Machiavelli's teachings from five centuries ago—continues to be a central challenge in the pursuit of an ethical politics, across various contexts and moral traditions the world over.

REFLECTIVE ACTIVITY 4.8

In what ways do the different ethical voices you reviewed in Sections 4.4–4.5 challenge and complement dominant Western accounts of ethics?

To answer this question, think of a major contemporary issue (e.g. the climate crisis, international development, civil war or military invasion, poverty, humanitarian intervention).

Choose at least one of these different voices (care, Confucianism, Ubuntu, Sumak Kawsay) in order to:

- *consider what political actions or policies you would suggest in response to this specific political issue.*
- *consider how your chosen ethical approach differs from (or is similar to) at least one of the ethical approaches you encountered in Section 4.3 (Deontology, Utilitarianism, Contractualism).*

4.6 CONCLUSION: GLOBAL ETHICS IN A MULTI-VOCAL WORLD

. . . On the most general level, we suggest that caring be viewed as a species activity that includes everything that we do to maintain, continue, and repair our 'world' so that we can live in it as well as possible. That world includes our bodies, our selves, and our environment, all of which we seek to interweave in a complex, life-sustaining web (Tronto, 2013, 19).

In this definition of care offered by Joan Tronto, we could substitute the word 'caring' for the word 'ethics' and we would touch upon one of the aims of this chapter—to highlight the ethical threads in this life-sustaining web which are central to our political pursuit of the common good. An exploration of three myths—of *The Prince*, of the law, and of the West—has highlighted the reality of politics as a realm of human endeavour informed by ethical judgement; has presented an alternative voice (care) to traditional (justice) framings of moral reasoning; and has outlined a number of rich and complex moral traditions which existed long before the international states system. As Kimberly Hutchings (2010) astutely argues, the real challenge of global ethics in this century is to determine how best to navigate the ethical questions and problems which arise out of the global interconnection of the world's people across multiple 'glocal' (global + local) contexts. She points to mass migration and direct intervention (e.g. military or foreign aid and development) as just two examples of the clash of values which will invariably occur.

Regardless of which mode of ethical reasoning we choose to apply to a particular glocal clash of values—Utilitarian, Ubuntu, Sumak Kawsay, or Contractualist—it is difficult to imagine political solutions which are not couched in *some* specifically ethical understanding of what is good or right. Furthermore, what a better appreciation for the multi-vocal nature of global ethics allows is the possibility of some *combination* of these modes of ethical reasoning to be applied to large-scale problems. In the case of the impending climate crisis, for example, a utilitarian ethic might inform the political decision of advanced industrialised nations to shoulder the burden of the cost of decarbonising the economies of lesser developed countries. Some combination of Sumak Kawsay and Contractualist modes of reasoning might further enshrine the rights of nature in various constitutions or international treaties. The deontological understanding of human beings as an *end* and never as a means to some other goal, combined with the more relational ethical accounts above (e.g. Ubuntu or care ethics) might help to reinforce laws and address the push–pull factors around people smuggling/trafficking which the economic dislocation of climate change is wreaking.

In other words, far from seeing these many ethical voices as an invitation to determine which of them provides the most universally applicable framework for political decision-making, these many voices might instead be seen as part of an ongoing discussion about the multiple values which inform our responses to specific political problems. The more that individual citizens or the *Ayllu* are in some way involved in the ethical debates and decisions which determine what constitutes the good or the right in particular political contexts, the stronger the link between ethics and politics becomes; and the stronger and more resilient we will continue to make that life-sustaining web in and of the world around us.

Access the online resources at www.oup.com/he/hirst1e for case studies to help contextualise your understanding of key concepts, further reading recommendations to guide you through your reading, and a library of web links to journal articles, blogs, and video content to help you take your learning further.

VIOLENCE

5

READERS' GUIDE

Chapter 5: Violence deals with the mystery of why, despite the rise of institutions and legal systems designed to prevent it, violence remains so pervasive in global politics. To do this, it challenges the myth that violence is only physical in character by setting out three interrelated types of violence: physical, structural, and immanent. From there, the chapter turns to the question of whether violence can ever be justified, and explores why we often assume in global politics that violence carried out by states is legitimate while nonstate violence is illegitimate. Having challenged this assumption, the discussion turns to the issue of whether and how, given the multiple forms of physical and nonphysical violence we can observe, we can work towards nonviolence in global politics. Against a fatalistic view that infers that because it is ubiquitous we should be resigned to the inevitability of violence, the chapter shows that we all have the power to reduce violence in global politics.

5.1 INTRODUCTION

In Chapter 4, we challenged the myth that ethics play no part in global politics, showing instead that human societies across the globe are deeply concerned with the 'why' questions of how the world is ordered. One key reason for people's scepticism about the possibility of ethics is that violence seems to be such an enduring part of the global landscape. Violence, it is often claimed, is everywhere and inevitable in global politics. Throughout history, states have engaged in armed conflict against one another and violently established empires, while domestic populations have fought civil wars and staged revolutions. Our news media are filled with stories of violence, for example police assaulting political protestors, the persecution of LGBTQIA+ communities, and humanitarian crises such as those in Syria, Palestine, and the war in Ukraine. Less well documented, but nevertheless important, are activities like lethal covert operations and remotely piloted aerial vehicles (drones) dropping bombs on civilian populations. Sometimes agencies created to reduce violence in global politics are caught perpetrating acts of violence, for example recent allegations of sexual exploitation by Oxfam executives and aid workers in Haiti following the 2010 earthquake. Violence even plays a role in our leisure activities as a source of fun and enjoyment, for example in videogames and movies set in theatres of war. As this suggests, violence is widespread at the grand, institutional level of global politics as well as in our everyday lives.

This ubiquity might lead us to believe that violence is simply a fact of life in global politics, that it is a regrettable but inevitable part of human existence. If we accept this position, there seems little point trying to reduce violence at the global level. If violence really is *inevitable*, there is simply nothing we can do about it. And yet this response serves to perpetuate a series of myths about the nature and architects of violence. The aim of this chapter is to explore the mystery of whether or not violence is inevitable in global politics by identifying and challenging three key myths. The chapter shows that while these myths might make violence *appear* inevitable in global politics, when we think a bit more about them it becomes clear that there *are* things we can do to reduce violence in global politics at both institutional and everyday levels.

The first myth explored in the chapter is that violence is necessarily physical in character. While acts of physical violence are widespread in global politics—such as war, torture, and various forms of bodily assault—the chapter shows this is by no means the only kind of violence we can identify. Instead, it proposes that there are three types of violence to which we should pay attention in global politics: physical violence, **structural violence**, and **immanent violence**. The first part of the chapter argues that developing an understanding of these three types of violence, and the ways they interrelate, will allow us to deepen our analysis of how violence works at the global level and, crucially, what might be done about it.

The second myth challenged in this chapter is that state violence is necessarily legitimate, while violence conducted by nonstate actors is always illegitimate. Prefiguring themes that will be discussed in Chapter 10, the chapter shows that while states are often able to *present* their violence—such as that done by an army or police force—as permissible or even laudable, this does not necessarily make it so. At the other end of the spectrum, the chapter shows, while violence enacted by nonstate actors—such as revolutionary groups or private citizens—is usually portrayed as illegitimate, illegal, or morally indefensible, some scholars argue such violence *can* be legitimate.

What this suggests, the chapter shows, is that acts of violence are often not simply justified or unjustified *in themselves*. Rather, they are *represented* as, and *judged to be*, legitimate or illegitimate based on political **narratives** and **discourses** (see Chapter 3). But these representations are political rather than value-free. Indeed, the state has *an interest* in presenting its violence as acceptable and the violence of other actors as unacceptable. Accordingly, using the ideas of philosopher Jacques Derrida, the chapter challenges the claim that the state has a monopoly on the legitimate use of force, showing instead that state violence is frequently illegitimate even in its own terms. From there, drawing on the thought of psychiatrist and political philosopher Frantz Fanon (see photo 2.1), it argues that nonstate violence—usually assumed to be illegitimate—is deemed by some to be legitimate in global politics, for example in the context of struggle against a colonial power.

The final myth to be examined in the chapter is that only elite actors have the power to reduce violence in global politics, and that even they face unfavourable odds because ultimately people are self-interested and prone to conflict. Against this, the chapter argues that individuals and **grassroots** groups can take, and indeed historically have taken, a leading role in challenging a range of violences in global politics, often facing resistance from elite global actors who have little incentive to challenge existing power relations. This will demonstrate that, just as each of us has a role to play in power relations (as discussed in Chapter 3), all of us have the ability to identify and reduce violence in global politics. The chapter ends by examining how we might pursue the goal of less violence in global politics by examining whether nonviolence is possible. It shows that while a concrete condition of complete nonviolence is likely impossible, we can nevertheless commit to nonviolence as a goal or aspiration and work to reduce violence in a number of ways across its physical, structural, and immanent levels.

REFLECTIVE ACTIVITY 5.1

Before we begin our exploration of violence, consider these questions:

What is violence in global politics and where does it take place?

What forms of violence are you most concerned about in global politics?

What can be done to reduce violence in global politics?

Make a note of your answers as we will return to them at the end of this chapter.

5.2 WHAT AND WHERE IS VIOLENCE IN GLOBAL POLITICS?

It is often said that political life is riddled with violence. Political philosopher Vittorio Bufacchi notes that in the 20th century, violence reached historically unprecedented levels through mechanised warfare, resulting in the deaths of 105 million people and the suffering of many millions more. Other estimates are higher still. Political scientist R. J. Rummel (1994) puts the figure at over 169 million. A desire to understand and work to reduce violence is often a key reason why students choose to study global politics. Some of you will have experienced physical acts of violence, like an assault or an armed conflict. Most of you will have witnessed violence of one form or another, whether in real life of via news or recreational media. Many of you will have wondered what drives people to commit acts of violence, such as terrorism or freedom fighting. You may have wondered why states and governments resort to invasions, wars, and ethnic cleansing rather than resolving disputes peacefully. And you may also have questioned why we seem so powerless to resolve violence in global politics despite the laws we have created to avoid it.

This might lead us to think, as Bufacchi (2005, 193) puts it, that 'violence is, and has always been, the essence of politics'. This links back to our discussion of power in Chapter 3. Philosopher Hannah Arendt (1970, 35) (see photo 2.6) explains that many view violence as 'nothing more than the most flagrant manifestation of power'. And yet, she continues, we need to distinguish between power and violence because they are different. Power occurs, she explains, when people act in concert with one another on the basis of some kind of agreement or consensus. Violence, in contrast, comes into play when this power to act in concert has been lost and the attempt is made to *force* people to do something. Such force, she argues, can destroy power but it cannot create it. This means that violence is not only different to power but actually its opposite—the more power a person or state has, the less they will need to resort to violence to achieve their ends (1970). Far from the *essence* of politics, then, according to Arendt violence occurs where politics *fails*, as when one state invades another or a civil war breaks out.

In his attempt to define violence, Bufacchi identifies two key approaches: one which frames violence as 'force', and a second which views it in terms of 'violation'. Those who define violence in terms of force, he explains, argue that to count as violent an act must be *intended* to cause harm. Key here is the idea that violence is something done *deliberately* by one actor to another. In this framing, the emphasis is on forceful physical actions carried out by one person or group against another. Examples of this would include wars, torture, invasions, shooting, stabbing, and so on.

In contrast, those who argue that violence consists in the violation of a person suggest that it can be both physical and nonphysical. An act of violence takes place, they suggest, if one person harms another's body but *also* if one person violates another's human rights or dignity. In this framing, in addition to physical acts, violence occurs in situations like economic exploitation, political repression, and psychological suffering. This definition of violence is significantly broader and can include acts which were not intentional. As development economist Jamil Salmi explains, in this framing violence is 'any avoidable action that constitutes a violation of a human right, in its widest meaning, or which prevents the fulfilment of a basic human need' (cited in Bufacchi, 2005, 197).

This leads us to two broad definitions of violence: a 'minimalist' account and a 'comprehensive' account, each of which has strengths and weaknesses. Minimalist conceptions of violence have the benefit of making it clear what is, and what is not, violent. As Bufacchi (2005, 197) puts it, this framing has the 'important advantage of delineating clear boundaries around what constitutes an act of violence, avoiding therefore the tendency to use the term violence as synonymous for everything that is evil or morally wrong'. The problem with this is that it excludes a host of things which we might think *should* count as violence, for example the fear, anxiety, and trauma that accompany drone strikes or domestic abuse.

Comprehensive analyses of violence have the inverse problem: while they allow for a more expansive understanding of violence which extends beyond the physical to include psychological, economic, and even symbolic violence (understood as violences that attack something of symbolic cultural or political value, like the attacks by Al Qaeda on the World Trade Centre on 9/11), this expansiveness risks an inability to distinguish between what is and what is not violent. This can lead to false equivalences between very serious physical violences—like being attacked—and apparently more minimal infractions—like name-calling. As political theorist John Keane argues, such definitions of violence 'stretch its meaning to include "anything avoidable that impedes human realization"' which 'effectively makes a nonsense of the concept . . . [by] making it indistinguishable from "misery", "alienation" and "repression"' (cited in Bufacchi, 2005, 198).

On the other hand, if we limit our examination of violence to purely physical manifestations, we ignore, and by ignoring minimise the importance of, a wide range of things we might consider violent, like misogyny and sexism, racism, political persecution, psychological abuse, and bullying or harassment. While it might appear as though these experiences should not count as violent because those who experience them have not been physically wounded, many people would argue that the psychological and emotional impacts, which can last for many years, should be understood as violences in themselves. In addition to causing enduring suffering and disenfranchisement, these kinds of nonphysical violences can lead to physical violences such as attacks, self-harm, and suicide. This troubles any attempt to draw a line between physical and nonphysical violence.

REFLECTIVE ACTIVITY 5.2

Pause here to reflect on these two framings of violence, and consider the following questions:

What are the strengths and weakness of minimalist and comprehensive definitions of violence?

Which should we use when studying violence in global politics, and why?

Discuss your answers with a classmate or friend.

We can observe from this discussion that violence occurs in ways which are not only physical or tangible. In other words, in addition to its physical manifestations, violence exists outside the material world to include the social, political, psychological, cultural, and even our inner subjective realms. In light of this, Section 5.2.1 sets out three types, or dimensions, of violence which we will use to develop our analysis: physical violence, structural violence, and immanent violence. As we explore these manifestations of violence, keep in mind that they should be understood as mutually interrelated rather than neatly separated. For example, while **genocide** might at first appear to be a physical form of violence because it kills people, it *also* includes structural and immanent elements through its erasure of economic and social systems, languages, and identities. Similarly, if a person of colour is the target of a racist attack, in addition to the physical violence suffered, there are *also* non-physical forms of violence at work in the racist ideas and beliefs that motivated the attack. This is important because these forms of violence are not only connected but actually rely upon and reproduce one another.

5.2.1 **PHYSICAL VIOLENCE**

When we begin to study violence in global politics, the form that likely springs to mind first is physical violence. Indeed, for many of you the decision to study global politics at university might well have been motivated by a desire to do something about violence of one form or another. Some of you might want to know why humanitarian intervention does not always happen, even when genocide takes place, as occurred in Rwanda in 1994 and is being perpetrated against Uyghur people in China today. Others might be interested in how international institutions try to prevent violence through diplomacy and interdependence, and why this is sometimes not successful, as in the case of the 2003 invasion of Iraq. And others might want to get involved with NGOs which provide on-the-ground assistance to people experiencing violence. What these concerns have in common is the desire not just to understand but to help prevent the *physical* harm caused by violence.

By physical violence we mean acts consisting of a direct attack on a person, including all forms of homicide (murder, war crimes, and so on) and other forms of bodily assault (torture, sexual violence, kidnap, fighting with or without weapons). We might also include things like forced displacement and labour camps, which compel people to physically move and/or work. Physical violence can also be perpetrated against nonhuman targets such as animals, for example battery farming and fox hunting. Property damage such as bombing a building, for example, would also count as physical violence. What distinguishes physical violence from other forms is that it is easily identifiable and involves a break from the norm. For example, if one person punches another, the perpetrator, the target, and/or bystanders will be aware that an act of violence has taken place.

In IR and global politics, mainstream theories often assume that violence refers to physical acts. For example, when Realists discuss violence, often euphemised as 'force' or 'operation', the emphasis is usually placed on the activities of states and militaries, such as invasions, wars, or occupations. As Feminists have argued, however, this framing excludes other forms of violence that are often more widespread in global politics. In particular, forms of violence at work in the so-called 'private' sphere, such as violence in the home, are frequently left out of IR's examination of violence on the grounds that they fall beyond the field's areas of concern. But, many scholars argue, this poses a problem for the field because it blinds us to a range of violences which affect large numbers of people across the world.

Since the 1970s, Feminists inside and outside academia have argued that 'the personal is political', meaning that people's everyday experiences should count as political issues. This challenges the assumption that what takes place 'behind closed doors' is not of concern to states and legal systems, and has paved the way for new laws around domestic and sexual violence. Indeed, as IR professor Annica Kronsell (2006, 127) has argued, 'the personal is the international' because women's lives are intertwined with global patterns and world politics. This marginalisation of gendered forms of physical violence is compounded, as law professors J. Oloka-Onyango and Silvia Tamale (1995, 701) argue, by forms of exclusion that run along colonial lines: 'for women in the south, the slogan "the personal is political". tells only half the story of the multiple dimensions of gender oppression by which they are confronted'. As Chapter 3 explored, an intersectional analysis is key to challenging the exclusion of these forms of physical violence from mainstream IR.

A further complication is the question of the physical forms of violence that take place in digital or virtual environments. Many people enjoy playing videogames set in real or fictional conflicts, such a first-person shooters like *Call of Duty* (see photo 5.1). The physical acts of violence that take place in a game, we usually think, are fundamentally different from those that happen in real life. After all, it's only a game. It's not real—we're only playing.

While some have made a connection between high school shootings in the US and violent videogames, for example through a series of Congressional hearings in the 1990s following the Columbine High School killings in Colorado, most players would never dream of harming someone in real life. However, some scholars argue that physical violence carried out in virtual worlds like videogames should count as violent even though no one in the real world gets directly hurt. This is because such violence desensitises players, normalises military responses to conflict, imparts gendered and racialised messages, and teaches military skills like weapons proficiency (Leonard, 2008).

The status of in-game violence becomes more complicated still when games are used by military institutions to train personnel for real-world combat. *Virtual Battle Space (VBS)*, for example, is used by the US Army to train soldiers, meaning that lessons learnt in a simulation can translate to real-world warfighting. Similarly, *America's Army* was developed by the US Army as a highly effective recruitment tool, further blurring the boundary between the unrealness of games and their real-world impacts (Hirst, 2022). The implication here is that the physical violences that take place in games can have effects in the real world,

Photo 5.1 **With the explosion of the videogames industry, controversies have arisen about extent to which games like *Call of Duty* can desensitise young people and turn violence into fun.**

including persuading someone to join the military, and training young people in military skills in their home (Robinson, 2016).

Scholars of violence have argued that, in addition to these physical forms, violence exists in ways that are less obvious and explicit. Postcolonial and Decolonial scholars, for example, have shown that enduring imperial and racist violences are at work across the global political system. In addition to the physical manifestations of these violences, such as police brutality towards Black people, scholars have explored the *nonphysical* aspects of imperial and racist violence which underpin and perpetuate the physical dimensions. These might include reduced access to education or healthcare, lower wages or employment opportunities, disproportionately high levels of surveillance by police, or everyday experiences of discrimination and marginalisation, such as being ignored by taxi drivers when trying to hail a ride or awarding gaps in university degree outcomes.

REFLECTIVE ACTIVITY 5.3

Take a pause to think about these questions:

What kinds of physical violence tend to be included in the study of global politics, and which are left out?

Should violence in videogames be considered violent? Why? Why not?

Is it enough to consider physical forms if we want to understand violence in global politics?

Discuss your answers with a friend or classmate.

In cases like this, even if no direct physical act of violence takes place, scholars like Johan Galtung argue violence is present because they have long-term effects on people's life chances, health, and well-being. Such violences, they have shown, are often invisible to us as they are *built into the structure* of the global system. This means that people perpetrating violence of this kind might not be aware they are doing so as it might look like common sense or simply the right thing to do. This occurs, for example, when a father prevents a daughter from going to school because of a belief that girls should not be educated. It also means that those experiencing such violence might not view it as violence, for example if the daughter also believes she should not go to school because she is a girl. Such a situation makes sense to the people involved because it is built into their political, social, and economic structures. Consequently, this kind of violence is known as 'structural violence'.

5.2.2 **STRUCTURAL VIOLENCE**

In addition to the physical violences at work in global politics, violence also occurs at a second and less visible level—our political, economic, and social structures. Structural violence of this kind exists when some people do better out of the status quo arrangements than others. Examples of structural violence include economic inequality like poverty and pay gaps, political exclusion such as the denial of voting rights, legal disenfranchisement including the inability to get a lawyer or receive a fair trial, and various forms of discrimination that limit people's life chances, such as institutional racism, sexism, homophobia, transphobia, or **ableism**.

While they might at first appear less obviously violent than physical violence, we need to pay attention to this second level of violence because, as sociologist Johan Galtung argues, a focus on the physical dimensions of violence alone is inadequate. This is because, he explains, the definition of peace that would arise from the absence of physical violence alone would be compatible with highly unjust social orders. What he means by this is that simply removing the physical aspects of, for example, gender violence would not deal with the *unjust structures* of patriarchy, sexism, and misogyny that *underpin* physical acts. It is also important to examine violences of this kind because they are more common than physical violences, and because they often create the conditions within which acts of physical violence take place.

While this kind of violence might be harder to see than physical violence, we can identify where structural violence takes place, Galtung argues, by comparing the *potential* and *actual* outcomes in a given situation. In other words, we need to compare what *could have* happened and what *did* happen in the situation. If something could have been avoided, for example a death from a disease for which we have a cure, but was not avoided, then violence *has* taken place. If, on the other hand, we did not have a cure for the disease, then violence *has not* taken place. In his words, 'violence is present when human beings are being influenced so that their *actual* somatic and mental realizations are below their *potential* realizations' (Galtung, 1969, 168. Emphasis added).

Galtung provides several other examples to illustrate what he means. A life expectancy of thirty years would not be a violence in prehistoric times, he claims, but it would be today because we have the medical knowledge to prolong life beyond this. This is the case even if the deaths were caused by war or the social injustices of neoliberal capitalism, for instance large price mark-ups on medicines that prevent people being able to buy them. Because we have the capacity not to go war, and to provide medicine, if we fail to do so we have acted violently. For example, uneven access to Covid-19 vaccines for people in different parts of the world would count as a violence of this kind. Similarly, in the case of global hunger Galtung (1969, 171) argues that 'if people are starving when this is objectively avoidable, then violence is committed, regardless of whether there is a clear subject-action-object relation, as during a siege yesterday or no such clear relation, as in the way world economic relations are organized today'. Because such violences are built into the system, he calls them 'structural violences'.

As this suggests, Galtung's framing of structural violence includes violences for which there is no clear perpetrator. As he puts it, in this type of violence '[t]here may not be any person who directly harms another person in the structure. The violence is built into the structure and shows up as unequal power and consequently as unequal life chances' (Galtung, 1969, 171). For example, he continues, 'when one husband beats his wife there is a clear case of personal violence, but when one million husbands keep one million wives in ignorance there is structural violence' (Galtung, 1969, 171).

Importantly, violences of this kind may not be immediately visible to us as violent. This is because they do not have a clear subject-action-object relation. Indeed, it may be the case not only that we do not *notice* structural violence but that we see the unequal relation as normal or even as a *good* thing. Unlike in cases of physical violence in which the object perceives the violence done to them and may complain or seek redress, when structural violences take place, the object 'may be persuaded not to perceive this at all . . . Structural violence is silent, it does not show—it is essentially static, it *is* the tranquil waters' (Galtung, 1969, 173). In cases like this, violence does not show even to the person who has experienced it. This is because nothing out of the ordinary has happened.

REFLECTIVE ACTIVITY 5.4

Pause here to reflect on the following question:

> *What is structural violence? What examples can you think of?*

Discuss your answer with a family member or friend.

Having established this second, less visible, type of violence, we might think our task of understanding what and where violence is in global politics is complete. After all, we have challenged the myth that violence is always physical in character, and shown that it ranges from shockingly visible to completely invisible. There is, however, a third dimension of violence to which we should pay attention. While physical and structural violences take place in the political world 'out there', there are also forms of violence which go on *inside* our ways of understanding and being in the world. These violences occur 'inside' us all in our patterns of thinking, speaking, and behaving. It is to this form of 'immanent' violence that this section now turns.

5.2.3 **IMMANENT VIOLENCE**

If structural violence is less immediately visible than physical violence, immanent violence is even more difficult to spot. The word 'immanent' means 'on the inside of' or 'within'. This is not to be confused with 'imminent', meaning 'soon to happen'. Immanent violence refers to the violences at work on the *inside of each of us* in the language, concepts, and thought patterns we use. Violences of this kind are, like structural violence, coded into systems in which we operate. But, unlike structural violence, immanent violence operates not in *external* structures like economic inequality or political marginalisation but rather in the *internal* realm of values, beliefs, and identity. Immanent violence of this kind might include sexist, racist, homophobic/transphobic, or ableist beliefs or assumptions that have been internalised. Such beliefs form the context within which structural violences, like **institutional racism**, and physical violences, such as a racially motivated attack, take place.

One element of immanent violence has to do with the concepts, theories, and ideas we use to create knowledge about the world. This is of interest to us in the context of our studies at university. Termed **epistemic violence** by literary theorist Gayatri Chakravorty Spivak (in Williams and Chrisman, 1994), this kind of violence occurs in, for example, when one way of thinking or producing knowledge presents itself as superior to other ways.

Spivak focuses on the way knowledge about the world has been produced in a colonial system (explored further in Chapter 8) in which the West frames itself as superior by claiming it is more rational and scientific than other parts of the world. In colonial ways of thinking and producing knowledge, she explains, colonised peoples are framed as 'other' by those studying them (in Williams and Chrisman, 1994, 76). The consequence of this **othering**, Spivak—quoting Foucault—argues, is that 'a whole set of knowledges . . . have been disqualified as inadequate to their task or insufficiently elaborated: naïve knowledges, located low down on the hierarchy, beneath the required level of cognition or scientificity' (in Williams and Chrisman, 1994, 76. Citing Foucault).

This prompts Spivak to pose her famous question: 'Can the subaltern speak?' By **subaltern** here, she means 'men and women among the illiterate peasantry, the tribals, the lowest strata of the urban subproletariat'. What she is asking here is whether, under conditions of epistemic violence of imperialist law and education, people outside the Western knowledge-producing elite have a voice audible to those producing knowledge in the West. Her response to this question is that the knowledge produced by colonised people is systematically discounted and overridden by Western forms of knowledge production. In this way, violence is done to such people as they are treated as passive *objects*, rather than active *subjects*, in the production of knowledge. To add another layer of complexity, Spivak continues by pointing out the gendered impacts of this epistemic violence, noting that '[i]f, in the context of colonial production, the subaltern has no history and cannot speak, the subaltern as female is even more deeply in shadow' (in Williams and Chrisman, 1994, 82–83). Because this violence occurs in the ways we think and produce knowledge about ourselves and other peoples, it is an immanent form of violence.

Such epistemic violence extends to the fields of IR and global politics. As IR scholar Siba Grovogui (2001, 426) explains, in current debates '"Africa" has emerged to the large Western public yet again as a metaphor for a number of evils: failed states, AIDS, poverty, corruption, and "fratricide". . . But such allusions still racialize international knowledge and thus provide a basis for the exclusion of non-whites from the essential decision-making fora of the moral order'. As this suggests, despite being at the level of thought and language, this form of violence has concrete real-world consequences. Literature professor Tirop Peter Simatei (2005, 86) makes a similar point when he argues that colonial scholarship's '(re)ordering of land and its inhabitants becomes a form of epistemic violence to the extent that it involves immeasurable disruption and erasure of local systems of meaning that guide the ownership and use of land. Because it actually suppresses the difference of the Other, colonial representation in this sense is a mode of violence'. This suppression of 'the other' functions, as many postcolonial scholars have argued, to instantiate a hierarchy of cultures and lives in global politics.

Some IR scholars have argued that this hierarchical epistemic violence extends to the heart of the Western philosophical tradition. Focusing in on the idea of 'reason', IR professors David Campbell and Michael Dillon have argued that the West's fixation with rationalist forms of knowledge production can be read as a form of violence because it seeks to make universal claims when only particular ones are possible. As they put it: 'As modern reason is deeply complicit in the violence of the modern political subject, then the political subject of violence not only exceeds the analytic of political violence so far offered by modern reason, it must also include reason itself, especially in view of reason's universality aspirations and claimed immunity to violence' (Campbell and Dillon, 1993, 2). Because Western value systems and identities are so bound up with this desire for rationalist knowledge and universal truths, according to

Campbell and Dillon, we are situated within relations of violence which operate along colonial, gendered, heteronormative, and a host of other lines. As they put it: 'The basic subject of modern politics is . . . also a subject of violence, in the sense that central figure, or agent, is a violent political subject by virtue of its very composition' (Campbell and Dillon, 1993, 1). The discomforting conclusion of this is that not only is immanent violence at work in our formal philosophical traditions but also in our everyday ways of thinking and behaving.

REFLECTIVE ACTIVITY 5.5

Pause here to reflect on the following question:

What is immanent violence, and what can we do about it?

What is the role of language in generating immanent violence?

Discuss your answer with a family member or friend.

As you may have noticed, the three forms of violence explored here are difficult to separate. Physical forms of violence are rooted in structural violences, which in turn are located and perpetuated through the immanent forms of violence at work in our language, concepts, and patterns of thinking. If we take the example of drone strikes (as shown in Photo 5.2), which have been used in recent years by the US in Afghanistan, Pakistan, Syria, Iraq, Somalia, and Yemen, we can see that all three forms of violence blend together.

Photo 5.2 **Drone strikes combine the three forms of violence: physical, structural, and immanent.**

© sibsky2016 / Shutterstock.com

First, physical violence is clearly in evidence in the dropping of bombs from remotely piloted planes. There have been over 3,500 deaths caused by drone strikes in Northwest Pakistan alone since strikes began in 2004, and many thousands more have been injured. Second, structural violence is present in the form of the long-term fear and distress caused by the ever-present possibility of an attack. As law professor Nasser Hussain explains:

> Because drones are able to hover at or above 30 thousand feet, they are mostly invisible to the people below them. But they can be heard. Many people from the tribal areas of Pakistan (FATA) describe the sound as a low-grade, perpetual buzzing, a signal that a strike could occur at any time. The locals call the drones machar, mosquitos. Because the drone can surveil the area for hours at a time, and because each round of surveillance may or may not result in a strike, the fear and anxiety among civilians is diffuse and chronic (Hussain, 2013).

This type of enduring psychological violence would fail Galtung's test of actual vs potential outcomes. It is within our power not to use drone strikes in this way; given that we choose to do so anyway, in his framework violence is at work. While this form of violence is less dramatic than the physical injuries associated with drone strikes, it affects entire populations over prolonged periods, causing a host of psychological and logistical problems. Third, the example of drone strikes also clearly indicates immanent violence. The rationale for this form of warfare is that it protects the lives of US personnel. Drone operators can control their aircraft operating in, for example, Pakistan, from the safety of the mainland US. However, as philosopher Grégoire Chamayou has argued, this changes the nature of war from one in which both sides are at risk of harm to one in which only one side is vulnerable. The consequence of this it that '[w]arfare, from being possibly asymmetrical, becomes absolutely unilateral. What could still claim to be combat is converted into a campaign of what is, quite simply, slaughter' (Chamayou 2015, np).

This logic, as Chamayou and others have argued, is thinkable only if one views the various lives at stake as of different worth. Against conventional Just War thinking, which provides immunity from harm to noncombatants, through the use of drone warfare the US privileges *combatant* immunity (for its own forces) at the expense of noncombatants of other states/areas. What is at work here is a violence at the level of thought, which entails the lives of those living under drones are of less worth than those of US military personnel. The killing of noncombatants is presented as insignificant as reflected in the use of the term 'bug-splats' to refer to them (Benedictus, 2014), and the recreationalisation of such attacks by showing them on YouTube and in videogames.

REFLECTIVE ACTIVITY 5.6

Take a break here to respond to the following questions:

What is the relationship between physical, structural, and immanent violence?

What other examples in global politics can you think of where all three types of violence are at work?

Discuss your reflections and answers with a friend or classmate.

The implication of this is that violence is at work not just in physical and structural sites *out there* but also *inside* each of us, in our ways of creating knowledge, the political and social concepts we use, and our language and thought processes. In other words, just as the third face of power shapes our internal preferences and values (Chapter 3), violence occurs *within*, as well as *outside*, each of us. These are troubling thoughts. Many of us study global politics because we want to do something to improve the world. The idea that we are bound up in a web of violent relations, many of which we do not even perceive, is certainly an unsettling one. And the claim that our language has the effect of reproducing violence, even as we try to challenge it, might make our good intentions feel hopeless.

Against such hopelessness, one path forward is to explore whether or not some of the violences we participate in may be more legitimate than others. If we cannot step outside violent relations, perhaps we can find ways to distinguish between more and less defensible violences. Section 5.3 addresses this question, examining the mystery of why state violence is often viewed as legitimate, while nonstate violence is treated as illegitimate.

5.3 CAN VIOLENCE BE JUSTIFIED?

We have so far conceptualised physical, structural, and immanent violence and examined how they relate to one another. What has yet to be addressed is the question of whether violence can ever be *justified* in global politics. Scholarly opinion varies widely on this issue. **Pacifists** claim that violence can never be justified. Just War Theory seeks to establish conditions under which certain violent acts can be justified. And some Post/Decolonial scholars claim violent revolution against imperial rulers can be justifiable.

Echoing the discussion of legitimacy and authority in Chapter 2, at the heart of the issue of legitimate and illegitimate violence is the question of to whom we are responsible in global politics. In other words, who can 'legitimately' use violence in global politics, and against whom or what? Traditional approaches in IR like Realism would suggest that states are the primary actors that use violent means in global politics. But, of course, so too do private citizens (for example in murders and mass school shootings), organised criminal networks (such as drug cartels and mafia groups), and past and present political and paramilitary groups and movements (like the Black Panthers, the IRA, and ISIS). Violence is also deployed by transnational corporations that force workers to produce goods such as textiles or mobile phones in unsafe buildings for poverty wages. To make matters more complex, if we're using a comprehensive analysis of violence which includes structural and immanent forms, perhaps we are *all* violent actors to the extent we participate in things like global banking or credit systems, pay taxes which are used to fund the arms trade, or enact unconscious biases in our everyday lives.

Just as important as the question of who *uses* violence in global politics is the question of who or what can *experience* violence. While most accounts privilege humans as the key actor of concern, recent scholarship and activist movements have emphasised that animals can experience violence, for example in battery farming, circus acts, or deforestation leading to loss of habitat. Advocates of this position offer a **post-humanist** framework to understand and challenge violence in global politics (Cudworth and Hobden, 2013). Moreover, in many legal systems the act of deliberately damaging property is a prosecutable offence. It is also possible to enact violence against less tangible things such as values systems, languages, or ways of life. In addition to the physical violences they experience, Indigenous communities in North America and Australasia emphasise the violences done to their cultures, economic and political arrangements, belief systems, and languages, by settler colonisers.

It is also vital to consider how the visibility of certain acts, and the invisibility of other acts, has the effect of making some forms of violence *appear* more serious than others. For example, the issue of gender violence has historically not featured centrally in security policy and international law as it was deemed a 'private' matter. Indeed, in some legal systems the idea of sexual violence within marriage is deemed nonsensical as sex between spouses is understood as part of the martial contract. This poses the key question of how a particular form of violence *becomes* visible in global politics.

While some of the examples discussed have been the focus of popular and scholarly discussions for a long time, others have only just been put on the agenda of current debate. While the violences associated with war and organised crime, for example, have long been key issues of discussion in global media and IR, other violences—such as violence against LGBTQIA+ people, or violence against animals and the environment—have tended to be marginalised from mainstream debates. As scholars working with Feminist, Queer, Post/ Decolonial, and **Green Theory** have argued, it has taken a good deal of struggle to get these violences on to the agenda, and many in the mainstream still resist their inclusion either by ignoring them or by being actively hostile.

What this shows is that particular forms of violence are not simply more or less visible *in themselves*. Rather, *power relations* affect the extent to which the global community takes notice of a specific violence. If we think back to the discussion in Chapter 3 of power, we can see that whether an instance of violence makes it on to, or is kept off, the agenda, relates to whether or not powerful actors allow them to become, or prevent them from becoming, a topic of debate. While power and violence are not one and the same, those who break norms prescribed by power relations risk violent reprisals.

Power relations function to establish hierarchies in society which frame people and lifestyles as more or less desirable or acceptable on the basis of their conformity with, or transgression of, particular norms of conduct. For example, heteronormative social norms which devalue queer relationships prescribe a series of behavioural expectations. Straight couples do not have to think twice about holding hands or kissing in public, while queer couples are frequently subject to verbal and physical abuse for displaying affection. Similarly, trans people who 'pass' easily as cisgender are statistically more insulated from attacks than those who do not; the latter are more frequently subject to abuse and violence. Despite the UK having passed the Equality Act, the prevalence of homophobic and transphobic attacks have increased rapidly in recent years; in 2019 *The Guardian* reported that hate crimes including stalking, harassment, and assault against gay and lesbian people had doubled, and against trans people had trebled, since 2014 (Marsh, Mohdin, and McIntyre, 2019). Similar patterns are in evidence in many other parts of the world.

In addition to the physical violences associated with attacks and assaults, people who transgress the norms of established power relations are subject to a series of violent disciplinary and exclusionary practices which function to instil fear, intimidate, and marginalise them. In the case of LGBTQIA+ people, these kinds of violences include lower chances of being promoted at work, poor treatment by state officials and medical professionals, and pressure to perform conventional gender norms in terms of dress, speech, and movement. Thus, the *visibility* of an act is closely linked to perceptions of its (il)legitimacy.

Furthermore, a specific act of violence can be understood as more or less legitimate depending on *who carries it out*. For example, in prevailing understandings, a soldier fighting in a war can 'legitimately' harm or kill soldiers of an opposing armed force, but a member of a nonstate armed group cannot 'legitimately' kill a member of an opposing armed group. The *act* in these cases is the same, but the *status* of the individual in terms of state sanction appears to make a significant difference in our framings of what counts as legitimate or illegitimate violence. If we extend the example, what would the status of the violent act be if the state which licensed the soldier's behaviour was defeated by another state? If the victorious state dissolved the defeated state, would the soldier's violence still enjoy the legitimacy of state sanction? Or would it turn overnight from legitimate state violence to illegitimate or terrorist violence? The following section explores these problems in detail with a view to challenging the myth that state violence is necessarily legitimate and nonstate violence illegitimate.

5.3.1 **LEGITIMATE STATE VIOLENCE?**

In prevailing philosophical and political traditions, a division is drawn between violence conducted by the state, which is thought to be legitimate, and violence conducted by nonstate actors, which is deemed illegitimate. The state, the story goes, has a unique right to exercise violence in the global sphere. Unlike other actors, it can use organised armed forces to harm and kill the armed forces of other states. It can use police forces to arrest, prosecute, and incarcerate individuals. It can use intelligence services to surveil and monitor individuals or groups. And in many cases, it can use legal systems to impose the death penalty on its citizens.

One key origin of this claim is sociologist Max Weber's essay 'Politics as a Vocation' (1919). Weber, who you can see in Photo 5.3, argued that one defining feature of the state is that it alone can claim that its use of violence is legitimate:

> [W]e have to say that a state is a human community that (successfully) claims the *monopoly of the legitimate use of physical force* within a given territory . . . Specifically, at the present time, the right to use physical force is ascribed to other institutions or to individuals only to the extent to which the state permits it. The state is considered the sole source of the 'right' to use violence (Weber, Gerth, and Mills, 2015, 78. Emphasis in original).

Here, Weber argues the state is the only actor that can claim legitimacy for its violent acts (with the caveat that it can extend this right to actors acting on its behalf). This might sound reasonable enough—we are used to this arrangement in the everyday working of global politics. But it is less than clear in this account *where* this legitimacy comes from.

Weber discusses the matter further, adding a statement which gives away something important: 'the state is a relation of men dominating men, a relation supported by means of legitimate (i.e. *considered to be legitimate*) violence' (Weber, Gerth, and Mills, 2015, 78.

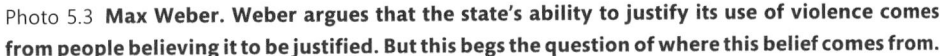

Photo 5.3 **Max Weber. Weber argues that the state's ability to justify its use of violence comes from people believing it to be justified. But this begs the question of where this belief comes from.**

© Keystone Press / Alamy Stock Photo

Emphasis added). Here, Weber draws attention to a central problem with this claim to legitimacy. Far from resting on solid ground—for example, the divine right of kings or a *bone fide* social contract—the state's claim to legitimacy depends on people *considering* it to be legitimate. In other words, rather than being grounded in something concrete, the state's right to a monopoly on the legitimate use of force derives from people—us—*believing in it.*

What this suggests is that Weber's account begs, rather than resolves, the question of what makes the state's claim to a monopoly on the legitimate use of violence valid. We are left wondering what exactly it is about the state that transforms the act of killing or wounding from an illegitimate to a legitimate act. If it is simply the existence of a popular consensus that the state has this monopoly, what happens if people's opinions change? Beyond people's perceptions, what precisely is the difference between a state-sanctioned soldier, a paramilitary soldier, a revolutionary, or a private individual conducting the same act of violence? Key here, as the next section sets out, is the role of language in *constructing* our ideas about legitimate and illegitimate violence.

REFLECTIVE ACTIVITY 5.7

Take a break here to respond to the following questions:

Why does Max Weber argue that only states can legitimately use violence? Do you agree with his justification of this claim?

Discuss your reflections and answers with a friend or classmate.

Rather than grounded in a solid rationale, then, the state's claim of a monopoly on the legitimate use of force rests in its ability to *convince us* that this is, and should be, the case. Weber himself points to the state's need to *persuade people* to accept this claim: 'Organized domination, which calls for continuous administration, requires that human conduct be *conditioned to obedience* towards those masters who claim to be the bearers of legitimate power . . . [and] the control of those material goods which in a given case are necessary for the use of physical violence' (Weber, Gerth, and Mills, 2015, 80. Emphasis added). Here, Weber suggests that far from spontaneously occurring, people's belief in the legitimacy of state violence must be 'conditioned'. So, how is this belief in the state's monopoly on the legitimate use of force conditioned?

One element is the selective use of particular words and phrases which imply legitimacy or illegitimacy when attached to particular violent acts and actors. Scholars like Claire Thomas have explored the ways states use language to construct favourable framings of their violence. One way they do this is by limiting the use of the word 'violence' itself. This is because, some commentators have argued, the use of the term 'violence' is enough to delegitimise an act. As Thomas explains, many canonical texts in the field use terms other than violence to describe states' activities, such as 'force', 'security promotion', or 'military offensive', reserving the term 'violence' for the actions of nonstate or 'rogue' actors.

Giving the example of Realist theorist John Mearsheimer's influential book *The Tragedy of Great Power Politics*, Thomas notes that despite it being 'about the subject of violence, the word violence is not used. This at least hints at the fact that "violence" is seen as illegitimate, and the use of military force between states is seen as legitimate' (Thomas, 2011, 1820). The choice of language is, then, crucially important not just in terms of accurately describing an act of violence but rather in establishing whether an act of violence took place at all. If the same act, say shooting a gun at an adversary, can be described variously as an act of heroism (if carried out by a state-sanctioned soldier) or murder (if carried out by an 'enemy combatant'), then language does not simply *describe* the act but rather contributes to *constructing* our normative understandings of its meaning and (il)legitimacy.

What this ultimately means it that actors can influence perceptions of a particular act by choosing to describe it as an instance of violence or not. As Thomas explains:

> By bringing the concept of legitimacy into the definition of violence, the term becomes a political tool. Governments are able to call something violent in order to condemn it, at the same time as using violence themselves to maintain the status quo where they have the power . . . The presumption is that the terrorists use violence and are illegitimate, and state authorities are legitimate and so use military force (Thomas, 2011, 1825).

REFLECTIVE ACTIVITY 5.8

Take a break here to respond to the following questions:

To what extent is language important in framings of legitimate and illegitimate violence?

Can you think of other examples of words which influence our view of whether or not an act or agent of violence is legitimate?

Discuss your reflections and answers with a friend or classmate.

A further, and crucial, question is explored by philosopher Jacques Derrida, who is shown in photo 5.4. Prevailing accounts which privilege state violence over nonstate violence tend to treat the state as though it simply exists, forgetting that in fact states have

Photo 5.4 **Jacques Derrida. Derrida argued that states rewrite their founding violences, presenting them as noble and heroic.**

© The Hebrew University of Jerusalem/Dr. Betty Rojtman

to be established, and that this is a violent process. States are established, Derrida argues, through processes of war, revolution, displacement, expulsion, ethnic cleansing, disenfranchisement of certain groups, and so on. States, however, rarely describe their founding as violent (Derrida, 1992). Instead, they alter the image of this violence by presenting it as noble and heroic, as we commonly see in the lyrics of national anthems, which celebrate the glorious revolution or other founding myths. This sleight-of-hand, Derrida shows, belies a paradoxical situation: while states claim for themselves the monopoly on the legitimate use of force, the state's own founding violence cannot be deemed legitimate in its own terms as it occurred *before* the state was founded.

Consider a revolution that led to the founding of a new form of government, for example in France in 1798, Haiti in 1804, or China in 1949. The revolutionary fighters who changed the way the state was run were not at the time state officials, so in this framework could not have exercised violence legitimately. What we often see following a revolution is that this nonstate violence is legitimised after the fact, through discourses of glory, heroism, and liberation. In spite of this, however, given that states claim for themselves a monopoly on the legitimate use of violence, the violence used in the founding of the state is not legitimate. This is because as nonstate actors at the time, the revolutionaries could not enjoy the state's claim to legitimacy. Once we notice this, Derrida argues, we have exposed the 'mystical foundations' of the state's claim to a monopoly on the legitimate use of force. The implication of this is that the state's violence is no more legitimate than violence enacted by any other agent in global politics. With this is mind, we will now address the question of whether or not violence carried out by nonstate actors is necessarily illegitimate.

5.3.2 ILLEGITIMATE NONSTATE VIOLENCE?

As the same moment as the legitimacy of state violence is called into question, so too is the assumption that nonstate violence is necessarily illegitimate. While the conventional story reserves legitimacy for violence carried out by state actors, scholars such as Frantz Fanon have argued that the nonstate actors can, under certain conditions, claim legitimacy for their acts of violence. Furthermore, they have shown that an uncritical acceptance of the legitimacy of state violence, and of the illegitimacy of nonstate violence, can result in processes of dehumanisation and othering which themselves amount to, and license, serious violences. The next section explores two key examples of this: post-9/11 designations of the 'terrorist', and the treatment of colonised peoples.

In the post-9/11 world, perhaps the most widely discussed form of nonstate violence has been terrorism. The notion of terrorism has a long history—from state terrorism such as the 'Reign of Terror' during the French Revolution (1789–99) and the 'Red Terror' in revolutionary Russia (1918–22), to nonstate actors such as the **IRA** or the **Baader Meinhof** group. In the post-9/11 context, the concept of terrorism took on a specific set of meanings which had powerful **depoliticising** and **dehumanising** effects on those to whom the label was attached. While many mainstream scholars focused on how the West might defeat terrorism in the post-9/11 world, others, like philosopher Judith Butler, focused on critically examining the effects of the label 'terrorist' and the kinds of actions it licensed. Against the usual framing of the terrorist as evil, barbaric, and inhuman, they argued that in a climate in which the label 'terrorist' authorised torture ('enhanced interrogation'), kidnap and indefinite detention ('extraordinary rendition'), and denial of legal rights and representation, we commit a serious violence by using the label at all. The violence here is to make people described as terrorists **ungrievable**.

Butler, who you can see in photo 5.5, explores the question of what makes some lives grievable, in the sense that we mourn their deaths, and others ungrievable, in the sense that we do not experience their deaths as something to mourn. They explain that in the current global order, '[s]ome lives are grievable, and others are not; the differential allocation of grievability that decides what kind of subject is and must be grieved, and which kind of subject must not, operates to produce and maintain certain exclusionary conceptions of who is normatively human: what counts as a liveable life and a grievable death?' (Butler, 2006, xiv–xv). In this framing, the terrorist is dehumanised to such a degree they become ungrievable—they can be disappeared or killed without any sense of loss. The consequence

Photo 5.5 **Judith Butler. Butler argues that the label 'terrorist' is violent because it dehumanises individuals and makes them 'ungrievable'.**

© Agencja Fotograficzna Caro / Alamy Stock Photo

of this, Butler explains, is that the 'derealization of loss—the insensitivity to human suffering and death—becomes the mechanism through which dehumanization is accomplished' (Butler, 2006, 148).

What this shows is that whatever we think of the legitimacy of nonstate violence, this should not give us licence to enact violences of our own by dehumanising those accused of it to such a degree they cease to be legible as human. Doing so entails and reflects important immanent violences. As Butler explains, for torture and rendition policies to be thinkable, processes of dehumanisation—as she puts it 'derealization'—must have already occurred in the minds and discourses of dominant powers: 'certain lives are not considered lives at all . . . [T]heir dehumanization occurs first . . . [and] then gives rise to a physical violence that in some sense delivers the message of dehumanization that is already at work in the culture' (Butler, 2006, 34).

A further important issue is the use of violence by nonstate actors against an unjust political system such as imperial rule. In addition to its physical and structural violences, European colonialism is immanently violent because it relies on an ideology of white supremacism which affects the self-image of colonised peoples. As psychiatrist and political philosopher Frantz Fanon (see photo 2.1) argued,

> [t]he colonial world is a Manichean world. It is not enough for the settler to delimit physically, that is to say with the help of the army and the police force, the place of the native. As if to show the totalitarian character of colonial exploitation the settler paints the native as a sort of quintessence of evil. Native society is not simply declared as a society lacking in values. It is not enough for the colonist to affirm that those values have disappeared from, or still better never existed in, the colonial world. The native is declared insensible to ethics; he represents not only the absence of values, but also the negation of values (Fanon, 2001, 31–32).

Because of this extreme violence, operating across physical, structural, and immanent domains, Fanon argues that violence on the part of colonised peoples is not only justified but necessary to expel the colonial powers, build a new society, and reclaim agency. As he puts it, '[a]t the level of individuals, violence is a cleansing force. It frees the native from his inferiority complex and from his despair and inaction, it makes him fearless and restores his self-respect' (Fanon, 2001, 74). Fanon's account shows that nonstate violence can be presented as legitimate. This suggests that a blanket delegitimisation of all forms of nonstate violence may have violent effects such as undermining challenges to colonial domination.

REFLECTIVE ACTIVITY 5.9

Take a break here to respond to the following questions:

What does Butler mean by grievable and ungrievable lives? How are these designations attached to particular groups or individuals in global politics?

Why does Fanon argue that violence in the service of decolonial struggle is justified? Do you agree with his rationale?

Discuss your reflections and answers with a friend or classmate.

This shows that the assumption of legitimate state violence and illegitimate nonstate violence rests on a series of myths rather than solid ground. As political theorists Elizabeth Frazer and Kimberly Hutchings argue, the distinction drawn between legal 'force' used by states and the illegal 'violence' used by nonstate actors is difficult to sustain (Frazer and Hutchings, 2019, 9). This is because, they explain,

> the distinction 'state' and 'nonstate' is too simple to capture that range of positions of the various members of the polity: those who exercise sovereign power and authority; police and security forces; civil servants; agents of the state who contract with governments to deliver public services; citizens (i.e. those who have the full set of rights to a passport, to vote, to stand for office); denizens (i.e. those who live on the territory of a state but are not citizens); aliens (visitors, illegal denizens) members of parties competing for office and governmental power; members of campaigning groups trying to put pressure on, or to oppose, governments; members of cultures which are positioned in opposition to the dominant cultural groups, or don't participate in political life. There are others. In the theory of popular sovereignty and democracy some of the people, but not all, constitute 'the state'—although which do varies from theory to theory (Frazer and Hutchings, 2019, 9–10).

It thus becomes unclear which actors are included in the state, and which fall outside, making it difficult to draw lines between 'legitimate' and 'illegitimate' violence.

Establishing legitimate and illegitimate violence in global politics is, then, more difficult than might be assumed. Rather than getting stuck in this puzzle, it is important to consider the question of how we might reduce or end violence in global politics. As the final section below sets out, however, this too is more complicated than one might think.

5.4 THE (IM)POSSIBILITY OF NONVIOLENCE

This chapter has established three dimensions of violence in global politics—physical, structural, and immanent—and has argued that prevailing assumptions about the legitimacy of state violence and the illegitimacy of nonstate violence are ultimately unsustainable. We are left, in this final section, to consider how to respond to this complex situation. If violence permeates not just our concrete political world but also our modes of thinking and being, what can we do about this? If our aim is to reduce violence in global politics, where can we start?

This seems like a daunting problem, but the final argument made in this chapter is that, despite its ubiquity, there are lots of things we can do to address violence. A good place to begin is the assumption that violence is inevitable. As mentioned in Section 5.1, if we start from the belief that people and politics are irredeemably violent, we risk removing the incentive to challenge and change violent relations. After all, if violence really is *inevitable*, there's no reason to try doing anything about it because any such attempt is doomed to failure.

Classical Realist scholars in IR, like Hans J. Morgenthau, take this view, arguing that violence and conflict are—tragically—rooted in human nature. In his famous book, *Politics Among Nations* (1978, 4), he argues that 'politics, like society in general, is governed by objective laws that have their roots in human nature', which he sees as evil because it is driven by a lust for power. This is, however, but one interpretation of human nature, based on the idea that the self has to dominate others to achieve a sense of wholeness. As IR scholar

Ty Solomon (2012, 210) explains, this understanding has been challenged by critical scholars who view the relationship between self and other not as one of competition and domination but rather mutual reliance and vulnerability. After all, if the self needs the other to be intelligible as the self, this means we rely upon, rather than compete with, one another.

The implication of Morgenthau's pessimistic view of human nature, we suggest, is that it has the effect not of *describing* a world which simply exists but rather contributes to *creating* such a world. In other words, by assuming the worst about people and violence we create an environment in which violence appears inevitable, *bringing about* what we claim merely to describe. If violence is framed as inevitable, violent actors legitimise their violence by claiming that there is nothing else that could be done. So, the first thing we can do to challenge violence in global politics is contest the myth that it is inevitable.

Once we have challenged this **fatalistic** myth, the bind we are left with is whether nonviolence is possible, and if so, what it looks like. Many of us study global politics precisely to make the world a better place in some way, often focusing on reducing or eliminating a certain kind of violence, whether physical (like conflict or war), structural (like economic inequality), or immanent (like racist forms of knowledge production). But is it possible to reduce violence in global politics? And how would a less or nonviolent world be organised?

Simply avoiding physical violence does not mean we have removed relations of violence. We can imagine a form of rule which contained little physical violence, but which could be thoroughly structurally and immanently violent. Indeed, a rigid commitment to physical nonviolence might well, in this example, serve to perpetuate an unjust system. Under such conditions, it is arguable that physical violence on the part of the oppressed—whether against property, symbolic objects, or people—might be the only way to address and remedy these less visible forms of violence.

On the other hand, such violence, even when well-intentioned, participates in processes of othering and destruction, and has harmful effects on those who carry it out, as Fanon noted. As literary critic and gender studies professor Deepti Misri argues, '[i]f the premature dismissal of violence from below prevents us from seeing the direct and structural violence to which such violence is often posited as a response, an uncritical (or sometimes barely qualified) embrace of such violence potentially obscures the ways in which such violence so often runs awry from its stated path, frequently turning inward (Misri, 2014, 165–166). She continues: 'the violence of the disempowered, while often a function of last resort, is rarely a pure ethical product despite its stated ends . . . [Consequently,] "conceptual distinctions between forms of violence, based on the ethical ends they seek to achieve, are largely unsustainable in practice"' (Misri, 2014, 166. Citing Roy).

Rather than judging it legitimate or illegitimate, Misri concludes, we should understand that

> violence is a complex ethical terrain that can only be assessed through deep contextualization. Therefore, rather than falling back into a framework that sorts the 'good' violence of the disempowered from 'bad' violence of the state and powerful groups, or declares both to be equally reprehensible in the end, I would propose . . . that we attend to the imaginative possibilities suggested by the violence of the oppressed (Misri, 2014, 176).

Also acknowledging that nonviolence can sometimes end up colluding with structural violence, Frazer and Hutchings argue that nonviolence is preferable to violence. Echoing discussions in Chapters 2 and 3, they note two key reasons for this: 'First, the practice of nonviolence itself instantiates relations of respect, inclusion and being with others, as opposed to contempt and exclusion. Second, nonviolence is much more likely to leave all political protagonists able to try again in case of failure, as opposed to tactics that will annihilate political opponents, yet are still likely to fail' (Frazer and Hutchings, 2019, 118).

They explain that this rejection is based on the idea that violence is not simply an instrument that actors use but rather that it has a politics of its own, rooted in 'hierarchy and exclusion . . . and structures of inequality, rejection and estrangement' (Frazer and Hutchings, 2019, 119). Political **liberation**, they conclude, comes not from violent action but rather from 'deliberately quitting one set of relationships and entering into, building, another set. A nonviolent power' (Frazer and Hutchings, 2019, 119–120). Instead of assuming that violence can, at least under certain circumstances, be justified, Frazer and Hutching argue that we should be cautious because

> [t]he idea of justification is that it makes something right. This mistakenly implies that the politics of violence is capable of being defused or controlled. The language of justification is also fundamentally permissive. It establishes thresholds for action. It is this part of gendering and racialized discourses that make political violence a practice in which it is not only possible, but rather easy, to engage, providing that participants are trained, and entrained, to embody the appropriate ideologies, skills, propensities, and habits' (Frazer and Hutchings, 2019, 120).

As yet, as Frazer and Hutchings are also aware, once we employ a comprehensive analysis of violence which includes structural and immanent forms the attempt to be nonviolent becomes much more difficult. It is one thing to renounce physical violence, but how, if our political, economic, social, and even cognitive and affective realms are bound up in violent relations, can we strive to be nonviolent? Is this an impossible goal?

Returning to the work of Butler is helpful to make sense of this problem. They make the following statement:

> I doubt very much that non-violence can be a principle, if by 'principle' we mean a strong rule that can be applied with the same confidence and in the same way to any and all situations. If there is a claim of non-violence or if non-violence makes a claim upon us, that seems to be a different issue. Non-violence then arrives as an address or an appeal (Butler, 2010, 165).

Here, nonviolence is framed not as an end point to be reached but rather an ongoing call to which we can respond. Our suggestion is that a key step towards reducing violence in global politics is to remain open to, and heed, this call. While nonviolence is not a condition at which we can finally arrive, we can actively interrogate, and challenge, the immanent violences inside us, the structural violences of our economic and political systems, and the physical violences which endure in global politics.

REFLECTIVE ACTIVITY 5.10

Take a break here to reflect on this question:

What is nonviolence and how can we work towards it?

Discuss your answer with a friend or classmate.

5.5 CONCLUSION

This chapter has argued that despite its ubiquity there are things we can *all* do to reduce violence in global politics. The first step in this endeavour, we have argued, is to reject the fatalistic view that violence is inevitable in global politics. By making violence appear inevitable, we have shown, this view undermines our attempts to tackle it. Against this self-fulfilling prophecy, in this chapter we have offered a path forward in the struggle against violence which involves becoming more attuned to the levels at which it takes places. This is important because the first step in challenging violence is becoming more aware of what and where it is.

To do this, the chapter challenged the myth that violence is necessarily physical. While acts of physical violence are widespread in global politics, the chapter showed this is not the only kind of violence we can identify. Instead, it set out three types of violence to which we should pay attention in global politics: physical violence, structural violence, and immanent violence. Importantly, these forms of violence are not separable but rather interrelated and mutually reinforcing. Just as importantly, it showed that violence is not something that happens 'out there' or 'far away' but rather close by and every day. Once we see that there are violences at work across our economic, social, and political structures, as well as in our ideas, belief, and language, we can begin to challenge them. This work might be as simple as challenging a racist joke, or as complicated as devising new economic systems. But they all count in the struggle to reduce violence in global politics.

From there, the chapter challenged a second myth about violence in global politics: that state violence is necessarily legitimate while nonstate violence is always illegitimate. Using Derrida's ideas to critique Weber's claim of the state's monopoly on the legitimate use of force, and Fanon's defence of nonstate actors' use of violence in the service of decolonial struggle, the chapter problematised common assumptions about who can legitimately use violence in global politics.

Finally, the chapter challenged the myth that only elite actors have the power to reduce violence in global politics, and that even they face unfavourable odds because ultimately people are self-interested and prone to conflict. Against this, it showed that individuals and grassroots groups can take, and indeed historically have taken, a leading role in challenging a range of violences in global politics, often facing resistance from elite global actors who have little incentive to challenge existing power relations. Our suggestion to you is that the more we pay attention to violence, including those in which we unwittingly take part, the more we are able to reduce violence in global politics.

> **REFLECTIVE ACTIVITY 5.11**
>
> Turn back to your answers from Reflective Activity 5.1 at the start of this chapter and consider these questions again:
>
> > *What is violence in global politics and where does it take place?*
> >
> > *What forms of violence are you most concerned about in global politics?*
> >
> > *What can be done to reduce violence in global politics?*
>
> Have your answers to these questions changed? Why or why not?

 Access the online resources at www.oup.com/he/hirst1e for case studies to help contextualise your understanding of key concepts, further reading recommendations to guide you through your reading, and a library of web links to journal articles, blogs, and video content to help you take your learning further.

LAW

6

READERS' GUIDE

Chapter 6: Law focuses on the mystery of how law has come to function as a form of authority in global politics. It explores the flaws in the myth that international law provides a form of moral authority justifying the rules, institutions, and enforcement mechanisms that will civilise global politics and make it more peaceful and just. At the same time, it demonstrates the limitations of the myth that international law is an impossibility, as global politics is dominated by the struggle for survival between states and their conflicting self-interest. In place of these myths, it shows how international law functions both as a mechanism for maintaining order, often unjustly, and as a way of acting politically, with distinctive advantages and limitations for making change.

6.1 INTRODUCTION

We all know something about the law, but when we examine its meaning it proves complex. We can think of law as a set of rules addressing specific aspects of life, such as traffic laws guiding our movements through cities and towns. Yet the law is rarely so simple, not least because we think of *legal* rules as different from other sorts of rules like the rules of basketball or other games. The law is presumed to have greater authority, reflected in the penalties we face for failing to follow the law, ranging from fines or imprisonment for individual criminals to the waging of war to uphold international law in special cases. As the law claims to justly take our money, freedom, or security when we do not respect its authority, it must therefore have greater legitimacy than the rules or conventions we find in other aspects of our lives. The law aspires to a degree of majesty, inspiring respect for its authority and fear of its power. Yet the law is never quite up to the task of commanding our complete respect. At times the law is ineffective, or even ridiculous, all too often it is unfair and discriminatory, and on occasion it's deeply boring and technical. Like any set of rules, the law reflects the interests of those who make the rules, bends all too easily to suit the interests of those with power and influence, and at times fails to provide adequate solutions to the problems we face. Given law's importance and ambiguity, it's vital to understand it, and its role in global politics.

In this chapter we prepare you to think critically about the role of law in global politics. Importantly, we won't introduce you to the practice of international law nor will we enumerate all the ways law is woven into global politics. Instead, we demonstrate that law is a central concept in global politics, arguing it is a fundamental form of authority structuring our political relationships (see Section 2.2.1). This means the law exerts power (see Section 3.2) over us, even as it is shaped by other powerful actors, and in the process threatens us with violence (see Section 5.2) in the form of punishment if we break the law. The law, however, aspires to legitimacy, meaning its distinctive authority, at least in principle, is grounded in its normative quality—such as serving a common good or respecting the fundamental rights of individuals, states, and other actors (see Section 4.3). Further, the law becomes a modality of global politics, entailing particular institutional structures and distinctive ways of acting politically. For example, European colonialism (see Section 8.3.2) was conducted within a legal framework, which provides the basis for modern international law, and today global economics (see Sections 7.2 and 9.2.1), despite the rhetoric of 'free' markets, is conducted in and through a tightly woven network of legal institutions and bodies of law.

To help you understand the law and its place in global politics, we examine the relationship between law and authority in global politics. Then, we explore two myths about international law. On the one hand there is the myth international law provides a form of moral authority justifying the rules, institutions, and enforcement mechanisms that will civilise global politics, making it more peaceful and just. While on the other hand there is the myth international law is an impossibility as global politics is dominated by the struggle for survival between states and their conflicting self-interest, meaning global politics cannot be effectively constrained by the aspirational authority of international law. Finally, in place of these myths we offer an understanding of international law as an ambiguous practice sitting between 'apology and utopia' (Koskeniemi, 2005), which both serves to legitimise the interests of powerful actors as well as inspire moral reform in global politics.

REFLECTIVE ACTIVITY 6.1

Think of the rules of a game you know well. Consider how they function to direct and limit your actions, what goals they orient you towards, and the penalties applied for breaking the rules. Then, compare this with a body of law that you know, such as traffic laws, domestic criminal law, contract law, or international human rights law.

What similarities and difference can you identify?

What makes a set of rules or body of law legitimate?

6.2 AUTHORITY AND LAW IN INTERNATIONAL POLITICS

We can see the fundamental role of law in global politics by beginning with an infamous moment of law's failure. On 7 June 1936, the Emperor of Ethiopia, Haile Selassie, appeared before the **League of Nations** (see photo 6.1) appealing for assistance against the Italian invasion of his country in October 1935. For nearly two years tensions had escalated between Ethiopia and Italy who were both members of the League of Nations, but the organisation was unable to prevent or respond to Italian aggression. When the League of Nations was created it was the first intergovernmental organisation with the capacity to enforce international treaties, and its covenant prohibited aggressive war, establishing a legal duty of **collective self-defence**.

In the build-up to war, Ethiopia and Italy both engaged with the League's dispute settlement arrangements and signed treaties. So, when Italy invaded Ethiopia, using chemical weapons banned under the Geneva Protocol, it was in clear violation of international law. By the time Selassie made his appeal in 1936, the authority of the League was highly tenuous. Italy had withdrawn from the organisation. The major powers had not abided by sanctions the League placed on Italy—and in fact the League voted to remove those sanctions after

Photo 6.1 **The League of Nations council chamber in the Palace of Nations, Geneva in 1922. In 1936, the League failed stop Italy's invasion of Ethiopia despite being the first intergovernmental organisation with the capacity to enforce international treaties.**

© Pictorial Press Ltd / Alamy Stock Photo

Italian forces occupied Addis Ababa in May 1936. In his appeal, Selassie made the stakes of the League's inaction clear:

> It is not merely a question of the settlement of Italian aggression . . . It is the confidence that each State is to place in international treaties. It is the value of promises made to small States that their integrity and their independence shall be respected and ensured . . . In a word, it is international morality that is at stake. (Selassie, 1936)

The League's failure to stop Italian aggression lays bare the conflict at the centre of international law: is the sovereign state's authority absolute, or can international law exercise effective authority over states? This question is as relevant today as it was in 1936, as time and again international law has come up short. It failed to constrain the aggression of powerful states when the United States of America invaded Iraq in 2003; it failed to rein in the power of multinational corporations by holding global clothing brands responsible for their contribution to the Rana Plaza building collapse in 2013; and it failed to bring international criminal and former Sudanese President Omar Al Bashir to justice, as he has evaded an arrest warrant issued by the **International Criminal Court** (ICC) in 2008.

The League of Nations, despite its failures, helps us see how legal authority is contested in global politics. Born of the tragedy of the First World War, the League was set up to constrain the absolute authority of sovereign states to wage war, sign treaties, and conduct their diplomatic affairs in secret. For many, the immense human suffering of the war gave new impetus to an older mission to bind the authority of states to a higher legal authority which would be capable of constraining their action, ensuring the peaceful resolution of disputes, and protecting individuals from the ravages of war. The idea that a universal moral and legal authority should constrain political authority has a long and diverse history (Keene, 2005), which we cannot consider, but modern international law arises out of the European **natural law** tradition, particularly the **Enlightenment** idea of **natural rights** (see Boucher, 2011). In Section 6.2.1, we look at the distinctive way this tradition conceptualises legitimacy, drawing out how this has shaped the development of modern international law.

6.2.1 INTERNATIONAL LEGAL AUTHORITY: FROM NATURAL LAW TO THE LAW OF POWER

The fundamental premise of natural law is that political authority is constrained by a special set of universally applicable rules limiting what political leaders can do. With the advent of natural rights thinking, these rules are expressed as a rational set of universal rights, which rather than having a divine origin get their content and force from human reason. This approach to legitimising authority finds its most famous expression in the idea of a **social contract** that imagines free and rational individuals living in a **state of nature** without government, who are willing agree to a basic set of rules to protect their natural rights, which provides the foundation for legitimate government. This submission to a common set of rules provides the basis for a distinctive kind of authority, namely the **rule of law**, which is essentially the idea that agreed and public rules have final authority rather than particular individuals with wealth, might, or social position. Further, the rule of law requires that individuals are treated in a consistent manner (though not always equally) and the law is applied impartially. While this is a simplified account, it is sufficient to draw out the tension between the rule of law and what we might call the rule of power, which suggests authority is fundamentally an expression of superior power and that, as the cliché goes, 'might makes right'.

In contrast to the idea of natural law, in the 19th and early 20th centuries it was widely held that in global politics authority rested with sovereign states—it's important to remember there were only a small number of mostly European states considered sovereign at this time. The primacy of state sovereignty limited the effectiveness of international law, as its authority was dependent upon the consent of sovereign states This meant international law had authority only so far as states agreed to abide by the treaties and covenants they signed and negotiated—and states could withdraw their consent at any time. In contrast to the idea of natural law, grounded in the idea of a universal law applicable regardless of whether a sovereign consented to it, the idea of positive law dominated in this period. According to positive law, the law's authority is grounded in its effective enforcement by legitimate political authorities, which was presumed not to exist in global politics. The terrible consequences of the First World War challenged this consensus and inspired numerous projects to establish an international rule of law, and while we will look at some of these developments in later sections, here we turn to the influential ideas of the 18th-century German philosopher Immanuel Kant (see photo 4.2), whose thinking about natural law and global politics were extremely influential in the aftermath of the First World War.

REFLECTIVE ACTIVITY 6.2

Today, rights claims are ubiquitous, in the law, in politics, and in our wider culture. But within this cacophony, many people promote human rights as a special universal set of rights, expressing a similar logic to the natural rights first developed during the Enlightenment.

What human rights do you have?

You may be familiar with human rights through organisations like Amnesty International and Human Rights Watch, or legal documents like the United Kingdom's Human Rights Act, the African Charter on Human and People's Rights, or, perhaps most famously, the United Nation's Universal Declaration of Human Rights. You can find details of these in your university library or online; have a look when you consider the following question.

What makes the human rights enumerated in legal documents true human rights?

6.2.2 KANT AND PERPETUAL PEACE

Kant covers a staggering array of topics in his work, but here we are concerned with his thoughts on international law and global politics. As was common in the late 18th century, Kant thought politics between states begins in a state of nature, meaning individual sovereign states are free and equal in standing with no higher political or legal authority above them. We commonly associate the state of nature with the domestic social contract and thinkers like Thomas Hobbes, John Locke, and Jean-Jacques Rousseau, but it has a longer and wider history, and was used by thinkers like the Dutch jurist Hugo Grotius to formulate a rule of law between sovereign states (Koskenniemi, 2019). Kant's idea of perpetual peace draws on this tradition. Because each state is free and equal, Kant argues the international state of nature is a state of war, meaning each state has a right to wage war against any other state (Kant, 1989, 96, 98). Importantly, he does not think this right to wage war is a moral right; he is not suggesting it is good to wage war but rather in the absence of a legitimate authority to constrain the actions of states, each state possess the freedom to go to war—and to conduct all their political affairs as they see fit. For Kant this is a problem, perhaps the fundamental problem of global politics, because it makes it nearly impossible to prevent war between states, and the resulting lack of order makes justice impossible.

In contrast to realist accounts of international law, which we will discuss in Section 6.3.2, Kant does not think global politics is stuck in a permanent state of unstable and conflict-prone anarchy, and his primary contribution to how we think about global politics is his plan for escaping the international state of nature and attaining a perpetual peace between sovereign states. For Kant, states are compelled to find a way to leave the state of nature because the absence of a legitimate authority to constrain their behaviour means the freedom of each state tends to limit and impair the freedom of every other state. This means the same pressures driving individuals to submit to legal authority within the state also drives states to submit to some form of international legal authority. The higher authority that states should submit to, however, is not a world state or a universal sovereign, as this would fail to solve the problem Kant identified. A universal sovereign would be yet another authority, which would also need to be constrained in order to be legitimate. What Kant thinks is needed is a form of political order ensuring an international rule of law while also maintaining the freedom of sovereign states.

The creation of a legitimate international political authority is justified by the moral imperative to respect the freedom of other states and the practical need for states to constrain their behaviour to ensure the preservation of their own freedom. For Kant, morality and self-interest work together. He suggests six 'preliminary articles' for establishing lasting international peace, which enumerate the constraints on their sovereignty that states must accept (Kant, 1989, 93–97).

1. A prohibition on the use of secret treaties, which appear to pursue peace while actively preparing for future wars.
2. A prohibition on the annexation of independent states by other states through inheritance, exchange, or purchase.
3. A commitment to the reduction of standing armies.
4. A prohibition on taking out national debt with foreign lenders to prepare for war.
5. A prohibition on interfering with the constitution or government of another state.
6. A prohibition on tactics, weapons, and methods of war that make future peace between states impossible.

These articles are preliminary because they set out the rules that states should abide by to preserve their freedom and equality, but they don't set out mechanisms for their enforcement. To achieve perpetual peace, legitimate legal authority must be embodied in a formal institution, which Kant provides in his 'definitive articles'.

Kant's first definitive article addresses the essential precondition of legitimate international legal authority: the constitution of each state must be a republican constitution (Kant, 1989, 99). What he means is the domestic authority within states must be legitimate if an agreement made by a state with other states is to be legitimate as well. According to Kant, a legitimate domestic authority is one (a) based on respect for the freedom of all members of society, (b) which subjects all members of society to a single shared body of laws, and (c) treats all members of society equally under the law. Kant defines legitimate domestic authority in terms of the rule of law, with the additional stipulation that the government must be representative to properly respect the rights of individual citizens. A representative government based on the rule of law is necessary to achieving international peace because only a rightfully constituted political authority can make legitimate and lasting agreements, which are necessary to establish an effective international legal authority. Further, representative government ensures those who bear the costs of war have a say in decisions about the use of force, which is a vital practical mechanism for encouraging peace. If this precondition is met, Kant thinks it is possible to establish a legitimate international authority, which he calls a league or federation of states. This aspect of Kant's thinking influenced democratic peace theory (Doyle, 1983a, 1983b).

Kant advocates for an international league of states dedicated to preserving peace. But why doesn't he advocate a world state to constrain the actions of individual states? As is often the case with Kant, he has both practical and principled reasons. Practically, he suggests a world state is highly unlikely given the difficulty of administering such a state and the unwillingness of sovereign states to giving up their authority (1989, 102–105). As important, however, is his principled reason, which is that a sovereign state with a representative government founded on the rule of law (what Kant calls a 'republican constitution') expresses the legitimate freedom of the national society bound together within that state. Therefore, forcing rightfully constituted states to submit to a world state would violate the rights of both the state and the individuals whose wills it represents. So, in place of a world state binding all individuals under a single universal authority, Kant advocates for an institution that preserves the rights and freedoms of legitimate states and their citizens, while also possessing the authority to ensure an effective international rule of law.

REFLECTIVE ACTIVITY 6.3

While it is tempting to agree with Kant that a world state is impractical, his principled argument against such an authority is more controversial. To draw out his reasoning consider the following:

Would you consent to follow a set of rules that you knew were morally justified but which you had no say in determining or interpreting?

Kant was an Enlightenment thinker and believed that being reasonable (becoming enlightened) required us to freely consent to moral and legal rules limiting our freedom.

Does this alter your response to the first question? What do you think it means to freely consent to be bound by a rule?

Kant's international league would be a voluntary institution states join to preserve peace through the mechanism of public international law. His proposed league would have the authority, granted by the consent of its members, to draft and enact legislation preventing conflict, and the capacity to punish violations of the law. While Kant does not suggest the league would be a representative institution, it would serve to establish an international rule of law, as it would be dedicated to preserving the freedom of all member states by holding them to a common body of law applied equally. Further, the positive law created by his proposed league would be grounded in the higher authority of the rational natural law, giving the league moral meaning and purpose. As we can see, Kant's ideas are reflected in the League of Nations discussed in Section 6.1, and in the United Nations set up at the end of the Second World War, even though there are important differences between his ideal and actual international organisations developed in the 20th and 21st centuries.

This brief account of Kant's ideas leaves out a great deal, including his discussion of the necessity of a cosmopolitan right protecting individuals' freedom to travel and engage in commerce across national borders, an early precursor to the development of international human rights law. Rather than offering a complete account of Kant, the purpose of engaging with his work is to draw out the political problems and intellectual ideas shaping the European natural law tradition that forms the background to modern international law. In Section 6.2.3, as we look at the myths about international law, it will be apparent these persistent myths grow out of the founding tensions of modern international law.

6.2.3 **THE CONTESTED AUTHORITY OF THE RULE OF LAW**

With Kant's idea of perpetual peace in mind, it's worth reflecting on why proponents of international law value the rule of law so highly—especially given the difficulty of achieving it. Why does law matter in politics? Intuitively, most of us think it that it does matter, but pinpointing exactly why is another of those difficult philosophical questions that arises when we think theoretically.

Law has an intimate relationship to politics to the extent much of what we think of as 'politics' is concerned with the making and enforcing of law, or electing representatives and leaders who make and enforce the law. However, as we argued in Section 2.5, politics is fundamentally concerned with the relationships constituting our common life, including the established rules, institutions, and norms of the political order that surrounds us, as well as our attempts to act collectively to make our common world anew. The law is a particular way of managing political relationships, which systematises the rules governing our interactions. We can think of the law as a way of organising political action that limits the worst aspects of politics, especially indiscriminate violence and the unrestrained use of power. To do this, the law claims a distinctive legitimacy based on its capacity to hold authority accountable to established rules, giving law a basis in morality. The legitimacy of the rule of law emerges from these dual functions. On the one hand, it provides a more rational form of order, as a set of rules that is well-structured, and interpreted and enforced by predictable institutions such as courts and legislative bodies. On the other hand, it provides a more just order, governed by rules applied fairly and serving the common good rather than by 'might makes right'.

In domestic politics we generally accept the law's legitimacy, at least in principle. Yet this habit of presuming the law is legitimate obscures a deeper question. Does the rule of law have legitimacy separate from the effective power of the state? Or does legal authority ultimately rest with the coercive power of the state, including its capacity for violence? This fundamental question gets transposed to the global level in interesting and complex ways, bringing this fundamental question about the law to the forefront. In Section 6.4, we argue that attending to law's role in global politics helps us understand the idea of law itself more clearly. Traditionally, however, the academic discipline of International Relations has treated the law as either impossible between sovereign states, at best serving as a type of political rhetoric, or facilitating the transcendence of the international state of nature, providing the mechanism to make international politics resemble domestic politics, where the pursuit of justice is possible (see Section 2.2.4). Famously, E. H. Carr (2016) rendered the question of international law's authority as a debate between 'utopian' and 'realist' approaches to global politics. To dispel the myths shaping our thinking about international law, we look at Carr's 'utopian' and 'realist' understandings of global politics, comparing them to the more complex and nuanced ideas of two influential 20th-century thinkers, Leonard Woolf and Hans Morgenthau, who offer contrasting accounts of international law.

6.3 TWO POLITICAL MYTHS ABOUT INTERNATIONAL LAW

The study of global politics is shaped by encompassing narratives and International Relations has been shaped by the story of a foundational debate between two opposing sides. On one side are utopian or idealist thinkers, and on the other, the realists. This narrative owes much of its structure to Carr's work, *The Twenty Years' Crisis*, but its reach and persistence comes from its mythic status (Carvalho et al., 2011). The debate between utopians and realists is a myth in two senses. First, it provides a stylised origin story through which many in the discipline of International Relations come to understand their own ideas and placement—though the myth has been repeatedly challenged and is less powerful than it once was. Second, it is more fiction that fact; the great debate did not occur in the way the myth suggests, and its participants did not hold the views the myth suggests they did. Here we return to that debate, and in particular the way it sets up the contest over the role of international law in global politics.

Carr's staging of the debate starts with a group of thinkers he describes as utopian. He claims that in the early years of the 20th century, and especially in the aftermath of the First World War, idealist scholars pursued utopian reforms intended to fundamentally alter the conduct of global politics, hoping to prevent the outbreak of future conflicts. Carr's utopians are guilty of a multitude of intellectual and political sins, but his case against them can be summarised in three central charges (Wilson, 2003, 20):

1. Their analysis of global politics was flawed, neglecting facts and a proper understanding of cause and effect, and instead focusing on visionary projects to attain far-off moral ends.

2. Their understanding of both global politics and its reform neglected the fundamental role of power, leading them to overestimate the potential for morality, public scrutiny,

and, most centrally, the rule of law to constrain states and alter the character of global politics.

3. Their utopian ambitions lacked self-reflection, as they were unable to see that the purportedly universal interests they claimed to pursue reflected their own self-interest.

Carr's stylised account of this foundational debate has been enormously influential, and is still reflected in contemporary retellings of the central divide, now embodied in realist and liberal theories of International Relations.

Part of Carr's influence has been to bequeath us two myths about law's role in international politics. The first myth is the rule of law has the power to fundamentally transform global politics, shifting from a primary concern with survival under conditions of anarchy to the creation of an international order supporting peace and human flourishing. In contrast, the second myth is international law is essentially impossible, as the conditions for an effective rule of law do not exist at the international level, and where international law is effective it serves as a tool for powerful states to pursue their self-interest. We have one story that tells us law will make global politics more like domestic politics, and another suggesting global politics is radically different from domestic politics.

REFLECTIVE ACTIVITY 6.4

The myths about the promise and impossibility of law in global politics depend on drawing a stark division between domestic and international law, with domestic law seen as more legitimate because it is effectively and consistently enforced. Consider the following questions:

Can you think of examples when domestic law is not enforced? Or is enforced ineffectively or unequally?

Can you think of examples where international law is enforced? What might the uneven effectiveness of international law tell us about the politics of its enforcement?

6.3.1 THE MORAL NECESSITY OF INTERNATIONAL LAW

The idea of international law as a civilising force for the reform of global politics is more myth than reality. Such ideas about the law's purpose and power draw selectively from the rhetorical flourishes that can be found in legal documents and statements from lawyers and legal scholars. Robert Jackson (1945), the lead prosecutor at the Nuremberg Trials in 1945, spoke of how the fact that 'great nations, flushed with victory and stung with injury stay the hand of vengeance and voluntarily submit their captive enemies to the judgment of the law is one of the most significant tributes that Power has ever paid to Reason'. He went on to say '[t]he common sense of mankind demands that law shall not stop with the punishment of petty crimes by little people. It must also reach men who possess themselves of great power and make deliberate and concerted use of it to set in motion evils which leave no home in the world untouched' (Jackson, 1945). Similar sentiments can be found still, for example, the international legal scholar M. Cherif Bassiouni (Bassiouni, 1999), speaking at the ceremony opening the treaty creating the ICC (see photo 6.2) to signatures, said '[t]he ICC reminds governments that *realpolitik*, which sacrifices justice at the altar of political settlements, is no longer accepted'.

Photo 6.2 **The ICC logo outside the entrance to the international criminal court in The Hague, the Netherlands. Is it possible that international legal bodies can have legitimacy which distances or totally removes them from politics?**

© oliverdelahaye / Shutterstock.com

Similarly, Louis Moreno-Ocampo (2010), the first lead prosecutor of the ICC, speaking about the relationship between the law and politics, said 'I shall not be involved in political considerations . . . my duty is to apply the law without political considerations. Other [political] actors have to adjust to the law.' Taken out of context these sorts of statements suggest supporters of international law believe the law has a special kind of legitimacy, and the power to transform and possibly even escape politics altogether.

It's this sort of rarefied rhetoric in international law that motivates Carr's dismissal of the utopian project of reforming global politics. The mythical reading of international law frames it as a functional necessity for international cooperation and the path to global peace and prosperity. International law's promise, then, lies not only in its capacity to provide a common code for the relationships between states but to articulate universal principles imbued with a rational and moral authority that constrains power and limits politics. This description, however, does not accurately reflect what even the most idealistic supporters of international law think or how international law is practised. For example, Kant's highly idealised plan for perpetual peace does not claim such power or purity for the rule of law itself. While this mythical account of international law is at times drawn on by supporters of international law in moments of moral appeal, it is more an imaginative creation of the critics of international law. Using Carr's diagnosis of the failures of utopianism, we will look at an early and influential account of the necessity of law to the pursuit of peace from Leonard Woolf (one of Carr's alleged utopians) to get a sense of the promise of international law and the ideas that motivate its advocates.

Carr claimed that utopian thinkers ignored the facts of global politics and failed to analyse cause and effect, while also missing out the central role of power and ignoring the self-interest expressed in their plans for reform. While this might be an accurate indictment against a mythical understanding of international law, how does it fare as an assessment of what the utopians actually thought and wrote? In his book, *The Framework for a Lasting Peace* (1917), Woolf makes the case for establishing an international rule of law to limit the recourse to, and destructiveness of, international war. Attending to the detail of Woolf's views, we see his account of international law is not utopian in the sense Carr suggests but rather provides a programme for the progressive reform of global politics grounded in both the reality of politics and the moral case for political change.

Far from ignoring facts, Woolf offers an evaluation of the facts of global politics in his day. Appalled by the consequences of modern war and despairing of the capacity of traditional **balance of power** arrangements to prevent or moderate war, Woolf develops an alternative project to establish an international rule of law, moving from an international order based on force and violence to one based on what he calls government. Government, according to Woolf (1917, 13), involves 'the regulation of relations according to general rules, which to a greater or less extent are understood vaguely to embody the idea in the community of what the *right* relations ought to be'. In questions of international governance, these general rules are international laws. Woolf (1917, 16) makes use of a domestic analogy as he argues we find it acceptable, and wholly unexceptional, that within the state there should be general rules and laws enforced by sanctions. Further, he details the many ways in which we accept such rules and laws at the international level already, drawing on both formal treaties and international custom (Woolf, 1917, 21–23). He acknowledges international law is partial and underdeveloped, with uneven and piecemeal enforcement, but Woolf also draws out that this often is, or was, the case with all forms of law. Rather than these limitations proving the impossibility or undesirability of an international rule of law, Woolf thinks it provides the strongest possible case for political action to create more comprehensive international law and more effective institutions of international governance able to make and enforce the law. Support for international law, and the effort to make it more comprehensive, hardly demonstrates ignorance of facts, or cause and effect; rather it involves acting to reform global politics to encourage cooperation and acceptance of rules, and to discourage conflict and the reliance on force and violence. Woolf argues this project of reform builds on existing aspects of global politics, but takes them further than they have thus far gone—he accepts that 'every new idea and proposal is Utopian. Everything is Utopian until it is tried' (Woolf, 1917, 58).

Contrary to Carr's claims, Woolf does not forgo a detailed analysis of global politics; rather his analysis differs from Carr's own. There is, however, one area where the realist critique of Woolf has force. While Woolf carefully draws out the extent of existing international law, and rightly notes there are similar gaps in the effectiveness of domestic law, he could be accused of failing to appreciate the difference between social order at the national versus international level. We can see this, for example, when he discusses the enforcement of international law (Woolf, 1917, 52–53). There is a categorical difference between the enforcement of domestic law by police and the enforcement of international law, especially when we consider the use of force. Collective self-defence, the model used by the League of Nations and the United Nations, still involves the waging of war, which is different to police using force to detain individual criminals. Not only is the extent and scope of violence far greater in war but collective self-defence would be akin to the victims of domestic crime forming a posse to engage in a form of vigilante justice. It is probably more accurate to fault Woolf for being too sanguine about the practical barriers to reform rather than accusing him of insensibility to the facts of global politics.

Carr's second accusation is utopian thinkers ignore the central role of power, leading them to place too much faith in the capacity of morality and law. This criticism is echoed by many realist thinkers (Krasner, 2002) sceptical of the desire to limit politics through the power of the law, often seen as a secularisation of the Christian ideal in which moral revelation leads humans to beat their swords into ploughshares. Again, this doesn't accurately reflect Woolf's argument. He doesn't claim the law has an independent moral or rational force that will magically compel individuals or states to act differently; rather he appeals to existing practices for managing social conflicts and argues that in global politics we have a choice between either accepting the inevitability of force as the method of resolving conflicts or creating a system of government in which law, as a stable set of rules and institutions, will resolve conflict. This does not suppose the law has a mysterious force that will change human behaviour; instead Woolf appeals to our capacity to choose another way of resolving conflicts. His account does not ignore the centrality of power but rather seeks to constrain and transform its expression by creating institutional space for pursuing the idea of a general right, which we might understand as a kind of chastened Kantianism where a minimal account of what is in the long-term best interest for all states justifies an international legal authority limiting the power and self-interest of individual states. Rather than misunderstanding the role of power, Woolf is setting out a political project to shift who has power and the mechanisms through which it is exercised.

Woolf's essentially liberal account of the international rule of law entails a contest not only over who holds power and authority but also its institutional form and practical expression. Woolf is explicit; we must make a choice to move authority from the sovereign state to international laws and legal institutions, from an order based on force to one based on government. He is less explicit about the way in which this alters the nature of power in global politics, as the move to an institutionalised form of legal authority depersonalises power, such that it looks less like Steven Luke's first dimension of power and more like his second and third dimensions of power (see Section 3.2). Woolf's project of reform would limit the ability of states to exercise power over each other by force and violence by subjecting their authority to the higher authority of an international rule of law. But the law itself exerts power by allowing some actions and prohibiting others—it is here Carr's third criticism of the utopians has real force. Woolf does not appreciate how the law is not only manipulated to serve the ends of those with privilege and power; rather it actually reflects those interests in its very structure. For example, international law did not simply fail to prohibit or condemn European imperialism and its attendant brutalities; it was a central tool of that project. From *El Requerimiento*, a legal document written in 1513 by the Spanish jurist Juan López Palacios Rubio requiring the Indigenous peoples of the Americas to submit to colonial rule in order to give imperialism a veneer of moral and legal legitimacy to the Berlin Conference of 1885, which formally portioned the African continent between imperial powers given authority by the law, which was simply denied to African peoples; law was a central mechanism for legitimising and administering violence and oppression. Woolf's blindness is perhaps evidence of the third dimension of power, of the ideological power of the European legal tradition to naturalise imperialism (see Section 8.3)—a problem we still face today when an ostensibly neutral legal mechanism such as the **Responsibility to Protect** framework and even the ICC seem to apply different standards to powerful Western states and leaders from those in the Global South.

Despite the shortcomings of Woolf's thought, it should be clear neither Carr's criticism of utopianism nor the mythical understanding of international law capture the reality of law's fundamental and growing role in global politics. Despite the rhetorical excesses and exaggerated moralism of some advocates, international law is actually a central tool in a rather sober, and at times conservative, project of reform and governance. Thus far we have focused on international law in the early 20th century, but these ideas and tensions are even more relevant today. The scope of global politics covered by the law has expanded greatly, as the body of public international law has grown alongside developments in international human rights law, **international criminal law,** and **private international law,** which expand the reach of international law to individuals, the conduct of domestic politics, and the regulation of the global economy. This growth involves not only an increasing number of treaties, international legal organisations, and expanding international case law but also the globalisation of law and the legal profession, leading Anne-Marie Slaughter to speak of a new world order built around a global legal system (Slaughter, 2004). Further, even as the growth of international law has not eliminated war, as Woolf had hoped, it has transformed it, such that the decision to go to war is bound by an extensive legal framework, and nearly all aspects of war by formal militaries are conducted in accordance with complex legal regimes. As David Kennedy (2006, 9) argues, 'warfare' has 'become a legal institution'. Finally, the ideological and structural power of international law remains problematic. While imperial practices have been outlawed and the self-determination of peoples guaranteed by right, the legacy of European imperialism continues to shape international law. For example, Siba Grovogui (2011) argues the legalised use of force against Libya in 2011 was viewed differently by African states worried the use of force, authorised by the United Nations, reflected a drift back towards an international legal order dominated by Western powers, which legitimises and facilitates the use of force against non-Western states. They were wary 'humanitarian concerns come once again to serve as pretext for widening the global democratic deficit and, in the case of the Middle East, re-inscribing the terms of past imperial relations under new guises' (Grovogui, 2011, 568). Understanding the nature and development of international law is necessary for understanding global politics. However, it is not the case the law is always progressive or promises the triumph of morality over politics. International law is highly politicised, leading to the question: should international law be considered law at all?

REFLECTIVE ACTIVITY 6.5

Woolf frames the development of international law a political project of social reform, which undermines accusations that international law is utopian.

Can you think of examples where domestic or international law has been used to achieve political change? Do you think projects of legal reform are naïvely idealistic?

6.3.2 THE IMPOSSIBILITY OF INTERNATIONAL LAW

The second myth about international law is it is not law at all. This myth draws from a long history of scepticism about the possibility of legal authority beyond the state, in particular because of the lack of effective international political authority able to make and enforce law. Thomas Hobbes is an early source of this idea, stating '[w]here there is no common Power, there is no Law' (Hobbes, 1996, 90). This sense that true law was impossible at the international level can be traced to both academic scholarship and the views of political actors. 'For many years most political scientists who studied international politics regarded international law as an oxymoron' (Krasner, 2002, 265). Krasner's sentiment is echoed by many US foreign policy actors. John Foster Dulles, US Secretary of State from 1953 to 1959, wrote: 'I confess to being one of those lawyers who do not regard international law as law at all' (Dulles quoted in Arend, 1988, 57). This sentiment still finds expression today, for example John Bolton (see photo 6.3), who has held numerous positions in the US foreign policy establishment writes: 'International law is not law; it is a series of political and moral arrangements that stand or fall on their own merits, and anything else is simply theology and superstition masquerading as law' (Bolton, 2000, 48). This scepticism of international law as law is, however, based on a mythical understanding of law, as much a falsehood as the notion that international law will allow us to transcend politics and achieve some perfect social harmony.

Photo 6.3 **John Bolton, who served as National Security Advisor to former President Donald Trump advocated for military action in Libya, and described international law as 'a series of political and moral arrangements'.**

Bloomberg / Contributor / Getty Images

Sceptics of international law often draw from, and identify with, the realist tradition of thought, but political **Realism** does not deny the existence or relevance of international law, and very rarely does it deny that international law *is* a form of law. Rather, Realism suggests we have to analyse and understand the law in a particular way. To illustrate this, we will look closely at the ideas of Hans Morgenthau to draw out a clearer sense of what his realist understanding of law actually entails.

Similar to Woolf, Morgenthau gives an account of international law that recognises its historical role in global politics. However, unlike Woolf, Morgenthau is pursuing an intellectual project rather than a political one. In his article, 'Positivism, Functionalism, and International Law' (1940) Morgenthau presents an account of what international law is and how it should be studied. Morgenthau (1940, 260–261) argues legalistic understandings of international law separate law from others spheres of social life and therefore misunderstand the nature of law. He thinks this criticism applies to positivist and natural law traditions, as both abstract from the realities of law and its social function (Morgenthau, 1940, 263). The result of this faulty understanding is that lawyers, diplomats, and politicians presume the legitimacy of law that is not actually legitimate, while also wrongly presuming the illegitimacy of otherwise legitimate norms and rules. According to Morgenthau, this occurs because legalistic understandings of the law divorce international law from the social forces shaping it (1940, 267). Where positivism locates the law's authority and meaning in formally agreed legal arrangements and customary practice, it presents the law as an independent system with its own sphere, separated from ethics, politics, economics, and other social spheres. The legalistic account of law locates its authority within a closed system.

Morgenthau argues the legalistic approach fundamentally misunderstands the nature of the law's authority, which results in misrepresenting international law's relationship to change and stability, as well as the importance of ethics and politics to international law. Law, whether domestic or international, is given meaning and force through the other social forces at work. What Morgenthau means is that laws gain authority partly because they express accepted ethical norms, and partly because they are expressed through political institutions able to effectively enforce legal decisions. Further, laws are written and decisions on legal questions are made within a wider social context in which economic forces, morality, culture, and a variety of other forces play a part. An effective and stable system of law requires these social forces are organised by an authoritative institutional structure, which is what the modern state does for domestic law. At the international level, however, Morgenthau thinks this authoritative structure is lacking. International law is unstable and prone to change, not because there is a lack of centralised political and legal authority but because the law is created and practised in a social environment where there is profound diversity and conflict over ethical norms, economic systems, political values, etc. For Morgenthau, it is the failure to appreciate how the function of the law is related to these other social functions that leads to the myths about law we have been discussing. If we fail to appreciate the instability inherent to trying to create a legal system at the international level, we are prone to believing the international rule of law is more settled and effective than it actually is. But, if we fail to appreciate international law is still a system of law, though under different social conditions from those found domestically, we will tend to discount appeals to international law made by states, and, thus, be unable to account for why states obey most of their international legal obligations most of the time.

By connecting international law to the social forces shaping it, Morgenthau thinks we will be able to properly understand its meaning and operation. In particular, his account of international law helps us deal with important questions about the validity, legitimacy, and interpretation of international law. The validity of international law depends upon the degree to which it reflects the existing constellation of social forces. Morgenthau argues this leads to two types of international law, one reflecting broad and stable interests persisting across different configurations of power at the international level, and the other, which he terms political international law, expressing emergent norms and interests arising from the particular constellation of power dominant at a particular moment. This dynamic quality of international law means determining the legitimacy of international law requires methods suitable to the subject, in particular methods focusing on the contestation and lack of consensus around fundamental ethical norms that shape international law, as well as those that can carefully analyse the overall political situation in which legal decisions are rendered, and new laws and institutions are created. Morgenthau's account does not deny the existence or importance of international law; rather it argues its meaning and content are shaped by the social forces which undermine the idea of a singular and unchanging international rule of law but also challenge the myth of the impossibility of international law.

While we have hopefully deflated both myths, we have also provided two contrasting accounts. Before we move on to think about how we might reconcile these, it is useful to consider if Morgenthau fares better in light of the criticisms we made of Woolf. Above we saw how Woolf relied on a domestic analogy to defend the effectiveness and legitimacy of international law, but suggested he failed to take sufficient account of the difference between the national and international levels. In Morgenthau's functionalist theory, the difference between these two levels is much clearer and he gives us an account of how this alters the meaning and practice of international law. An opposite concern is raised by Morgenthau's account: does he overemphasise the anarchic character of international politics? While he makes room for a stable canon of international law responding to the enduring interests of all states, in contrast to what he calls political international law, he does not give sufficient attention to the historical contingency of those 'enduring interests' or the way in which the mechanisms of political coordination in global politics he focuses on—the balance of power, for example—operate within a wider social structure that is dynamic and historical. There is a tension, if not an outright contradiction, in Morgenthau's focus on how social forces shape international law while also presuming there are stable state interests—which is linked to his view that global politics is inherently anarchic because of a universal and constant lust for power that makes a more ordered global politics impossible (Morgenthau, 1985, 38).

Compared to Woolf, Morgenthau has a fuller grasp on the politics of the law. His functionalist theory focuses on how the structure and purpose of international law is subject to change as different constellations of social forces emerge. However, like Woolf, Morgenthau still misses the way in which legalisation has its own force and can lead to more profound political shifts. Morgenthau is able to trace the interplay of law and politics in global politics, and, therefore, he gives international law a more central place than sceptics allow for, but his account also suggests law is essentially dependent on politics, and international law is a tool of state interest that allows powerful states to impose rules and structures to suit their interest. Stephen Krasner (1999) describes this dynamic as a type of 'organized hypocrisy', in which powerful states create and accept limits on their sovereignty, up to the point that it serves their interests. On this account, when the constraints on sovereignty created by international law fail to serve the interests of the powerful, or who holds power changes, then the primacy of sovereignty will re-emerge. Similarly, Jack Goldsmith and Eric Posner (2006) trace out the way states use international law when it is to their advantage. While Morgenthau's account hints at the possibility of more critical and historical understanding of international law, he fails to develop this, as has much of the realist literature on international law he has inspired.

What Morgenthau misses is that rules, and the law especially, exercise a kind of independent power in shaping the possibilities of political action. Anthony Lang Jr (2007) demonstrates this by looking at the United States invasion of Iraq in 2003. Lang draws out how the US and its allies, as well as those opposed to the war, made their case through international law (2007, 257–258). While it is tempting to see this as a confirmation of what Morgenthau argued—the **hegemonic** power of the US allowed it to manipulate and remake international law to pursue its own interests—Lang suggests something more is going on. By appealing to international law, particularly a duty to engage in collective self-defence, the US ensured debate over the invasion would be conducted through the United Nations and within a legal framework. This shows law constrained the US in some ways while at the same time the US could ignore aspects of the law. Lang, however, argues it also showed the law tends to constrain our capacity for creative political action. 'An alternative critique of rules is that they are inherently coercive or, in stronger terms, actually violent' (Lang, 2007, 258). His point is the law does have force; it does change the nature of international politics over time, but not in a way that either reliably leads to justice, or is only an expression of the interests of powerful states. Lang's criticism suggests the politics of international law is more complicated than either utopian or realist readings can account for; in the final section we will consider this idea in greater depth.

REFLECTIVE ACTIVITY 6.6

Morganthau's functionalist theory of law has important implications for how we understand law at the domestic and the international level, as he suggests the law has distinct institutional and political dimensions.

Can you identify the political dimension in the domestic law of your home country?

6.4 EMBRACING THE POLITICS OF INTERNATIONAL LAW

Taking a very brief and partial look at the history of international law, considering both common myths and the specific ideas of some key thinkers, an overarching narrative emerges suggesting the question of international law is centrally about whether or not the law can constrain politics. As we have tried to show, this narrative is too simplistic, and in its place, we argue the question should be what kind of politics the law enables. To explore this, we look at two final thinkers to help us understand the ambiguous role international law has in shaping global politics, while also considering the possibilities it opens up for political action and change. In this final section it will be useful to think back to Sheldon Wolin's distinction between 'politics' and 'the political' from Section 2.4.2.

6.4.1 LAW AND INTERNATIONAL ORDER

Hedley Bull (2002) provides a more critical understanding of international law. On the one hand he accepts many of the sceptic's criticisms: international law lacks institutions that effectively and consistently enforce the law; states, historically the primary subject of international law, are often able to avoid compliance; and when states do follow the law it can be argued they do so out of self-interest. On the other hand, Bull demonstrates these criticisms do not undermine international law as legitimate law, showing how law is fundamental to maintaining international order. He does this by making two conceptual distinctions: first, he offers an alternative understanding of law that is more historical and contingent than either Woolf or Morgenthau; and second, he gives us an account of international order that rejects the idea there is an international state of nature, instead suggesting we have an international society, which while anarchical is nonetheless a structured social order, and therefore more political than is generally understood.

For Bull, international law is fundamentally a system of rules binding states and other international actors together (2002, 122). It is the binding function that makes Bull's understanding distinctive as it emphasises the social function of law rather than its effective authority or political usefulness. The social function of international law is to provide a medium for interaction between states and other institutions; it provides a set of rules they use to navigate their relationships and uphold the core values of a distinctive international form of society. Bull draws on the work of the legal philosopher H. L. A. Hart to explain how there can be a legal system without effective, coercive enforcement. The idea he uses is Hart's distinction between primary and secondary rules (2002, 128). Primary rules set out what those subject to the law must do, or refrain from doing. Secondary rules concern how new rules are added, existing rules are enforced, and disputes between rules are settled. For Bull, this allows us to recognise international law clearly contains a set of primary rules widely recognised and agreed upon, even as there is no uncontested and final account of the secondary rules. This clarifies the function and limits of international law, proving an answer to the question of why states' interests are so often compatible with international law despite the lack of unambiguous secondary rules (Bull, 2002, 134).

In contrast to Woolf and Morgenthau, Bull abandons the notion there is an international state of nature that international law alters. Instead, he posits an international society existing between states and other international actors, and the interactions between these actors form a kind of second-order society with its own rules and institutions. Working with this idea of international society, Bull argues international law is an accepted institution and has the status of law because the members of society broadly accept its authority, even if the form law and society take at the international level are distinct from domestic law and society. Bull enumerates three functions international law has in maintaining order within international society. First, it provides a universal principle of political organisation between members, which would be the norms of sovereignty and nonintervention; second, it sets out the basic rules of coexistence in international society; and, third, it outlines the ways international society can mobilise to ensure compliance, which focuses of self-help mechanisms, such as the balance of power and collective self-defence (Bull, 2002, 135–366). Bull's argument suggests law is essential to maintaining international order—as a fundamental institution of international society, it provides a language and practice for resolving disputes and guiding social interaction, which we can see in the continued expansion and development of international law.

Bull, however, goes on to highlight the limits of international law. First, he acknowledges the social function played by international law is essential, but the particular form of modern international law is not; other institutions could fulfil the role played by law, or international law could have taken another cultural form not drawn from European political developments. That modern international law has taken the form it has is an historical accident (Bull, 2002, 136–137). Second, while Bull thinks international law is necessary, on its own it is not sufficient for maintaining international order. International law provides a set of rules for social interactions, but it is dependent upon a set of accepted social norms (Bull, 2002, 137), which means when these norms change or are challenged, international law will be destabilised. For example, the creation of the ICC in 2002 directly challenged the legal immunity of state leaders, who had been shielded from individual criminal liability by legal norms of state sovereignty. Third, the principles of international law can and will clash, leading to tensions and conflicts in the international order it is meant to serve (Bull, 2002, 138). Finally, law can serve as a vehicle for purposes other than order, especially as the norms of international society change; for Bull a key tension arises between the pursuit of order versus justice (2002, 139). This means international law at times actively seeks to upset international order, echoing the kind of ambiguous and dynamic interaction Wolin finds in politics more broadly.

Bull's account better enables us to understand contemporary international law, which has grown and expanded in ways neither Woolf nor Morgenthau anticipated. As the institution of international law develops, it gains greater sophistication through institutionalisation, giving increasing clarity to its secondary rules, and it expands into new areas of global politics, reflecting wider contests over the fundamental purpose of international society. Bull himself characterises this as a possible shift from international to world society, with the later entailing a greater degree of normative consensus and institutional integration as well as an increased focus on justice for individuals. By socialising international law, Bull better accounts for the persistence of international law despite its seeming inconsistency and lack of enforcement, while also providing space to understand the law, and rules more generally, as a central part of global politics. However, if law is a social institution it suggests some rather unhappy things about international society, in particular that it is hierarchical and highly unequal, as it is not only that the law is applied inconsistently but the law is applied consistently but unequally, suggesting the order Bull thinks it should serve is potentially unjust—though he does acknowledge this tension is one of the motivations for a shift from international to world society.

Attending to law's role in upholding international order enables us to engage with the substance of international law more critically, tracing the ways it has institutionalised and upheld inequality. For example, if we attend to the history of European international law, which Bull characterises as central to contemporary international law as a matter of historical accident, we can see his account is inadequate. International law as we know it, and the order it upholds, is structured by a hierarchy between European peoples and states, seen as legitimately sovereign and civilised, in contrast to non-Europeans seen as lacking civilisation and incapable of self-government. Antony Anghie (2006) traces out how this racialised hierarchy is written into international law from the start, as the question of how to justify European imperialism was always central to international law. Further, he argues this hierarchical structure continues to this day, even as international law has formally repudiated imperialism. He notes, for example, how there was a double standard at play when Western powers (especially the United States and the United Kingdom) opposed Third World proposals, enacted through the United Nations General Assembly in 1974, for a New International Economic Order on the grounds that states cannot be bound by laws to which they have not consented. But, as Anghie (2006, 748) notes, Western powers hypocritically expected the Third World to accept existing international economic law they did not author or consent to, as this law was premised on their exclusion from it. Similar impositions negating the formal notion of sovereign equality can be found in international human rights law, which seeks to limit state sovereignty with universal moral norms, and practices of intervention legalised through the responsibility to protect doctrine, which justifies political and military interference if normative standards dictated by Western states are not fulfilled. The point here is not that there shouldn't be moral constraints on state sovereignty but that the existing constraints are established through imperial hierarchies, resulting in a normative order criminalising and pathologising some violence, while legitimising and normalising other violent acts. Mahmood Mamdani (2010) illustrates this by comparing the different international responses to the violence of Sudan's civil war (especially from 2004), which was characterised as genocidal, and the violence of the US' invasion of Iraq, which after the 2003 invasion was framed in terms of counter-insurgency despite comparable levels of violence. Attending to the colonial legacy of international law reveals the international order is in fact built upon the displacement of disorder and violence from one sphere to another, such that order achieved in the legal relations between European sovereigns led to, and naturalised, disorder and violence in the colonised world. Law as a social institution is not simply about order; it is about the exercise of legal power, both de facto power upholding the existing state of affairs as well the power to determine the conditions under which we pursue political change within established legal institutions. This returns us to Lang's insight; the expansion of law into more and more of global politics can increase predictability and stability, but it also structures our political relationships, privileging particular actors, values, and practices, while limiting the space for the *political*, limiting space for more profound change to the global order.

REFLECTIVE ACTIVITY 6.7

Like Morgenthau, Bull's account of international law has important consequences for our understanding of law more generally. Understanding law as a social institution with a contingent history motivates Bull's attempt to understand its ongoing evolution, but he is less attentive to how that past may have contributed to historical and contemporary injustice.

Can you think of examples where historical legal inequalities contribute to contemporary injustices?

6.4.2 FROM APOLOGY TO UTOPIA

We have seen how international law is central to global politics and is itself an object of political contestation. The final element of international law we consider is how politics arises within the law, looking at the work of the Finnish international lawyer Marti Koskenniemi. Sharing much with both Morgenthau and Bull, Koskenniemi begins with the question of how conflicts within international law are decided, arguing:

> our inherited ideal of a World Order based on the Rule of Law thinly hides from sight the fact that social conflict must still be solved by political means and that even though there may exist a common legal rhetoric among international lawyers, that rhetoric must, *for reasons internal to the ideal itself*, rely on essentially contested—political—principles to justify outcomes to international disputes (Koskenniemi, 1990, 7. Emphasis in the original).

Koskenniemi draws our attention to international law's political effects, as it shapes the international order in important ways, and how decisions made within the practice of international law inevitably involve the exercise of political power. But, crucially, this aspect of international law is commonly disavowed within the practice of the law. Koskenniemi identifies an unspoken tension at the heart of international law, which maps on to the sceptical and utopian myths of international law we examined, leading critics to reject the law either because it is excessively dependent on the self-interest of states, or because it is excessively utopian. 'According to the former criticism, international law is too *apologetic* to be taken seriously in the construction of international order. According to the latter, it is too *utopian* to the identical effect' (Koskenniemi, 1990, 9). Koskenniemi argues international law is caught between apology and utopia, which leads to a constitutive incoherence in the law. We might think of this as the seed from which the myths about international law germinate—like all truly powerful myths they find their origin in a truth we would rather not accept. The power of Koskenniemi's critique is its revelation that unless we accept, and embrace, the inevitable politics of making decisions in the practice of international law, then it will remain incoherent and problematic.

Rather than embrace the political element of international law, Koskenniemi argues most lawyers adopt one of two opposed approaches, either justify the law and legal decisions by appealing to rational rules that ground the law in an underlying normativity, or by appealing to established practice of states, both of which are unable to fill the gap left by lawyers attempting to avoid the necessity of truly political judgement. This leaves contemporary international law in a state of 'happy confusion, unaware of its internal contradictions' (1990, 12) in which it is silent 'about theoretical justifications' and satisfied with merely '*ad hoc* compromise' (1990, 20). Koskenniemi goes on to argue the continued expansion and success of international law depends upon its procedural formality, which is incapable of setting down determinate legal standards and principles (1990, 28). Because of this formality, states and other international actors are able to read their own substantive principles into international law, making international legal practice a sight of political contestation—but one in which the conflicting parties do not acknowledge the substantive aims they pursue. This highlights another danger in the legalisation of international politics, as the structure of legal decision-making and the law's disavowal of its political role make the law vulnerable to being co-opted to serve the ends of powerful actors, which then gain legitimacy from their legal status. Further, progressive political action can be stymied, as the disavowal of the politics of the law by legal practitioners promotes suspicion of those using the law for emancipatory purposes, undermining the contribution law can make to political change (Koskenniemi, 1990, 31–32).

As a way to understand the significance of the politics inherent to international law, we can look at the example of feminist scholars and lawyers, who have diagnosed and challenged the patriarchal structure of international law. Feminist approaches to international law have done vital work in drawing out how the international order systematically excludes and oppresses women (Charlesworth et al., 1991). Catharine MacKinnon, for example, traces the ways violence against women is not captured in international human rights law. She argues that as both laws and moral norms have their root in human experiences, the injustices of society get written into law. 'Human rights principles are based on experience, but not that of women' (MacKinnon, 1993, 59). This is significant because it means human rights are drawn from a limited range of human experience, and they incorporate the injustices of patriarchal oppression into the law. MacKinnon shows how violence against women is not adequately covered by human rights law, either because the violence women suffer as women is the 'wrong' type of wartime violence, such as systematic rape and forced impregnation as part of ethnic cleansing campaigns, or because the violence women are subject to is not exceptional enough, such as ongoing violence against women that occurs during times of 'peace' (Mackinnon, 1993, 59–61; 2006). While some progress has been made in making human rights law more reflective of women's experience, such as sexual violence being included as a war crime in international criminal law, this progress is the result of legal activism that does not stop when formal legal statues are changed—the work of effectively preventing wartime sexual violence goes on, and formal legal changes only address part of the problem (MacKinnon, 2008). MacKinnon, and other feminist legal activists, are willing to confront the incoherence in the law Koskenniemi identifies, making use of the code and practice of established law where possible, but pushing the law forward in the name of the substantive goal of gender justice.

What Koskenniemi and feminist legal scholars help us see is progressive change in the law is neither automatic nor impossible—contra the myths we have been examining. Expanding human rights law to better address the harms faced by women was not achieved simply by properly analysing the underlying norms of international law, nor was it changed because states decided the law needed to change. Rather, the law and state practice had to be interpreted in ways that took emancipatory goals forward, and those progressive interpretations were pushed for by individuals and groups acting politically to try to reshape both the law and the order of global politics. Political contestation over the norms and practice of international law is always ongoing and unsettled, as the law is an ambiguous thing, a set of rules we give ourselves, but which develops profound capacities to order the world around us. The law affects us every day, enabling us to do some things, preventing us from doing others—empowering and coercing us differently depending on our race, gender, nationality, and class. The law is more than the naked self-interest of the powerful, but it will not save us from politics; rather it calls on us to act politically to make the law more reflective and supportive of the common world we want to share.

REFLECTIVE ACTIVITY 6.8

Attending to the politics of international law reveals law can be both a mechanism of oppression and medium for emancipatory change. This dynamic is particularly well understood by feminist scholars of international law. Reflecting on various feminist movements for legal reform, such as feminist human rights law or other campaigns you know, answer the following:

Why does legal contestation and reform require collective and sustained political action? Does political change require the law?

6.5 CONCLUSION

In this chapter we examined international law as a fundamental feature of global politics, acknowledging the ambiguity this entails. The law is both a way of maintaining global order and a medium of political change, depending on our intentions and how we use it. While we have tried to show the law does not promise an escape from politics, it does have the capacity to alter the political order, in large part because it opens up space to ask questions about the justification and legitimacy of authority in global politics. We have also argued, however, that the law must be approached with humility and caution, as it has been and continues to be an institution that perpetuates and justifies exclusion and injustice. The key questions to keep in mind when we think about the role of international law in global politics is how has it shaped us up until now, and what we want to use it to do in the future.

 Access the online resources at www.oup.com/he/hirst1e for case studies to help contextualise your understanding of key concepts, further reading recommendations to guide you through your reading, and a library of web links to journal articles, blogs, and video content to help you take your learning further.

MONEY

READERS' GUIDE

Chapter 7: Money examines the mystery of the origins and function of money in global politics. It challenges the myth that money developed in a politically neutral way as the most functional mode of exchange, showing instead that the power and violence of empire—including conquest and enslavement—were central to the emergence and functioning of money. It also explores some possible futures of money, such as cryptocurrencies and local currencies, and the challenges these might pose to the historically strong link between money and state power.

7.1 INTRODUCTION

If, as we said in Chapter 1, our everyday understanding is something we come to rather like a native language (see Section 1.3), to unravel the myths surrounding the role of money in global politics, it makes sense to start from how money is usually presented to us the first time we come across it in the classroom. When we encounter economics in high school or in introductory modules at university, we are usually told that money has three functions: it can serve as a unit of account, a means of exchange, and a store of value. We are taught that the origins of money are to be found in the limitations of the barter system. The latter is based on what is called a 'double coincidence of wants'. For me to successfully get the wood needed to warm up my house in the winter, I need to find someone willing to exchange it for the cow's milk that I can offer in exchange. Money can then provide the universal means that enables me to sell milk to a household that might need it, even if they have no wood to exchange. I can then use the proceeds of my milk sale to buy wood from someone else. This is intuitive enough. It is also historically inaccurate, as extensive evidence from anthropology shows that money first emerged as a way of recording debts, leading Humphrey (1985, 48) to argue that '[n]o example of a barter economy, pure and simple, has ever been described, let alone the emergence from it of money'. Similarly, the threefold functions of money barely begin to capture the political relevance of money, as we will see in this chapter.

Why has this myth about the origins of money, and these simplifications about its functions, been so influential despite being historically inaccurate? Why does it still constitute the most common entry point to the study not only of money but of all economic interactions? As with all myths, a story that captures something real and intuitively understandable at the same time conceals an aspect of reality of at least equal importance. It is undoubtedly true that money has historically played, and still plays, a key role in facilitating exchange, as it enables strangers to buy and sell goods and services without necessarily having to trust each other. It is the actual means of exchange—money itself—that must command the trust of buyers and sellers. Hence, through the mediation of money, exchanges become more and more impersonal. At the same time, this origin myth presents money as emerging naturally from the economic needs of society, and as politically neutral in mediating economic exchange. David Graeber's (2011, 230–250) work on the 'military-coinage-slavery complex' provides an interesting perspective in this regard. It is now well established that coinage—that is, the physical minting of money—was originally associated with the establishment, consolidation, and expansion of kingdoms, principalities, and empires. Looting was only one of the forms of violence produced by territorial conquest, the other one being the uprooting and enslavement of much of the local population, then put to work in mines to extract metals (silver and gold especially) that would be melted and minted into coins to pay soldiers. Hence, war, slavery, and coinage were central to the establishment of vast empires in the Mediterranean, the Indian Ocean, and China during the so-called 'Axial Age' (800–200 BC). At a polar opposite to the political neutrality of the barter myth, this view presents power and violence, which we encountered in Chapters 3 and 5, as central to the emergence and functioning of money. This is why money inevitably matters to whoever is interested in politics. As we live in a world of many monies, what we usually call currencies, and as power relations also exist between different currencies, then money also concerns whoever is interested in global politics. This is apparent both when we consider decisions with global repercussions at the individual level (can I afford to pay the travel costs associated with migrating and settling in a new country?), and when we look at international decisions traditionally associated with IR, including for instance waging war (how does a government pay for the military equipment needed to wage war?).

REFLECTIVE ACTIVITY 7.1

Consider the following questions:

What was your last purchase? Would it have been possible under a barter system?

Can you identify any power relations directly or indirectly involved in your purchase?

This chapter proceeds as follows. In Section 7.2, we start by focusing on the myths outlined above regarding the origins and functions of money, but also introduce a new myth about the effects of money, and see what unveiling these myths means for issues of power, ethics, violence, and law as covered in previous chapters, and of empire, capitalism, and the state, which we will cover next. In Section 7.3, we then outline the importance of money in contemporary global politics with reference to theories from IR, and the cognate field of International Political Economy (IPE), which focuses more specifically on the relations between power and wealth, as well as powerlessness and poverty, in global politics. More specifically, following the work of Susan Strange, we will focus on the twin roles of money as both credit and currency (Sections 7.3.1 and 7.3.2 respectively), in the process providing some details on the political dimension of international financial and monetary arrangements. Such a discussion enables us to address the following mystery: how is it that in so much IR and IPE literature money and power are seen as pertaining to different spheres (the economic and the political, respectively) rather than intimately connected organising principles of social life both in history and today? In Section 7.4, we look at the possible futures of money, understood here as a social technology, and thus briefly discuss the prospects for cryptocurrencies on the one hand and local currencies on the other hand, and the challenges these might pose to the historically strong link between money and state power.

7.2 WHEREFROM AND WHAT FOR? THE ORIGINS AND FUNCTIONS OF MONEY

If power relations are shot through the origins and functioning of money, we are then in a position to better contextualise Hay's point that 'power is to politics what the economy is economics' (2002, 168, see also Chapter 3). Having exposed the myth of the origins of money, we can already say that power is inherent to money and by extension to the economy. In light of this, constructing a discipline studying the economy around the idea that power is an anomaly in economic interactions, and indeed when it usually affects them it only brings problems and distortions, might appear unduly limiting. Yet this is how the field of economics has consolidated itself, especially in the wake of the so-called **marginal revolution** in the late 19th century. This shifted the attention of the academic field away from the analysis of the emergence and transformation of economic systems in history towards an increasing reliance on mathematical models, in turn based on the assumption that economic choices and interactions are better understood by focusing on what happens at 'the margins'. This explains why microeconomics classes heavily focus on marginal costs, marginal revenues, marginal profits, and so on. Crucially, this reference to margins has very little in common with the attention to marginalised groups that characterises for instance postcolonial and critical feminist approaches to global politics (see Section 3.3). If anything, it invites the student to disregard anything that happens before an additional (i.e. 'marginal') unit of a product is produced, bought, or sold. This is why the 'marginal revolution' is essential to make sense of the neglect of power relations in dominant approaches to economics. It is also why in the wake of the 2007–08 global financial crisis, and the government response of bailing out the banks (see Picture 7.1) and then compensating for the public sector outlay through years of austerity for the general population, triggered a movement to contest the economics curriculum in universities, especially in the United Kingdom (Husnain and Parekh, 2013).

This argued that the failure of orthodox economics not only to predict, but even to make sense of, the crisis should be addressed through a radical revision of the economics curriculum. The point of this movement, and the one we are making here, is not that we should disregard altogether issues pertaining to markets, prices, demand, and supply. Rather, we suggest that one must not confuse the neat disciplinary distinction between economics, politics, and sociology, important and perhaps necessary in the production of knowledge about our contemporary world, with the everyday reality of this very world in which economic, political, and social considerations intertwine in ways at times impossible to disentangle. Power relations are crucial to this intertwining: if we look at the effects of austerity in the UK, for instance, there is now substantive evidence showing that it has hit disproportionally disadvantaged groups in society, including for instance women, the elderly, lower-income households, and Black, minority, and ethnic groups (Women's Budget Group, 2018).

Photo 7.1 **After the 2008 financial crisis, the UK government intervened to bail out the banks.**

© Norman Chan / Shutterstock.com

It is exactly at the intersection between politics and economics, between power and wealth, that the field of International Political Economy has emerged. At times presented as a subfield of IR, it was once provocatively presented by Susan Strange, one of its founding figures, not as a subfield but rather as a macrofield of which IR itself was a subfield (Strange, 1989). At the end of the day, why should a field of research that studies both the political and the economic dimensions of international interactions be considered smaller than, and subordinated to, a field that concerns itself only with the political dimension (see also Chapter 2)? As you can see, the very definition of disciplines, fields, and subfields of academic research is itself a product of contestation and—yes—of power relations. But we will come back to this issue, and to Susan Strange and IPE, in Section 7.3.

7.2.1 POWER IN THE TRADITIONAL ACCOUNT OF MONEY AND ITS FUNCTIONS

Returning to money in economics textbooks, power permeates the three different functions as unit of account, store of value, and means of exchange mentioned earlier. In an increasingly integrated world, even the use of money as a unit of account is in crucial respects politicised. Let us take for instance a young Egyptian student, coming from a family earning their living in Egyptian pounds (EGP), and spending it largely in the same currency, who enrolled for an undergraduate degree in International Relations at a UK university in September 2015. Back then, fees of 9,000 British pounds (GBP) amounted to slightly less than EGP 107,000. When her sister enrolled for the same degree at the same university three years later, the same GBP 9,000 would have nearly doubled to about EGP 208,000.

Photo 7.2 **Fluctuating currency exchange rates affect purchasing power.**

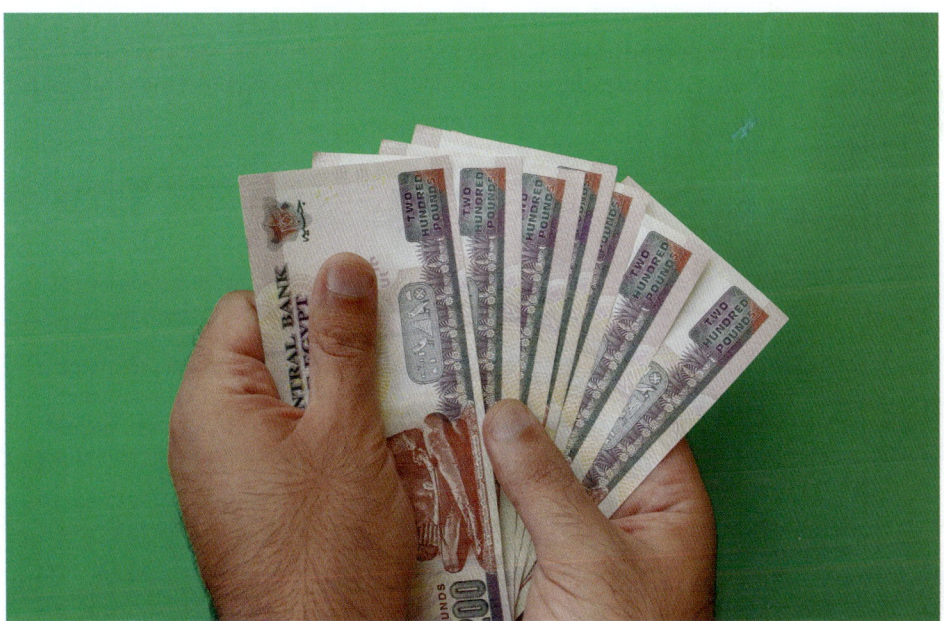

© ViktoriyaFivko / Shutterstock.com

Tuition for the same degree has become twice as expensive in a three-year span. Insofar as there is not a global *unit of account*, the changing exchange rate between different currencies affects purchasing power (see Photo 7.2 above), not only for the more mobile individuals but more generally for anyone buying and selling goods and services in currencies different from the one in which they earn their income. As fluctuations of exchange rates depend on a range of factors, from monetary policy to government spending plans, to the very stability of a political regime and its position in international relations, one can see how politics factors into these swings in ways not necessarily captured by a traditional supply and demand model.

Staying in Egypt, the official devaluation (a state-mandated fall in the exchange value of the domestic currency) led to the dramatic drop in the EGP exchange value. This was followed not only by a depreciation (a fall in exchange value of a currency related to the increasing unwillingness of investors to conduct transactions in that currency) but also and more importantly by higher inflation. This is primarily because foreign products that need to be imported into Egypt, including staples such as wheat, must be paid for in a foreign currency worth considerably more EGP than in 2015. As a result, the same wage in local Egyptian currency will be able to afford a much lower amount of foreign goods: the function of money as a *store of value* has thus also been eroded. Additionally, if you own a company that relies on foreign inputs purchased in another currency, as is often the case in an increasingly globalised world (see Chapter 9), the collapse in EGP exchange rate drives input costs up and might force you to scale down production and even lay off employees. This in turn lays to rest one of the consequences of the origin myth of money discussed earlier. If money is just a way of simplifying the barter system and represents a notional value attached to the goods and services exchanged, then it cannot have an impact on real economic variables. This is the same assumption underpinning the **quantity theory of money**: in the long run, nominal variables do not have an impact on real variables. Yet, through the example about Egypt above, we see changes in two nominal variables: the fall in the value of the local currency on the one hand and the generalised increase in price levels (i.e. inflation) on the other. These changes have material repercussions (i.e. increase in import prices) that trigger a set of decisions in the 'real economy' whose consequences will not be limited to the short run only. For instance, these decisions might lead to falling production levels and rising unemployment.

REFLECTIVE ACTIVITY 7.2

One of the flipsides of Egyptian students paying higher fees to study abroad is that after graduation their UK wages will be worth much more when converted to EGP. Consider the following questions:

It is now the student's turn to help her parents. Let's assume that exchange rates remain stable in the foreseeable future (GBP 1 = EGP 21). Working and living in London, our student can send back home GBP 400 per month. Doing the same job in Cairo, she will be able to give her parents EGP 1,200 per month. How long would it take to return their original investment of EGP 320,000?

How is this likely to affect the student's decision to stay in the UK or go back to Egypt?

If she decided to remain in the UK, would there be consequences for the Egyptian economy?

Finally, and perhaps more intuitively, the function of money as a *means of exchange* is also laden with power relations. Richer people can afford more goods and services, and of higher quality, than poorer people. Asymmetry in means also produces asymmetry in exchange that can manifest itself as unequal exchange between rich and poor countries, but it can also present itself as unequal exchange among people between and within countries (see Section 9.5). In an economy faced by a shortage (again, Egypt in the wake of the 2007 and 2010 global food crises provides a case in point), limited availability of goods depending on foreign inputs (in Egypt: bread produced from imported wheat) might mean that—in the context of weak price controls—wealthier people are able to outbid poorer people and secure access to bread while denying it to others (Cook, 2012, 177–178). This was central to the demands of 'bread, freedom, social justice' of the 2011 mass uprisings in Egypt, which led to the overthrow of then president Hosni Mubarak (see photo 2.5).

If in democratic elections one of the key principles is that one person equals one vote, in market transactions—as economist Joseph Stiglitz (2012) put it—the driving principle is that one dollar equals one vote. If politics is then redefined and regulated as a market-place, wealthier people and groups can exert more influence over key decisions. Given the ever more pervasive corporate influence on democratic politics, it is then not especially surprising, and is certainly not a sign of health for democracy itself, that over the past three decades we have seen the rise of billionaire politicians, perhaps best embodied by the for-mer US President Donald Trump, but with forerunners including Italy's Silvio Berlusconi, Thailand's Thaksin Shinawatra, and Lebanon's Rafic Hariri. With billionaires as key politi-cal actors, not only has it become harder to ignore how politics and economics intersect, overlap, and interact, but this very issue has turned into a matter of political contention, becoming for instance a central plank in the platform of rising political figures such as Alexandria Ocasio-Cortez in the US (see for instance this video: https://www.youtube.com/watch?v=Kz1lxKF2hDY).

REFLECTIVE ACTIVITY 7.3

The labour market provides another vantage point for examining the effects of inequality of access to money as a means of exchange. Discuss with a classmate the following questions:

You are offered a paid summer position at one of the major consulting firms after several rounds of tough selection. However, the position fails to cover for all your living expenses. Is there any chance you could negotiate a raise? How? If you are unsuccessful, would you still take the position? Why?

What are the alternatives available to your employer? Would these make them more or less likely to reach a compromise that allows you at least to break even?

Once reduced to its simplest definition, 'money is essentially a provisional "promise" to pay' (Ingham, 2004, 12). However, at least four major implications stem from this succinct definition. First, insofar as this promise is made by someone to someone else, money is a social relation, and more specifically a social relation between a debtor owing money and having made a promise to pay it back and a creditor who is owed money that was lent under the promise that it would be paid back, usually with interest. Second, there must be an authority that the creditor expects to intervene should the debtor not repay the money. Hence, political authority and its codification in law are necessary for money to fulfil its role: 'money has its origins in law' (Ingham, 2004, 93, see also Section 6.4). Third, as mentioned earlier, money stems from the creditor–debtor relation, and emerges as a way of counting and regulating it. It is only later that it becomes a generalised means of exchange. Fourth, and following directly from this, money is fundamentally a **social technology**, understood as the harnessing of material, intellectual, and digital resources with the aim of organising and regulating 'social' processes through reference to an objectified—and hence allegedly impersonal—'technology'. This also affects money's material manifestations. Clay tokens that later became the first recorded means of payment were originally used as bookkeeping devices. As over time these means of payment became based on metals, we can once again see the centrality of power and politics: more than the actual availability of gold and silver, for instance, it was first and foremost their use as coins symbolising power and prestige that made them 'precious' metals.

7.2.2 MONEY CREATION AND THE BANKING SECTOR

Once we have settled on this baseline definition of money, we must still account for its workings: in a modern economy, where does money come from? Economics textbooks tell us that money creation is a process in the hands of a country's central bank. As it sets interest rates, the central bank turns on its printing and minting machines and puts into circulation an amount of money commensurate with a given interest rate. This dominant role of central banks in money creation is another persistent myth regarding money, and one recently acknowledged by the Bank of England (BoE), the UK's central bank. In a recent paper (Bank of England, 2014, see also short video here: https://www.bankofeng-land.co.uk/quarterly-bulletin/2014/q1/money-creation-in-the-modern-economy),   the BoE admits that central banks today set the parameters within which money is created by individual, usually private, banks. Hence, rather than driving the show, the central bank as a state institution is better seen as a cog in the broader process of money creation.

   To move beyond this myth of the central bank as the primary money creator, we must confront a series of questions, concerning for instance the relation between the state and the private sector with respect to money. While it may have lost direct control over its creation, political power remains relevant insofar as social trust in money does not derive exclusively, or even primarily, from its intrinsic qualities but rather depends on how it is backed and underwritten by a political authority, usually but not exclusively (think of the euro, but also of cryptocurrencies, to which we will turn later in Section 7.4.2) associated with a state. An element remains undoubted: financial institutions, including commercial and investment banks, insurance companies, and various types of investment companies including hedge funds, are among the most powerful actors in contemporary global politics. Similarly, finance is increasingly central to how we think about the economy, with major repercussions within and between states. To understand why this is the case, we must venture a bit further into the field of IPE.

7.3 MONEY IN THE AGE OF GLOBALISATION

Together with the state–market dynamics mentioned in Section 7.3, the relation between public and private authority is another of the main concerns of IPE (see also Sections 2.2.1 and 2.2.2). This has produced a lively debate on the nature and drivers of globalisation, usually presented as one of the most relevant transformations in global politics over the past half century. In its economic dimension, globalisation identifies the quantitative increase in the cross-border movement of goods, services, capital, technologies, and people across the world. This is in turn enabled by technological transformations—most notably, the information and communication technology (ICT) revolution, and container shipping as part of the so-called logistics revolution (see Photo 7.3 below)—that have qualitatively altered the functioning of the world economy (Mittelman, 2000).

A sceptical tradition, usually associated with the realist school of IR, argues that increased economic interconnections across borders are not a new phenomenon, and are better understood as new channels through which states, still seen as the most powerful actors in global politics, exert their influence (Hirst and Thompson, 1999). Other traditions, including for instance liberal scholars and more critical ones such as Susan Strange, argue instead that globalisation is a structural game-changer, as the rise of cross-border interactions, often bypassing the state, have transformed significantly the location and distribution of power and authority in global politics. This literature highlights especially the rise of the transnational corporation (TNC) as a major actor in international affairs, one that negotiates with

Photo 7.3 **Advances in container shipping mean that goods can be more easily transported across the world, a key function of globalisation.**

© nobleIMAGES / Alamy Stock Photo

states, and at times directly with other TNCs, on economic and also political issues of global relevance. Strange went as far as suggesting that this transformation entailed a 'retreat of the state' (1996, more on this in Section 9.3.2). A third tradition, often called 'transformationalist' suggests instead that the state has not so much retreated but rather has experienced a transformation of some of its key functions, accepting greater levels of economic integration across countries while retaining a regulatory role.

Globalisation is inextricably intertwined with the rise of financial institutions as major players in global politics. This is because one of the key channels of globalisation has been the removal of barriers to capital movement while the other one is the removal of barriers to trade in goods and more recently services (we will return to this in Chapter 9). Greater capital mobility allows us to transfer money to another country with a click on our devices. It also has the more systemic effect of empowering those who own resources that can be moved easily across countries over those owning fewer mobile resources. In a world with high levels of capital mobility, and generally low barriers to trade, this means empowering first financial capital, then—to a lesser extent—manufacturing capital, while limiting the options of those who rely on their ability to generate a wage through labour as their ability to move across borders is limited by increasingly restrictive migration policies.

REFLECTIVE ACTIVITY 7.4

Let us return one moment to Reflective Activity 7.2 and to the Egyptian IR graduate. We were suggesting that she would have an incentive to find employment in the UK to help her family in Egypt. Now, consider the following question:

In your view, why do wealthier countries like for instance the UK have immigration policies giving new graduates a short timeframe to seek employment in the UK, after which they are expected to leave the country if still unemployed?

Reforms dismantling barriers to the movement of capital and goods have traditionally been implemented by states, which have thus surrendered much of their power to curb those movements. The question then becomes: why have states given up on such a powerful source of authority? The classical economic argument, often echoed by the liberal institutionalist tradition in IR, is that technological transformations have on the one hand outflanked states' ability to control people-to-people flows and on the other hand have created opportunities for 'efficiency gains', that is, the reorganisation of production in ways that allow higher quantities of a good to be produced at lower average costs. As a result, there are strong incentives for economic cooperation between states, but also between corporations and people. This enables greater openness, which in turn produces greater wealth and prosperity for all. Within IR, Keohane and Nye most forcefully advanced this case, first with reference to interdependence and then to globalisation (Keohane and Nye, 1977, 2000). The evidence in support of this argument, however, is limited at best (Wade, 2017).

Given the weight it lends to ideas and meanings in influencing how we understand the world around us, and how we act within it and eventually shape its own development, the constructivist tradition, in this respect, argues that at times belief in certain ideas and discourses might even trump economic evidence. Hence, states continue to pursue policies stimulating financial and trade openness because they have been persuaded that this is the best way of securing wealth and prosperity for their own country (Abdelal, 2007). Realists, and economists like Ha-Joon Chang (2003, 2007), argue instead that economic openness is a tool in the hands of powerful states, which—often with the help of international economic organisations like the International Monetary Fund (IMF), the World Bank, and the World Trade Organization (WTO)—force poorer states to open up their economies so that TNCs from powerful states can more easily access their markets in order to set up more competitive production plants, purchase raw materials at lower costs, or sell their products (see Photo 7.4 below).

While agreeing on the exploitative nature of this arrangement, the Marxist tradition pays more attention to how the capitalist class, and within it more specifically its financial component, has become increasingly influential on state policy, both through direct representation and through the threat of moving their investment out of a country should its policies threaten their perceived interests.

REFLECTIVE ACTIVITY 7.5

Discuss with a friend the following questions:

What does globalisation mean in your everyday life?

Which of the traditions outlined in Section 7.3 reflects more accurately your everyday experience of globalisation?

Are there any elements of your everyday experience of globalisation that are not captured by any of these traditions?

Photo 7.4 **International economic organisations like the IMF force less wealthy states to open up their economies, enabling corporations from richer states to access their markets.**

7.3.1 **MONEY AS CREDIT**

Susan Strange was one of the first scholars to grasp the extent to which money and its fungibility (it can be used to consume goods, buy production plants, pay wages, trade in stocks and shares, and much more) was one of the key determinants of who stood to win and to lose from globalisation. Strange also provided a very helpful way of distinguishing what money does in the modern global economy. One can think of money as credit and of money as currency. Credit is 'the lifeblood of a developed economy' (Strange, 1994, 91), but, as we will see in this Section, also of so-called 'developing' and 'underdeveloped' ones, if one is to still use these terms even though they are profoundly steeped in paternalism and teleology. Deriving from the Latin word *credere*, to believe, credit leads us back to the point made earlier regarding the importance of trust. The decision of a bank to extend a mortgage to a first-time buyer is based on the *expectation* that the buyer will be able to repay the mortgage and interest in monthly instalments. This is in turn related to the borrower's *credibility*, ascertained through what is called credit rating. A system of credit rating also exists for states. As governments seek to borrow from international financial markets, the rating provided by credit rating agencies (CRAs) such as Moody's, Fitch, and Standard & Poor's is a crucial signal of whether the borrower is trustworthy, or—better—'creditworthy' (see Photo 7.5 below).

While they have historically denied having any formal regulatory role, CRAs undeniably perform crucial monitoring and assessment functions, thus constituting one of the major forms of private authority in contemporary financial markets.

As demonstrated by David Graeber's groundbreaking anthropological research (Graeber, 2011), credit and debt historically precede both barter and money as coinage. Indeed, up until the violent imposition of specific power relations through the 'military-coinage-slavery complex', mentioned in Section 7.1, 'human economies' understood debt, and symmetrically credit, as community-building mechanisms, insofar as financial obligation went

Photo 7.5 **Credit-rating agencies are powerful private authorities as they signal whether borrowers are trustworthy or not.**

© Tim Remer / Shutterstock.com

hand in hand with the moral obligation of the debtor towards both the creditor and the community at large. There was also by and large an expectation that those in a position to give credit would do so, further consolidating their community as well as their own status within it. Without any need to become apologists of a bygone era, and remaining fully aware of the challenges that such a system would face at larger scales, it is possible to suggest that economic arrangements that took into consideration issues of fairness, justice, and reciprocity provided for a moral economy built on shared expectations (Thompson, 1971).

Credit and debt are once more central to global political and economic arrangements for reasons related to our earlier discussion of globalisation. If financial capital can move more easily in and out of countries, TNCs can much more effectively threaten to leave a country if, say, taxation levels are not internationally competitive (read: low enough). It is now established that not only top income tax but also corporate tax rates have fallen significantly throughout the wealthiest economies, grouped in the Organisation for Economic Cooperation and Development (OECD). The power of TNCs is also increasingly enshrined into law, especially through the so-called Investor-State Dispute Settlement (ISDS), a mechanism included in investment and trade agreements that enables an investor to bring a claim against a state it invests in, should the investor believe that the state is breaching the terms of the agreement. Crucially, rather than being assessed through public international law (see Section 6.3.1), the claim is adjudicated through private international law. Such an approach has effectively reduced the capacity of governments to legislate around public concerns, such as health, environmental protection, labour, and human rights, whenever new laws might affect the profitability of investing TNCs. Once more, we see the extent to which the strengthening of private corporations brought about by globalisation can clash not only with state power but also with the public interest (see also Reflective Activity 9.8).

Returning to the tax revenue side, the lower receipts states get from corporations operating on their territory have two major implications for us. On the one hand, they force states to rely less on tax revenues and more on public debt to finance their spending. On the other hand, given the disciplining power of CRAs outlined earlier, states also find themselves under increasing pressure to cut spending, which usually means cutting the public services that it provides, which might include healthcare, childcare, education, subsidised transport, pensions, and so on. As public services are disproportionately needed by marginalised groups in society, including for instance the elderly, single mothers, the unemployed, and people with disabilities, public service cuts not only hit these groups harder but also place them in a position where a larger portion of their budget gets allocated to services not provided by the state anymore, including for instance the introduction of university tuition fees. This has in turn contributed to much higher levels of household debt, especially but not exclusively in Anglo-Saxon economies, as discussed in Section 9.2.2.

REFLECTIVE ACTIVITY 7.6

In the wake of the so-called Eurozone crisis beginning in 2009, during which the public debt of several states using the euro ballooned out of control, Greece was mandated by the European Central Bank, the European Commission, and the International Monetary Fund to undertake a series of draconian economic reforms, aimed at reducing Greek public debt, but eventually producing the largest nonwar-related economic decline in recent history. This poses urgent ethical questions regarding the relation between private and public interests. Consider the following questions:

Should public debt be repaid irrespective of the hardship that this might impose on the population of the indebted country?

Given that they stand to gain an interest out of their loan, should creditors hold any obligation towards their debtors? Should this change whether the debtor is an individual, a corporation, or a state?

Increased indebtedness is a prominent feature not only in the wealthiest economies but also affects public sector debt and development lending in many of the poorest economies. Around the turn of the century, the provision of small loans, usually at low interest rates directed towards poor households, often rural women, emerged as an important trend in international development policymaking. Muhammad Yunus was awarded the Nobel Peace Prize in 2006 for his work on microcredit, with the interest of the World Bank, regional development banks, and many public and private international donors generating a wave of microcredit lending throughout the Global South. Especially in light of this scaling up, however, the original objective of poverty reduction has been accompanied, and at times sidelined, by a range of other considerations. First, institutions involved in microfinance, historically ranging from the World Bank to Grameen Bank founded by Mohammed Yunus himself, have become more interested in recouping their loans by whatever possible means, at times relying on forms of violence such as forced eviction of borrowers from their house and land (see for instance Al Jazeera, 2019 on the case of Cambodia, also discussed in Reflective Activity 7.7.). Second, microcredit has been directed less towards the poorest, and more towards those already living above the poverty line within their communities, as these are more likely to successfully pay back their loans. Third, and in this case with a strongly gendered dimension, the social relations of the pre-existing moral economy have been mobilised towards using honour and shame as mechanisms through which women are encouraged to take microloans and then pushed to prioritise repayment as a way of preserving family honour. This interaction between moral economy and financial deepening produces 'political economies of shame' (Karim, 2008, 9). As a result of these pressures, 'the best estimate of the average impact of microcredit on the poverty of clients is zero' (Roodman, 2012).

REFLECTIVE ACTIVITY 7.7

Cambodia is arguably the country that has seen the largest expansion in microcredit lending in the world. As Bylander (2015, 540–544) details in her fascinating study of the rural community of Chanleas Dai, repaying microloans often means relying on remittances from relatives working abroad. As a result, resources that could be used for developmental purposes are often diverted towards financial institutions in the form of debt repayment and interest. In light of this finding, consider the following questions:

In your view, is the profit orientation of microfinance institutions an obstacle to the emergence of partnerships that benefit both lenders and local communities?

Can philanthropic initiatives by wealthy individuals and corporate social responsibility initiatives by large corporations provide a better alternative to microcredit for rural development?

What are the potential and limitations of migrant remittances in fostering rural development?

As also witnessed by this brief discussion of microfinance, credit and debt are among the channels that empowered finance in the age of globalisation, relative to other forms of capital, to workers, as well as to the state. Strange's second dimension of money—as currency—enables us to explore further this finance–state nexus with reference to the international system.

7.3.2 MONEY AS CURRENCY

As already mentioned, the exchange rate identifies the amount of a currency that can be bought with one unit of another currency. Among the currencies of wealthy countries, these rates typically fluctuate on a daily basis, reflecting changes in the demand and supply for each of the two currencies considered. The demand for a given currency is related to how much economic actors need that specific currency to conduct their own transactions, which in turn depends on how sought after goods and services produced in that country are, whether these must be paid in local currency, whether the local currency is also considered to fulfil an international role, and lastly on the specific monetary policy adopted by the central bank of that country. These elements, in turn, are also related to political considerations. To give one example, in the summer of 2015, GBP 1 was worth 1.44 Euro (EUR). One year later, in the wake of the referendum on UK membership of the European Union, GBP 1 exchanged for less than EUR 1.20, where it has been hovering since. While originally uncertainty around the shape of Brexit might have contributed to the original fall in the exchange rate of the British pound against the euro, its stabilisation around the same level suggests there might be something else at play too.

While currencies of major economies, such as for instance the US, the UK, Japan, and members of the European Union adopting the euro, have floating exchange rates, this is often not the case for currencies of poorer countries. Many West African countries, for instance, have their currency pegged to the euro, while many states in Central America and the Caribbean have their currency pegged to the US dollar. Until the early 1970s, floating exchange rates were not the case for major economies either. For the best part of the previous two centuries, exchange rates between major currencies have been fixed (or pegged). This was the case with the **gold standard**, when all currencies exchanged at a fixed equivalent in gold, and with the **Bretton Woods** exchange rate regime, established towards the end of the Second World War. Gold was still a prominent part of the Bretton Woods exchange rate arrangement, but in this instance only one currency—the US dollar (USD)—was directly pegged to gold, with all other currencies instead pegged directly to USD rather than gold. This gave the US what then French finance minister and future president Giscard d'Estaing called 'exorbitant privilege' (Eichengreen, 2010): by declaring the US dollar effectively as good as gold, the Bretton Woods system created an incentive for other countries to accumulate USD as the main component of their foreign exchange reserves (that is, the amount of foreign currency that states keep as a buffer in case of problems with the local currency). This was the beginning of what the literature often calls 'dollar hegemony': the US central bank (the Federal Reserve, also Fed) provided liquidity in an internationally desirable currency. This arrangement established a hierarchy between currencies, which played a crucial role (together with reconstruction projects such as the Marshall Plan, and security provision through the North Atlantic Treaty Organization, NATO) in consolidating the so-called Western bloc along lines of political, economic, and security subordination to the US. One of the main sources of dollar demand internationally was the denomination of oil contracts in USD. Oil was needed by all economies undertaking a reconstruction effort, which in turn demanded industrialisation, to be powered not anymore by coal but by petrol (Mitchell, 2011). Importantly, this period after the Second World War also marks the beginning of the so-called 'great acceleration' in environmental degradation (McNeill, 2014).

The dismantlement of the Bretton Woods arrangement is instructive with respect not only to the tensions inherent to the dollar-centred exchange rate regime but also to the economic forces and transformations that it unleashed. The constantly increasing supply of USD far outstripped the increase in the amount of gold discovered and accumulated as metal reserve. As a result, in the late 1960s it became apparent that there were far too many dollars around for them to be exchanged at USD 35 per ounce of gold. Anticipating a fall in the USD–gold exchange rate, governments started exchanging their accumulated USD reserves into gold. Under President Richard Nixon in 1971, the US decided first to suspend convertibility of USD into gold (i.e. you could not exchange the former for the latter anymore), and then eventually removed the peg altogether, initiating the move towards the floating exchange rate regime outlined earlier.

As the Bretton Woods system was predicated on major restrictions to international capital movements unrelated to trade, its dismantlement also enabled the move towards capital mobility. Here, the credit story discussed earlier in Section 7.3.1 and highlighting the global rise of finance—or rather its re-emergence (Helleiner, 1994)—intersects with the currency story of post-Second World War US dominance. As oil contracts were still denominated in USD irrespective of the collapse of the Bretton Woods arrangement, international demand for USD if anything increased. Additionally, removal of barriers to capital movements meant that USD-denominated proceeds from oil sales could now be reinvested wherever they promised to provide the highest rate of return. Wall Street, then financial district of Lower Manhattan, became the outlet of choice for these 'petrodollars'. In the wake of the spike in oil prices following the 1973 October War, the petrodollar boom meant that US-based banks could now increase their lending dramatically, particularly towards Latin American governments.

REFLECTIVE ACTIVITY 7.8

Launched during a holy period for both Judaism and Islam, the October War (also known as the Yom Kippur or Ramadan War) was fought between 6th and 25th October 1973 with a coalition of Arab states attacking Israel with the aim of recovering Sinai and the Golan Heights, occupied by Israel since the 1967 Six-Day War. Angered by Western support for Israel, the Organization of Arab Petroleum Exporting Countries proclaimed an oil embargo against those states perceived to have more strongly supported Israel. The oil price increase that followed the embargo is also known as the 'first oil crisis'. Consider the following two questions:

Why is an increase in oil prices characterised as a crisis?

For whom was this a crisis?

As US commercial banks thought it safer to lend in their own currency rather than in local currency, Latin American governments saw their USD-denominated public debt soar by about 20 per cent a year in the second half of the 1970s. This also means that the nominal value of this debt was tied to the monetary policy of the Fed in the US. In sum, the size of public debt for these countries was influenced by the decisions of a foreign central bank with a mandate expecting it to focus on US macroeconomic indicators, not on Argentinian, Brazilian, or Mexican ones. A sudden change in US monetary policy in 1979, known as the 'Volcker shock', produced a strengthening of the USD exchange rate, increasing both the nominal amount of the debt to be repaid and debt servicing costs (that is, the cumulative interest paid on the loan). Between August and December 1982, the Mexican peso, for instance, lost nearly 50 per cent of its value against the USD, with the ballooning debt burden becoming unsustainable for the Mexican government, which decided to default on its debt, with the associated money outflow and economic collapse. The Argentinian and Brazilian governments found themselves in a similar position, and dynamics typical of this first 'Third World debt crisis' have reappeared since in many other countries in the Global South.

REFLECTIVE ACTIVITY 7.9

This activity requires you to first address the questions prior to coming to class, ideally conducting some research online enabling you to draft a short answer to each of the questions below. Once in the classroom, compare and contrast your answers in small groups:

What does the term 'Third World' refer to? What were the 'First' and 'Second' worlds? If you are not familiar with these terms, feel free to look them up online.

Does this imply a ranking between 'First', 'Second', and 'Third' Worlds? If yes, which criteria underpin such ranking?

Why, in your view, is the term 'Third World' no longer used?

Strange's distinction between credit and currency has given us a good sense of the relevance of money in contemporary global politics. The fungibility of money in the age of capital mobility and trade openness has enabled the rise of finance as one of the central determinants of global economic and political relations. As capital becomes increasingly footloose, its owners can more effectively exert their leverage against those owning factors that do not enjoy as much mobility (workers especially), and those who cannot move at all (states). This constraint however does not apply in equal measure to all states: the existence of a clear currency hierarchy limits significantly the ability of poorer states to influence global financial arrangements. These power relations will undoubtedly play a major role in shaping the future of money, but this will also depend on technology, to which we now turn our attention.

REFLECTIVE ACTIVITY 7.10

As part of its Belt and Road Initiative (BRI) (see photo 1.2), China demands that the majority of transactions connected to BRI are conducted in renminbi, the Chinese currency. In light of our discussion in Section 7.3.2, briefly consider the following questions:

Why is China promoting the international use of its currency?

What are the likely consequences of this for regional and global politics?

7.4 WHERE TO? 'SOCIAL POWER' AND THE FUTURES OF MONEY

We have explored three myths related to money and its role in global politics. First, we have contested the widespread narrative that locates the origins of money in the limitations of the barter system. This has enabled us to start unveiling how money is constituted by, and itself helps constitute, power relations in society. Second, we have dispelled the myth that sees money creation as the domain of central bank activity. This opens a clearer view on the fundamentally political struggles underpinning the material and symbolic uses of money. These struggles cut across states and international organisations, public and private actors, creditors and debtors. Last, we have also seen that the value of precious metals in history has derived more from their use as money, rather than the other way around. As the dollar no longer needs the fiction of a gold anchor to present itself as 'the money of all monies' (Marazzi, 1995), the role of social power, and the struggles around it, in defining relations between currencies becomes impossible to ignore.

Both terms in 'social power' help us define what money does in global politics. The social element is crucial not only in framing and 'regulating' the interpersonal relations between creditors and debtors but also in attributing money—as both credit and currency—the trust necessary to function as a social lubricant, usually backed by state institutions. Conversely, this very role of political authority points once more to how power shapes hierarchical relations between different currencies and eventually the actors issuing and using them, as much as between who owes and who is owed money, and between who can access and who cannot access valuable resources, goods, and services. Additionally, thinking of money as an expression of social power also enables us to shed light on the mystery pertaining to the separation of money and power, as inhering respectively to economics and politics, common to many IR and IPE approaches. If money is, and is about, social power, and if money is also a social technology, how can technological developments such as cryptography and blockchain, underpinning bitcoin and other cryptocurrencies, affect the power relations between and within states? In what ways does technology shape the future(s) of money? This is what this section focuses on.

7.4.1 MONEY AS SOCIAL TECHNOLOGY IN HAYEK AND MARX

Before we get to cryptocurrencies (explored in Section 7.4.2), we must first briefly outline how money itself has been presented as a social technology by major thinkers. The technological power of money as a means of both coordination and transformation is for instance at the heart of two thinkers often presented as polar opposites of the political spectrum: Friedrich von Hayek and Karl Marx (see photo 2.3). For Hayek (2008), money performs a fundamental coordinating function within and between markets. This is linked to the ability of prices, expressed in money form, to act as aggregators and synthesisers of information about the goods and services available on the market. Prices thus act as a signal for market actors, who can decide whether to buy or sell a given good or service. In reaction to changes in the demand and supply for goods generated by individual transactions, the price also changes, thus modifying its signal in a feedback loop where prices orient individual decisions and at the same time synthesise and transform them in a collective yet impersonal coordination device. According to Hayek, this impersonality is constantly imperilled by state intervention in markets, for instance in the form of central bank increasing the amount of money in circulation in a stalling economy to stimulate people to invest, spend, and consume. In this account, state intervention implies a movement away from 'natural money', as the intrusion of state authorities in the market mechanism generates not only pressures towards more public spending (for instance in the form of 'unaffordable' welfare programmes), but also a distortion of the signalling function of prices, which in turn leads individual decisions astray, especially in the form of 'malinvestment', that is, investment directed towards inefficient and unprofitable ends. In his later work, this line of thinking leads Hayek to call for the denationalisation of money, to be issued not by central banks and hence underwritten and distorted by state power, but rather by private institutions. This would be the most effective way of establishing 'sound' money, which could potentially have a global reach, and one untouched by the polluting power of politics.

As we shall see in detail in Section 9.2.1, Marx names our economic system 'capitalism' after the domination and exploitation of capital over labour for the sake of profit. Money has coordinating and transformative functions also in Marx's analysis. Insofar as it permits the purchase and sale of commodities, including raw materials, machinery, equipment, intermediate inputs and finished products, but also workers' ability to work (what Marx calls labour power), money acts as an organiser and synthesiser of the system of commodities (Dodd, 2014, 82). While not buying into the price system as the autonomous and objective coordinator of market exchange, Marx is in this respect not so far from Hayek. Marx's (2004 [1867]) view is however drastically different when we look at the two major transformations that money enables within capitalism. First, money is central to the realisation of profit. Profit is generated through the extraction and appropriation of surplus value on the part of the capitalist. Following a tradition in classical political economy including Adam Smith and David Ricardo, but whose lineage goes even further back, including in the writings of Ibn Khaldun, Marx argues that value is produced by labour. Capitalism then revolves around an unequal exchange, as workers' wage is lower than the actual value they produce, with the exceeding (surplus) value appropriated by capitalists (see Section 2.3.3). This surplus value is however realised, that is, it becomes real, only once a commodity is sold on the market for a monetary value. This enables the capitalist to expand production by purchasing more commodities, including labour power, than was originally the case. For instance, my employees' labour in building a chair out of wood enables me to sell it for a price higher than the sum of my employees' wage, the tools they employ, and the price of wood. This enables me to hire another employee, buy more wood, and produce more chairs to be sold on the market.

Money (M) is also used to produce commodities (C) that, because of the labour power they embody, command more money (M'), leading to the common formulation M-C-M': after selling chairs I have more money than before I invested in the production of those very chairs I just sold. But there is an interesting implication at this point: once profit is realised, it is not necessary for money to go towards purchasing more commodities: money might well be hoarded by capitalists. The very possibility of hoarding, then, implies that money cannot be understood exclusively as means of exchange, and in fact we need to consider alternative ways through which money circulates in the economy, most notably through the financial sector.

Following from this, the second transformation is related to the ability of credit money to become a way of accumulating that does not depend on production: put into circulation as interest-bearing capital, credit money generates more money (M-M'). According to Marx, this creates the illusion that capital is self-expanding, which in turn leads to ever more credit money, generating cycles of speculative bubbles and crashes. As it sidesteps production and only circulates within finance, money exacerbates what Marx considers the crisis tendencies of capitalism. If in its first transformation money enables capitalism to function through the transformation of surplus value into profits, in this second one money can threaten capitalism by increasing the likelihood of crises, to which we will return in Section 9.4.

7.4.2 CHALLENGES TO TRADITIONAL MONEY

While neglected in this necessarily abbreviated outline, the state has a very important role in Marx's account of money and crisis. Internally, it seeks to perpetuate capital accumulation through underwriting the monetary base, but also through securing the acquiescence, if not necessarily the support, of the exploited through coercion and consent (see the discussion of Gramsci's view of power in Section 3.2.3). In global politics, states also play a key role in the expansion of capitalist social relations, through imperialism and primitive accumulation (see respectively Sections 8.2 and 9.2.1), and in mediating competition between capitals, for instance through the exchange value of the local currency. The fact that when this mediation is unsuccessful, and states resort to more confrontational means, we refer to **currency wars** speaks volumes about how power, and here more specifically state power, is part and parcel of the global politics of money in both its credit and currency form.

One of the elements on which Hayek and Marx agree is that competition between capitalists produces innovation and technological advances. Two of the most notable in recent times, especially in terms of potentially undermining state power over money, are cryptography and blockchain, the technological foundations of countless cryptocurrencies including bitcoin (see Photo 7.6 below).

Cryptography consists in the use of algorithms (complex mathematical equations) and secret keys with the aim of building and solving 'codes' used to simultaneously authenticate and anonymise our communications and data. Based on this, blockchain enables the recording of the transaction history of each given unit of value in a way that is both publicly known and anonymised. The former feature allows users to bypass state and bank checks, providing an extreme form of what is called **disintermediation**, while retaining trust between users. Hence, the security of electronic banking can be guaranteed from within the network itself without relying on supervisory authorities, while also preserving the anonymity of cash transactions. Despised and feared by financial authorities, cryptocurrencies based on cryptography and blockchain have been presented as the most advanced example of Hayek's dream of denationalising money, as their ability to generate trust from within the system allows them to bypass states and financial authorities and to empower currency users through radical decentralisation.

Wild fluctuations in the value of cryptocurrencies have shown that with the increasing number of users, traditional banking practices have become more common, for instance in the form of short-term speculation geared towards gaining easy profits out of the rise and fall in the exchange value of a (crypto)currency. While state authorities may be bypassed, this

Photo 7.6 **Cryptocurrencies include bitcoin, ETC Ethereum, ADA Cardano, LTC Litecoin, IOTA Miota, and ZEC Zcash.**

need not entail that power disappears in the world of cryptocurrencies. Rather, it is still central in the functioning of bitcoin, for instance. The supply of bitcoin is strictly regulated both in the maximum amount of coins issued (21 million) and in its yearly rate of growth (halved every four years). While one may agree or disagree with the principles guiding this choice, the fact that it was a choice in the first place implies that a specific set of power relations are embedded in bitcoin's own structure. Additionally, if bitcoin production (called 'mining' perhaps to evoke the mythologised past of gold-backed currencies) becomes twice as hard every four years, then the expansion of the user base over the past decade creates a situation where every individual user will be able to produce lower amounts of the fixed pot of bitcoins. As this crucially depends on processing power, the ability to scale up early is crucial to individuals amassing bitcoins, thus generating an issue of bitcoin, and hence of power, concentration within the system. Indeed, the most efficient mining method might well be having all mining concentrated in a single pair of hands, and there are reasons to believe that this is slowly materialising, with a cluster of 1,600 investors holding about one third of the available bitcoins, far away from the original dreams of radical decentralisation. State power is expelled from the system to be replaced by private power. This is then compounded by the negative **externalities**—i.e. the collateral damage—of bitcoin, including the possibilities that anonymity opens up for illicit, illegal, and criminal transactions and activity, and the devastating environmental impact of the extremely energy-intensive production process, estimated by a University of Cambridge study to exceed 121 terawatt-hours annually, more than the energy consumption of countries like Argentina and the Philippines.

REFLECTIVE ACTIVITY 7.11

Cryptocurrencies have been used by some states to circumvent economic sanctions, that is, commercial and financial penalties imposed against a country, its officials, or private citizens, usually as a form of punishment or to make it more costly to engage in a specific course of action. For instance, in 2018 the Venezuelan government created its own cryptocurrency, 'petro', allegedly with the aim of bypassing US and EU sanctions against its own economy. Large investments in cryptocurrencies have also been reported by other countries under sanctions, including Iran, North Korea, and Russia. Together with the strong suspicion that cryptocurrencies provide cover for various types of money-laundering activities, not necessarily or even primarily conducted by states, this has led to growing calls for regulating these markets. Given these developments, consider the following questions:

Is the proposed international regulation of these markets an attempt to reassert state power over money creation?

Even if this were the case, do you consider regulation a lesser evil than the threat that sanction circumvention and money laundering pose to international stability?

Can attempts at circumventing and violating economic sanctions ever be legitimate?

If scale has historically been the problem, is it possible for the future of money to be local? Already at the start of this century, and more after the global financial crisis, local currencies have taken an increasingly important role. Their rise and appeal comes from a consideration that resonates with many of the themes discussed in this chapter: the traditional financial sector diverts resources out of local communities, either to invest them elsewhere, through the technological advances of globalisation, or to keep them circulating directly within the financial circuit; governments in turn appear either unable or unwilling to alter this state of affairs, and in the wake of the crisis have decided to bail out the banks, and then condemn the rest of the population to austerity. Within this context, local currencies become a way of establishing and consolidating economic relationships within the community, through a system designed to keep money circulating locally, or—in more advanced cases—to exchange with similar local currencies elsewhere.

One such example is the Brixton pound established in South London in 2009 and aimed at increasing the resilience of the local economy after the global financial crisis, for instance by seeking to shorten supply chains and increase benefits for local residents. Variously configured to respond to the specific needs of local communities, some of these currencies have been remarkably successful in making sure that more of what is consumed is produced locally, and more of what is earned is also spent locally. However, it is harder to claim that these initiatives pose a systemic threat to global capital. These schemes are usually designed as complementary, rather than alternative, to legal tender issued by central banks. Hence, these initiatives tend to post positive results in hard economic times (which is no mean feat), only to stabilise or decline as national and global macroeconomic conditions improve. At the same time, and despite these limitations, both cryptocurrencies and local currencies demonstrate that it is possible to think money differently, away from the legal and coercive shield of state power and the global reach of major banks.

7.5 **CONCLUSION**

Thinking of global politics without thinking of money has become increasingly difficult. From the consequences of global economic crises to the rise of billionaire politicians, the ways politics and economics influence one another on a global scale are impossible to ignore for any student of contemporary global politics. This chapter has shown that to analyse this we must first and foremost challenge some of the myths concerning the origins, functions, and effects of money. We have then seen that it is helpful to think of money by distinguishing between credit and currency, while keeping an eye on how these two dimensions connect. This approach enabled us to learn a bit more about recent international economic history, and most importantly it has put us in a position to highlight the connection of power, ethics, violence, and law to money. Power has received more direct attention. As a result, we have explored the mystery generated by the separation between money as essentially economic and power as essential political common to much IR and IPE literature. But this chapter also touched on how money relates to the concepts and themes discussed elsewhere in this book. For instance, whereas it has now become commonplace to speak of the amorality or even immorality of money, we have seen how credit and currency systems in the past have also been inspired by principles of reciprocity, often associated with the idea of a 'moral economy', which we have only touched upon briefly here. The recent surge in the popularity of local currencies appears to signal the continuing relevance of these considerations. Additionally, we have also explored some of the ethical questions pertaining to inequality of economic means, and have invited you to think about the prospects and limitations of philanthropy and corporate social responsibility as strategies to address this inequality. We have also discussed how money has been and still is used as a way to exert violence, from its early days through the 'military-coinage-slavery complex' to forced evictions in the face of inability to pay back mortgages to debt crises in the Global South. Finally, we have seen how the power of money is not simply inherent in its properties but is enshrined through law, from Ingham's annotation about law laying at the very origins of money to TNCs resorting to private international law mechanisms to protect their interests in ways that constrain the range of policies states can pursue. As we strive to connect these concepts when we encounter them, we start to unveil the rich tapestry that makes up contemporary global politics. And as we seek to emphasise the importance of everyday life and experiences, we are also increasingly aware that we are all part of this rich tapestry, and that by understanding it better we can more meaningfully contribute to it.

Access the online resources at www.oup.com/he/hirst1e for case studies to help contextualise your understanding of key concepts, further reading recommendations to guide you through your reading, and a library of web links to journal articles, blogs, and video content to help you take your learning further.

EMPIRE

8

READERS' GUIDE

Chapter 8: Empire explores the mystery of why people claim that imperialism is a thing of the past, why some people are nostalgic about empires, and why the field of IR has conventionally sidelined issues of imperialism and racism. The purpose of the chapter is to contest the myth that imperialism has come to an end, showing instead that many of the imperial attitudes, racialised power hierarchies, and material in-equalities that structured the era of empires remain in place today. In light of this, the chapter invites you to consider whether and how IR might take account of its imperial origins, and the ways in which academia more generally could work in promotion of decolonisation and anti-racism.

8.1 INTRODUCTION

If the conventional story is to be believed, empires are a thing of the past. This story tells us that **decolonisation** began shortly after World War Two, and independence and statehood were granted to many colonies from the mid-twentieth century. However, the inequalities that structure the current global order have led many scholars to question whether imperialism has really ended. Using **Postcolonial** and **Decolonial Theory**, these scholars argue that the distribution of wealth and power in the international system today is similar to that of the era of empires, and that despite international norms and legal protections, racism and **xenopho-bia** remain widespread. These scholars also claim that IR is rooted in imperial history and attitudes, and that its core concepts and theories are infused with a colonial legacy.

In addition to these academic debates, questions of empire and racism are receiving increasing attention in the global press, political debates, and popular culture. The BLM movement, sparked by the killing of Black people by police in the United States, for example, has become global in scope, while universities across the world are under increasing pressure to decolonise their courses and address systemic biases in hiring staff and grading assessments. Blockbuster movies such as *Black Panther*, *Sorry to Bother You*, and *BlacKkKlansman* have challenged racist stereotypes, and drawn attention to white supremacism in the US and beyond. And the discriminatory policies of governments run by leaders such as Donald Trump, Narendra Modi, and Jair Bolsonaro—in addition to Europe's inaction on the deaths of migrants in the Mediterranean Sea—have prompted widespread concern about the ways lives are hierarchised along racialised and colonial lines in global politics today.

The purpose of this chapter is to challenge the myth that imperialism is a thing of the past. While formal decolonialisation did indeed take place from the mid 20th century, the chapter shows that many of the imperial attitudes, racialised power hierarchies, and material inequalities that structured the era of empires remain in place today. Having established that we live in an 'imperial present' (Morrissey, 2013), the chapter explores the mystery of why discussions about empire and racism remain rare in mainstream IR. As an academic field focused on war, conquest, and power, one would expect empire to be among its chief concerns. However, the chapter shows that mainstream IR suffers from what political scientist Debra Thompson calls **colonial and racial aphasia**, meaning a wilful forgetting (in Anievas et al., 2015). The chapter seeks to understand the mystery of why the mainstream might wilfully forget empire, and what might be done to correct this.

The chapter opens in Section 8.2 by exploring what empire and imperialism are and their key effects. It clarifies the relationship between colonialism and empire, sets out how they work in both material and immaterial ways, and outlines three key types of colonialism: territorial, economic, and cultural. Having done this, the chapter then explores why it might appear that the era of empire is over and why some people are nostalgic about empire and defend it.

Having done this, the chapter then turns to the mystery of why, given the past and present harms of empire and its global reach, mainstream IR remains reluctant to engage with it. To understand and challenge this mystery, the chapter examines two 'origin stories' of the field. The first story—the one that is told in most introductory courses and textbooks—describes how IR was established in the aftermath of the First World War by scholars and statesmen committed to avoiding another terrible conflict. By understanding how the international system works, this story suggests, IR would promote global peace and security for all. The second story—an alternative that rarely appears in IR's teaching materials—claims that IR was founded by Western powers to preserve their material interests and spheres of influence in the non-Western world. In other words, according to this second story, from the very beginning IR has worked to preserve and promote empire. By putting IR's founding under the microscope in this way, the mechanisms of, and vested interests served by, its imperial aphasia will be exposed.

Having explored how empire and imperialism continue to structure global politics and the academic field of IR, the chapter explores the complicated topics of race and racism, showing that although the idea of race as a biological category has long been discredited, racism is nevertheless a very real problem in global politics. It argues that, contrary to common-sense assumptions, racism is not necessarily intentional in character, and explores how structural racism is at work in both global politics and the academic field of IR, even if people don't deliberately act in racist ways.

The chapter turns finally to the question of what might be done to address the problems of imperial and racial aphasia, both theoretically and practically. It discusses current moves to decolonise the curriculum and our minds, symbolised in the defacing and removing of statues of imperial figures like Cecil Rhodes at the University of Cape Town, British monarchs and colonial administrators in India, and Confederate and Conquistador figures in the US and Latin America. It also notes the problem that a commitment to be anti-imperialist and anti-racist does not automatically mean one avoids participating in and reproducing imperialism and racism. Accordingly, this requires ongoing reflection and effort which the chapter invites readers to contribute to in promotion of a decolonised field of IR.

Before we begin our analysis, it is worth explaining why we take an explicitly critical view of empire in this chapter. Some might suggest that it would be better to provide a more 'neutral' for-and-against approach, organised around weighing up the pros and cons of empire. Others might say we should dedicate more space to discussing the claimed benefits of empire, such as modernisation, industrialisation, and the aggregation of wealth and resources. Still others might believe we should be proud of empire and celebrate the military might and glory of conquest. The problem with these approaches, we argue, is that they downplay, ignore, or defend the violence of empire: 'Across history, empires have involved the imposition of force by one power or people upon others. That imposition generally involves violence, including cultural and linguistic violence, such as the suppression and subsequent loss of native languages ... [E]mpires divide humanity into the rulers and the ruled, the wounders and the wounded. The rulers harm with guns and bullets, but also by using more subtle forms of destruction and domination' (Boehmer and Holland, 2020).

As this suggests, unlike some other forms of rule, empire is not based on the consent of the governed. Rather it is imposed by force and resistance is often violently supressed. This makes empire inherently antidemocratic: '"empire" as a form of political organisation remains deeply objectionable because it is premised on the complete denial of agency of those ruled without representation' (Rao, 2004, 160). This is because empires 'invariably entail a relatively small political community ... conquering other peoples and territories, often settling among them, and always absorbing them through a combination of coercive, legal, cultural and economic mechanisms'. This involves 'the hierarchical rule over a periphery from a metropolitan centre or "motherland"' (Colás, 2007, 6–7). Consequently, just as we think it correct to take a clear position against atrocities like gender violence, slavery, and genocide, we believe it is important to take a stand against empire by acknowledging and challenging both its past and contemporary violences.

8.2 **UNDERSTANDING EMPIRE AND IMPERIALISM**

There is no single or stable definition of empire. Across the centuries, and in different parts of the world, empires have manifested differently. The word 'empire' derives from the Latin '*imperium*', which means command, authority, control, or rulership (Bell, 2011, 864; Colás, 2007, 5). A useful distinction can be drawn between 'empire', which is a geographical place or territory, and 'imperialism', which is a set of political power relations in which one group of people dominates another group or groups. As Chapter 3 explored, power relations structure the political world in both obvious and invisible ways. Imperialism can be understood as a particular set of power relations which seek to establish and maintain empire. As such, imperialism is not a physical 'thing' but rather something that resides in the beliefs, intentions, and actions of people who approve of or want to create an empire (Colás 2007, 11).

Imperialism is related to, but different from, colonialism. Colonialism derives from the Latin '*colonus*', meaning farmer. Colonialism refers to the practice of acquiring land, resources, and wealth, sometimes but not always including the transfer of population from the colonising to the colonised region—this is called **settler-colonialism**. In that sense, it is a policy or process of acquisition. Imperialism, in contrast, relates to the ruling of colonised peoples and their land in a range of ways, and is thus more directly about wielding power. Colonialism is thus a type, but not the only type, of imperialism (Saurin, in Gruffydd Jones, 2006).

Empires have existed since the days of the Greeks, Romans, and Aztecs. Many lasted over multiple centuries, including the Chinese Imperial dynasties (from 221BC to 1912AD) and the Ottoman Empire (14th to 20th centuries). Known as the **Age of Empire**, the European empires of the 19th and early 20th centuries far exceeded those of earlier periods in size and scope. As literature professor Edward Said (see photo 8.1) explains, at the start of the Age of Empire, the European colonial powers held approximately 35% or the world's land. By 1878 this had increased to 67%, and by 1914 it reached 85% (Said, 1994, 8). The largest of these—the British Empire—alone encompassed 24% of the world's territory in 1920. Spanning at different times the Indian subcontinent, North America, North, East, and South Africa, the Middle East, East and Southeast Asia, and Australasia, the British Empire was fuelled by, and fuelled, the Industrial Revolution. Because of this, some argue that it brought economic and technological innovation to parts of the world which would otherwise not have had them.

One problem with this account is that ignores the extent to which scientific innovations were developed outside the West, but often appropriated through empire, for example in the fields of mathematics and engineering. A further serious problem is that such claimed benefits are far outweighed by the extreme violence of empire. For example, concentration camps were first used not by the Nazis but by Spanish imperial forces in Cuba in 1896–97 and the British in the Second Boer War between 1899 and 1902 in South Africa. The former led to the deaths of more than 10,000 people through disease and starvation, while the latter caused the deaths of 25,000 Boer people (mostly women and children) and an unknown number of Black African people (Stone, 2017, 11–13). The British 'scorched earth' policy in this war included the destruction of homes, farms, and livestock and systematic sexual violence against women and children with a view to wholesale depopulation in the service of imperial conquest. Similarly, when India was under British control, between 12 and

29 million people starved to death in a series of famines because Britain exported millions of tonnes of wheat to Europe. As late as 1943, between three and four million people starved in Bengal because Winston Churchill diverted food to European countries and militaries in full knowledge of the devastation this was causing (Kuchay, 2019). And as recently as the 1950s, Kenyan people numbering in the tens to hundreds of thousands were subject to torture in the form of electric shocks, burning, mutilation, and sexual violence by British colonial forces during the Mau Mau uprising, as the British government admitted in 2012 (Taylor, 2012).

A key element of the Age of Empire was the slave trade. Beginning in the 15th century, over a period of 400 years slave-trading states including Portugal, Britain, Spain, France, and the Netherlands shipped around 12 million enslaved people across the Atlantic from Africa to the Americas. Several million more died in transit or in camps following arrival (Segal, 1995). Driven by the desire for greater profits and inter-imperialist rivalries in Europe, the slave trade stripped Africa of both people and natural resources. In addition, enslaved people were treated as subhuman and denied fundamental rights. As IR professor Robbie Shilliam explains, 'in 18th and 19th century European thought, the body of the enslaved African was systematically denied any coeval relation to the civilized bodies of white European men' (Shilliam, 2012, 103).

As this suggests, imperialism is closely connected to questions of race and racism. To return to the example of Churchill, his own statements show he was a white supremacist who valued people differently on the basis of their skin colour. For example, when Kurds rebelled against British rule, he said: 'I am strongly in favour of using poisoned gas against uncivilised tribes ... [It] would spread a lively terror.' During the famines in India, he said: 'I hate Indians. They are a beastly people with a beastly religion', and claimed that the famine was their own fault for 'breeding like rabbits'. He similarly referred to Palestinians as 'barbaric hordes who ate little but camel dung' (Duffield, 2020).

REFLECTIVE ACTIVITY 8.1

Take a moment to pause here and consider the following questions:

Are you surprised by Churchill's use of language like this? Why/why not?

What might be the concrete effects of describing groups of people in this way?

How can we make sense of the tension between these statements and Churchill's opposition to Nazism?

Discuss your answers with a friend or classmate.

8.2.1 THREE LAYERS OF COLONIALISM

To understand how empires work, it is helpful distinguish between three types of colonial rule. First, and most obvious, is territorial colonialism. This is most closely associated with classical and modern colonisation which involved **dispossessing** people from their land and extracting their wealth. Sometimes this involved the settling of large populations, such as the French in Algeria or the Dutch in South Africa, with a view to establishing permanent new societies. Such settler-colonialism sought to replace the existing population with another by killing, displacing, and assimilating them, as Europeans did to **Indigenous** people in the Americas and Australasia. Other territorially-based empires involved the rule of land distant from the colonising power, such as the British in India and Nigeria. This form of colonialism involves the rule of a colonised place by small groups of administrators rather than relocating populations. A key difference between these forms of colonialism is that 'whereas colonialism reinforces the distinction between colony and metropole, settler colonialism erases it'. It does this by working to '"tame" a variety of wildernesses, end up establishing independent nations, effectively repress, co-opt, and extinguish indigenous alterities' (Veracini, 2011, 3).

In both colonial and settler-colonial conquest, land was acquired by violence and the threat of violence in addition to deceit and theft. Also in both cases, racial hierarchies were established through legal and informal mechanisms which served to place white colonisers in positions of control and subjugate colonised people. The use of so-called 'colour bars' was common in colonised countries, for example in Zambia and Zimbabwe. Such practices were used in the UK as recently as the 1960s to ensure that only white people could get particular jobs (Mohdin, 2020).

With the end of the period of formal colonisation from the mid 20th century, however, a second form of colonialism developed. Writing in 1965, politician and theorist Kwame Nkrumah called this **neo-colonialism**. While some argued that the end of the territorial colonies meant the end of empire, others insisted that new forms of neo-colonial and neo-imperial domination replaced the territorial version. As Nkrumah explained, '[t]he essence of neo-colonialism is that the State which is subject to it is, in theory, independent and has all the outward trappings of international sovereignty. In reality its economic system and thus its political policy is directed from outside' (2004). In this form of empire, the economies of colonised states and peoples are exploited, creating wealth and profit for colonising powers in much the same way as under territorial colonialism. After all, territorial colonialism was less about the land itself, and more about extracting raw materials and gaining access to free and cheap labour. Importantly, this form of colonialism appears less objectionable today as the label 'empire' is no longer used and because the states involved are officially independent.

Many scholars argue that the West continues to have a disproportionate influence in institutions of global financial governance. Such influence, they argue, is colonial in character. They provide examples like the **structural adjustment programs** (SAPs) of the International Monetary Fund and World Bank which have provided loans for many states in the Global South. Such loans come with conditions, specifically that recipient states adopt neoliberal economic principles like privatisation, trade liberalisation, and austerity. In light of this, scholars suggest that this amounts to a neo-colonial or neo-imperial arrangement—while the West no longer has formal territorial control, it retains a tight hold of the economies and resources of the Global South and requires the suppression of domestic resistance to reforms (Ibhawoh 1999, 160). As Fanon noted, this represents a continuation of the exploitation of the Global South by the West: 'colonialism and imperialism have not paid their score when they withdraw their flags and their police forces from our territories. For centuries the capitalists have behaved in the underdeveloped world like nothing more than criminals' (Fanon 2001, 80).

Finally, we can identify **cultural imperialism** (Said, 1994). As the least obvious of the three kinds, it is often hard to spot. Said argues that imperial assumptions and standards are at work in our cultural sites and products, such as novels, theatre, and poetry.

For example, he argues, colonialism is used to confer power and moral status in Jane Austen's books. In *Mansfield Park,* he explains, 'Thomas Bertram's overseas possessions are threaded through; they give him wealth, occasion his absence, fix his social status at home and abroad, and make possible his values, to which Fanny Price (and Austen herself) finally subscribes'. The effect of this, he shows, is that 'the right to colonial possessions helps directly to establish social order and moral priories at home' (1994, 73).

We might extend Said's analysis to consider popular culture, for instance movies, television, and videogames. Take, for example, the issue of beauty standards. Much has been made in the press in recent years about the dominance of light-skinned Black people in leading roles in blockbuster movies. Because of these representations, darker skinned people have described feeling social pressure to have lighter skin, to such a degree they sometimes use bleaching products. The **colourism** at work in this process has a series of effects; one recent

Photo 8.1 **Edward Said, a founder of Postcolonial Studies, was best known for his 1978 book** *Orientalism* **which analysed cultural representations of Middle Eastern, Asian, and North African societies. He contended that Orientalist scholarship was, and remains, inextricably tied to the imperialism of the societies that produced it.**

© CPA Media Pte Ltd / Alamy Stock Photo

study showed that in Mexico, lighter-skinned people experience a series of social privileges in terms of income, education, and occupation (Reeskens and Velasco Aguilar, 2020).

Similarly, consider the expectation that people around the world should speak English. Whether to communicate with tourists, work for transnational corporations, or publish in academic journals, people outside the West are often expected to learn English. In contrast, first-language English speakers often feel no such obligation to learn other languages. While English is a first language for 360 million people, 20% of the world's population speaks it. That's 1.5 billion people. And despite it not being widely spoken on an everyday basis, English remains the official language of many former colonies in Africa and South/Southeast Asia. As this suggests, empires and imperialism function in a web of political, economic, and cultural practices. This is because '[i]mperialism is a "full spectrum" social phenomenon, reworking economies, cultures, and polities through agencies as diverse as missionaries, businessmen, soldiers, poets, and state officials' (Barkawi, 2017).

REFLECTIVE ACTIVITY 8.2

Before moving on to the next section, take a break and think about the nature of empire.

How does your everyday understanding of empire and imperialism differ from the academic framing offered here?

Do you agree that imperialism operates at territorial, economic, and cultural levels?

What other forms of 'cultural imperialism' can you think of?

Discuss your answers with a friend or classmate.

8.2.2 EMPIRE TODAY

As discussed in Chapter 3, language matters. In the context of understanding empire today, it matters especially because whether or not we choose to call a particular political relationship 'imperial' has a strong bearing on whether or not we approve of it. Interestingly, we tend to use different terms to describe empires that we do or do not agree with. While it is widely accepted that the US and USSR sought in similar ways to expand their spheres of influence during the Cold War, we refer to the latter's 'Evil Empire' while the former's activities are euphemised in other more benign-sounding ways such as **hegemonic stability** or alliance. But, as Said explains, the global activities of the US are similar to those of empires, including for example the genocide against Indigenous peoples and wars over spheres of influence. And yet, he continues, because the US has been so successful in presenting itself in a positive light in global politics, we do not normally refer to it as an empire:

> [S]o influential has been the discourse insisting on American specialness, altruism, and opportunity that 'imperialism' as a word or ideology has turned up only rarely and recently in accounts of United States culture, politics, history. But the connection between imperial politics and culture is astonishingly direct. American attitudes to American 'greatness', to hierarchies of race, to the perils of *other* revolutions (the American revolution being considered

unique and somehow unrepeatable anywhere else in the world) have remained constant, have dictated, have obscured, the realities of empire, while apologists for overseas American interests have insisted on American innocence, doing good, fighting for freedom (Said, 1994, 8–9).

What is suggested here is that we are reluctant to call 'empire' those hegemonic powers for which there is broad approval (at least in the West).

REFLECTIVE ACTIVITY 8.3

Take a pause here to consider the following question:

Is the USA an imperial power? Why or why not? What leads you to this conclusion?

Discuss your answer with a friend or classmate.

Empire can be described as 'world ordering through accumulation by dispossession' (Saurin in Gruffydd Jones, 2006, 25). Dispossession refers to taking something from someone, in this context land, wealth, property, or goods. Despite the variations in territorial, economic, and cultural manifestations, empire is about taking things that belong to other people. The thing in question might be physical—like gold or fertile land—or more intangible, for example the ability to self-govern or live by one's own cultural or value systems. What unites these various forms of dispossession under conditions of empire is that it is done for the sake of accumulating wealth, goods, and property.

Accordingly, Decolonial and Marxist theorists argue that there is a close relationship between imperialism and capitalism (for further discussion, see Chapter 9). Because capitalism entails the endless **extraction of surplus value**—in other words, the creation of profits—imperial conquest was Europe's solution to its own finite resources. In this reading, both imperialism and capitalism are ideological, as well as material, phenomena. Said explains:

> Neither imperialism nor colonialism is a simple act of accumulation and acquisition. Both are supported and perhaps even impelled by impressive ideological formations that include notions that certain territories and people *require* and beseech domination, as well as forms of knowledge affiliated with domination: the vocabulary of classic nineteenth-century imperial culture is plentiful with words and concepts like 'inferior' or 'subject races', 'subordinate peoples', 'dependency', 'expansion', and 'authority' (Said, 1994, 9).

Key here is that idea that an imperial mindset includes the idea that certain people should subjugate others—that there is a responsibility to rule some groups otherwise they will not 'progress' properly. As IR professor John Hobson notes, while some assume that 'imperialism is defined by the *exploitation* of the weak by the strong' it is also 'conceptualised as a **civilising mission** precisely because it entails the West engaging in the "paternalist uplift" of the non-West' (in Gruffydd Jones, 2006, 90). What is important here is that benevolent intentions can be just as imperial as violent ones if they involve 'teaching' or directing people to adopt a set of values or practices presented as superior. Indeed, such rationales have often been used to justify the violences of empire.

This also suggests that empire did not end with the formal decolonisation process that began following the Second World War. Indeed, far from being over, 'imperialism is one of the most influential forces which has shaped, and is still shaping, the world' (Bush, 2006, 7). If imperialism persists because capitalism persists, the idea of decolonisation amounts to nothing more than a myth. As sociologist Ramón Grosfoguel argues, '[o]ne of the most powerful myths of the twentieth century was the notion that the elimination of colonial administrations amounted to the decolonization of the world. This led to the myth of a "postcolonial" world.'

The myth of the end of empire has important effects. Specifically, it 'obscures the continuities between the colonial past and current global colonial/racial hierarchies and contributes to the invisibility of "coloniality" today' (Grosfoguel, 2011). In this framing, the greatest trick colonialism and imperialism ever pulled was to claim they no longer exist.

One important concept here is **coloniality**, originally developed by sociologist Aníbal Quijano. Coloniality refers to the unequal political, economic, and cultural arrangements that remained in place after the end of formal colonialism. In this reading, decolonisation is incomplete—coloniality endures even without colonialism in the classical sense. The key contribution of the concept of coloniality is that it allows us to make sense of the ongoing inequalities that reflect the empires of the past.

REFLECTIVE ACTIVITY 8.4

Take pause here to consider the following question:

Is empire a thing of the past?

What are the implications of the idea that we live in an 'imperial present'?

Discuss your answer with a friend or classmate.

All of this makes it difficult to understand why people in the West are sometimes nostalgic about, and defend, empire. As you can see in photo 8.2, a 2020 YouGov poll shows that significant proportions of people in Europe think empire is something to be proud of. In the Netherlands 50% of people hold this view, in Britain 32%, France 26%, Belgium 23%, Italy 21%, Spain 11%, and Germany 9% (YouGov, 2020). Only 6%–26% of people in these countries think empire is something to be ashamed of. But how do we make sense of this?

Few people would defend the use of genocide, murder, starvation, displacement, internment, and sexual violence in global politics. And yet, when empire is discussed in the UK media or general public, a veneer of glory and nostalgia for a time when 'Britannia ruled the waves' is sometimes perceptible.

Part of the reason for this is that many Western people are simply unaware of the horrors of empire. Recent campaigns in the UK have drawn attention to the absence of the British Empire in school curricula, which tend to focus on the 'good wars' of the 20th century that present the victorious European powers in positive light (Owen, 2016). Similar campaigns in the US, Australia, and other settler-colonial countries are under way to ensure the genocides perpetrated against Indigenous people in the founding of these states is taught as part of the school curriculum. A further reason is that people feel reluctant to take responsibility

Photo 8.2 **Despite the horrors and violence of empirical rule, 32% of British people in 2020 thought that empire is something to be proud of.**

© Andrew Fare / Alamy Stock Photo

for things that their ancestors did, resulting in a 'recurrent need to disavow' responsibility for empire (Veracini, 2010, 14). Having examined how empires have functioned historically and today, the next section turns to the question of why, despite its world-historical significance, mainstream IR has broadly remained silent on the topic.

8.3 EMPIRE IN IR

Despite its global significance and enduring character, mainstream IR does not talk much about empire. The terms 'empire' and 'imperialism' are strikingly absent from leading journals, conference presentations, and research grant applications. Many introductory IR courses present mainstream theories—like Realism and Liberalism—that share this silence. And the history of the international system is often taught as though untouched by imperial and colonial relations. Indeed, it is quite possible that a student could complete a degree in IR in many Western universities without having examined in any depth the role of empire in the world order.

Where there is engagement from the mainstream, it often follows the logic of the 'oops theory' of empire, as though it were just a minor blip on the historical radar (Sabaratnam, 2020, 26). In these accounts, empire is framed as a thing of the past in which the case is now closed, the problem now solved (Nisancioglu, 2019). Such engagements even manage to congratulate the West for the territorial decolonisation that began in 1947 as though it was a reflection of its upstanding moral character—a 'benign gift that was graciously bequeathed by Western civilisation' (Hobson in Anievas et al., 2015, 86). This erases the anticolonial struggles of colonised people which undermined empires, and the forms of economic and cultural colonialism that continued. Equally troublingly, the violence and horrors of empire are often erased in mainstream IR. In such accounts, by 'subtracting the racism and governing correctly … colonialism [can appear] a desirable model of governance for our times' (Muppidi, 2012, 8).

However, conversations about race and empire *have* in fact taken place in the field for several decades, even if the mainstream hasn't paid much attention. Beginning in the 1990s, a number of texts have been published which explore these topics (Doty, 1993; Krishna, 1993; Henderson, 1995; Nair, 1999; Vitalis, 2000; Persaud and Walker, 2001). Today there is a rapidly growing community of scholars dedicated to studying the past and present impacts of empire on global politics. These scholars argue that a focus on race and empire is vital for the field. This is because 'studying the origins, dynamics, evolution and decline of empires offers the shortest route to identifying and understanding both the enduring hierarchical structures and the powerful forces of change across human societies' (Colás, 2007, 2).

Scholars working in this area draw on Postcolonial and Decolonial Theory. Postcolonial Theory builds upon the work of Edward Said, Homi Bhabha, and Gayatri Spivak, focusing on cultural colonialism and imperialism. Decolonial Theory, in contrast, is associated with the work of Aníbal Quijano, Maria Lugones, and Walter Mignolo, and focuses on the economic and material continuities of colonialism and imperialism (Bhambra, 2014, 115). While they differ in several ways, both traditions argue that colonialism is a thing of the present— at work in Western knowledge production as much as trade and foreign policy—and that as such it urgently requires analysis and challenge. Some scholars working in these traditions integrate gender into the study of empire through an intersectional analysis, showing how the paternalistic attitude of colonial states operated to feminise colonised places and peoples as part of their justification for ruling them (Patil, 2013). Others use Queer Theory to examine how sexuality is utilised and governed by colonial practises (Rao, 2020).

Importantly, these scholars draw attention to the injustices of empire. They also demonstrate the intimate connections between imperialism and racism, showing that contemporary forms of discrimination have their roots in imperial practices and mindsets. This raises the important question of why this work is often ignored by the mainstream. It cannot be that academics in the field are unaware of empire—after all, as we explored in Chapters 2 and 3, their field is explicitly dedicated to the study of global politics and power. So why else might a discipline so well placed to study these topics have neglected to do so?

REFLECTIVE ACTIVITY 8.5

Take a pause to consider the following question:

> *What reasons can you think of which might explain IR's past and present marginalisation of empire?*
>
> *What are the effects of this marginalisation, and who stands to benefit from it?*

Discuss your answer with a friend or classmate.

To explore these important questions, we need to revisit the account IR gives of its founding as an academic field of study. Specifically, we need to explore two 'origin stories'.

8.3.1 ORIGIN STORY ONE: GLOBAL PEACE AND SECURITY

If you have read a textbook account of the origins of the academic discipline of IR, it will likely have gone something like this. The international system as we know it came into being with the **Treaties of Westphalia** (1648) that ended the **Thirty Years War** and brought the modern sovereign state into existence. In this new world order, states have **sovereignty** because there is no higher form of authority. Organised as a system of states, all more or less functionally the same, the international system has since been characterised by a condition of **anarchy**. Under anarchy, each state governs itself but must compete for survival with other states along the way. States must preserve their existence by finding ways to maximise their interests in this system of anarchy.

From there, you will learn that the academic discipline of International Relations came into existence following the end of the First World War. Horrified by the death and destruction of mechanised warfare, the story tells us, important statesmen and scholars from the victorious powers resolved to domesticate the dangerous anarchic system by subjecting it to rigorous study and creating international institutions. If only the causes of war could be understood, it might be avoided. If global institutions could facilitate diplomacy and deal with troublemakers, violent conflict could be a thing of the past. In this light, the **League of Nations** (see photo 6.1) was established to preside over disputes and promote global peace and security for all. Whatever the successes and failures of the League itself, the story tells us, it reflected Liberalism's goal of a **harmony of interests** in global politics. With these lofty aims in mind, International Relations was established in 1919 via a professorship at the University of Wales, Aberystwyth. The position was named the Woodrow Wilson Chair, after the US President who pioneered the League and the spirit of cooperation in the interwar period.

These two dates—1648 and 1919—are treated as the 'big bangs' of the discipline (de Carvalho et al., 2011). Westphalia is viewed as

> the place where the big modern idea of the *sovereign* state and the *anarchic states-system* exploded into being and where the life of empires and other hierarchical political formations ended, while 1919 was presented as the year when the discipline itself exploded into existence with IR scholars becoming for the very first time enthused with theorising about the international as a subject matter in its own right insofar as it constituted an autonomous domain (de Carvalho et al., 2011, 736).

However, far from painting an accurate picture, these big bangs are in fact powerful myths which continue to be repeated in materials used to teach future IR scholars. While it may offer a 'heart-warming rendition' of the discipline's origins, series of important challenges have been posed to this orthodox account (several of which will be explored in more detail in Chapter 10).

This conventional story presents Europe and the West as entirely independent of the rest of the world, as though all the good ideas and important actions came from there alone. This 'presents Europe as a unique world-making agent and a prime mover of history, where the innovation of modern sovereignty is first generated within its pristine boundaries and then "diffused" elsewhere. This claim rests on a geohistorical abstraction whereby European states are viewed as self-propelling actors that are hermetically sealed from external—non-European—relations' (Nisancioglu, 2019, 5). This tendency to present Europe as the most or only important actor in global politics, and to assume that all useful knowledge comes from Europe, is called **Eurocentrism**.

Eurocentrism presents Europe—and states culturally close to it like the US, Canada, and Australia—at the centre of things. In Eurocentric accounts, Europe is conflated with the world, and the roles played by other actors and forces are marginalised. Eurocentrism can lead to imperial amnesia: 'Forgetting empire is often a function of Eurocentrism, of the un-reflective assumption of the centrality of Europe and latterly the West in human affairs. In IR this often involves placing the great powers at the center of analysis, as the primary agents in determining the fate of peoples' (Barkawi, 2017). Eurocentrism might be perceptible in, for example, a course or module which claims to teach global or world history, but actually only teaches European history. It might also be at work in classes which explore a particular part of the world—say East Asia or the Middle East—but which assigns readings from European academics rather than those written by people from the region. Eurocentrism thus suggests that you can know everything you need to know about global politics from Western ideas and traditions of thought: 'Eurocentrism is most evident in the unspoken assumption that we do not need to attempt to travel to intellectual terrains outside the ideal West' (in Shilliam ed., 2011, 24).

This story presents Europe in a suspiciously favourable light. As we know from our everyday lives as much as global politics, people's and states' actions are motivated by a range of both noble and self-interested concerns. Framing Europe, or indeed any global actor or region, as squeaky clean should cause us to wonder if something has been left out of the story. In this case, the orthodox story serves to present Europe as wholly peace-loving and altruistic. However, this 'conceals more than it reveals. This messianic narrative about IR's "birth", rising from the ashes of war to bring peace to the world, has, almost for a century now, linked IR's identity to world peace while conveniently erasing its racial and imperial origins' (Thakur et al., 2017, 22).

By presenting Europe in this suspiciously positive light, the orthodox account paints a picture of the colonised world in a less positive light. As Chapter 3 explored, our thinking and knowledge often relies on **binary opposites**—like good/evil, masculine/feminine, or light/dark—in which one term (the former in these cases) in treated as better than the other (the latter in these cases). The conventional story of the birth of the modern international system and IR does precisely this by relying on the binary of West/Non-West. In the story of domesticating global anarchy, the West is presented as taming and managing an unruly system. If the West must do this, this can only be because the rest of the world is responsible for this unruly condition. This narrative serves 'to refurbish the image of the West as regenerative, progressive, and redemptive in contrast to other variably regressive, repressive, and reactionary models of society' (Grovogui, 2009, 6).

The key structure of this inequality between states is past and present forms of empire. Indeed, far from signalling the end of hierarchical global order, 'the *post*-1648 era witnessed a *proliferation* of international imperial-hierarchies, which comprised a series of single sovereign colonial powers, each of which stood atop a conglomerate of dependent non-sovereign polities' (de Carvalho et al., 2011, 741). The effect of the myth of a system comprised of equal state actors is to erase the highly asymmetric power relations between different states, namely colonial and colonised ones. This has the effect of naturalising and legitimising this inequality—if they do not appear as a problem, or appear at all, we don't have to do anything about them. Thus, colonial and imperial relationships go unchallenged because they are unacknowledged.

REFLECTIVE ACTIVITY 8.6

Take a pause here to reflect on origin story one and consider the following questions:

What are the strengths and weaknesses of this origin story?

Whose interests are served by this version of events? Whose experiences are marginalised or erased?

To what extent is origin story one convincing, and why? What is left out?

Discuss your answer with a friend or classmate.

Seeking to expose the violence of empire, however, a second story has been offered by critical scholars in IR, which will be explored in Section 8.3.2.

8.3.2 ORIGIN STORY TWO: COLONIAL ADMINISTRATION

While the mainstream story of the birth of the international system and the discipline of IR fails to acknowledge it, empire and imperialism have long been written about and theorised. Indeed, in 1920, just as the discipline of IR was being founded, sociologist W. E. B. Du Bois (who you can see in Photo 8.3) published a prescient analysis of the role of empire and racism in global politics. In one of his texts on the subject, 'The Souls of White Folk', he argued that 'it is expansion overseas; it is colonial aggrandizement which explains, and alone adequately explains, the World War' (Du Bois, 2003, 51–52).

Such colonial expansion was, he argued, the result of limits to the extraction of profits from European working classes. With the rise of labour movements from the mid 19th century, European workers were calling for better working conditions, shorter hours, and higher pay. This meant a reduction in profits for the wealthy elite. The solution arrived at by this elite was, Du Bois shows, colonial expansion. As he explains, this solution involved

> the exploitation of darker peoples. It is here that the golden hand beckons. Here are no labor unions or votes or questioning onlookers or inconvenient consciences. These men may be used down to the very bone, and shot and maimed in 'punitive' expeditions when they revolt. In these dark lands 'industrial development' may repeat in exaggerated form every horror of the industrial history of Europe, from slavery and rape to disease and maiming, with only one test of success—dividends! (Du Bois, 2003, 53).

Photo 8.3 **W. E. B. Du Bois. Du Bois argued that economic competition between European states was a key driver of colonial expansion, though his work has been ignored in the field of IR until very recently.**

© Library of Congress Prints and Photographs Division Washington, D.C. 20540
USA http://hdl.loc.gov/loc.pnp/pp.print

This led, as Marxist revolutionary Vladimir Ilyich Lenin argued, to **inter-imperialist rivalry**. This competition between the powers of Europe for colonial aggrandisement ultimately led, as Du Bois explains, to the outbreak of the First World War.

So, what was the role of IR in all of this? Surely an academic field cannot be held responsible for the decisions of European leaders. Several scholars have argued that, if we look again at the founding figures of IR, we can see strong support for this imperial expansion. This challenges the founding story of the promotion of global peace and security. For example, early texts in the field were imperial in character. P. H. Kerr's *An Introduction to the Study of International Relations* (1919) argued that 'one of the most fundamental facts in human history' is that 'mankind is divided into a graduated scale ranging from the civilised to the barbarian, which necessitated colonisation of the latter by the former' (Henderson in Anievas et al., 2015, 21). Similarly, the founding journals of the field focused on race and empire. IR's first academic journal, then called *The Journal of Race Development*, explored how Western states might best administer their empires and prevent uprisings (Vitalis, 2015). This journal is still with us today, having changed its name to *Foreign Affairs*.

Such attitudes did not change following the First World War. For example, Norman Angell, who in addition to an IR scholar was also a Labour MP and won a Nobel Peace Prize, argued in *The Defense of Empire* (1937) (Kirby, 2022):

> 'absolute' self-determination, or sovereignty, or independence, is incompatible with civilisation. To talk, as anti-imperialist critics sometimes do, as if a few thousand desert tribesmen or Hispano-Indian peasants, if only they will call themselves a 'nation', should have complete control of raw materials indispensable to the world as a whole, or the right to block some world highway, is to set up standards which in fact will not be observed, and the ethics of which perhaps do not deserve observance.

Such a view was shared by others in the field. As late as 1955—when formal decolonisation was underway—political scientist Quincy Wright argued in *The Study of International Relations*:

> Colonial government is the art of organizing, administering, and developing backward peoples and areas, geographically separated from the governing state ... The art is a progressive one. It is assumed that backward peoples like adolescent individuals will eventually graduate from that condition into full maturity. Consequently, the art of dealing with them involves not only control of guidance ... but also development of the area and people so that they will cease to be in the unequal situation of backwardness ... The people must be organised, controlled, guided, educated and advanced to bring them to a condition of responsibility ... The area must be developed economically and its resources converted to use (Kirby 2022).

These passages paint a rather different picture to the orthodox story. Far from a commitment to autonomy, freedom, and equality, IR's leading figures argued for empire and paternalist control of the non-Western world. In doing so, they displayed an imperial mindset and a will to dominate the global system. As another leading figure in early IR—E. H. Carr—argued in his famous *The Twenty Years Crisis* (1939):

> [w]hat is this thing called International Relations in the 'English speaking countries' other than the 'study' about how to 'run the world from positions of strength'? In other places, at other times, it might be something else, but within those states which had the influence—as opposed to those that did not—it was little more than a rationalization for the exercise of power by the dominant over the weak. There was no 'science of International Relations' ... The subject so-called was an ideology of control masking as a proper academic discipline (Kirby 2022).

Here, Carr hits on a key point shared by many contemporary critical scholars in IR. Far from promoting peace and security for all, IR was really developed to help Europe better govern the world. In other words, IR facilitated Europe's desire 'to divide up the darker world and administer it for Europe's good' (Du Bois, 2003, 52). Read in this way, international institutions like the League of Nations (and later the United Nations, the World Bank, and the World Trade Organization) celebrated in IR as serving the global common good, actually serve the interests of the Western powers.

This alternative story suggests that International Relations was, and in many ways remains, a colonial field of study: 'IR was from the moment of its disciplinary conception, together in substance and spirit, imperial and national in character', and inherited 'the coloniser's model of the world' that rested on a white supremacist worldview (Saurin in

Gruffydd Jones, 2006, 24–26). In other words, in this reading IR's imperial mindset is rooted in a racist vision in which different peoples are of unequal worth in global politics. This is a big and unsettling claim. So, let's pause to reflect.

REFLECTIVE ACTIVITY 8.7

Consider the following question:

What are the strengths and weaknesses of origin story two?

Is it fair to suggest that IR is an imperial or racist academic field? Why/why not?

If so, what should be done? Should we scrap it entirely and come up with a new one? Or can we change it to make it better?

Discuss your answers with a friend or classmate.

Even if we accept this version of events, surely things have improved today. The successes of anticolonial movements in bringing about formal decolonisation from 1947, we might think, brought an end to the violences of empire, and consequently IR will have seen the error of its ways. Surely, imperialistic arguments would no longer be acceptable in IR texts and racialised ones less still.

Unfortunately, Postcolonial and Decolonial IR scholars argue, several hallmarks of the imperial mindset remain today, only in a different form. Much like the form of colonial domination changed from territorial to economic and cultural from the mid 20th century, these scholars argue that the *language*, rather than the extent, of Western domination has altered. What happened, they show, is that the explicit language of empire has been replaced by euphemisms and code words which appeared to respect formerly colonised states' sovereignty. This is the case, for instance, in IR's dominant theories. For example, **Hegemonic Stability Theory** (HST) is a Realist-inspired theory which argues that the world is likely to be most stable if there is a dominant power—a hegemon—in charge. Critics argue that such a hegemonic power is none other than an imperial power. In HST, Eurocentrism has gone from being explicit to be 'subliminal', cloaked in the language of value-free social science (Anievas et al., 2015, 95). The difference is that the language is sanitised so that the theory appears more benign. In addition to imperial tropes becoming subliminal, so too have issues of race and racism, to which this chapter now turns in Section 8.4.

8.4 RACE AND RACISM

Conceptualising race is difficult because it is at once real and not real. We have all experienced or witnessed moments when issues of race come into play in everyday life, such as how people are treated differently by airport security personnel, noticing whether or not our teachers and professors are from the same ethnic groups as us, or experiencing an increased risk of being targeted by police when walking through a particular neighbourhood. And yet, in scientific terms, the idea of race and racial difference has long been discredited.

As anthropologist Franz Boas demonstrated over one hundred years ago, the claim that different races exist which exhibit specific behaviours and biological characteristics is false. In doing so, he showed that race is not a biological or natural phenomenon but rather located in cultural assumptions and stereotypes.

These ideas were further developed by philosopher Alain Locke, who showed in 1916 that race was a 'sociological construct'. He argued that so-called races 'have neither purity of blood nor purity of type'. Instead, they maintain their cultural meaning because of a cultural 'fetish of biological [purity]' (Henderson in Anievas et al., 2015, 23). These insights showed that races do not exist biologically. They are, rather, social constructs which impose meanings and hierarchies on people and their bodies. What this means, importantly, is that racial categories are *not biological* but rather *political* in the sense that they develop and change through *power relations*: 'race is neither objective nor neutral ... There is power involved in constructing race' (Thompson in Anievas et al., 2015, 46).

Scholars of race and racism argue that this social construct is specific to the modern era. This might at first seem unconvincing—we can certainly think of xenophobic acts carried out in the ancient world and Middle Ages. However, scholars argue that race and racism are products of modernity:

> [T]he practice of assigning properties of the human body onto 'character', which began with seventeenth-century European travellers, paved the way for the later emergence of race as a biological fact and a social problem. Pre-modern peoples also engaged in colonialism, but this type of colonialism did not produce, and was not produced by, race-based hierarchies. So while the ancient Aztecs, Athenians and Azande were sexist, slave-holding and xenophobic in matters of citizenship and language, they were probably not racist in either the ordinary or scholarly sense of the term. In contrast, modern-era Europeans, whose expanding empires moved to establish boundaries between the superior whites and the inferior non-whites, were certainly racist because they purposefully ordered and re-ordered people on the basis of assorted physical (biological) traits such as skin colour, hair and nose (Vucetic in Anievas et al., 2015, 102).

This suggests that the emergence of 'race' as an organising theme is linked to the modern European imperial project and the rise of 'scientific' modes of study which claimed that biologically distinct races existed.

During the late 19th and early 20th centuries, proponents of scientific racialism claimed it was possible to rank people on a scale broadly corresponding to the lightness or darkness of their skin, with the white race (of which all the researchers were members) attributed the highest levels of intelligence, perseverance, instinct for order, and love of liberty (Vincent, 1982, 659). This coincides with the heyday of European empire. Indeed, imperial conquest was justified by **Social Darwinist, eugenicist,** and white supremacist ideas which ranked people on the basis of race. Such ideas were used to justify enslavement, genocide, ghettoes, land grabs, and apartheid (Vucetic in Anievas et al., 2015, 102).

This leaves us with something of a problem. If race has been shown to be a scientifically obsolete concept, why do so many people feel the effects of racism in global politics? Despite its constructed character, it is undeniable that race and racism have serious real-world consequences. It would be both empirically and morally wrong to suggest that because race is socially constructed its effects are not real. So how do we make sense of this contradiction?

Racism can be described as 'the belief, practice, and policy of domination based on the spurious category of race' (Henderson in Anievas et al., 2015, 20). Here, while race as a category is treated as 'spurious'—meaning false or unconvincing—racist actions and attitudes are real. A major source of confusion in current debates, from Black Lives Matter to decolonising the curriculum, is whether or not you have to *mean to be racist* to be racist. When we think of the word 'racism', we might think of speech or actions which deliberately target a person or group because of how they look, where they (appear to) come from, or how they talk or dress. In this framing, racism involves intentional forms of violence, abuse, or intimidation. It follows, in this rationale, that if you don't behave in these ways, you are not racist.

While these aspects of racism are certainly very important, they are not the end of the story. Racism is not limited to specific acts of violence or aggression. It is similarly not limited to intentional behaviours. IR scholar Olivia Umurerwa Rutazibwa gives the example of the children's Christmas tradition of *Zwarte Piet*, meaning 'Black Pete', a figure who accompanies Saint Nicolas' arrival in the Netherlands and Flanders, Belgium. *Zwarte Piet* is a group of individuals who paint their faces black, wear afro wigs and period costume, and mimic a Caribbean accent, as they help Saint Nicolas distribute toys and sweets, and scare children into behaving well though the year. In the story, if they do not behave, *Zwarte Piet* will kidnap or beat the children. *Zwarte Piet* is presented as both threatening and absurd, a bogeyman who needs to be told what to do and repeatedly gets things wrong.

Since 2015, there have been protests and demonstrations to end this tradition because it is harmful to Black people. In the wake of the murder of George Floyd in the US and the increasing momentum of the BLM movement, as shown in photo 8.4, these campaigns have grown.

Photo 8.4 **BLM protests aim to end violence against Black people, but have been met with anger and backlash.**

© Matteo Roma / Shutterstock.com

And yet they face considerable opposition. Protests have been met with anger, violence, racial slurs, and even Nazi salutes. Many people in the region argue that the tradition of *Zwarte Piet* is not racist, and that campaigners are making a fuss over nothing. As Rutazibwa explains, they ask: 'How can a children's tradition be racist? It was not meant to be racist, hence it is not racism … [I]f it doesn't look like something Hitler would have done, it's not racism' (Rutazibwa, 2016, 194).

And yet protestors against *Zwarte Piet* argue that the tradition is racist even if people do not intend it to be. They claim the tradition is rooted in colonial and imperial hierarchies in three key ways: first, it presents Black people in the slave labourer narrative; second, it depicts them as stupid, clumsy, and absurd; and third, it frames them as dangerous and frightening to children. This is a form of representational harm. As Amma Asante, a member of the Dutch Parliament of Ghanaian origin, explains, while she would look forward to Christmas as a child, she recalls being called *Zwarte Piet* as an insult: 'So there comes a moment that you're like, oh, my God. Something doesn't feel OK, you know, especially when somebody is mad at you and they call you Zwarte Piet. Oh, my God. So it's an insult? You mean me? You think I'm Black Pete? You think I'm dumb, I'm stupid?' (Warner, 2020). As activist Jerry Afriyie also explains, 'I was a child and not politically aware, but I realized realized we played this dress up with this character who is dumb, who is silly, who doesn't know much, who needs someone to lead the way, who keeps messing up, who is looking very ugly, and then realising that I am the butt of the joke, I was 12 years old when I realised it' (Garen et al., 2019).

Importantly, this representational harm has serious real-world consequences for Black people both in terms of how they are treated by others and how they see themselves. As Afriyie explains, 'we have seen many examples of children coming home and jumping in the shower trying to wash their skin off because the children at school are teasing them that they are ugly, that they are dirty. One girl recently was asking why can other kids get clean, but I can't? Why is my dirtiness permanent? And she was referring to her skin.' Campaigners say that such incidents are related to the dehumanisation and hierarchisation of people in traditions like *Zwarte Piet*, which is why the tradition should end.

REFLECTIVE ACTIVITY 8.8

Take a pause here and reflect on the example of *Zwarte Piet*.

Why is it that some people do not view the tradition as racist?

What does this example tell us about the nature of racism in global politics?

Discuss your answers with a friend or classmate.

As this example shows, racism exists beyond individual acts that someone does deliberately. If we think back to Chapter 5, we showed that violence can be direct and physical, but it is often structural and immanent, within the structures of society and our patterns of thought and language. As such, racism is not always something one intends to do. Equally, it is not always immediately visible, especially to those of us not on the receiving end. Such structural rather than deliberate individual racism has also been shown to be prevalent in academia, as Section 8.4.1 explores.

8.4.1 **RACE AND RACISM IN ACADEMIA**

Students from all over the world who come to study at Western universities often find themselves being taught by white professors. In the UK, for example, just 1% of professors are Black; that's just 160 out of a national total of 22,855 (White, 2022). This ongoing problem has prompted students to ask: 'Why isn't my professor Black?' (Jahi, 2014). Over the last several decades, many academic fields have been taking account of their racist origins and practices, and developing new theories and methods which seek to be non- or anti-racist. New approaches such as **Critical Race Theory**, Postcolonial and Decolonial Theory, and Black, Intersectional, and **Third World Feminism** (as discussed in Chapter 3, Section 3.4.2) have challenged conventional hierarchies between the subject (researcher) and object (person or group studied) in academic research. These approaches have shown that academic research has often led to Western scholars presenting the non-West as viewed from their perspectives. This involves biases, inaccuracies, and stereotyping.

This process can be described using Edward Said's (see photo 8.1) notion of **Orientalism**. Said uses this term to describe the ways Western scholars across a number of scientific and social scientific fields have for centuries created dominant understandings of what people and cultures from non-Western parts of the world are like. This process is closely associated, he argues, with imperial conquest. As the West conquered and occupied non-Western countries, it sent with its armed forces a large number of scholars from fields including biology, botany, and mathematics. These scholars studied the colonised world in order to understand it, and gain a foothold in it. In doing so, they created knowledge about the people and places of the colonised world. As we explored in Chapters 2 and 3 however, the production of knowledge is never free of *power relations*.

The knowledge produced by European scholars about the colonised world presented an inaccurate picture of the people and places studied because it was infused with European assumptions and stereotypes. Said gives the example of the 60,000 books that were written by European authors about the non-West between 1800 and 1950. These books contained, and kept repeating, tropes about the places and people they depicted. They painted a picture, Said explains, of the Orient's 'sensuality, its tendency to despotism, its aberrant mentality, its habits of inaccuracy, its backwardness' (Said, 1979, 204–205). Because people from these areas had no way of responding to and correcting them, excluded as they were from Western academic and public debate, these portrayals were perceived by readers as true.

Following the logic of binaries, discussed in Section 8.3.1 and in Chapter 3, by representing the non-West in these unfavourable ways the West presented itself as the polar opposite of these things—as serious, democratic, rational, accurate, and progressive. The Orientalist knowledge produced had the effect of creating a caricature of 'The Oriental' which, Said explains, has the effect of 'obliterating him as a human being' (Said, 1979, 27). These tropes furthermore legitimised the West's imperial mindset by implying that it had a duty to help the non-West rid itself of their inferior modes of thinking and governing.

This theme of the West controlling the representation of the non-West relates to Du Bois's (see photo 8.3) idea of **double consciousness**. Writing about racism in the United States, Du Bois describes how white people's prejudicial assumptions about Black people come to distort how Black people see themselves, creating a split in their sense of identity. On the one hand, Du Bois explains, Black people understand themselves as normal, good, and valuable people. On the other hand, however, white people's negative assumptions about them stick in their minds and alter this self-perception. He explains that Black people are compelled to see themselves through the eyes of the white people who look at them unfavourably:

It is a peculiar sensation, this double-consciousness, this sense of always looking at one's self through the eyes of others, of measuring one's soul by the tape of a world that looks on in amused contempt and pity. One ever feels his two-ness, – an American, a negro; two souls, two thoughts, two unreconciled strivings; two warring ideals in one dark body, whose dogged strength alone keeps it from being torn asunder (Du Bois, 1903, 3).

REFLECTIVE ACTIVITY 8.9

Take a pause here and consider these questions:

What does Said mean by 'Orientalism'? How useful is this for understanding academia today?

What does Du Bois's idea of 'double consciousness' mean? What does this tell us about the relationship between imperialism abroad and racism at home?

Discuss your answers with a friend or classmate.

Prefiguring debates about *intersectionality* (as discussed in Chapter 3), early Black liberation activist and scholar Anna Julia Cooper (see photo 8.5) corresponded with and influenced Du Bois. Cooper's book *A Voice from the South* (1892) can be read as setting out a

Photo 8.5 **Anna Julia Cooper. Cooper was born into slavery in 1858 in North Carolina, and later became an accomplished author, educator, and public speaker. She was one of the founding figures of Black Feminism and the fourth Black woman in the USA to earn a PhD.**

C.M. Bell Studio Collection (Library of Congress)

'triple consciousness' that included being a woman (Staton-Taiwo, 2004). In a speech to the World's Congress of Representative Women in 1893, she argued: 'Let woman's claim be as broad in the concrete as the abstract. We take our stand on the solidarity of humanity, the oneness of life, and the unnaturalness and injustice of all special favoritism, whether of sex, race, country, or condition. If one link of the chain is broken, the chain is broken.'

These ideas were taken up later by Audre Lorde (see photo 8.6), who argued that even within the feminist movements of the mid 20th century, ideas and texts authored by women of colour were excluded. These exclusions functioned, she argued, as a form of 'othering': 'As white women ignore their built-in privilege of whiteness and define woman in terms of their own experience alone, then women of Color become "other," the outsider whose experience and tradition is too "alien" to comprehend' (1984, 110).

REFLECTIVE ACTIVITY 8.10

Take a pause here and consider these questions:

How does Cooper's discussion of avoiding favouritism and instead considering sex, race, country, and condition affect Du Bois's idea of 'double consciousness'?

Is Lorde correct to argue that the exclusion of women of colour from feminist debates amounts to a form of 'othering'?

Discuss your answers with a friend or classmate.

Photo 8.6 **Audre Lorde highlighted how women of colour were excluded from feminist movements, ignoring the 'built-in privilege of whiteness' of such movements in the Western world (1984, 110).**

Having examined these themes in academia in general, Section 8.4.2 examines how they manifest in the field of IR.

8.4.2 RACE AND RACISM IN IR

While academic disciplines as diverse as history, philosophy, sociology, cultural studies, literature, media studies, feminism, and linguistics have spent a good deal of time reflecting on their racist origins and changing their methods and assumptions to correct this, mainstream IR for the most part has neglected to do so. Indeed, the topics of race and racism remain taboo in mainstream debates, arguably even more than questions of empire. Raising them is treated as somehow impolite, biased, or politically loaded. Such questions are better left, it is suggested, to other fields of study like domestic politics or area studies. This suggests a 'norm against noticing' race and a 'racial aphasia' in IR (Henderson in Anievas et al., 2015, 26).

In recent years, however, more and more scholars are challenging this avoidance and asking: 'Why is Mainstream International Relations Blind to Racism?' (Bhambra et al., 2020). These scholars argue that issues of race and racism are of growing importance in global politics, not least because we are currently in the midst of a global 'racist resurgence' (Nisancioglu, 2019, 3), with anti-immigrant, Islamophobic, and white supremacist discourses and groups on the rise. Du Bois argued a century ago that '[t]he problem of the twentieth century is the problem of the color-line, – the relation of the darker to the lighter races of men in Asia and Africa, in America and the islands of the sea' (Du Bois, 1903, 13), and this question remains crucially important if we are to understand and rectify the unequal distribution of power and wealth in global politics.

Scholars in IR have noted several ways that race and racism play key roles in the discipline. First, they suggest, IR theory draws heavily upon explicitly racist traditions of thought. Indeed, somewhat embarrassingly, several of the key 'founding fathers' of the field turn out to be deeply racist. Woodrow Wilson, after whom the first professorship in IR was named, was in fact a white supremacist who supported the Ku Klux Klan and worked to re-segregate the US government and civil service. Recognising this, Princeton University in the US has recently announced their decision to remove his name from their School of Public and International Affairs (Lehr, 2015). Yet most IR scholars still present him as a pioneer of freedom and democracy, particularly in their teaching. And the University of Aberystwyth's website continues to refer to him as 'the man whose name is synonymous with the creation of a League of Nations for the maintenance of international justice and the preservation of peace' (see here https://www.aber.ac.uk/en/interpol/about/#our-history).

Similarly, Immanuel Kant (see photo 4.2), often taught as a key inspiration for Liberalism in IR, was explicitly racist: 'Kant developed a theoretical scheme positioning races in a hierarchy on the basis of cultural and intellectual capacity and civilisation. Kant places white Europeans at the top, followed by Asians, with black Africans and Native Americans at the bottom, arguing that both Africans and American Indians were incapable of intellectual advancement or education to a high level and incapable of self-government' (Gruffydd Jones in Anievas et al., 2015, 70). Much of Western Enlightenment philosophy, which underpins Liberalism, shared or built upon in different ways Kant's racial hierarchies, resulting in the Occidentalism and white supremacism of the 19th and 20th centuries. In this framing, far from a consensual social contract underpinning global relations of governance, global politics has long been organised through a **racial contract** (Mills, 2011).

Second, as with the shift from explicit to subliminal imperialism, the language of race and racism may have been removed from IR—including avoiding discussion of the racism of the field's founding fathers—but the racial hierarchies underpinning key terms and concepts persists. For example, while the explicit invocation of racial difference has disappeared, the **failed states** discourse 'reproduces in new ways features of earlier modes of racialised thought' (Gruffydd Jones in Anievas et al., 2015, 72). Such subtle racialised hierarchies are also at work in terms like **development**, which places humanity on a linear trajectory on which the West has arrived at an ideal point while the non-West lags behind, which legitimises Western intervention like SAPs to bring them up to speed. Such examples suggest that IR has become good at invoking race without speaking its name (Younis, 2018, 354).

The reason these issues are not widely discussed, scholars argue, is that they are wilfully ignored. Like questions of empire and imperialism, talking about race makes people uncomfortable. To admit that IR has a problem when it comes to race is to admit the possibility that IR scholars are doing something wrong, that we might be doing things that are race-blind or racist. One can, of course, see why the orthodox story remains popular among IR scholars. After all, it is far easier to stand in front of a lecture theatre full of students and tell them about a field characterised by lofty goals of peace, justice, and security than it is to confess problems of enduring imperialism and structural racism.

So, what should be done to tackle the enduring problems of racialisation and racism in global politics and IR? One option might be to do away with the category of race altogether. As a scientifically obsolete term, it may be that its use causes more harm than good. Alternatively, we could substitute 'race' with a different term, such as **ethnicity**, which is more accurate and less politically charged. On the other hand, it is possible that we should keep referring to race because it is an important marker of identity with which many people identify. In a context where cultural imperialism seeks to absorb and appropriate difference, racial identities can be important to minority groups. Some scholars, such as Rutazibwa, argue that we should continue to talk about race even though it may be difficult and uncomfortable. As she explains, we should keep using the 'R word' 'because we still live it on a daily basis and it somehow seems impossible to think it away or beyond it … [The] strategic use of the R-word has an important role to play, as both a critical and analytical device in the study of IR' (Rutazibwa, 2016, 198–199). As scholar and activist Angela Davis has argued, in a racist society it is not enough to be nonracist; we must be *anti-racist*.

REFLECTIVE ACTIVITY 8.11

Before we conclude, take a pause here and consider these questions:

Does it matter that the founding fathers of IR and its theories were racist?

Should we get rid of the term 'race' in IR or is it important?

Is Davis correct that nonracism isn't enough, and that we should rather be anti-racist? What might this look like in practice?

Discuss your answers with a friend or classmate.

8.5 CONCLUSION: DECOLONISING IR/GLOBAL POLITICS

This chapter has challenged the myth that empire is a thing of the past and examined the mystery of why it is broadly sidelined by mainstream International Relations despite its clear importance for the field. It has argued that while their manifestations may be different to earlier historical times, imperialism and racism remain alive and well today even where we do not intend or recognise them. So, what can we do to improve the situation of those who are harmed by imperialism and racism?

In recent years a series of movements to decolonise the university and end structural racism have emerged which combine Postcolonial and Decolonial Theory with concrete campaigns such as Rhodes Must Fall and Why Is My Curriculum White? These activities have resulted in new publications (Bhambra et al., 2018) and toolkits (SOAS, 2018) on how to decolonise the university. A number of universities now have working groups, action plans, and student-led initiatives to decolonise their curricula. And academic associations like the International Studies Association and British International Studies Association have begun to examine and reform the structural racism at work in our institutions and societies (Shilliam, 2020, 152).

However, dismantling structural racism and imperialism is a big task and involves long-term work on many fronts. The intention to decolonise, much like the intention to avoid racism, is not in itself a guarantee of success. Accordingly, campaigners have noted a series of key areas which will help promote this agenda. First, it is necessary to decentre or 'provincialise' Europe (Chakrabarty, 2000). This involves admitting and rectifying the Eurocentrism of the university. When analysing an event or problem, we should consider not just how it appears from the West's perspective but also from other vantage points.

Second, we must learn to think differently about how we study and relate to people in different times and places in global politics. Because Orientalist scholarship that frames the (usually assumed to be Western) researcher as the active subject of knowledge production and the non-West the raw material or passive object of study is still prevalent, we need new research methods and practices which emphasise the agential co-production of knowledge by all parties concerned.

Third, we need to include new topics, concepts, and materials in our scholarly activities. Instead of assuming that knowledge only exists in formal academic spaces, we need to explore artefacts like oral histories, media publications, and philosophical traditions from all over the world to gain a clearer picture of how people think about themselves, their histories, and their activities in the global arena.

Fourth, it requires that we reconsider how and what we teach students about the field by 'decolonising the curriculum'. This should involve rewriting programmes, modules, and reading lists to include voices and perspectives from outside the West. While these steps are important, however, they are not sufficient according to many Post- and Decolonial scholars. Because, as this chapter has shown, colonialism and imperialism are at work at the level of our core disciplinary concepts and theories, we need to dig deeper and seek to address this by 'decolonising our minds' (Thiong'o, 1986).

REFLECTIVE ACTIVITY 8.12

Take a moment here to consider the following points:

Should we seek to decolonise the curriculum? If so, how can this be done? If not, why not?

What does it mean to 'decolonise our minds'? How might this be accomplished?

Discuss your answers with a friend or classmate.

As noted above, there remains considerable resistance in IR to admitting and tackling these problems. This chapter has argued that such reluctance is a problem because it discounts the harm done to people who are affected by imperialism and racism. A denial of, or indifference to, this harm is itself a manifestation of the imperial mindset because it implicitly (and sometimes explicitly) explains it away through abstract ideas of progress or—as we saw in the case of *Zwarte Piet*—through claims it is not really a big deal. As such, making light of or denying the violence of empire amounts to a *perpetuation* of colonial violence because these behaviours ignore or mock the sense of injustice felt by many previously colonised people and their descendants. Breaking with such an imperial mindset involves hard and long-term work to expose and challenge the power relations which even today structure how the world is ordered and whose lives matter in global politics. The good news is that challenges to imperialism and racism are gaining momentum, and that everyone can get involved in working towards positive change.

 Access the online resources at www.oup.com/he/hirst1e for case studies to help contextualise your understanding of key concepts, further reading recommendations to guide you through your reading, and a library of web links to journal articles, blogs, and video content to help you take your learning further.

CAPITALISM

READERS' GUIDE

Chapter 9: Capitalism addresses the mystery of why many people claim that capitalism is the only viable economic system. The chapter contests the myth that capitalism operates as a system of free enterprise independent of state involvement. Instead, it shows that rather than operating in a separate economic sphere, capitalism is a deeply *political* system with far-reaching effects on the international system today. In doing so, it invites you to think about how adopting a new way of thinking about capitalism, as well as how a world after capitalism might look like, can prove insightful in both academic and practical terms.

9.1 INTRODUCTION

We have discussed throughout this book how globalisation has transformed our economic lives. This is also visible on an everyday level. Our grocery shopping customarily includes apples from Chile, peppers and vine tomatoes from Spain, kiwis from Greece, prawns from Vietnam, and so on. As surprising as this may sound, the mass availability of these products coming from all over the world is a rather recent phenomenon. The more complex the product, the greater the chances that a number of companies, located in different countries, have been involved in its production process. Some of you might own an iPhone (see also discussion in Chapter 1), which you will most likely have bought not far from where you live, but which has been assembled and produced elsewhere. This is what Richard Baldwin (2016) has called globalisation's 'unbundling': over time, much more of what we consume is produced in remote places in ways that, despite the long history of transregional sea routes (Abulafia, 2019), were certainly not as common before the Industrial Revolution.

According to Baldwin, this process of unbundling began in the period often referred to as the 'first globalisation', but it has accelerated dramatically in the wake of the technological transformations of the past half-century, most notably the information and communication technology (ICT) and the logistics revolutions. These have led to the emergence of what we usually call **global value chains** (GVCs) or global commodity chains (GCCs). This is why we own shirts proudly claiming to be 'designed in London' and made in Sri Lanka or Malaysia, and French-brand furniture built in China with Malagasy wood.

Returning to the iPhone, its production requires Apple to provision raw materials, turn them into manufactured components meeting specific standards, assemble them, and sell the final products wherever customers can afford to purchase them. Typically, at least forty countries are involved in the iPhone's value chain (see Photo 9.1 below). Raw materials come from a range of countries spanning from Bolivia to the Democratic Republic of the Congo. While Apple exerts control from the mines to the post-sale repair and maintenance operations, it does not own all facilities involved in the extraction, production, and assembling process. Rather, through **outsourcing** and **offshoring**, it relies on a large and constantly shifting network of suppliers.

This has implications for instance in terms of who bears legal responsibility for exploitative work practices along the iPhone's value chain, such as the reliance on child labour in parts of the mineral extraction process, well documented by reputed organisations such as Amnesty International (2016) and more recently addressed by Apple.

The total cost of extraction, production, assembling, and transportation, including labour costs, is in the USD 400–450 range depending on the specific iPhone model

Photo 9.1 **Though you may have bought your iPhone locally, components will have come from about forty countries: a global value chain.**

(Tricontinental Institute for Social Research, 2019). Why is it then that iPhones typically cost nearly twice as much? Two main explanations are usually given. First, the activities adding most value to the iPhone, most notably in the form of research and development (R&D) making the iPhone an innovative product, but also activities related to marketing, advertising, and branding, are not factored in the production process. Second, Apple's owners and shareholders need to be compensated for the risk they take in investing in a product that might fail. Profits and dividends are the reward for the far-sighted investment strategy of CEOs. While we should not discount the intuition and endeavour of individual entrepreneurs, this narrative neglects the fact that a number of power relations impact on this outcome. These involve for instance relations between Apple and its suppliers, but also more generally between these corporations and both their home governments and the governments hosting part of their operations. It also depends on the relations between entrepreneurs, management, and workers at each step of the relevant global value chain.

While more than half-century has passed since their emergence, GVCs as we know them are a recent development in the history of capitalism. To better understand their importance as a key feature of today's capitalist economy we need to discuss capitalism and trace its transformations over time. This is what we do in Section 9.2 of this chapter. Section 9.3 then returns to GVCs and the functioning of contemporary capitalism, and how it affects global politics today. Sections 9.4 and 9.5 shift the focus on how capitalism relates respectively to crisis and to poverty and inequality. Through this journey, we will expose some of the myths about capitalism, from defining it in terms of free enterprise to understanding it as a self-equilibrating system to the so-called 'retreat of the state' in the age of globalisation. This will in turn allow us to explore the mystery regarding how dominant approaches to IR neglect the formative and continuing influence that capitalism has on the international system.

9.2 WHAT IS CAPITALISM? WHY DOES IT MATTER FOR GLOBAL POLITICS?

The working definition of capitalism adopted in this chapter is a straightforward one: capitalism is a system in which immediate producers do not own the means of production required to guarantee their subsistence; instead, capitalists do. While staying within the parameters of this definition, capitalism has changed considerably over time. To make sense of these transformations, we can look at how the literature on the international division of labour identifies three main periods in the modern era. The first sees an international division of labour along colonial lines, organised around hub-and-spoke relations of exploitation between the imperial cores and their respective colonies. Built on the back of slavery and dispossession enforced by colonial trading companies—the first modern transnational corporations (TNCs, see Section 7.3)—since the 16th century, this model was predicated on the imposition of high tariffs against manufactured products coming from the colony (most notably India's craft textiles), accompanied by the tariff-free transfer of raw materials (in this example, cotton) to the imperial metropole, where it would become a manufactured product to be exported back in the colony as cloth. This import/export model became even more pronounced as other European countries followed Britain on the path towards industrialisation and empire-building, leading to the concentration of industrial manufacturing in Western Europe.

The second period, the so-called classical international division of labour, consolidates after the Second World War. While the term 'classical' is itself problematic, as it presupposes a rather Eurocentric gold standard of 'appropriate' division of labour, in many respects this is the period in the history of modern capitalism in which economic growth was most sustained in most regions of the world and with some measure of distributional equity. This phase was characterised by mass production and mass consumption, according to the so-called 'Fordist model'. Crucially, and here we see the Eurocentric element, it was based on the dramatic concentration of manufacturing in the 'triad' of North America, Western Europe, and Japan, which also absorbed about four-fifths of the primary products from the rest of the world.

It is only with the third and 'new' international division of labour, characterised by the fragmentation and geographical dispersal of the production process, enabled by the ICT and logistics revolutions, that GVCs become possible. Again, the role of TNCs in this process cannot be underestimated, not only in the form of **foreign direct investment** (FDI) but also of sheer trade volumes: TNCs currently account for more than two-thirds of world's trade in goods and services, with a significant share covered by intrafirm trade in intermediate inputs (i.e. components transferred between facilities of the same company located in different countries).

Hence, capitalism has changed significantly over time. In fact, capitalism has not always been with us. Rather, capitalism is a historically specific system for organising the production, distribution, and consumption of goods and services. Insofar as these activities are essential for sustaining human life on this planet, in the form for instance of food, shelter, clothing, the effects of capitalism on human societies go well beyond what we normally conceive of as 'the economy'. For instance, capitalism reaches deep into the organisation of family life, as highlighted by the literature on social reproduction (Bhattacharya, 2017), which shows how an extensive set of practices and norms must be prevalent on a rather capillary level in order to shape how we grow up and are socialised as workers, as consumers, and so on.

This arguably banal observation on the historical specificity of capitalism enables us to go beyond a rather common myth, which presents capitalism as the expression of a universal human disposition. This view was perhaps most eloquently expressed by Adam Smith, with reference to the very idea of division of labour, though admittedly Smith conceived of it on a much smaller geographical scale. In his words (1982 [1776]: Book I, Chapter II):

> This division of labour, from which so many advantages are derived, is not originally the effect of any human wisdom, which foresees and intends that general opulence to which it gives occasion. It is the necessary, though very slow and gradual consequence of a certain propensity in human nature which has in view no such extensive utility; the propensity to truck, barter, and exchange one thing for another.

When looking to the consolidation of IR as a scholarly field in the early 20th century, one cannot but notice the limited attention devoted to the historical specificity of capitalism just discussed. To make sense of this mystery, we need to return briefly to the foundational myth of modern international relations (see also Chapters 1 and 7). Insofar as it presents the 1648

Treaty of Westphalia as its founding moment, IR has had the privilege—and the limit—of a historical view where the emergence and consolidation in north-western Europe of statehood and sovereignty on the one hand and capitalism on the other blur into one another. It should then not come as a surprise that major IR traditions have effectively bracketed out capitalism as a constant throughout the history of modern international relations. As a result, many IR classics speak directly of 'the economy' or 'the market' (see for instance Gilpin, 2001), often treated as synonyms. However, while capitalism is undoubtedly an economic system, and hence a type of 'economy', it is only one among several, as demonstrated for instance by the prevalence and diffusion of feudalism in the past, and by attempts at building communist economies in the second half of the 20th century. Additionally, capitalism is both broader and narrower than the idea of 'the market'. It is broader because the market focuses chiefly on the mechanism of exchange, which is only one of the organising principles of economic systems in history. Karl Polanyi (2001[1944]), for instance, emphasised the importance of redistribution and reciprocity as organising economic principles. The former is based on a central entity—be it a government or a feudal lord—redistributing part of what is produced and exchanged to members of their society, while reciprocity identifies a form of exchange of goods or labour based on the expectation that this will be reciprocated, typically at some point in the future. Even within exchange itself, scholars like Marcel Mauss (1990[1925]) outlined how dynamics of gift exchange are altogether different from those of commodity exchange. But capitalism is also historically narrower than the market, insofar as markets have empirically existed long before any form of economic organisation that could be construed as capitalist, and are likely to exist also after capitalism.

REFLECTIVE ACTIVITY 9.1

Take a few minutes to reflect on the economic activities that you conduct in a given week, pertaining to how you ensure that you reproduce yourself, meet your basic needs, and contribute to the welfare of other people. Then, consider the following questions:

How many of these activities are driven by the principle of exchange? How many by redistribution? How many by reciprocity?

Among the activities driven by reciprocity, how many occur in your relations with your loved ones? Why is this?

The tendency to conflate economy, capitalism, and market in classical IR literature is a symptom of the mystery regarding IR's silence on capitalism, which is expressed in a contradictory relation. On the one hand, the economy has been kept outside of the core remit of IR, and indeed since the marginal revolution (see Section 7.2) it has been conceptualised as a sphere of social activity outside of politics. If power is central to politics, as discussed in Section 3.1, the depoliticisation of the economy is bound to lead to the neglect of those power relations that predominantly assert themselves in the economy. This will produce limited analyses of global politics that are unable, for instance, to account for unequal power dynamics between TNCs and small and medium enterprises (SMEs), or between employers and employees. Such an approach contrasts with how foundational thinkers of the liberal canon such as Adam Smith and David Ricardo foregrounded relations of production, distribution, and consumption in their work. On the other hand, somewhat paradoxically, microeconomics has long served as the ground for the analogical modelling of IR. This is central to Kenneth Waltz's hugely influential *Theory of International Politics* (1979). As outlined by Teschke and Wenten (2016), Waltz makes two key moves. First, he considers states as akin to the *homo oeconomicus* of microeconomics: rational, with a clear ranking of their preferences, and maximising their utility, here understood in terms of security as survival in the international system. Second, Waltz's work posits a law of how units in such an international system interact that is meant to apply throughout history, no matter whether we are talking about the Maya civilisation, the Greek city states, or the British Empire. Similar tendencies also permeate realist IPE. Gilpin (2001, 211), for instance, accepts that 'the market has its own logic', but this is one that fails to include power considerations, entirely left to the politico-security sphere. As a result, the specificity of capitalism, and of the multiform configurations that this takes, are largely overlooked.

We have thus already established two important points. First, capitalism is not the expression of a timeless and universal human disposition. One of the inferences from this first finding is that we have very little reason to believe that capitalism will go on indefinitely into the future. It is more likely that, like feudalism and other economic systems before, capitalism will also have an end. This opens up the possibility of thinking a world beyond capitalism, to which we will return in the conclusion to this chapter. Second, capitalism is not a stable economic configuration, and it has experienced significant transformations in its history, with GVCs a defining feature of capitalist production today. These morphing abilities pose an interesting question to which we now turn our attention in Section 9.2.1: if capitalism has changed rather dramatically throughout its history, what are the distinctive and persistent features that enable us to speak of 'capitalism' to begin with? How can we define 'capitalism'?

9.2.1 **TOWARDS A DEFINITION OF CAPITALISM**

One answer to the definition of capitalism is that it is a system based on free enterprise. This view is common for instance among authors associated with the **Chicago school of economics**, and it was popularised by the Nobel laureate Milton Friedman. In *Capitalism and Freedom*, Friedman develops an analogy inspired by Hayek, whom we have already encountered in Section 7.4.1. Insofar as it is free of the arbitrary whims of government intervention, an economic system based on free enterprise is not only the best guarantee of a free economy but also protects the exercise of political freedom, as the private sector will act as a counterbalance against government power. However, the conflation of capitalism with a free enterprise system is both theoretically problematic and historically incorrect. Already in 2012, *The Economist*, one of the most influential liberal publications (see Zevin, 2019), published a special report focused on 'the rise of state capitalism'. While this was presented as a distortion of how economic systems should function, it nonetheless conceded an important point: economic systems like the Chinese one, which rely extensively on government intervention and state ownership of major corporations, are still capitalist (see Photo 9.2). This is very much in keeping with a long tradition acknowledging the active role of the state in capitalist development. In the early 20th century, German sociologist Max Weber (1978

[1922], see photo 5.3) wrote about 'political capitalism', an expression recently revived by Branko Milanovic (2019) to capture the main features of the Chinese economic system.

While one may argue that because of the imbrication of power, violence, and the law, capitalism is always already political, we need not go that far to dispel the myth that free enterprises are an essential condition of capitalism as an economic system.

In sum, in the liberal view of economy, buyers and sellers are only constrained by their own free will, and interact with one another as equal under the law, each of them disposing of their property as a commodity exchanged equivalent for equivalent (my labour power, your money as wage). A utilitarian motive drives each person entering the market. Such an understanding of equality under the law, however, neglects the position from which individuals enter into any market exchange. A delivery courier might well decide to sell their labour power to Amazon for a wage, and both enter into this contract as equal under the law. Does this imply that they also enjoy the same leverage in determining the conditions of that exchange? Do power differentials (i.e. substantive inequality despite legal equality) affect how these exchanges occur in the marketplace? The individualist approach underpinning much liberal thinking fails to provide a satisfactory answer to these questions. As a result, the relevance of pre-existing social property relations is entirely sidestepped. Their historical centrality comes into full view if we look at the historical transition from feudalism to capitalism.

REFLECTIVE ACTIVITY 9.2

The Economist special report mentioned in Section 9.2.1 suggested that '[t]he crisis of liberal capitalism has been rendered more serious by the rise of a potent alternative: state capitalism, which tries to meld the powers of the state with the powers of capitalism'. It then claims that state capitalism can claim 'the world's most successful big economy for its camp [and] some of the world's most powerful companies'. Back in 2012, the analysis was primarily focused on so-called BRIC economies (Brazil, Russia, India, China). With more than a decade of hindsight, consider the following questions:

Would you agree with the central assertion of the article that 'state capitalism is the most formidable foe that liberal capitalism has faced so far'?

To what extent does this opposition between liberal and state capitalism shed light on contemporary global politics? How does this obscure other important dynamics?

According to Marx (see photo 2.3), this transition cannot be understood without referring to **primitive accumulation** (Marx, 2004 [1867]), that is, the process by which workers and direct producers are dispossessed of the means of subsistence and production. This occurred through a variety of measures, including for instance the violent eviction of peasants from the land they collectively cultivated, sanctioned by law, during the enclosures in the late 18th- and early 19th-century Britain. It also occurred much earlier, most notably through the Spanish and Portuguese conquest of the Americas from the late 15th century onwards, through the appropriation of land and natural resources on the part of colonial administrations, which would then typically reallocate them in the hands of individuals and corporations hailing from the metropole. According to Marx, this very accumulation of means of production and subsistence makes up for capital, which accrues in the hands of a minority (capitalists), while forcing producers to sell their ability to work in order to guarantee their

Photo 9.2 **Recent research has focused on the rise of 'state capitalism', for example with reference to China, given the role of government intervention in the Chinese economy.**

© ESB Professional / Shutterstock.com

own subsistence. This systemic power imbalance means that propertyless wage labourers must accept a wage below the value they add to the products now owned by capitalists. In Marx's terminology (2004 [1867]), ownership of the means of production means that capitalists extract **surplus value** out of their employees' labour. Hence, the exploitation of workers is part and parcel of the functioning of capitalism: it is a feature, not a bug.

We are thus approximating a working definition of capitalism as a system where immediate producers do not own the means of production required to guarantee their subsistence; capitalists do.

9.2.2 CAPITALISM BEYOND PRODUCTION

If this definition of capitalism is primarily centred on production, it also has wide-ranging implications for reproduction, distribution, and consumption. It is worthwhile to outline them here. Dispossession of immediate producers from the means of production and subsistence has implications for how workers, their families, and communities reproduce themselves not only biologically and physically, but also in terms of the roles they are expected to perform in society. The first, and most immediately visible, consequence is that social reproduction also becomes increasingly dependent on the legally equal but substantively unequal exchange that occurs on the market. If you lack other sources of income such as profits or rent, a wage is a necessary condition to put food on your table and provide shelter and clothing for yourself and your loved ones. As long as these basic needs are exchanged as commodities, a wage is a precondition for accessing them. This market dependence for social reproduction also had, and still has, heavily gendered and racialised consequences. The 'male breadwinner model' that prevailed since the emergence of capitalism imposed disproportionately large social reproductive duties on women, who were tasked with the physical, emotional, and social upbringing of younger generations as well as with household chores. In times of globalisation, women's greater participation in the workforce has often had two effects on social reproduction. On the one hand, it has led to women carrying a 'double burden', insofar as an active working life has not been accompanied by a reorganisation of the gendered division of domestic and reproductive labour. On the other hand, women's participation in the workforce has displaced social reproduction onto migrant women, establishing what Arlie Hochschild (2015) aptly termed 'global care chains'. Whether in the US, Sweden, or Qatar, this displacement of reproductive care is demarcated along a colour line that is symptomatic of **racial capitalism**, which refers to how the functioning of capitalism presupposes and reinforces racial hierarchies be they in global care chains or in the crew composition of container ships (Khalili, 2020).

REFLECTIVE ACTIVITY 9.3

The spring of 2020 saw protests in a number of countries on issues such as the commemoration and celebration via statues of slaveholders and slave traders, as well as police brutality, and inequality. All these issues cut primarily across racial lines, finding a key catalyst in the Black Lives Matter movement. In light of your knowledge of these events, consider the following questions:

To what extent, if at all, does capitalism play a role in creating these grievances?

Do you find the concept of racial capitalism helpful in making sense of the protests?

Does this matter for global politics? How?

When discussing distribution, it is helpful to refer to the state, which in its capacity as enforcer of the rule of law and holder of the monopoly of violence plays a major role in 'protecting' and legitimising the gendered and racialised imbalances just discussed. Law is essential to sanctioning and entrenching the ownership of means of production, and to shielding it from attack, insofar as it is presented—problematically but often successfully— as existing and operating outside politics rather than being itself a product of politics and power relations, as discussed in Section 6.2.1. Coercion and punishment are used against those who fail to follow obligations as enshrined in law, irrespective of the responsibilities of the individuals under consideration, as witnessed for instance by the wave of home evictions in several US states in the wake of the Covid-19 pandemic. Legally sanctioned violence also featured prominently in how states and empires facilitated primitive accumulation via dispossession in the colonies. Much like primitive accumulation itself, these mechanisms are very much still in place, for instance in the form of private militias (or even local police forces) shielding the activities of extractive companies in areas where the law and coercive state forces might not reach successfully.

On the other hand, however, the state has also provided a mechanism for addressing these systemic imbalances via redistribution. Forms of progressive taxation, whereby people earning more are expected to pay a proportionally larger share of taxes, have enabled the development of free healthcare, free education, a pension system, unemployment allowances, and more in a number of countries, for instance in Nordic countries such as Norway, Sweden, and Finland. As a result, especially following the Second World War, many Western European countries 'decommodified' key services, to use Esping Andersen (1990)'s influential term. Government policies effectively removed from the realm of market transactions, and hence of commodities, a range of activities and services such as education, which in some cases not only became free for all but also entailed a monthly grant from the government to university students, which still exists in the countries mentioned above.

REFLECTIVE ACTIVITY 9.4

Decommodification can make some services available to everyone for free irrespective of income and status. As a result, a young member of the Swedish royal family, or an heir to the IKEA business empire, could go to university for free exactly like the child of an unemployed parent. Consider the following questions:

Do you find this to be a fair arrangement?

From an equity perspective, would you favour a fee-paying system? Why/why not? And from an efficiency perspective?

Recent literature has brought into focus how the features of the welfare state, at times truly progressive, are themselves predicated on the perpetuation of unequal power relations dating back to the colonial era (Bhambra and Holmwood, 2018), as also evidenced by the hierarchy implied in the 'classical' division of labour mentioned in Section 9.2 between the industrial Global North and a Global South conceived primarily as natural resource reservoir, and occasionally as outlet market. Rather than enabling the emergence of welfare policies in poorer states, globalisation and the shift in global production away from the Global North appears to threaten the conditions enabling the existence of the welfare state in wealthier economies to begin with. Offshoring production leads not only to fewer manufacturing jobs domestically but often also means that companies pay fewer taxes to their home government, which thus finds it hard to sustain similar levels of welfare expenditure. Finally, receiving a disproportionately large share of income and wealth also has implications for consumption. Wealthier individuals and households often engage in what Thorstein Veblen (1994 [1899]) termed **conspicuous consumption**. This phenomenon shows the extent to which what we desire to own does not depend solely on individual cost–benefit calculations but is fundamentally social. Some goods have not only the benefit of being enjoyed by their owners, but also of conferring a specific status upon them. Owning a private jet, for instance, is often taken as a key element of distinction between the super-rich and the 'merely' rich. Such a consideration is relevant from our perspective in light of the globalisation of consumer culture, which is arguably more pronounced among elites, who are more likely to come into contact with one another while also sharing a medium of communication (more often than not the English language). Very much in line with what is discussed in constructivist IR, this enables processes of socialisation, whereby the consumption preferences and patterns of the new elites from historically poorer countries are presented as a variation of those of Western elites, at times with features exaggerated almost to the point of caricature, as depicted in popular culture products such as the 2018 film *Crazy Rich Asians*. This contrasts starkly with the dramatic increase in household indebtedness in countries like the US and the UK, with credit card spending, mortgages, car loans, student loans, and the like compensating for stagnant or falling real wages (that is, wages once inflation is deducted). In times of precarious employment, lower-income households might become even more dependent on short-term credit and find themselves unable to repay their debt, while often victimised for their lack of financial savvy in a way entirely abstracted from the systemic features of low pay, insecure employment, cheap and poorly supervised credit provision.

Hence, capitalism is the dominant system for organising production, reproduction, distribution, and consumption. It has in many ways reshaped our planet and our life within it. Despite this importance, capitalism has received scant attention in much classical IR literature, on the grounds of what we can now see as a limited and limiting distinction between politics as the sphere where power operates and economics as the realm of market relations. While fundamentally defined by capitalists' ownership of means of production, which in turn compels workers to sell their labour power so as to ensure their subsistence, capitalism has taken different forms over time, and for this reason we need to pay closer attention to its contemporary configuration. We thus need to return to GVCs.

9.3 GLOBAL RESTRUCTURING, STATES, AND CORPORATIONS

In the introduction to this chapter we primarily focused on Apple because it is arguably the most thoroughly researched corporation. There are few reasons to believe that other tech giants would fare much differently if they were similarly put under the microscope of investigators and researchers. Hence, the brief outline of the iPhone's GVC in Section 9.1 holds broader implications. On the one hand, as with all transformations in global politics, we should ask the *cui bono* question emphasised by Susan Strange, whom we have already met in Chapter 7. Who benefits from this global restructuring of production? On the other hand, we should also consider the specific role of states and corporations in this latest transformation of capitalism. These are the primary concerns of this section.

9.3.1 WHO BENEFITS?

The question pertaining to the 'winners' and 'losers' in the restructuring of capitalist production that has occurred over the past half-century can be addressed on a number of levels: first, with respect to which companies and workers are integrated and which ones are marginalised by this restructuring and, second, with respect to the distinction between capital and labour. To understand this, we should cast a critical look at reports published by international organisations on the effects of GVCs. A large number of studies have been extolling the virtues of GVC integration as the most effective route to development: the 2020 World Development

Report (WDR) was significantly titled 'Trading for Development in the Age of Global Value Chains' (World Bank, 2020). While corroborated with a number of examples primarily from East and Southeast Asia, this narrative neglects the fact that it is materially impossible for all small companies to be integrated in GVCs, because of both the limits to global demand for goods and the concentration of power and wealth in the hands of **buyer firms**, which benefit from diversifying suppliers and generating competition among them, but have no incentive in integrating any companies that might adversely impact their profit margins. These companies benefit from what we might call a 'reserve army of suppliers' to draw upon to address temporary surges in demand and keep costs in check. While exacerbated in the present, these unequal power relations, as we saw earlier, are an inherent feature of capitalism.

REFLECTIVE ACTIVITY 9.5

Since the 1990s, argan oil has become a globally sought-after hair, beauty, and health product to the point of becoming the world's most expensive oil (see Photo 9.3 below). Argan oil is produced by cracking, roasting, grinding, and kneading the kernel of the argan tree nut, which grows only in the forests of southwestern Morocco. Argan oil production has existed for centuries, and it has historically been carried out by Amazigh women. As global demand for argan oil boomed, major corporations in the cosmetics industry moved towards establishing a GVC for argan oil, primarily based on local cooperatives. As detailed by Kate Meagher (2019), these elements coalesced into a narrative of women empowerment, local empowerment, and minority empowerment, and it has had a positive impact on Morocco's balance of payments, as argan oil exports increased from 1 ton in 1996 to 1,387 tons in 2016 in a period in which the price of argan oil increased twelvefold.

Photo 9.3 **As argan oil became a valuable commodity, corporations in the cosmetics industry established a GVC, which ultimately increased the economic vulnerability of the Indigenous women who harvest argan nuts.**

© Luisa Puccini / Shutterstock.com

However, a closer look at the argan oil GVC shows that through this process of integration via cooperatives global firms gain 'greater control over women's labour with minimal changes to their precarious economic situation', that 'connections into value chains have also provided rather minimal improvements in women's access to resources', and that 'evidence at the household level confirms the limited economic benefits of argan oil production'. In more general terms, '[i]ntegration into the global argan oil value chain tends to increase dependence on a low-return forest product among people with few other options, intensifying rather than reducing vulnerability' (Meagher, 2019, 81–83). In light of these outcomes, consider the following questions:

Are the 'minimal improvements to women's access to resources' worth the costs and risks brought about by integration in the argan oil's GVC for the local community? On whose perspective are you basing your answer?

Is the concentration of benefits in the hands of global cosmetics corporations problematic? Why/why not?

Is GVC integration in sectors such as argan oil desirable? Why/why not?

The example in Reflective Activity 9.5 shows how local companies often become 'captive' of buyer firms. As a result, their negotiating power is limited and limits the benefits they can accrue, while simultaneously exposing these companies more to sudden shocks in their value chains. Companies specialised in the most labour-intensive parts of the production process are often at a disadvantage, even when they employ more people than the lead firm they work with. This is the case for the largest company in Apple's supplier network, Foxconn, whose profits are not only much lower than Apple's but have also declined sharply over time (Chan, Pun, and Selden, 2013).

Costs and benefits of global capitalist restructuring are unequally distributed at a second level: that between capital and labour. Is it only businesspeople, in the form of owners and shareholders, who benefit from this process or are workers also better off? There is no doubt that the share of workers employed by globally integrated companies has increased dramatically in recent years. However, the 2020 WDR also claims that the labour share of the proceeds from GVCs has declined: as more companies and workers are drawn into global networks of extraction, production, assembling, distribution, and sale, a smaller share of revenues is paid as wages. This does not necessarily imply a loss for workers as they may be getting a smaller share of a much larger pie. However, it certainly shows that the benefits of GVC integration are distributed unevenly. This depends on the one hand on the much greater mobility of capital vis-à-vis workers, which provides a formidable exit threat, for instance moving investments elsewhere. This is leveraged by lead firms to extract more favourable conditions pertaining to labour and environmental regulations, tax rates, and so on. On the other hand, these conditions are not a given but are instead influenced by policies set not only at state level but also at larger (e.g. international organisations) and smaller scales (e.g. regions, cities, municipal authorities).

When it comes to the distributional impact of GVC integration on workers, we must consider two main elements. First, the different geographical location and jurisdiction of workers matters, as does the position and power of the employing company within the GVC. As a result, workers in the R&D department of Apple in Cupertino or of L'Oréal in Paris are most likely better off compared to colleagues working for Foxconn in Taiwan or for a women's cooperative in the Souss Valley, Morocco. Second, one of the greatest purported benefits of globalisation is that it brings about a much greater availability of a wider variety of goods and services at more competitive prices than was previously the case. While these improvements (in type, quantity, availability, and price competitiveness) are themselves still subjects of debate, what is more interesting for us is how this presupposes and indeed creates a tension between the respective subjectivities entailed by work and consumption. As consumers, we have an interest to buy laptops of similar quality and durability at a lower price. As a result, demands for higher wages and better working conditions on the part of workers extracting the coltan necessary for producing our laptops, or of those involved in producing and assembling their microchips, might result in the final seller passing on at least part of these extra costs onto the consumer. While often geographically at a distance, this opposition between consumer demand for lower prices and worker demand for higher wages and better working conditions is not difficult to see.

REFLECTIVE ACTIVITY 9.6

Cambridge economist Joan Robinson (2006, 21) famously argued that 'the misery of being exploited by capitalists is nothing compared to the misery of not being exploited at all'.

Do you agree with this view? Why/why not?

Finally, another level at which the distributional implications of global capitalist restructuring is the geographical one. In 2010, the Organisation for Economic Cooperation and Development (OECD) argued in its *Perspectives on Global Development* annual report that 'the world's economic centre of gravity has moved towards the East and the South, from OECD members to emerging economies. […] This realignment […] represents a structural change of historical significance' (OECD, 2010, 15). The phenomenal rise experienced by China over the past four decades, and the relocation of large portions of global production into East, Southeast, and to a lesser extent South Asian countries has led some IR analysts to suggest that 'the future is Asian' (Khanna, 2019). Following this line of reasoning, globalisation appears to be producing the equalising effects heralded by its advocates, as countries specialise in sectors where they are comparatively more productive, thanks to liberalising policies that facilitate flows of capital, goods, and services. Regrettably, the concrete unfolding of economic restructuring on a global scale does not really appear to conform to this neat logic.

9.3.2 STATES AND CORPORATIONS IN THE GLOBAL ECONOMY

Industrialisation has historically been key to successful development under capitalism. This is of course the case with the Industrial Revolution in Great Britain and then the European mainland. But it has also been the case much more recently with the countries of East Asia (Chang, 2003), as discussed below. Even the most notable outliers, including for instance oil-rich Saudi Arabia and Qatar, are currently pursuing diversification plans to shield themselves from the extreme volatility in oil prices, best visible in the short venture of oil prices into negative territory in April 2020. GVCs have significantly transformed industrialisation away from the concentration of manufacturing in the triad of North America, Western Europe, and Japan, typical of the classical international division of labour mentioned in Section 9.2. Now, the manufacturing process is not only dispersed across a larger number of countries but also fragmented and specialised in discrete components throughout the production process. As a result, according to Gereffi (2014, 18):

> [W]hile industrialization under the EOI [*Authors' note*: export-oriented industrialisation] model became easier and faster (countries could just 'join' supply chains by performing specialized tasks, rather than 'build' them), it may also be less meaningful. If countries are only engaged in the simplest forms of EOI, such as assembling imported parts for overseas markets in export-processing zones, then they would develop neither the institutions, nor the know-how, nor the consumer markets needed to create and sustain entire industries.

In this context, long-term development prospects hinge not simply on industrialisation but on **upgrading** successfully within existing GVCs, moving from labour- to capital-intensive production. Most successful cases of upgrading are located in East Asia, where the relative geographical proximity of Japan and so-called newly industrialised countries (NICs, also referred to by the orientalising label of 'East Asian tigers': Hong Kong, Singapore, South Korea, and Taiwan) was crucial to enabling a regional division of labour within the global restructuring of production, creating a pattern well captured by the so-called 'flying geese model' (Akamatsu, 1962, see Figure 9.1). This implies selective incentives and temporary trade barriers aimed at fostering internationally competitive exports initially in low added-value sectors (garments in Figure 9.1) to then move incentives and trade barriers to a higher value-added sector to do the same, 'upgrading' towards increasingly more sophisticated exports. Importantly, this successful upgrading creates an opening in the lower rungs of the ladder, historically filled by neighbouring countries adopting similar policies. This regionalisation within globalisation, rather than as a paradox, should be seen as a key ingredient of East Asia's successful integration in the global capitalist economy.

A key distinction between the first and the more recent waves of East Asian late development is well known to IR scholars. While Japan and the NICs were all US allies, and during the Cold War were under the US security umbrella, China is in an altogether different position insofar as it is perceived as an economic and geopolitical rival to the US. This might explain why discussions about containing China's rise have been central to US foreign policy in the region. Very much in line with the focus of the realist tradition in IR on power and security in an anarchic international system characterised by competition and conflict (see for instance Section 8.3.1), a focus on relative gains suggests that dominant powers might be concerned with states that, from their own perspective, are upgrading their economies 'too much' or 'too fast', thus risking upsetting established power hierarchies. At least since the 'great divergence' that saw the West pull ahead of the rest (Pomeranz, 2000), international dominance has since been located on either side of the North Atlantic. Within this broader historical context, the US–China trade conflict can be seen as the most recent attempt on the part of the US to slow down China's return to the status of great power, in line with times when China and India accounted for more than half of global manufacturing (as late as 1800, see Bairoch, 1993) and global output (as late as 1820, see Baldwin, 2016).

Figure 9.1   **The 'Flying Geese Model'.**

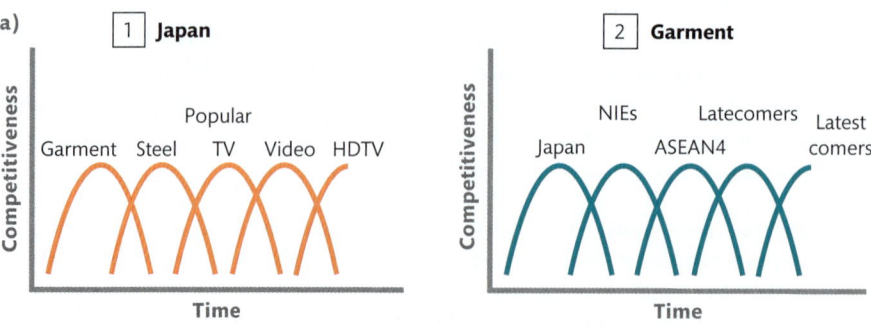

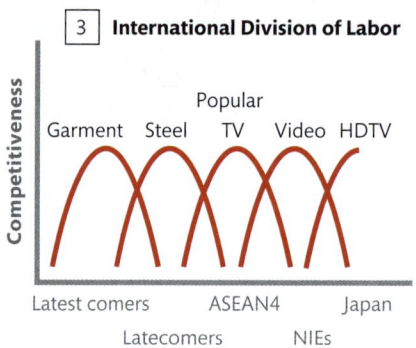

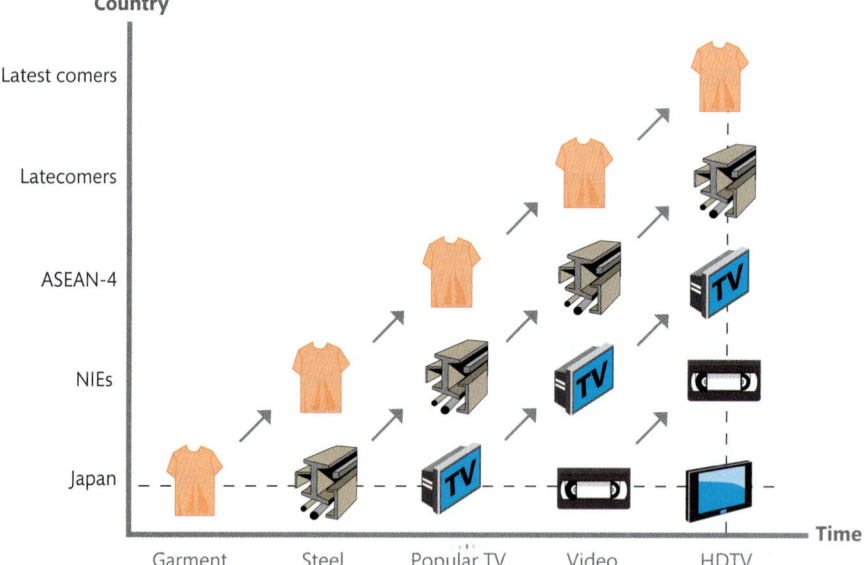

Source: Dr Saburo Okita, "The Flying Geese Pattern of Development", 1985

REFLECTIVE ACTIVITY 9.7

Photo 9.4 **US President Joe Biden meets with China's President Xi Jinping during a virtual summit from the White House, November 2021.**

© MANDEL NGAN / Contributor / Getty Images

In light of the discussion in Section 9.3.2, it might appear that the global restructuring of production, which the US has been instrumental in promoting, has led to the emergence of a major geopolitical rival in the shape of China (see Photo 9.4 above). Consider the following questions:

From a realist perspective, could one argue that the US promotion of globalisation has been a strategic error? Why/why not?

Does this mean that the US imposition of trade tariffs towards Chinese goods is a rational response to China's economic and geopolitical rise?

How does the point above in the main text regarding the historically large size of China's economy affect, if in any way, your judgement of its current rise?

The US reaction to China's ascent highlights the continuing importance of states, but the targeting of increasingly global companies such as Huawei also shows the limitations of a state-centric approach to studying contemporary global capitalism. It is for this reason that we now turn our attention to how states relate to TNCs (transnational corporations). Attracting foreign direct investment (FDI) has become one of the main international economic functions performed by states, especially in the Global South. Up until relatively recently, the majority of FDI occurred within the triad of North America, Western Europe, and Japan: all advanced economies, with comparable levels of infrastructural and technological development. For most other economies, technologies and infrastructures are not really the main draw for potential investors, and a different set of incentives is expected by TNCs.

This typically includes low corporate tax and capital gains tax rates, taken to extreme levels in so-called 'tax havens' such as the British Virgin Islands and the Cayman Islands that do not have a general corporate income tax. It has often also meant lower taxation on those receiving the highest income, with examples such as Egypt, where the maximum tax rate applied to the highest part of income—the so-called 'top marginal income tax rate'—has halved from 80 to 40 per cent between 1979 and 2002 (see *Our World in Data*). Other investment-friendly policies focus on deregulating labour markets, with measures including very low or no minimum wage, and relaxing regulations pertaining to working conditions, often aided by the reforms imposed by international economic organisations (IEOs) as a condition for their loans (see Wade, 2017). Through this so-called **conditionality**, the International Monetary Fund (IMF) and the World Bank have promoted policies that accelerate globalisation, while simultaneously limiting the range of policies that governments can adopt to shield themselves and their population from the adverse effects of this process, especially in the Global South. As evidenced by Ha-Joon Chang (2003), limiting the chances of resorting to these protective measures also amounts to 'kicking away the ladder': after having selectively employed tariffs and other protective measures to aid their industrial and economic development, wealthy countries are now kicking away the ladder that allowed them to climb to the top of the world economy.

REFLECTIVE ACTIVITY 9.8

In Section 7.3.1, we covered the Investor-State Dispute Settlement (ISDS) mechanism, a clause typically included in international and bilateral investment treaties which subjects to international private law controversies between TNC and the host government. Following a 2011 law introducing plain packaging on cigarettes, Philip Morris launched a court case against the Australian government arguing that such a measure breached foreign investment provisions related to trademark rights included in a 1993 trade agreement between Australia and Hong Kong. Philip Morris lost the case and had to pay a multimillion bill covering legal costs.

In other cases, however, it goes rather differently. In 2014, an ISDS tribunal ordered Peru to compensate a Canadian mining company following the cancellation of a mining licence, decided by the government as the company had failed to obtain informed consent for the mine from Indigenous landowners. You can find many more examples of ISDS cases here https://investmentpolicy.unctad.org/investment-dispute-settlement.

In light of the tobacco and mining examples, discuss with a friend the following questions:

In your view, why do governments agree to sign treaties that curtail their policy options and might lead them to incur major costs should they lose an ISDS court case?

Would you characterise the relation resulting from signing bilateral investment treaties as an exploitative one? Why/why not?

What benefits do Western states gain from supporting the international operations of 'their' TNCs? Why do they do it?

Global value chains thus put to rest two pervasive myths, often presented as opposing one another, about the key drivers of capitalism. On the one hand, presenting capitalism as a function of the interests of dominant states fails to account for two major developments: power shifts within capitalism leading to changes in which states are dominant at different points in time; and increased power concentration in the hands of TNCs. On the other hand, this latter trend has produced a diametrically opposed myth, suggesting that globalisation entails a 'retreat of the state' (Strange, 1996), with TNCs becoming the primary driver of contemporary capitalism. If the discussion in this section might lend some support to this thesis, the references we have made throughout to policies, laws, and international organisations show that states and political authorities more generally still have a fundamental role to play in enabling more and more power to be concentrated in fewer and private hands.

9.4 **CRISES IN/OF CAPITALISM**

Another of the myths in the representation of capitalism is that competitive markets act as a self-equilibrating system, enabling prices to adjust until demand and supply meet, that is, until the amount that buyers are willing to pay matches what sellers are willing to accept. The flaws in this myth of self-equilibrating markets have become apparent to anyone growing up in the age of the global financial crisis, and living through the seizing up of the global economy in the wake of the Covid-19 pandemic, with a decade of low growth and high inequality in between. This has in turn led more and more people towards critiques both of real-existing contemporary global capitalism and of capitalism as an economic system.

The instability of capitalism has been noted by some of its prominent defenders and advocates, who argued that crisis provides the conditions for creative solutions and breakthrough innovations. Austrian economist Joseph Schumpeter went even further, suggesting that this is in fact the very operational logic of capitalism, which 'is by nature a form or method of economic change and not only never is but never can be stationary [...] **Creative Destruction** is the essential fact about capitalism' (Schumpeter, 2006 [1942], 82–83). The destruction will have negative economic and social consequences, but clearing the deck—so to say—is an inevitable part of the process and builds the foundations for the next wave of innovation and growth. Such an approach acknowledges the fundamental ambivalence of capitalism, which has provided phenomenal technological advances that for instance enable us to communicate for free with our friends on the other side of the world, but which also devastates the livelihoods of hundreds of millions of people through countless financial and economic crises. The latter, with companies going out of business, entire sectors becoming obsolete, and large numbers of people losing their jobs, is presented as an inescapable wake-up call enabling new innovations. Beyond the questionable calculus between technological advances and human suffering, another often neglected element requiring attention is the uneven distribution of the ambivalences of capitalism: low-income groups not only get to enjoy less the consequences of the economic upswing but also find themselves bearing the brunt of crises and of their management.

Karl Polanyi's work is often invoked to make sense of these tendencies of capitalism. One of the central theses of *The Great Transformation* (2001[1944]) is that economic development is caught within an insoluble tension between improvement and habitation, that is, between technological progress and the emancipatory potential that it holds on the one hand, and the social dislocation and marginalisation that this creates on the other (see Photo 9.5). This is arguably even more salient today, since the shift towards production techniques that are more technologically advanced, for instance in the form of artificial intelligence, entails a reduced need for human work, thus creating the prospects of higher unemployment and of the broadening of the **surplus population**. This element is well captured in the literature on automation and the future of work (Benanav, 2020; Smith 2020).

REFLECTIVE ACTIVITY 9.9

Photo 9.5 **Polanyi (2001[1944]) states that technological progress can enable emancipation, but at the same time causes social dislocation.**

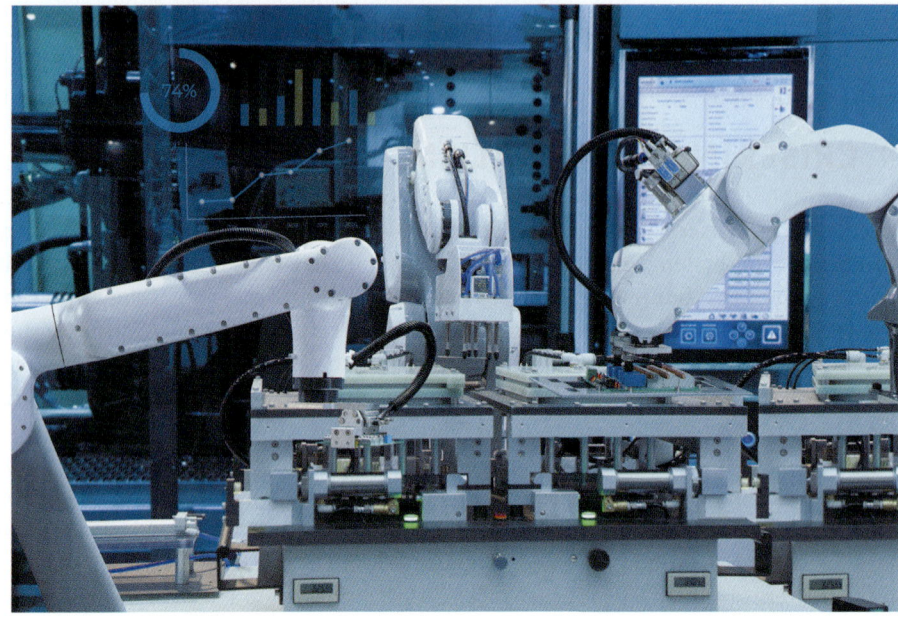

© Suwin / Shutterstock.com

The effects of automation on the present and future of work cannot possibly be underestimated. Most existing research has focused on what automation means for workers in wealthy economies. In the context of poorer economies, automation poses severe risks, including most notably: stunting the potential for manufacturing to drive convergence in incomes; increasing returns to capital vs labour; increasing income inequality between workers; putting rural smallholders under increased strain; increasing insecurity and isolation for workers in the digital economy; and eroding solidarity in wealthy countries (see Norton, 2017, including also possible positive effects).

Consider the following questions:

Does Polanyi's distinction outlined in Section 9.4 between improvement and habitation hold any sway in accounting for these dynamics?

Is the social dislocation produced by automation inevitable?

How many of the risks outlined above also apply to wealthy economies? What does this mean for contemporary global politics?

The myth of self-equilibrating capitalist markets is problematic for another reason: all complex economies require planning, and it is hence misleading to present equilibrium as the spontaneous outcome of the interaction of producers and consumers intermediated only by the price system. The diffusion of logistics from its origins as a predominantly military set of concerns (e.g. How to ensure that a battalion reaches the most favourable position before a battle? How to ensure that weapons are delivered to them when needed?) into a subfield of business and management shows the relevance of coordination problems in a complex and globally integrated economy. In many respects, the turn to logistics is an attempt to address and overcome coordination problems among private transnational actors.

The centrality of logistics to our everyday life often comes into full view only when it fails to produce its intended outcomes. In the wake of the Covid-19 pandemic, supermarkets in several wealthy countries, including for instance the US, experienced shortages in several products, and most notably milk, flour, and eggs (see Photo 9.6 below).

In a situation of lockdown where most of the population is expected to stay at home, it is not surprising that these staples are widely sought after. This was reported in the press in the context of panic-spending on the part of consumers and hoarding on the part of individual intermediators. In the following weeks, a different picture related to the supply side began to emerge. There was no shortage of food, but over the preceding decades the food supply chain for retail and the one for commercial activities, including hotels, restaurants but also schools, had grown apart. In most circumstances, food produced and entering the US would be split about halfway between these two chains. As lockdown measures forced the closure of restaurants, schools, and hotels in many US states, there was a surge of demand in the retail sector. Because of the separation between the two supply chains driven by logistical decisions on the part of private companies, however, it was nearly impossible to divert goods from the commercial to the retail supply chain. As a result, supermarkets experienced major shortages, while a large amount of fresh produce was left to rot in the fields or—in the case of milk—was poured into rivers, thus adding environmental insult to the injury of manufactured shortage.

Photo 9.6 **Empty shelves at a Target store in Montana, USA. Essential supplies were sold in limited quantities during the Covid-19 pandemic as a consequence of supply chain breakdowns.**

© Lyonstock / Shutterstock.com

People who had experienced first-hand the final years of the communist era in Central and Eastern Europe did not hesitate to draw parallels between the two situations, particularly with respect to shortages in food and essential items and the subsequent rationing. So, if planning is also part of what private corporations do, and if both state- and private-led planning can go equally wrong, we find ourselves facing another question: which (and whose) purposes does planning serve? Under capitalism, it is the logic of profit that drives any form of coordination. Free market supporters often invoke Adam Smith's image of the **invisible hand** to outline how what has historically been understood as a private vice turns into a public virtue, as the pursuit of self-interest creates the preconditions for the flourishing of society as whole. As Smith put it in one of the most quoted passages from *The Wealth of Nations* (1982[1776]: Book I, Chapter I), '[i]t is not from the benevolence of the butcher, the brewer, or the baker that we expect our dinner, but from their regard to their interest'. However, neither Smith nor his followers have been able to demonstrate logically and empirically this transformation of private selfishness into public altruism. Additionally, Smith's argument invites us to accept what can be a concretely problematic behaviour today (the pursuit of self-interest) because of the abstract good (greater prosperity) that will, or might, come out of it in the future. In Foley's words (2006, 3), this 'requires a strategy of wholesale denial of the real consequences of capitalist development, particularly the systematic imposition of costs on those least able to bear them, and the implacable reproduction of inequalities that divide people from one another'.

This is not to deny that state planning can also be deeply problematic, and it has proved to be so time and again in history. As Hayek pointed out, the question is not 'whether planning is to be done or not' but 'whether planning is to be done centrally, by one authority for the whole economic system, or is to be divided among many individuals' (Hayek, 1945, 520–521). While the former route led the Soviet Union and its Central and Eastern European satellite states to organise the economy along dictatorial lines, the latter strategy, favoured by Hayek, fails to acknowledge that the production of wealth under capitalism is also profoundly undemocratic, insofar as it gives a much greater weight to capitalists. As Martin Hägglund put it (2019, 4986–4996):

> As an individual capitalist, I am not concerned with the best use of available resources but with the most efficient way to make a profit. Moreover, as a capitalist society, we are not collectively committed to producing for the sake of consumption. Rather, we are committed to producing for the sake of extracting surplus value that can be converted into the growth of capital.

As a result of these dynamics, a capitalist market economy cannot be a rational economic order, and is thus prone to generating multiple crises, 'both through the *overproduction* of commodities we do not need or cannot afford and the *underproduction* of goods we do need but cannot purchase'. The many ways demand and supply diverge under capitalism all 'follow from a principle of production that privileges the accumulation of profit over the satisfaction of needs and the provision of resources for spiritual development' (Hägglund, 2019, 5005–5013).

REFLECTIVE ACTIVITY 9.10

Discuss in pairs the following questions:

According to which principles should economic planning occur?

Can you rank these principles and provide a justification for your choice?

Who should do the planning?

Are these principles the same for different countries? You may want to compare and contrast one country from the Global North and one from the Global South.

Would the same planning principles also extend to the global economy?

Finally, the myth of self-regulating capitalist markets is also dispelled by the tendency towards market power concentration in the hands of few companies. In these conditions, technological innovation tends to slow down, prices go up, and informal agreements between leading companies proliferate. In this regard, we must not reject the insight that competition is an essential precondition for technological advancements under capitalism. The point here, however, is that when left unchecked capitalist markets end up stifling the very competition that makes them so good at innovation. An objection is often raised to this argument: if there are no barriers to entry even monopolies are contestable and hence investors and consumers would recognise a good idea, which would eventually gain traction and challenge the complacent monopolist. In the current era, however, the ability for newcomers to truly contest these monopolies has been curtailed in at least two ways. First, while there may not be formal barriers to entry, the amount of start-up investment needed to challenge platform-based giants such as Amazon, Google, and Facebook are so high that they are beyond reach for pretty much everyone. Second, the amount of wealth and cash reserves that these companies have amassed, in excess of the yearly GDP of many countries, means that they can quite simply buy their way out of trouble, for instance acquiring companies providing a genuinely innovative service. A case in point is Facebook's acquisition first of Instagram and then of WhatsApp, two of the greatest challengers to its own position as a social media and instant communication platform. All these companies and brands, and several more, are now housed within the parent company Meta, providing a vivid sense of the dynamics of market power concentration in the age of 'platform capitalism' (Srnicek, 2016).

9.5 CAPITALISM, POVERTY, AND INEQUALITY

By now, the nature of capitalism as an acutely contradictory system should be clear: its impressive technological transformations have been deeply intertwined with dispossession and poverty. These dynamics are nowhere clearer than in the trajectory of development as a concept and as a practice. Well before it emerged as the language of international organisations like the World Bank, development existed as part of the practice of colonial domination, often inserted in efforts aimed at 'civilising' natives. From its outset, it was a profoundly Eurocentric endeavour, positing the present of the imperial metropole as the future of its colonies.

In the wake of the Second World War, as India's independence from the British Empire gave impetus to decolonisation, newly independent states sought to craft their own path towards development but were soon forced to confront the distance between formal political independence and effective economic dependence. Kwame Nkrumah, anticolonial leader and first prime minister and president of independent Ghana, was acutely aware of this contradiction. In his famous pamphlet *Neo-Colonialism: The Latest Stage of Imperialism* (1965), he argued that relations of economic dependence were perpetuated after decolonisation, most notably through economic channels such as trade and investment on the one hand and resource transfer on the other.

Nkrumah was not alone in pointing out the exploitative nature of the international economic order. Two influential approaches in IPE, dependency theory and world systems theory, study the global economy by focusing primarily on the polarising tendencies of capitalist development, which is understood in terms of the relationship between core and periphery. With its roots in Latin America, dependency theory focuses especially on how global economic integration under capitalism makes rich economies (the core) richer and poor economies (the periphery) poorer. This is often referred to as the 'development of underdevelopment' (Frank, 1966), which according to Raul Prebisch was due to the deterioration of the terms of the trade: over time, underdeveloped countries are able to purchase fewer and fewer manufactured products with the same amount of raw material exports. Along similar lines, Walter Rodney showed the role of European imperialism in the underdevelopment of Africa, with consequences that still reverberate today (Rodney, 1972). While retaining the focus on polarisation, scholars in the world systems tradition have argued that dependency theory excessively simplifies the functioning of the capitalist world system. More specifically, the binary distinction between core and periphery makes it hard for dependency theory to account for cases of successful industrialisation in formerly peripheral states. To this end, Immanuel Wallerstein, the most influential world systems theorist, introduced the concept of semi-periphery, which covers states that have achieved even significant levels of industrialisation but have remained dependent on the core in other respects (Wallerstein, 1976). As the polarising tendencies of capitalist development have become more visible empirically and more salient politically, approaches focusing on the constraints posed by having a peripheral place in the global economy are experiencing a revival (Kvangraven, 2020).

At least partly influenced by these views, many postcolonial states began to call for a New International Economic Order (NIEO) in the late 1960s and the early 1970s. This aimed at restructuring the global political economy in a way that systematically factored in the issue of justice, and hence of how the riches of Europe and North America were based on the dispossession and exploitation of the colonies, but also how current patterns of trade and investment continue to perpetuate these relations of domination. For instance, Utsa Patnaik (2018) has calculated that the wealth that first the East India Company and then the British Raj 'stole' from India in the era between 1765 and 1938 amounts to approximately USD 45 trillion. As it not only identified but also sought to address these historical patterns of exploitation and dispossession, the NIEO provided an alternative view of 'worldmaking after Empire' (Getachew, 2019), which proposed justice as a central principle for reorganising the global economy.

REFLECTIVE ACTIVITY 9.11

The key economic demands advanced raised in the UN General Assembly Declaration 3021, adopted in 1974, which called for 'the establishment of a New International Economic Order', were the following:

1. Price floors below which commodity prices would not be allowed to fall.
2. Preferential tariffs allowing 'Third World' manufacturing exports to enter 'First World' markets with lower tariffs than exports from other industrialised countries.
3. Increase in foreign aid.
4. Alleviation of debt burden.
5. Reform of multilateral institutions to increase the voice of 'Third World' countries.
6. Legitimation of developing country protectionism to promote industrialisation (including greater control over TNCs operations).
7. Enhancement of technology transfer deriving from TNCs investment.

In light of your knowledge of subsequence historical developments, discuss the following:

Do you find an international economic order based on these demands to be preferable to the one we currently live in? Why/why not? On whose perspective are you basing your answer?

Do you find these demands to be realistic today? Why/why not?

The aftermath of the 1973 oil embargo and the increased dependency of governments in the Global South on lending from US commercial banks and international institutions (see Section 7.3.2) ultimately ushered in a major change in the development paradigm in the opposite direction to that pursued by the NIEO. The **Washington consensus** advocated for structural adjustment, privatisation, and liberalisation, and governments throughout the Global South were encouraged, and if necessary cajoled, into pursuing export-led growth as the solution to their developmental challenges, but—contrary to the East Asian experience—without the freedom to selectively use incentives and trade barriers.

Over the past four decades, we have seen several changes in development discourse on the part of IEOs, and the World Bank especially, shifting from structural adjustment to human development and 'good governance', then to the Millennium Development Goals, and most recently to the Sustainable Development Goals. In the process, the definition of development, and hence the scope for intervention on the part of international agencies, has been broadened to include not only poverty but health, education, infant mortality, gender, and environmental issues. While this move away from a growth-obsessed view of development is to be welcomed, none of the fundamental assumptions around the centrality of ever greater market integration into capitalist markets to developmental 'success' has been challenged in any meaningful way.

Despite this broadened definition of development, the ability to lift people out of poverty is often presented as sufficient evidence of the global success of capitalism. World Bank data shows that the share of the world's population in extreme poverty (living on less than USD 1.90 per day) has fallen from 36 per cent in 1990 to 10 per cent in 2015. This is good news that should undoubtedly be celebrated. At the same time, we should always seek to understand the complexities behind these headlines. For instance, demographic growth in some of the poorest regions of the planet means that the headcount of people in extreme poverty has declined much less than the percentage headline. Additionally, two large countries like China and India account on their own for most of this global decline in extreme poverty rates, with China alone lifting more than half a billion people above the extreme poverty line. This is clearly not to say that we should discount their experience, but rather to highlight that we should be aware that this success is heavily concentrated in a handful of countries. Finally, the World Bank itself acknowledges that much work remains to be done: by 2017, over a quarter of the world's population lived on less than USD 3.20 a day, and well over 40 per cent lived on less than USD 5.50 per day (see *Our World in Data*, https://ourworldindata.org/grapher/distribution-of-population-between-different-poverty-thresholds-up-to-30-dollars?country=~OWID_WRL). These figures suggest that large numbers of people are vulnerable to a sudden drop in living standards that might result from major shocks such as famines or economic crises.

REFLECTIVE ACTIVITY 9.12

As late as 1978, China and Malawi had approximately the same level of GDP per capita in current US dollars (156 and 161, respectively). By 2018, China's GDP per capita stood at USD 9,776, whereas Malawi's was below USD 400 (see here: https://data.worldbank.org/indicator/NY.GDP.PCAP.CD?locations=MW-CN).

This is just one, admittedly extreme, example of the extent to which poverty reduction has been concentrated in a handful of countries.

Consider the following questions:

In your view, what explains China's phenomenal economic growth?

Do you find the distinction between 'developed', 'developing', and 'underdeveloped' economies to be of any help in making sense of the dramatic divergence between China and Malawi?

Especially since the late 2000s global financial crisis, this focus on poverty has been complemented by greater attention to the relationship between capitalism and inequality, particularly following the highly influential work by French economist Thomas Piketty (2014). It has now been established that, at comparable levels of GDP per capita, higher levels of inequality are associated with greater incidence of issues pertaining to mental health, obesity, drug, and alcohol abuse, and also erosion of trust both towards government and in communities (Wilkinson and Pickett, 2010). Hence, if we take a broad definition of development, its prospects appear to be weakened by high levels of inequality. In fact, IMF economists have suggested that high inequality has a damaging effect also on economic growth, hampering development also in its narrow economistic sense (Ostry et al., 2014; Dabla-Norris et al., 2015).

Inequality takes a number of forms, but all relate to resources and access to them. These can be material, in the form for instance of income and wealth, but can also relate to unequal access to education, healthcare, legal advice, and much more. Additionally, resources are unequally distributed along different axes, from gender to class to race and beyond, and we should resist collapsing them into one another. By way of illustration, and taking advantage of the amount of data available, a brief discussion of income inequality helps us see how these dynamics play out.

Each measure of income inequality yields a different picture, but it also tells us something about how inequality is affected by capitalism and contemporary processes of globalisation. For instance, inequality within countries as measured by the **Gini index** has increased in most countries over the past four decades. Importantly, inequality has increased more in countries that have gone further on the path of privatisation, liberalisation, and deregulation associated with Neo-Liberalism and the Washington consensus. Such a finding is also confirmed by the literature, spearheaded by Thomas Piketty and his research team and available on the World Inequality Database website (see for instance Chancel et al., 2021), focusing on another indicator of within-country inequality: the share of total income that goes to the top 1 per cent of the income distribution.

Once we shift our focus to international income inequality, the measurement adopted by the World Bank shows a decline since the 1980s. The indicator used by the World Bank—population-weighted income inequality—compares changes in GDP per capita of all countries, weighted by their population size. This measure not only does not tell us anything about inequality within countries but it is one where declining international inequality results simply from large poor countries having higher growth rates than wealthy ones. As detailed by Milanovic (2016), if one excludes China and India from this count, international income inequality has in fact increased since the 1980s. Again, the argument here is not that we should not be considering the impact of the world's two most populous countries on these statistics but rather that when the benefits of capitalist globalisation are so heavily concentrated we should take triumphalist claims with a pinch of salt.

Hence, many of the discussions around 'global convergence', often couched also as 'the rise of the rest' in opposition to the historically dominant West, appear to be based on rather unstable foundations. Indeed, even the convergence in the metrics presenting more positive data needs to be placed in context. For instance, it is true that the ratio between US' and China's GDP per capita has reduced from a factor of 24 to less than 4 in the space of three decades (1990–2019). However, if we look at absolute numbers, the distance has grown much larger, from 22,906 international US dollars in 1990 to 48,495 in 2019 (see here: https://data.worldbank.org/indicator/NY.GDP.PCAP.PP.CD?locations=CN-US for full data). If this is the case even for the most successful developmental story in the history of post-Second World War capitalism, then one may understand why scepticism about the balance sheet of contemporary capitalism has increased so significantly in recent times.

9.6 CONCLUSION

The entry into this decade was marked by two dramatic transformations likely to have long-term implications on our daily lives. Capitalism is implicated in both. One of the first consequences of the Covid-19 pandemic has the been the freezing and contraction of GVCs, lamented by international institutions and global talking shops such as the World Economic Forum. This not only highlighted the centrality of China, and East and Southeast Asia, to the global economy today but it was also the first indicator of the global economic crisis that followed. The second dramatic transformation is the emergence of a transnational movement explicitly demanding social and racial justice. In the Black Lives Matter campaign these demands are framed within an understanding of the current political and economic order as fundamentally unequal and unjust. Within it, asymmetric power relations not only produce forms of violence structurally biased towards specific groups but also generate systems of law that either ignore this violence altogether or at times enshrine and legitimate it. Such an interpretation of the current predicament is at one and the same time ethical and political, and it reaches back into history to highlight the foundational role of empires and colonial rule not only in the emergence of the current global order but also in its continuing logic of operation in a formally decolonised world. Capitalism is once again implicated, and at times explicitly invoked, as one of the globalising and 'worldmaking' processes demanding that we look at global relations beyond the straightjacket of interstate relations.

This element is emphasised throughout this book, as signalled by our preference for speaking of global politics over international relations: all politics is global, and the global increasingly permeates our everyday experiences if in highly uneven and differentiated ways. We have seen this recently for instance in terms of how the global spread of a virus might have long-lasting implications on how we lead our lives, or how protests against police violence in the US can galvanise movements for social and racial justice elsewhere in the world, from similar protests against police brutality in Latin America to the removal of statues of colonisers and slave traders in the UK to, more mundanely, sportspeople 'taking a knee' in solidarity with the Black Lives Matter movement.

Both the material and the moral crisis of the contemporary global order are intimately linked to capitalism but should not be reduced to it. As mentioned in Section 9.2, this crisis poses the question of the temporal finitude of capitalism, and of whether and how capitalism will become primarily part of our history, much like the economic systems that preceded it, rather than the dominating force in our lives that it is today. Literature on post-capitalism and alternative practices of economic organisation have begun to prefigure a world beyond capitalism (see for instance Srnicek and Williams, 2015). Whether, when, and how this will come about is likely to be determined as much by how groups and communities will organise within and across countries as by the 'high politics' of diplomatic cables and G20 summits. For global politics is also the networked articulation of local lived experiences, and insofar as we are able and willing to connect the dots of our everyday lives to the global forces shaping them, we are not simply passive recipients of global politics but can contribute to its making and remaking.

Access the online resources at www.oup.com/he/hirst1e for case studies to help contextualise your understanding of key concepts, further reading recommendations to guide you through your reading, and a library of web links to journal articles, blogs, and video content to help you take your learning further.

THE STATE

READERS' GUIDE

Chapter 10: The State explores the mystery of why the state is treated in IR as the most—or in some theories the only—important actor in global politics. To do this, it challenges the interrelated myths that the state was founded by some divinely inspired social compact (reflected in an ultimately minor 17th-century European Treaty), and that the versions of *sovereignty* (within national boundaries) and *anarchy* (in the international realm) that we know today are the only way to truly understand the mechanics of global politics. These IR building blocks have led us to think that the locus of all power in global politics lies almost naturally and exclusively with the state. Instead, as we have already demonstrated (throughout this book), it is more often states which are shaped and maintained by myriad power relations which operate beyond the remit of state authority.

10.1 INTRODUCTION

It may strike some readers as odd that a discussion on the state should come at the very end of our study of global politics. It is, after all, as philosopher Quentin Skinner once described it, the 'master noun' of modern political discourse (Skinner, 2007). Regardless of what part of the world we find ourselves in, and even from an early age, we have come to gain an almost intuitive sense of the power and presence that is wielded by at least one state over some aspects of our lives (if not most aspects). And yet as the preceding chapters have demonstrated, so many of the concepts and phenomena that we understand to be deeply political in nature—from ethical decision-making to power relations, from cryptocurrency to the codification of rules/regulations—can (and do) often occur without the state looming large as an explanatory variable, cause, or factor. This in no way diminishes the role that it has played—and continues to play—in the experience of these other phenomena.

In the academic study of International Relations, the state—and specifically its modern European variant—has taken on a mythical status of its own. For Realists, it remains *the* central unit of analysis in the study of global politics. According to this particular mode of academic thinking, approximately two hundred sovereign units currently operate around the world, all within a state system defined by anarchy (or the absence of a single overarching authority). This, in turn, creates the defining problematic for the discipline: 'how to conceive of an order without an orderer and of organizational effects where formal organization is lacking' (Waltz, 1979, 89).

To be clear, our slightly unorthodox ordering of topics in no way diminishes the state as a significant *object* of analysis. Indeed, one might argue that, as the 'master noun' of political discourse, it too demonstrates the incredible power of myth and mystery, for it to have retained for so long its vaunted status at the centre of the study of IR. As citizens, we think of national, independence, or liberation day parades which feature our fellow citizens in military uniform, the pageantry of lock-step precision and synchronicity, the plumes of jet fuel exhaust (dyed in national colours) emitted from fighter jets overhead, and prized military hardware rolling through city streets, as state leaders and dignitaries watch on with solemnity.

Photo 10.1 **A display of the British Royal Air Force Red Arrows, and a display of hard power by the state.**

© Becky Stares / Shutterstock.com

This is the colourful, if sanitised, spectacle of hard power (see photo 10.1)—the deployment of which is understood to be solely within the remit of the state in the modern world. In the offices and government buildings at the edges of these events—whether along the Champs-Élysées, Red Square, or Tiananmen Square—we might instead expect to find bureaucrats and mandarins engaged in the diplomacy we have come to associate with the soft power of a State.

Conventional theories of the state (and of IR) tend to treat it as the locus of all power in political life, or at least of the power necessary for the maintenance of the broader global order. But as we saw in Chapter 3, political power exists *before* the state and does not necessarily come *from* it. Rather, the 206 officially and unofficially recognised states in the contemporary system were formed and are maintained *through* power relations, both within those states and across their borders. One of the problems with naturalising our understanding of this political entity as the *given* unit of analysis in the discipline is that it only helps to mask and obscure the power relations involved in both its formation and perpetuation throughout the modern era.

In order to better expose these founding myths—and to better understand their impressive 'staying power' within IR narratives—we will consider in Sections 10.3 and 10.4 three closely related myths. To be more precise, two of the myths relate to the perceived foundation and functioning of state and global politics in the current international order. They are the myth of the social contract, and the myth of the sovereignty/anarchy dyad. The third myth—a chronological one relating to the Treaties of Westphalia (1648) and Versailles (1919)—actually holds a more glorified status within the *discipline* of IR, specifically, than it does in the theorising about *how* global politics operates. Westphalia is understood as the origin of the modern state, and Versailles as the origin of the contemporary state system. In that sense, then, these so-called 'big bang' theories of IR (see Section 8.3.1) are perhaps more 'half-myths' in terms of importance, as they relate to an event and idea which only a small group of people ever deemed crucial to understanding their academic discipline, and germane to our discussion in Section 10.2. But before outlining in detail the problematic contours of these important myths, it would be useful to return to the basic approach we have employed throughout this text, which is to orient our initial appraisals of this 'object' of our analysis (the state) around those personal and lived experiences which give it most meaning. While they may not be *your* lived experiences of state power and pervasiveness, they will hopefully help you to reflect on your own daily lives, and to notice the ubiquity of our relationship with this modern phenomenon, from cradle to grave.

10.2 WHAT AND WHERE IS THE STATE?

One way to think about the ubiquity of the state in modern life is to see it as a constant background to key human milestones—the *hatchings, matchings,* and *dispatchings,* which for centuries had been the purview of religious communities and ceremonies. With regard to births (hatchings), consider that the majority of the 385,000 babies which are estimated by the UN to be born in the world each day are born in hospital. Normally, before a child can even be released from hospital it must be issued a birth certificate, which must list one of two sexes, male or female. If even only 1.3 in 1,000 of these babies are born intersex (i.e. with the physical characteristics of both sexes), as a recent Turkish study suggests

(Aydin et al., 2019), then we begin to understand how even the simple act of completing a birth registration carries far-reaching implications for the life and legal status of those individuals.

In terms of marriage (matchings), consider that the General Register Office in the UK (which lists all births, marriages, and deaths in the country) did not exist before about the middle of the 19th century. From this moment it was the British state which determined who could and could not be legally married (with the attendant rights and privileges bestowed upon such unions). So too with death (dispatchings), the fact that in most countries in the world euthanasia (or assisted suicide) is a criminal offence indicates the role that the state plays even in how an individual might be allowed to die. It need not even be such an obvious example. Consider the recent Covid-19 pandemic, during which healthcare systems around the world—stretched to breaking point by the numbers of hospitalisations—required medical professional bodies (mandated by the state) to draw up plans for who should receive care and who should be allowed to die in the event that such unfortunate choices needed to be made.

For its legal and administrative roles, we tend also to think of the state as the arbiter of national moral and ethical life (see Section 2.2.4), by means of the laws it enacts and as the examples above would also imply. When mores and customs in a society change, we can expect the state to reflect this in the laws it enacts or rescinds. In debates around homosexuality in society, for example, former Canadian justice minister (and later prime minister), Pierre Trudeau, was famous for having stated in 1968 that 'there is no place for the state in the bedrooms of the nation', thereby ushering in changes to the Canadian criminal code which saw the decriminalisation of 'homosexual acts'. Similarly, but with opposite moral intent, Section 28 of the UK Local Governments Act 1988 was introduced so as to outlaw the promotion of the acceptability of homosexuality as a 'pretended family relationship' in state schools during the administrations of Prime Minister Margaret Thatcher. It is worth remembering that this law, which prevented any discussion of homosexuality in school sex education classes (or with much openness even in wider public discourse), was enacted at the height of the AIDS epidemic, which at the time claimed the lives of thousands of people in the UK alone.

Liberalisation or criminalisation of relationships has been a constant tool used by governments, and enforced through the mechanisms of the state, the world over. In 1997, homosexuality was effectively decriminalised in China, even though throughout Xi Jinping's (see photo 4.7) presidency, we have seen systematic government crackdowns on LGBTQ+ NGOs and organisers, reflective more of a government concerned with group organising and protest than with individual personal behaviour (Zhu and Jun, 2021). In 2013, the Russian Duma unanimously passed a law which criminalised the distribution of 'propaganda of non-traditional sexual relationships' which might cause minors to 'form non-traditional sexual predispositions'. Again here it has been suggested that the law reflected more a desire to clamp down on foreign donations to Russian NGOs (a possible threat to Russian state power) than on the private behaviour of citizens (even if this was one clear effect).

Again, as Quentin Skinner suggests (2007), it is near impossible to arrive at a 'neutral' definition of the state, so present is it in all facets of daily life, which still vary across culture, time, and location. We can however identify a number of key roles and functions that have come to be associated with the state in modern times. The list is by no means exhaustive, but almost always includes:

- the ability to tax a population and to redistribute or allocate those revenues;
- the maintenance of law and order; the administration of social welfare provisions;
- the waging of war, and protection of the integrity of a designated territorial area;
- the enactment and enforcement of laws which govern the conduct between legally defined entities (e.g. individuals, groups, organisations, institutions) within that designated territorial area;
- the regulation of the economy and industry (taxes, import tariffs or quotas, the creation of 'free ports', etc.);
- the administration of social welfare programmes.

Through engagement in these activities—combined with the formal recognition of the legal ability to do so by other states—it then operates within the wider context of a state system which, among other things, is tasked with the maintenance of its own relative order. So ubiquitous is the state in contemporary power relations that it becomes *the* primary referent against which other forms and practices of power are judged. We speak of 'global superpowers', of 'failed states', and of 'quasi-states'. And when the private interests of a specific family come to dominate the very operations of state ministries and departments, or to cause the disappearance of billions of dollars of public finances—as was alleged to have occurred by the Gupta family in South Africa in recent years—we refer to it as 'state capture'.

The state is, quite simply, implicated everywhere, if we pause long enough to look for traces of it. Furthermore, one common theme which connects all of the state functions listed above—as well as your own daily observations of the state—is the concept of **sovereignty**. At its most rudimentary, sovereignty is simply the power or authority to rule. For IR scholars, modern debates around the nature of sovereignty can be traced back to the 16th-century jurist and philosopher Hugo Grotius, whose 1625 *De Iure Belli ac Pacis* (The Law of War and Peace) defined the highest ruler in any given context as he 'whose actions are not subject to the legal control of another, so that they cannot be rendered void by the operation of another human will'. And while this definition was written in a European world of kings (and later emperors)—the 'sovereigns' invested with this specific power—we can see how the definition could easily be applied to *any* state where some person or group of people hold this specific type of power.

In recent times, processes of economic, political, and cultural globalisation have led politicians and citizens alike to question whether their own state's sovereignty is being eroded by these global processes. An example of this was the decision of the British electorate in 2016 to withdraw the UK from the governance structures and institutions of the European Union. After four decades of membership in this supra-national organisation, Britain decided to 'take back control' (of money, laws, and borders) from the EU. A decision marked by acrimony (the measure passed in a consultative referendum by a narrow margin), its implications for UK sovereignty will be analysed for many years to come. So, if the state is the 'master noun' of modern political discourse, then sovereignty is clearly the concept which imbues the state with that mastery. Much like the variations of 'state' listed above, so too for sovereignty there are many contemporary iterations (pooled or shared sovereignty, popular sovereignty, absolute vs partial sovereignty).

Finally, before we dive into the three myths of this chapter, it is worth repeating that there is no single useful or sufficient definition of the state. In order to answer *what is* a modern state, we simply cannot rely upon any single set of distinguishing features. Rather we must avail ourselves of the sociological studies developed over many years which suggest the functions and processes we have come to associate with the modern state. This is not to say that certain well-known definitions don't exist. For example, from a 1918 lecture by German sociologist Max Weber (see photo 5.4), entitled 'The Vocation of Politics', we now take as a given the idea that the state is 'a human community that successfully claims the monopoly of the legitimate use of physical force within a given territory'. This three-part definition means that the state is understood to be a state by virtue of territoriality, (monopoly over) violence, and the legitimacy of the use of violence within that territory. On the one hand, this simply yields further questions for exploration (what is meant by legitimate? Does this mean that a state can grant another actor the right to use violence, and do so without losing its monopoly?). On the other hand, it also tells only a very fragmented version of what a state does in the modern world.

More than definition, then, it helps to think in terms of 'definitional contours' to the concept of the state, or a toolkit of functions we can reliably assume most states to engage with. These might include the enforcement of specified rights within a community, the power of taxation (and the concomitant power to distribute that revenue); the provision of certain services (provision of law and order being the primary one); the waging of war (and/or diplomacy) and related to this the assumed desire to maintain the international order within which it operates. Regardless (or perhaps because) of the ubiquity of the state, there are good reasons to ask, challenge and explore the reasons for its primacy in modern life. We now turn our attention to how modern theorists have tended to conceive of the state, how it was thought to have come about (much like with the empires of Chapter 8, its own 'origins story') and how 'the state' came to dominate so completely the thinking, grammar, texts, and practices of contemporary international relations.

10.3 THE MYTH OF THE SOCIAL CONTRACT

In answering the question '*where did the state come from?*' or '*how did the state arise?*', we need look no further than the myth of the social contract. In political philosophy, traditional social contract theory can be defined as one which 'grounds the legitimacy of political authority, and the obligations of rulers and subjects (and the limits thereof), on a premised contract or contracts relating to these matters' (Lessnoff, 1990, 3). That we may not have actual historically documented contracts to refer to need not worry the theorist. As with much of social contract theory, this is often a thought experiment which serves to demonstrate the logic of a particular ordering of affairs. It goes without saying, however, that such thought experiments take place within the minds of specific individuals, with their own lived experiences, histories, and positionality (see Section 1.4). As such, far from the abstract and universal 'origin story' we might wish them to be, social contract theories will often obscure the very power relations that they seek to illuminate.

10.3.1 CLASSICAL SOCIAL CONTRACT THEORY

In the traditional social contract variations of Thomas Hobbes (1651), John Locke (1689), and Jean-Jacques Rousseau (1762), this thought experiment served to explain why an individual or group of individuals might leave the state of nature—where they enjoyed more freedom over their own affairs—in order to join together within a society, under the legitimate rule of a specified political authority. The historicity of an actual contract does not trouble these theorists so much as the basic moral principle '*that men perform their covenants made*'. To modify slightly the questions above, then, our traditional contract theories are mostly concerned with *why* the state arose in the first place, in order to justify a certain ordering of political power to meet certain ends. For the purposes of this brief discussion, we take the 'myth' aspect of the social contract to refer more to its status as a fully fledged 'origin story' of both the modern European state and, by extension, the contemporary global order. Furthermore, in addressing this particular aspect of the myth, we are able to point out the exclusionary power relations (regarding race and gender) which were then hard-wired into the machine of the modern state—in other words, power relations which were justified by a retrospective social contract. To call the social contract a 'myth' is more to question what it obscures rather than to point out what it reveals. As a philosophical mental exercise, it may well still serve a purpose in helping to think through how we would envision the ideal relationship between different components of the modern state. This was briefly touched upon in our discussion of John Rawls in Section 4.3, and will be examined again below.

Thomas Hobbes (see photo 10.2), throughout his life, would often regale friends with the tale that his mother had gone into labour with him in a moment of panic when she learned (incorrectly) that the Spanish Armada had begun its invasion of England in 1588. He joked that for this very reason, he was born '*twinned with fear*'—with a brother who would accompany him throughout most of his life. Indeed, from Hobbes' account of the social contract, we understand that the primary purpose of such an arrangement (moving from a state of nature to the legitimate rule of a political authority) stems from his belief (and fear) that the state of nature is truly a '*state of warre, as in of every man, against every man*'.

In his famous *Leviathan* (1651)—considered by many to be one of the greatest texts of political philosophy, but also certainly the first truly modern political tract—Hobbes sets out what he sees as the reality of a state of nature, wherein basic human diffidence and the desire for each of us to fulfil our own individual desires will always inevitably lead to conflict. He was a sceptic, not a cynic, and his views were no doubt guided by his experience with the wars over religion which ravaged Europe throughout his lifetime, with the beheading of an English monarch (Charles I), and with the never-ending low-grade conflict which Hobbes understood to tear at the fabric of society, in the absence of *security*. His response was to envision a sovereign (or leviathan) whose chief aim was to determine what constituted a threat to the body politic and to counter that threat.

We associate this version of the social contract with the doctrine of absolutism: the idea that once a group of self-interested individuals agree to form a covenant—to create a sovereign tasked with their security—the resulting sovereign has *absolute* authority to decide, to command, and to enforce. A famous version of this idea, taught in many history books, is the statement by the Sun-King Louis XIV of France (1638–1715) who remarked '*l'État c'est moi*' (I *am* the state). What is often omitted, however, is the second

Photo 10.2 **Thomas Hobbes was an Enlightenment-era thinker who contributed to the development of 'social contract theory', a thought experiment to explore how authority is legitimised in a society.**

© IanDagnall Computing / Alamy Stock Photo

part of his declaration, namely '*je m'en vais, mais l'État demeurera toujours*' (I will leave [this world], but the state will always remain). What Hobbes' theory of political authority accomplished was to devise an explanation for political authority which satisfied the shifting political bases of authority in a Europe in deep turmoil in his day. The mechanistic pact he envisioned—for Hobbes' writing at the start of the scientific age was replete with mechanical imagery—forever locked the ruler and the ruled in a mechanical grip. It is not without irony, then, that we suggest that the biblical sea monster (Leviathan)—and specifically its allusions to anarchy and 'warre' in the absence of sovereignty—truly has become a 'ghost in the machine', haunting our notions about perceived threats in the international realm, even today.

The absolutism of the Hobbesian sovereign gave way to an argument for the protection of liberty found in John Locke's *Two Treatises of Government* (1689). For Locke, the state of nature was not as dire as the one depicted by Hobbes. In simple terms, his social compact first creates a society in which individuals agree to come together in order to better protect their individual pursuits (especially private property), and then agree on a sovereign power which will protect those fundamental pursuits. For Locke, life in nature is not bad, but it could be better if we banded together, fostering and protecting social interactions (including trade and commerce). This two-part original contract opens the door, in limited circumstances, to a revolt against the authority if it is not fulfilling its primary aim or purpose. From here, then, it is not a difficult mental leap to arrive at our most detailed account of this foundational theory in *Du Contrat Social* of Jean-Jacques Rousseau (1762).

The famous first line from his text, tells us that '*man was born free, and everywhere he is in chains*'. By this Rousseau (see photo 10.3) meant to suggest that the state of nature was actually the most ideal of places and that society and the state had eroded the true freedoms once enjoyed by man. For Rousseau, only through a social contract—establishing a government which acted upon the 'general will' (of the people)—could our civil freedoms be secured.

Photo 10.3 **Jean-Jacques Rousseau. In contrast to Hobbes' idea that in the state of nature life is 'poor, nasty, brutish, and short' (*Leviathan*, i. xiii. 9), Rousseau presents the state of nature as a place of true freedom, and suggests that the introduction of the state eroded these freedoms.**

© Pictorial Press Ltd / Alamy Stock Photo

In contrast to Hobbes, we already begin to see a curtailing of the power of the sovereign in that it may only have authority over matters that are of *public* concern.

Furthermore, in Rousseau we have a more detailed understanding of the different roles and functions played by different *organs* of the body politic. He distinguished between legislative and executive functions and, although he believed aristocracy to be the most stable form of government, he argued that any foundation for political authority was only legitimate insofar as it was able to capture and act upon the general will of the citizens of that territory. Less mechanistic than the Hobbesian version, Rousseau developed his anatomical imagery for 'the body politic' in a 1755 article on *Economie politique*. Here, he describes it as a single organism or entity. In this account, the sovereign is the head, laws and customs are the brain, the sensory organs are the judges and public officers, commerce/industry/agriculture are the mouth and stomach ('making nourishment available to all'), public finance is the blood, and the citizens are the limbs and body (6). In a later formulation of the same idea (1762), he describes sovereign authority as comprising two parts: legislative power is the heart, and executive power is the mind. He then astutely points out that while a man could conceivably live without a mind, without a heart he would surely die (121). For Rousseau, then, this tongue-in-cheek analogy serves the deeper political aim of advocating for the primacy of legislative over executive power as a better reflection of 'the general will'.

Rousseau's use of anatomical imagery to describe the foundations of legitimate political authority leads us to a series of observations about the effects that the social contract and the foundations of the modern state have had on different bodies and different people. As Charlotte Epstein (2021) suggests, the state and the modern political subject (the citizen) are actually 'co-constituted', insofar as neither of these two things existed before the relationship itself. This juncture in history was not simply one of political and religious turmoil. If anything, these were symptomatic of a much deeper ontological and epistemological rupture. As Epstein explains:

> . . . This is how the problem of origins came to be formulated as a political problem, not simply as a matter of birth or generation, but of founding and ordering. The state of nature is but one of its expressions. Autonomy was at stake, or how the subject learned to rely on itself to find its own sources of law (nomos) and to wean itself from a heteronomy, a law received and imposed from without, in the dual sense of from authority and from a 'nature' that was fast disappearing anyway (Epstein, 2021, 266).

In a world in which meaning itself was in chaotic flux (where the Earth no longer sat at the centre of the known universe, where kings were no longer divine), the search for the source of knowledge turned inwards and so, logically, many of the signs, symbols, and meanings that we arrived at in seeking our new truths—political or otherwise—became internalised in the human body. More importantly, the constant construction and repetition of the contrast between inside and outside allowed for the perpetuation of a rational (and ranked) internal order, and the exclusion of a chaotic or anarchical outside nonorder. In light of this, it is no surprise that discussions of liberty and equality, meticulously thought through in Locke's contract, did not apply to the 'savages' of the newly 'discovered' colonies.

REFLECTIVE ACTIVITY 10.1

Consider for a moment the three versions of the social contract you just reviewed from Hobbes, Locke, and Rousseau.

Does one of them appeal to you more than the others, in terms of explaining the legitimacy of the political authority of a state over your life and individual freedoms?

How necessary is it to appeal to the idea of some original 'contract' in order to justify current/contemporary power arrangements within the state?

10.3.2 CONTEMPORARY CRITIQUES: THE SOCIAL CONTRACT REVISITED

While we already considered questions around 'Orientalism' and race in our discussion of empire in Chapter 8, we should also pause here to consider the implications of the social contract on questions of race and the non-Western world, as they developed into the contemporary global order. For Charles Mills (1997), the 'racial contract' actually *underwrites* the modern social contract insofar as it created not simply racial exploitation (through colonialism, slavery, and empire), but helped to create the category of 'race' itself. This is in line with Epstein's analysis in Section 10.3.1. Mills considers the racial contract a 'naturalised' version of the social contract. In other words, rather than representing some ideal (for clearly, it was not), an understanding of the racial contract provides a guide for the actual historical record which blossomed from the abstract thought experiment. He understands the 'racial contract' as a necessary conceptual bridge between two segregated worlds in political philosophy—between the abstract discussions of rights and justice on the one hand and:

> . . . the world of Native American, African American, and Third and Fourth World political thought, historically focused on issues of conquest, imperialism, colonialism, white settlement, land rights, race and racism, slavery, Jim Crow, reparations, apartheid, cultural authenticity, national identity, indigenismo, Afrocentrism, etc. (Mills, 1997, 4).

In locating this theory within a proud tradition of oppositional Black theory, Mills contends that the racial contract not only has better explanatory power than the nonracial social contract theory but that, in laying these truths bare, it ultimately opens space for the normative potentials of social contract theory to finally be realised. One contemporary example of the critique of the naturalised social contract can be seen in the activism of the Movement for Black Lives (M4BL). If the very purpose of the contract is to consider questions of justice and the rights of all individuals within a society, then the murder by police of George Floyd in May 2020 focused the debate around the actual lived freedoms and liberties (or lack thereof) within the American state. By highlighting this one specific crime—combining as it did questions of race/racism, arbitrary state power, and the historical impunity of officers of that state—M4BL have advocated specific policies of redress including reparations (for slavery), wealth redistribution, and an overhaul of the criminal justice system. These demands for systemic change can be seen as doing the work of Mills's 'conceptual bridge'—in better aligning the abstract discussions of rights and justice with the injustices experienced by Black Americans.

Contrary to the naturalised reading of the racial contract, but no less damning of the traditional social contract model, Carole Pateman's *The Sexual Contract* (1988) presents the original version as one of 'conjectural history', which omitted an equally important sexual contract by upholding patriarchal right (while claiming it to be contractual) and presenting it as 'universal'. For that reason, she suggests that it is more appropriate to think of it as a sexual-social pact from which the original sin of patriarchy blossomed to replicate itself within all subsequent forms of contract in the modern state. While social contract theory presented itself as a new inquiry into the political foundations for legitimate rule in the modern world, it was actually a retrospective justification for unequal power relations between husband and wife. In the pre-modern world, modelled on divine right, political power was 'paternal' power (the procreative power of the father thereby considered the origin of political right). Where the social contract theorists now suggested that contract represented the origin of political right, what they ignored according to Pateman was that even the original formulation of paternal power only existed by virtue of a previous patriarchal right of husband over wife (3). This original power relation remained entirely intact even in the new modern formulation of covenant, compact, or contract.

For Pateman then, it is no surprise that all of the individual rights which are eventually granted to the citizen are based on this original 'fraternal' patriarchal contract (i.e. of all men over all women). She explores various examples from marriage law to property law, employment law to parental laws and divorce. In support of this reading of the historical-philosophical record—and by means of just a few short examples—it would be worthwhile remembering that, before the 1970s, women in the US could not: open a bank account, if married, without their husband's permission; could not adopt a baby, if single; and could not discuss sex in public. Furthermore, until well into the 20th century, most pharmaceutical companies tested their medications on male subjects, thus (inadvertently) discounting the different physiological responses to these medications, experienced by women.

While most of the examples cited by Pateman can be seen at the domestic level, there are also international implications which flowed from this sexual contract. As Helen Irving (2016) has traced in great detail, for much of the 19th and early 20th centuries, in the majority of countries around the world, marital denaturalisation occurred any time a woman married a foreign man. Women would, in other words, be stripped of their own citizenship, with the expectation that in marrying a foreign man, they had 'switched allegiance' and would be acquiring the citizenship of their husband (which was not always the case, and certainly not automatically). As a result, millions of women over this period faced difficulty of mobility across international boundaries and many were made stateless as a result. The issue was only resolved when it was finally taken up by the international community, with the United Nations Convention on the Nationality of Married Women in 1957.

Finally, in addressing the myth of the social contract—and especially with the powerful critiques levelled at it by non-white, non-male, non-Western voices—one could simply think of it as a theory to be consigned to the pages of history. And yet, as even Charles Mills argued, its potential as a useful tool of **normative theory** (see Sections 2.3.2 and 2.3.3) is great, especially in times of social upheaval. As a more contemporary variation of 'classical' social contract theory in Rawls's *Theory of Justice* (introduced in Section 4.3) showed, it is possible to employ the thought experiment of the social contract, *not* to determine the origin of political society but rather to envision the future possibilities for it. Minouche Shafik, former vice-president of the World Bank and current director of the London School of Economics, has recently proposed the need to do exactly this—to conceive of a new 'social contract' in order to better address our mutual obligations to one another.

Shafik conceives of the social contract not in the classical versions described by Hobbes, Locke, and Rousseau but rather as a 'partnership between individuals, businesses, civil society and the state to contribute to a system in which there are collective benefits' (Shafik, 2021, 10). She pictures our mutual obligations as sitting within concentric circles (see Figure 10.1) which expand outwards to include the international. At the core likely resides our care for self, family, and friends. The next circle considers our community (e.g. local government, or the religious and voluntary associations and groups we are members of). Next, as members of a state (and possibly regional bloc), we imagine the various rights and duties we might have with respect to other members. The last circle, the world at large, may involve fewer obligations from individual citizens, but is nonetheless important for the functioning of the *entire* system (think here of climate change or humanitarian crises). For each of these circles, she suggests that we could think through the obligations that we might have in order to make the system function better. This is an approach to social contract theory open not simply to legal and political scholars. It invites reflection by all of us to consider the myriad ways in which our decisions might affect the lives of near (and distant) others. To guide us in this pursuit, Shafik suggests that the approach to fashioning a new social contract should be grounded in three broad principles (Shafik, 2021, 26–27):

1. The minimum requirements needed for a decent life should be guaranteed to all (education, healthcare, pension, employment rights), within the limits of what each society can provide.

2. We should all be expected to contribute as much as we can to this common cause, but can also expect, in return, to be provided with the maximum opportunities by which to do this (whether through lifelong training or childcare).

3. An understanding that certain vulnerabilities in life (old age, sickness, unemployment) are better attended to collectively rather than by individual (e.g. person, family, or employer) contribution alone.

For Shafik, these concentric circles, and related principles, demonstrate the value of revisiting the social contract, as illustrated in Figure 10.1. Doing so 'recognises the primacy of expectations and mutuality, the efficiency and value in collective provision and sharing risks, [and] the importance in adapting to a changed world if we are not to witness a destructive fracturing of the mutual trust on which citizenship and society is based' (Shafik, 2021, 3). This project of societal renewal, with 'nested' rights and obligations, is a response to the disappointment and disaffection currently experienced by many communities around the world. Shafik's proposal is at least one, more concrete, way of adding political detail to the 'complex, life-sustaining web' described in our discussion of care ethics in Sections 4.4 and 4.6. We might also remember here Rousseau's analysis of the body politic from

Figure 10.1 **Shafik's 'New Social Contract': Here, concentric circles demonstrate the idea of 'nested' responsibilities', with each arrow representing obligations and/or rights. This figure is drawn from Shafik's proposals in _What We Owe Each Other_ (2021, 4).**

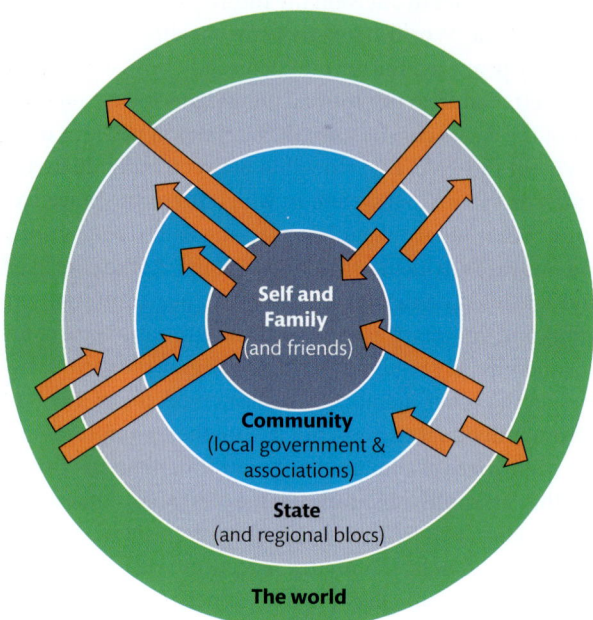

over 260 years ago. In Book III of _Du Contrat Social,_ he warns us that 'the political body, like the human, begins to die as soon as it is born, and carries within it the cause of its own destruction . . . but the one and the other can be more or less robustly constituted, so as to be preserved for a longer or shorter time' (121). As political theorists and engaged citizens alike, we do well to heed this warning, not as some gloomy prognosis from the grave but rather as an invitation to seek out new (and old) ways to keep the body politic healthy and to help our societies become more resilient.

REFLECTIVE ACTIVITY 10.2

Consider the accounts of Mills and Pateman.

Can you think of examples from your experience with the contemporary state, still today, which reflect the structural biases they both highlight?

Now consider the 'concentric circles' notion of mutual obligations described by Shafik, as well as her three broad principles.

Make a list of the obligations you might conceivably wish to see for each circle. Are they realistic or achievable? Why or why not?

10.4 LEVIATHAN REDUX: 1648, 1919, AND THE MYTHICAL BEAST OF SOVEREIGNTY-ANARCHY IN IR

Each of the concepts we have explored in this volume (from ethics to law, capitalism to empire, and to politics itself), has been analysed with reference to the explanatory myths which circle in their conceptual orbits. For academic IR, the most common origin stories deployed—in order to explain the state, sovereignty, or the state system—are the 'big bang' theories of 1648 and 1919. With regard to the first, the Treaty of Westphalia was traditionally seen as the legal epicentre of the modern international order of sovereign states, bursting forth onto an international scene. It was the moment, supposedly, from which the life of empires and all other hierarchical political formations began their inexorable decline. It is worth emphasising here, however, that as far as 'big bangs' go, the empirical record shows this one to have actually been a damp squib. Indeed, as Chapter 8 demonstrated, for the vast majority of the time between 1648 and today, the world of 'modern statehood' was relegated to a relatively small area of the planet.

Even so, eventually (slowly but surely), 'the state' terraformed the globe, leaving in its wake a map dotted with territorially bounded sovereign 'units', now existing in an anarchic state system. The new or supposedly modern view of political life which came about with the Treaty (marking the end of the Thirty Years' War, a 17th-century religious conflict fought primarily in central Europe from 1618 to 1648), we are led to believe, revolved around the confluence of three principles—territoriality, sovereignty, autonomy—which would define this 'new' system of states. And the expansion of this system simply accelerated with the end of the Great War and the Treaty of Versailles in 1919. As some scholars have noted, however, despite countless historical revisions of the content, context, and significance of Westphalia—1647 did not actually look much different from 1649—what is written and reproduced in IR textbooks about 1648 is rarely referenced, maintaining its status to the discipline as one of orthodoxy (de Carvalho et al., 2011, 745).

10.4.1 THE MYTHS OF 1648 AND 1919

It is true that great changes occurred to the way that politics functioned in Western Europe from about the 14th century. It is also true that, from the late Renaissance right through to the 20th century, the development of a new 'pan-European inter-state sphere of political interaction [occurred], and it was the development of this new political sphere that would eventually merge into a truly global international system that is the study among IR scholars today' (Ashworth, 2014, 20). In parallel with the protracted religious conflict which gripped the continent for centuries (not simply limited to the Thirty Years War), a new 'fiscal-military state' emerged in the modern era, focused on a taxation whose goal was to ensure war preparedness. Concomitant tools of statecraft also emerged over time, including an emphasis on the securing of borders, but also on diplomacy. As already discussed, the discipline of International Relations has responded to the question about how the modern international order arose by locating its origin in the Peace of Westphalia (see photo 10.4)—the name given to the two peace treaties signed in Münster and Osnabrück in 1648—which ended the Thirty Years' War. By this account, the European order which emerged from the treaty was marked by sovereign states which now adhered to decidedly modern principles—co-operation or conflict determined by an acceptance of new formalised relations between (and respect for) sovereign actors.

As Benno Teschke (2003, 3) describes it, the narrative of the Westphalian peace is that it brought about a 'consolidation of exclusive sovereignty, resting on the internal monopolization of the means of violence, [and which] translated into rulers' exclusive control of the instruments of foreign policy—the army, diplomacy, and treaty-making'. The plural allegiances which previously existed (of a feudal lord to both a king and to the Pope, for example) were now no longer possible. In fact, the emphasis on bounded territoriality, and the consolidation of the means of violence in fewer hands (those of monarchs), meant that the myriad actors which previously existed were now no longer deemed actors of international politics. The ripple effects were many—relations between 'sovereigns' were institutionalised within embassies, treaties, and diplomatic processes; these territorially bounded, secular modes of statecraft now stood in opposition to the unbounded aspirations of a 'universal' Catholic Church; distinct domestic and international spheres of activity were established; the number of legitimate actors within this arrangement were greatly reduced. Given these ripple effects of Westphalia, the IR narrative suggests that 1648 is therefore where we see the birth of modern International Relations and the international

Photo 10.4 **Painting by Gerard ter Borch of the ratification of the Peace of Münster, 15 May 1648, marking the end of the Thirty Years' War and the beginning of the Westphalian Peace.**

Peace of Munster: © Geheugen van Nederland / Wikipedia

state system. In contrast to this, Teschke contends instead that the settlement actually only marked the historical highpoint of European absolutism. In other words, Westphalia was more notable as a power grab by absolute monarchs than it was as a recognition of the international, and the various states within it. While there was a new understanding of the international, it was much more about 'inter-dynastic relations of absolutist, dynastic polities' (Teschke, 2003, 3).

The Westphalia myth can be challenged on the grounds that the treaty did not actually bring the modern state and international system into being. Indeed, 'neither the modern state nor the anarchic states-system originated in 1648, and . . . the enshrining or initiation of sovereignty was all but missing within the Treaties of Westphalia, which in fact comprised a constitutional document for the Holy Roman Empire' (de Carvalho et al., 2011, 739). Moreover, the big bang stories position the state as *the* key actor in global politics. This might seem to make good sense. After all, the field of study in question is called Interna*tional* Relations, implying a focus on the nation state. But this is problematic as the anarchy story (see Section 10.4.2) assumes that states are functionally the same and broadly equal. As such, it is reasonable for them to go about their respective business promoting their interests. What this story leaves out it that states are, and have been throughout modernity, organised hierarchically in global politics. In other words, far from a more or less level playing field, some states enjoy far more power, privilege, and wealth than others. It also excludes from focus those groups which identify themselves through framings other than the state, for example Kurdish people, an Iranian ethnic group, who refer to themselves as a nation without a state.

Because of these critiques, the orthodox story of the birth of the state system and the field of IR is increasingly rejected in academic debates. However, it remains firmly entrenched in mainstream theory and introductory modules: 'criticisms and re-evaluations of the story of Westphalia and the story of the origins of the field that have been quite central within the field have not been reflected in textbooks. The reason behind the reticence to break with the myths of the field is primarily because it would mean "to fundamentally confront the Eurocentric identity of the discipline"' (Capan, 2017, 6). Similarly, the so-called 'idealist' (vs 'realist') theories of the interwar period actually found their roots in the often racist and imperialist discussions of the decades which preceded the First World War. President Woodrow Wilson, famous for the advocating of self-determination—thus garnering a place in the pantheon of 'liberal' greats—did not actually believe in the extension of this principle to colonies, or to non-white races. In other words, much like 1648, 1919 serves as no better a marking point for some deeper understanding of the nature of the state or of the state system within which it operates. According to de Carvalho and co-authors, the myth of 1919 actually consists of three related elements: first, that the discipline was born in 1919, at the end of the First World War; second, that from the destruction wrought by the 'war to end all wars' there was an idealist attempt to solve the very problem of war itself; third, that this idealism eventually lost out to the realist scholars who highlighted the inability of idealism to explain or prevent the violence between states in the interwar period culminating in the Second World War (de Carvalho et al., 2011, 745). In effect, this would mean that the entire contemporary state system we inhabit today found its origin on the battlefields of Europe, much like (no surprise) the state itself did.

The danger, then, in perpetuating these myths, rests in the exceptionalist and isolationist (mis-)readings they give to the historical record. In the case of 1648 and 1919 as foundational myths of the discipline of IR, they create a false perception of reality whereby:

in the Eurocentric imaginary, 1648 constitutes the first step of the two-step Eurocentric big bang theory of modern international relations. The first step entails the single-handed creation of the sovereign state, which could only have occurred in Europe owing to its civilisational exceptionalism. And having created sovereignty in the absence of non-European help and non-European encounters, so the second step flows on ineluctably, where Europe expands outwards and graciously bequeaths sovereignty and Europe's panoply of civilised and rational institutions to the inferior Eastern societies, thereby remaking, as far as possible, the world in its own image (de Carvalho et al., 2011, 756).

In contrast to this, various historical records paint a very different picture indeed. For example, Robert Hommon's *The Ancient Hawaiian State* (2013) traces the thousands of years of pre-contact Polynesian societies to demonstrate the well-established origins of state society in these ancient kingdoms. Through centralised leadership, hierarchical bureaucracy, autonomy, scale, durability (of political processes), power, heterarchy, and tasks, he effectively demonstrates that by the time of Western contact (1778–79), Hawaiian polities had already organised themselves as 'state societies' (Hommon, 2013, 117), independently from the wider world.

With reference to the second part of de Carvalho's description of the big-bang myth above—the idea that Europe 'graciously bequeaths' sovereignty and rational institutions to the world—is deeply problematic. As Benjamin Hopkins (2020) makes clear, several British wars in the late 19th century—the second Anglo-Afghan War, the Anglo-Zulu War, the Argentine conquest, and the American Apache campaigns—all occur at the same time (anywhere between 1875 and 1885). Engaging in so many far-flung conflicts, argues Hopkins, would not make strategic sense to most armies unless it were being waged this way by design—parallel imperial engagements which, viewed together, he refers to as 'frontier governmentality' (192). The important point that Hopkin's emphasises is that, in all of these cases, the wars being waged involved acts of violence against Indigenous frontier dwellers 'who occupied the intervening space between recognizable state forms' (193). In other words, 'sovereign reality' of the time was more pluralist than we conceive of it today. Indeed scholars such as J. C. Sharman (2019) have also pointed to the role of 'company sovereigns' in the expansion of European state power across the world. Chartered companies like the Hudson Bay, Dutch, and English East India companies were in many respects the forerunners of modern multinational corporations—enterprises run for profit, but with the added benefit of being able to wage war (with the implied or stated permission of their home states). By some estimates, during the 17th century, the Dutch East Indies Company boasted the most powerful navy between East Africa and the Americas, and shortly thereafter the English East India Company had conquered much of the Indian subcontinent—effectively ruling over one-fifth of the world's population (Sharman, 2019, 67). These 'commercial' and 'frontier' realities, however, do not fit the neat (and benign) progress of the state, as outlined in our myths.

10.4.2 THE MYTH OF THE SOVEREIGNTY–ANARCHY DYAD

So, having addressed the two specific (chronological) myths most pertinent to the role of the state in International Relations scholarship, we noted that 1648 and 1919 did not actually create, with the stroke of a pen, the contemporary state system. What they did do, however, was to create a whole new series of binaries or dichotomies (domestic/international, secular/religious, inside/outside, friend/enemy), which culminated in the most significant conceptual dyad (think of this as a concept with two equal parts) for IR scholars—sovereignty/anarchy. Richard Ashley describes the 'anarchy problematique' as a theoretical phenomenon in academic IR which is not so much linked to individual scholars or works but rather by 'a tension that appears to animate it' (Ashley, 1988, 227). On the one hand economic and environmental interdependence are taken for granted in the global sphere of politics. Yet there is no central international leviathan or sovereign (remember here our discussion of Hobbes in Section 10.3.1), or agency of rule, and there is a multiplicity of states in this system, all of them sovereign. As such, the underlying tension results in a straight-forward problem: 'how, under a condition of anarchy, might lasting co-operation—policy coordination—become the norm?' (228).

Hedley Bull's response to this question, over a decade earlier—in *The Anarchical Society* (1977)—sought to counter the prevailing realist view that anarchy made the idea of 'international society' impossible. He did so through three related lines of critique. First, the modern international system cannot be said to resemble a Hobbesian state of nature, which was typified by an absence of 'industry, agriculture, navigation, trade or other refinements of living' (45). Second, it is simply not true that government is the only source of order within the modern state. Such a thin claim overlooks other reasons which might lead individuals to orderly coexistence, including (though not limited to) 'reciprocal interest, a sense of community or general will, and habit or inertia' (46). Third, for Bull the realist account overstates the domestic analogy (i.e. a state is simply not the same as a Hobbesian, or any other type of, individual human being). While for Hobbes the life of an individual in the state of nature is likely 'solitary, poor, nasty, brutish, and short', the same cannot be said of the life of a state. While individuals in the anarchy of nature might not be able to protect themselves against violent attack, 'groups of human beings organised as states [...] may provide themselves with a means of defence that exists independently of the frailties of any one of them (47). So for Bull, a proponent of the **English School** of International Relations, the response to the anarchy question posed above can be found in the maintenance of an international society which is (among other things) bound by common rules (e.g. treaties), based on a mutual recognition of states' sovereignty, and in shared institutions and norms (e.g. diplomacy, a balancing of power, international law, or even war).

Yet for Ashley (1988), any direct response to the problematique misses the more important point. He instead seeks to understand *how* it operates (and how it has become so entrenched in IR discourse). He suggests that by examining its rhetorical methods (i.e. the ways in which both sovereignty and anarchy are *described* in the literature), it might be possible to understand how it has come to close off the possibility of alternate productive avenues of inquiry into the nature of states operating in the international sphere. In his words:

> By doing so, we might finally come to understand this problematique 'not as a necessary condition that the "realistic" conduct of politics must take to be beyond question, but as an arbitrary political construction that is always in the process of being imposed' (229).

By seeing these conditions as imposed upon us, by the discipline upon its practitioners, we might better explore the chinks in its armour in order to cut through, to transgress, and to explore different modes of acting, communicating, and thinking in the international (i.e. outside of the logics of the sovereignty–anarchy dyad).

Ashley describes this theoretical imposition as 'heroic practice' (just as in high litera-ture, fables, or graphic novels, a 'hero/heroine' is set up against their nemesis in order for 'good' to prevail over 'evil'), and as monologic vs dialogic readings of the anarchy problematique. Under this monologic reading, the only ordering principle (i.e. the only 'hero') *is* sovereignty, whereby anything (an actor or process) which cannot be subsumed within its neat ordering is viewed as dangerous or as a problem to be solved. Again, he powerfully argues:

> Despite the fact that the state is an intrinsically contested, always ambiguous, never completed construct—a construct that is itself always in the process of being imposed in the face of never-quieted resistances—theoretical discourse of the anarchy problematique must 'find' the state to be a pure presence already in place, an unproblematic rational presence already there, a sover-eign identity that is the self-sufficient source of international history's meaning (231).

In other words, not only is the state the master noun of politics but in the context of our study, the master organising myth of global politics, the ideal against which all else is judged. Let us consider this monologic/heroic reading of one of the most significant events in global politics of recent times. On 24 February 2022, the armed forces of the Russian Federation invaded the Republic of Ukraine (see photo 10.5) on multiple fronts (from both Russian territory and that of neighbouring Belarus). Russian motives have been couched in statist terms by insisting that Ukraine never 'actually' existed independently of Russia before the collapse of the Soviet Union; that Ukrainians were 'little Russians'; that ethnically Russian Ukrainians in Eastern Ukraine needed protection from a 'Nazi administration' in Kyiv; and that this neo-Nazi administration was working in concert with 'Western aggressors' (read: NATO) in order to threaten Russia. The narrative around NATO has seen the return to prominence of realist scholars in IR who, for some time now, have argued that NATO had 'provoked' Russia with its own expansion eastwards. By this logic, they suggest, it is only correct that a large nuclear power such as Russia should wish to balance power against a foreign military alliance by keeping a 'buffer' country (just like Belarus) between itself and that foreign threat.

Yet apart from the galling implications of this reading (which effectively suggests that Russia's unprovoked and unacceptable behaviour is at least logically correct by realist IR standards), this narrative is entirely the product of a monologic reading of sovereignty/an-archy. There is no understanding in it of the complex histories of this region where Kyiv, as a thriving metropolis, existed at least a century before Moscow was even a village, or where Russian foreign policy logic is at least partly informed by an imperial logic which had been suppressed by decades of Soviet rule. The monologic reading also posits here that NATO is prevented from engaging more directly in assisting Ukraine to fend off the attack, because 'anarchy' in the international would simply be exacerbated. The entire framing of this tragic situation—by realists in particular—is one which Ashley would refer to as 'the blackmail of the heroic practice' (233).

We can also think of his analysis specifically in response to one of the best-known elabo-rations of 'anarchy' in academic IR, namely Kenneth Waltz's *Theory of International Politics* (1979). For Waltz, anarchy is taken simply to mean the presence of various state actors and

Photo 10.5 **April 2022. Broken tanks, combat vehicles, and other burnt-out military equipment of the Russian invaders in Hostomil in the Kyiv region of Ukraine.**

© Drop of Light / Shutterstock.com

the absence of any clear, historical presence of an effective centre of rule. It is a definition based on three related ideas:

1. The state is (in almost cookie cutter fashion) identical to other states in being a decision-making actor, with command and control over a specified domestic polity.

2. Any example of cooperation between states is merely an example of the advancing of private (i.e. the individual state's) aims.

3. The overarching reality of anarchy beyond the state makes for a reliable situation for limited co-operative conduct (limited to the second factor).

In this sense, co-operation is simply understood as a relationship based on instrumentality alone ('what's in it for me?'). But as Ashley points out, 'the power of the anarchy problematique is attributable to the effectiveness of the heroic practice in the disciplining of interpretation and conduct in modern life' (239). If the 'overarching reality' beyond the state is 'anarchy' for Waltz, then it becomes impossible to escape this hierarchical ordering of sovereignty over anarchy in each instance of global politics that we seek to understand. It is, in effect, a paradigm which girds itself against subversion.

A dialogical reading, Ashley instead suggests—one that prioritises contestation of meaning over the fixity of some overarching principle—provides us with a different means by which to recognise the heroic practice (in this case a rigid organising principle of sovereignty/anarchy) for what it is: 'a practice that is more or less successfully replicated in a wide variety of ambiguous and indeterminate sites to discipline interpretation, fix meanings, impose boundaries, discipline what people can know and do, and, among other things, dispose people to the further replication of the practice itself' (243). It is almost a built-in logic replicator. If Thomas Hobbes (see photo 10.2) is the ghost in our machine, then the machine to which Ashley is referring here is a self-automated photocopier or 3D printer. Returning to our example of Russia–Ukraine, a dialogical reading would bridle against the simple Russia-buffer state-NATO solution. It would recognise the multiple layers of shared identity across these borders, and it would propose a much more nuanced understanding of Russia's motives—an anachronistic, expansionist imperial exercise, simply posing as a statist, balance-of-power response to a country (Ukraine) wanting to forge a more European (and less Russian) political and economic future.

The real point to emphasise here, then, relates more to the very nature and structure of myth and mythologising as practices. The 'heroic practice', as Ashley calls it, of setting up a simple dichotomy (sovereign vs anarchic, hero vs anti-hero, good vs evil) and then using that dichotomy to order, limit, or 'police' what we can know or do in the international *is* the problem. What a dialogical reading allows for, he contends, is an examination of this heroic practice in order to identify where and in what instances it operates. Specifically, by including nonstate actors in the discussion of global politics, it becomes possible to chip away at the certainty that the hard core of the anarchy problematique has consistently built up. More than affirm a specific relationship or hierarchy here, a dialogical reading poses questions, raises doubt, or reaffirms historical contingency to our discussion of state relations.

REFLECTIVE ACTIVITY 10.3

Apart from the 'anarchy problematique', can you think of any other examples of 'heroic practice' as it pertains to the establishment of some organising myth or principle within the discipline of IR?

Think back to any of the other concepts and themes we have looked at so far in this volume in order to identify any problematic dyads or binaries which serve to circumscribe or limit our understanding of global politics.

10.5 THE FUTURE OF THE STATE

As Lucien Ashworth (2014) succinctly points out, the academic study of International Relations is both a 'product of and a reaction to an ongoing social revolution that occurred over the last four centuries'. Furthermore, in relation to a ubiquity of the state which we have described above, he suggests that:

> . . . this revolution has been so successful that few of us alive today, especially in the West, can contemplate a world without states (indeed, they have reached the status of being a natural part of our lives). Yet, a few centuries ago the idea of the sovereign state (let alone the sovereign nation state) was something accepted and experienced by a minority of the Earth's population (Ashworth, 2014, 20).

In continuing on this theme of social revolution, former editors of *The Economist*, John Micklethwait and Adrian Wooldridge (2014), trace what they see as the 3.5 (three and a half) revolutions already experienced by the modern state, in order to contemplate a fourth revolution—a truly 'global' race to reinvent the state. Here they refer to the different roles that the state has taken over the centuries. As already partly outlined in Section 10.3.1, the first of these was the Hobbesian revolution, which could be said to have centralised the locus of power within the sovereign—whatever form that might take. With a burgeoning small business and industrialist class emerging in the 18th century, the second revolution represented the desire to prize some power away from the vested interests and crony networks in the centralised power structure. In particular in the UK, the 'economisers' of the early Victorian era, similar to the theoretical firebrands who would follow almost a century after them, believed that their version of the 'night watchman' state—where government was viewed almost as an enemy to the success of individual pursuits—would represent the last stage in the development of the state. This was of course not the case.

With a parsimonious central government directing most revenues to expansionary pursuits (empire), and a yawning chasm opening between the small group of wealthy industrialists and the rest of the population, it was only a matter of time before another rethink was needed. The development of the welfare state in the 20th century is the third 'revolution' that many readers will be familiar with, because it is the provision of goods and services that has come to dominate contemporary discussions on the functions and feasibility of the state in the 21st century. We can point here to the work of Beatrice Webb, tasked with leading a Royal Commission on the Poor Law in 1909. Here she already suggested the creation of a national health service. Or we could jump back a few decades and look to Bismarck's pension reforms in Germany. However, in the UK, it would not be until the Beveridge Report of 1942 that a comprehensive welfare state—at least one recognisable today—would come about. The report sought to create the framework which would meet the needs of citizens from cradle to grave. Such a system would do this by 'vanquishing the five giants' of 'squalor, ignorance, want, idleness and disease'. This, especially by virtue of the language used, would in turn become the basis for the newer myths we would go on to tell about the role of the state.

And while to a certain extent, the welfare provision role is the aspirational goal of states all over the world, rising inequality, shrinking tax revenues, and even the radical notion that, perhaps, states should *not* be entirely responsible for this sort of provision (or at least not to this extent) have necessitated the fourth revolution that the authors welcome. The 'half revolution' noted by Micklethwaite and Wooldridge, incidentally, was the free market or neoliberal wave which began in the 1980s. Here they suggest it was only a half revolution because while much was privatised, and taxes were reduced, entitlements were not scaled back. Ballooning public debts will likely factor greatly in the decisions around how to move forward. Furthermore, the pandemic which raced across the globe in 2020, shutting down the productive capacities of many economies and—through furlough schemes and subsidies further added to the debt load of many economies—has brought into sharp focus at least two things: first, the truly global and immediate nature of certain issues which individual states cannot be equipped to deal with entirely on their own. Second, the need to consider once again the priorities and values that each polity might wish to see prioritised in the functions of the state.

While one might argue that this chapter has been an exercise in 'decentring the state', we instead suggest that —much like the concepts it explored—its aim was to leave you with some crucially important questions about the future of the state. While much had been made in recent years about the inevitable decline of state sovereignty, due to the increasing roles of international institutions and the 'multinationalization of previously domestic activities' (Held, 1989), recent events paint a more nuanced picture. Whether in the lengthy national pandemic lockdowns which curtailed international travel, or in the full-scale military invasion of Ukraine by Russia (an act which many believed had been relegated to the continent's bloody past), it would appear that this modern arrangement of political authority (the state) is not yet ready to leave the stage. Furthermore, while it is equally important to highlight the fatuously exceptionalist and Eurocentric constructions of the origins and proliferation of the modern state, it is equally important to take note of the changes it might be currently undergoing. As has often been the case throughout history, the advent of new technologies leads to new and unexpected changes. Equally important to note is that, although it is the modern era which was marked by the declared exceptionalism of European states, this does not make mythologising a strictly European undertaking.

In fact, the combination of technology and the notion of being a 'civilisational state' might well mean that a new dominant mode for the organisation of political authority will be found with the Chinese state in coming decades (see photo 10.6). Since 2014, the government of the People's Republic of China has been engaged in one of the most extensive (and intrusive) social experiments in human history. Linking government agencies to businesses, credit providers, and all individual citizens, each person will possess a permanent

Photo 10.6 **Advances in technology have enabled Chinese police to be equipped with smart glasses with facial recognition in order to spot suspects in crowded train stations.**

© Contributor / Shutterstock.com

digital record which keeps track of any infractions, merits, or demerits accrued over the course of daily interactions with these other institutions. Speaking out against the party, failure to pay taxes, even jaywalking can cause a drop in one's social credit score. This in turn can result in a 'blacklisting', which prevents a citizen from travelling on planes or trains, or even from obtaining a loan or renting a flat. Furthermore, the social credit aspect is only one part of a wider technological omnipresence of the state. With a network of over 170 million CCTV cameras, linked to the ever-growing skill of artificial intelligence technology, Chinese officials are able to track down and find any individual within a matter of minutes (Kobie, 2019).

For some this represents a coming dystopian nightmare, reminiscent of George Orwell's *1984*. For others it is simply the crude efficiency of state power in an era of scarcity of resources. It should, however, also be understood alongside increasing acts of Chinese state aggression and power projection, including the alleged torture and enslavement of its ethnic Uighur population, the severe crackdown on democratic protest in Hong Kong, the 'infilling' and securitisation of the internationally contested Diaoyu Islands, and the *Belt and Road* trade initiative (see photo 1.2), which stipulates a role for the Chinese military in protecting Chinese 'interests' abroad. The world has never seen such a large centrally governed state before. For anyone curious about the future of the state, or international state system, China is likely the most important country to observe in the coming decades.

REFLECTIVE ACTIVITY 10.4

Consider for a moment the new system of social credit and surveillance being rolled out across China (a country of over 1.4 billion citizens).

Do you think any of the social contract theorists we explored in this chapter consider this a sound and legitimate organisation of authority and power in a modern state?

What is your assessment of this possible evolution of the state and what are the effects likely to be? Good? Bad? Unlikely to become widespread? Most likely to be the technological breakthrough which brings about the demise of all states everywhere, to be replaced by an even larger or unified political ordering?

10.6 CONCLUSION

In this chapter we considered the myths of the modern state in the context of academic IR. We explored the myths of the social contract as founding blueprint for the modern state, and the myths of 1648 and 1919 as founding blueprints for the study of IR. It may well have been important for the evolution of Liberalism, for thinkers like Hobbes or Locke to seek to understand what would cause individuals in a state of absolute liberty (i.e. a state of nature) to choose to band together with other individuals, and to 'hand over' control (over at least some of that liberty) to some overarching authority. Equally, in imagining a shift from monarchical fiat to a 'general will', Rousseau likely found metaphorical inspiration in shifting bodily focus from the 'head' (i.e. Louis XIV) to the various vital organs of the 'body' politic. These clever literary descriptions of their day, however, do not actually help us to better understand *how* the modern state came about. If anything—much like with 'the myth of the law' outlined in Section 4.3 (in relation to ethics being a substantive part of politics only insofar as they can be codified into law)—what the classical contract theories demonstrate is that the 17th and 18th centuries in Europe were marked by great social upheaval and an overturning of power relationships which occurred before and through the state (rather than as a precursor to its founding). Furthermore, as so eloquently argued by both Pateman and Mills, the veneration of these classical 'foundational' social contract theories served to obscure *other* insidious forms and modes of power (based on gender and race), which contradicts the liberal/egalitarian myth of that original social compact.

Finally, we considered the means by which a pervasive myth (the sovereignty–anarchy dyad) became so engrained in our political discourse—by means of the heroic practice—and how it began to shape (and more importantly limit) the possible avenues of meaning available to us in our understanding of international relations and global politics. The social contract was also explored in its 'thought experiment' context, so that you might think of the ways in which *all* of the concepts you have considered in this volume might be used in *your* thinking about the best way to organise political authority in the 21st century. To return to the concentric circles described my Minouche Shafik, the social contract (as thought experiment rather than founding myth) asks you to consider what you have learned so far about the nature of politics, power, ethics, capitalism, violence, and the state in order to expand your own imaginary of 'the global' or 'the political', and to think about how and where you might wish to create political change and theoretical renewal in the world around you.

 Access the online resources at www.oup.com/he/hirst1e for case studies to help contextualise your understanding of key concepts, further reading recommendations to guide you through your reading, and a library of web links to journal articles, blogs, and video content to help you take your learning further.

CONCLUSION
MAKING CHANGE

11

11.1 INTRODUCTION

We began this book with the claim that before you begin studying global politics, you already know a good deal about it. In your everyday lives you encounter power relations and participate in political relationships as a matter of course. When you cross a border, play a videogame, or buy groceries, global politics happens. The conversations you have with friends and family about the problems of capitalism, the role of ethics, or the inevitability of violence are all part of global politics. From paying taxes to voting in elections to the Covid-19 pandemic, the political decisions we and others make shape our lives in complex ways. The key point is that global politics takes place not just at the level of states and international institutions 'out there', but also in the everyday practices, beliefs, and ideas that are much closer to home. As such, you are *already* an active political subject, even before you begin studying global politics. This also means you already have more power to make changes in global politics than you might have thought.

The core aim of this book has been to present a new approach to learning about and using theory. Rather than presenting a list of established traditions, or '-isms', to choose between, we think it is vital that you learn to *theorise*—that is, to *think theoretically*. To us, then, theory is a verb, an *active* practice. To *do theory* well is to think independently, critically, and deeply about the big questions of global politics, such as power, ethics, violence, law, money, empire, capitalism, and the state. Rather than leave these discussions to long-dead philosophers or today's experts, we believe we should *all* take part in them. And as our societies grapple with rectifying the historic underrepresentation of women, people of colour, queer and trans people, disabled people, and other marginalised groups in processes of knowledge production, it is all the more important that everyone takes part in debates about these big questions. The more you develop your critical thinking skills, the more you will be able to contribute effectively to these conversations.

Such critical thinking will transfer to all elements of life, allowing you to make informed and well-reasoned decisions about who to vote for, what kind of job to do, and what's right and wrong. Indeed, it is not an overstatement to say we believe thinking theoretically is the most important tool at our disposal, both as students of global politics and in our everyday lives, if we want to understand and improve the world around us. In an age of fake news and post-truth politics, where opportunistic companies like Cambridge Analytica offer to manipulate public opinion for their clients, and world leaders like former President Trump use social media to incite insurrection though false claims of voter fraud, developing the critical thinking skills to weigh up and evaluate information is a vital life skill.

To assist you in learning to theorise we have taken an unconventional approach, focusing on fundamental mysteries that structure global politics. Looking at politics, power, ethics, and violence (Chapters 2–5), we examined essential dynamics at work in global politics to see how these concepts are understood in various ways and are central to thinking theoretically. We then turned our attention to money, law, empire, capitalism, and the state (Chapters 6–10), looking at these topics as both theoretical ideas and political institutions, revealing how our theoretical understanding is intimately tied to dynamic political practices. Our hope is starting with content that is central to theorising about global politics, rather than reviewing existing theories, helps you see the value of theorising and see yourself as participating in this activity. Our goal is to avoid presenting a catalogue of theories to be memorised, to avoid thinking in terms of '-isms' that we either endorse or reject—we want to encourage you to think independently, critically, and theoretically about global politics.

The stories we tell in academic fields should be subject to critical scrutiny. While not intended to mislead, they can have the effect of producing a consensus which is more myth than fact. This book has invited you to put your academic field of study under the microscope by asking questions about its founding stories and the myths at work in its core theories and concepts. We encourage you to continue this practice as you proceed through your studies so that established myths do not limit or deter new ways of thinking and acting in global politics. Every module has been put together by someone; every reading list involves inclusions and exclusions; and every academic uses some myths and challenges others. Students who engage with the politics and power relations at work in their fields of study produce the best work and get the most out of their degrees.

Further, critical thinking also allows us to put *ourselves* into question. Because we are influenced by, and carriers of, myths we need to ask ourselves not just what we think but *why* we think what we think. Critical thinking allows us to question how much our opinion on a given topic is our own and made consciously, and how much is a product of habit, environment, or apparent common sense. If we find we are basing our opinion on an assumption that turns out to be flimsy, we can change our view to one with more weight. To fully develop your own positions, ideas, and arguments, you need to turn your critical thinking skills *inwards* to reflect on and sometimes change your own assumptions.

In that same reflective spirit, we should say something about the theoretical and political views of the authors. First, throughout the text we have written in terms of 'we' and 'us' in order to cultivate a sense of being on a common journey into learning about global politics. This rhetorical device, however, conceals differences and tensions. This book has been written by four authors, across several years, and therefore contains differences in perspective and a range of views. We hold a variety of different theoretical, ethical, and practical viewpoints, and of course our thinking is always evolving. This variety is reflected in the book's content and claims. While we share a critical sensibility and a commitment to **praxis** (the combining of theory and action), the book is not grounded in any specific theoretical tradition or '-ism'. Rather, we see theory as an active and ongoing process, which means we have sought to avoid ossifying theories into traditions or identities that one adopts like a partisan allegiance. Furthermore, just as we hold a range of views, you will no doubt have different commitments and perspectives to each of us. You may well have found yourself disagreeing with ideas we have presented or wondering about how we have presented or interpreted authors, ideas, and events. This is, we think, a good thing—and a vital aspect of thinking theoretically.

The question that remains, then, is where do we go from here? How can we go about making change in global politics? In an era of late capitalism in which our political, economic, and social systems appear deeply entrenched, what can ordinary people do to improve things? In this final chapter, we show how learning to think theoretically can open up new pathways for political action. In doing so, we challenge the myth that theory is politically ineffectual or abstract. On the contrary, we show that how we *think* is intimately connected to how we *act*. If we want to act differently, in other words, learning to think differently can show us how and where we might usefully intervene in concrete terms. Such critical thinking can also help us avoid accidently reproducing one set of power relations even as we try to challenge another. Before doing so, some further reflection on myths and their politics effects is important.

11.2 FROM MAKING MYTHS TO MAKING CHANGE

In popular culture we tend to associate the term 'myth' with either something that is simply untrue or a mode of thinking which is somehow outdated or inconsistent with the rigours of reason and logic now associated with Enlightenment modernity. Much like the disciplinary myths of IR which we have explored and disrupted through this book, it is worth pausing for a moment to consider these two popular misconceptions in order to better situate the role, purpose, and power of myth in making sense of the political world around us.

A myth is not a lie. Indeed, for much of human history, myth-making has been integral to the most basic expressions of the human condition. As anthropologist Claude Lévi-Strauss argued, it's not so much that mythology *uses* language to convey some deeper meaning but rather that it *is* language in its own right. It is a human language which exists alongside all other languages, across time, space, and cultures. Rather than dissect the words used in the retelling of a particular myth, we might instead glean meaning from the purpose or context of that myth. For example, a story often told by Realists in IR is of the shift from nature to society through the establishment of a *Leviathan*—a coercive political authority we create and consent to in order to protect ourselves from a life that is solitary, poor, nasty, brutish, and short (see Sections 2.1 and 10.2). Rather than a watertight explanation for the relationship between citizen and government, or the arrangement of 'anarchy' in the global system of states in the 21st century, however, this myth tells us more about the fears experienced by Thomas Hobbes (see photo 10.2) during a lifetime spent under the spectre of war, fleeing from conflict and impending social collapse in 17th-century England. Rather than providing a solid foundation from which to theorise global politics, then, myths can often tell us other things about their creators and proponents.

As this suggests, myths often recount events in history, not as factual chronology but rather as reflecting some deeper pattern of signs, symbols, or meanings. As historian Karen Armstrong has suggested, much like opera or poetry or any other artistic expression of human 'truths', mythology is like a 'game that transfigures our fragmented, tragic world, and helps us to glimpse new possibilities by asking "what if?"' (Armstrong, 2005, 8). For millennia, this was its role and intended purpose in guiding daily social life, activity, and human endeavour. By understanding it as a game, as an expression of the human penchant for *play*—and you will recall from Section 4.3 that 'play' is considered by Martha Nussbaum to be one of the ten central human capabilities we should most value and promote—we begin to understand the importance of being able to imagine the world differently in order to imagine it better. Armstrong goes on to argue that in the shift to modernity, European cultures replaced *mythos* with *logos* (or an emphasis on logic, practicality, and scientific enquiry). Yet this does not mean myth—or an ongoing search for deeper organising meanings of life—has simply disappeared. Indeed, as indicated in the quote above by Lévi-Strauss, politics is almost the most logical place for *mythos* to operate, as we seek answers to social and species problems, old and new.

This is not to say there is necessarily a self-evident truth out there to be discovered. Nor is the idea to suggest some different myth to take the place of existing ones. The critical thinking we advocate is not an exercise in 'truth-seeking' as finding a singular or ultimate truth behind the myths of global politics. Critical theorists discussed throughout this book, including among others Jacques Derrida, Cynthia Enloe, and Gurminder Bhambra, remind us that we are limited in how objective we can be about the world because we are always analysing it from a certain perspective, in a certain place and time, using a certain language. This means what might appear to us to be true might in fact only appear as such from our own perspective. Rather than seeking a singular truth, then, theoretical thinking allows us to dig into and evaluate the truth claims made by various actors in global politics. By unsettling such apparent truths through this book, we have highlighted the roles that myths play in our formalised understandings of global politics. In doing so we have sought to demystify the '-isms' which abound in IR, and to instead reconnect the reader—by means of their own intuitive understanding of politics—to the concepts, questions, historical processes, institutions, and ethical conundrums which animate the political world. Our critical examination of these myths is just a first step in developing the ability and confidence to decide for ourselves what we think about the stories we are presented with.

While they are not lies, then, there is a growing sense that dominant myths, and their attendant rituals, require demystification as a way to guard against harmful forms of meaning-making. In an ever more deeply connected world, beset by intractable problems which require concerted and global responses, there is a danger that some myths serve only to fuel the perceived age of discontent that we find ourselves in. In author and columnist Nesrine Malik's recent book, *We Need New Stories* (2019), she examines a number of contemporary myths (gender equality, political correctness, the free speech crisis, among others) in order to highlight the political dangers of mythologising.

Likening these myths to Ponzi schemes, Malik (2019, 241) suggests that 'the success of a myth depends on how well it can convince enough people that they are exempt from its consequences'. Myths and rituals, she argues, can limit or reinforce existing patterns of power and privilege, shifting focus away from those who seek to maintain that 'apex' status at the top of the power hierarchy, and towards invented threats to that status from below. But her suggestion that we need *new* stories—and the four *tools* she proposes by which to write these new narratives—also recognises the place of myth-making in our need for some 'galvanising, sense-making framework, a narrative, in order to instil order and a sense of purpose to our lives' (Malik, 2019, 6). Each of these tools will be outlined below. To the age-old political question—*What is to be done?*—we suggest that making change in a complex political world requires thinking differently, communicating differently, and acting differently, in our common pursuit of new stories. More importantly, such change can only come about when we recognise these three modes of political engagement not as discrete activities (e.g. 'ivory tower thinking' vs elections or street protests) but rather as tightly interwoven expressions of the same shared global political narratives. Crucially, we think each of us has a role to play in creating new stories through which to understand and live in the world.

Accordingly, in the following sections we examine how we might go about making change in global politics. This is important because it might be asked how we go from thinking in new ways to acting in new ways. If our aim is to change the ways we think, what does this mean for concrete action in global politics? Some might be worried that all this thinking remains abstract and ask how we can apply it to the real world in order to make some positive change. Our answer to this question is that thought and action are much more closely related than we might at first realise. This is because the ways we think have a direct bearing on how we act. The below explores how we might go about making changes in global politics by examining (1) thinking differently (Section 11.2.1); (2) communicating differently (11.2.2); and (3) acting differently (11.2.3).

11.2.1 **THINKING DIFFERENTLY**

Malik (2019) suggests four tools that can help us think differently in and about global politics:

1. *questioning the myth or dominant narrative*;
2. *looking beyond the story*;
3. *not picking a side*;
4. *arguing better, or not at all.*

These strategies have been employed across the chapters of this book. We have invited you to *question* established ideas and assumptions about politics, power, ethics, violence, law, money, empire, capitalism, and the state. We have encouraged you to *look beyond the story* of the founding of the state system and the academic field by critically interrogating the 'big bangs of IR'—the stories of 1648 and 1919. By suspending the rush to *pick and stick with a side*, we can forgo the tribalism that often creeps into forms of academic thinking dominated by '-isms' (**Realism**, **Liberalism**, **Poststructuralism**, etc.), and instead learn to *theorise for ourselves*, viewing theory as an active process which we use to navigate and interrogate the world. And instead of relying on an established theory to legitimise your views, we have encouraged you to *argue better* by developing your own ideas and original insights.

Malik's suggestions for active and disruptive thinking bring to mind the idea of **deconstruction**, often associated with philosopher Jacques Derrida. Deconstruction is an approach to critical thinking in which readers examine the tensions, contradictions, and omissions in a text. This involves asking yourself questions like: Does this argument make sense? What has been assumed here? What is left out? From whose perspective is this text written? What are the hierarchies and binaries that structure this text? On what does the argument rely for its coherence? Have these assumptions been justified? Asking questions of this kind can expose, for example, a **Eurocentric** or gendered bias in a text or theory. Importantly, by 'text' here we do not mean only written documents but rather the social and political fabric around us too. If we think of the political world as a text to be deciphered, we can see that both Malik's and Derrida's framing of active critical thinking have important concrete effects.

Critical thinking of this kind can be read, as Martin McQuillan argues, as a kind of 'textual activism'. What this means is that how we read and think about a text can be a site of political action. McQuillan (2008, 6–7) explains: 'Reading in this sense has very little to do with the quiet spaces of university libraries . . . Rather, this reading is an interminable, unconditional critical liveliness to the world around us, its histories and its futures.' While we often think theory and action are separate, what this means is that our patterns of thinking and our ways of acting in the world are closely connected. In order to demystify the myths and violences explored in this book, as McQuillan (2008, 9) puts it, 'critical reason and deconstruction are more important now than ever and this textual activism will be affiliated in unpredictable ways . . . to the material processes of the political'. Paul Bowman expands on the usefulness of deconstructive thinking, comparing it to t'ai chi, and arguing both are often misunderstood as 'philosophical, isolated, inward-looking, navel-gazing: as not *really real*'. Against this misunderstanding, he shows that both work by 'responding to challenges, intimately attentive, listening, sticking, yielding, inverting and displacing, always patient, calm and adaptive' (2010, 40–41). He argues that deconstructive thinking is attentive to 'the other' and emphasises listening to rather than denouncing and dismissing interlocutors: deconstruction 'listens by *sticking* to the other . . . Derrida listened, stuck and yielded to the texts and institutions of philosophy, in order to invert and displace conceptual orders and foci' (2010, 44).

A vital first step, then, in bringing about change in global politics is learning to think differently. This will allow us to amend or challenge established theories and assumptions and put our academic fields, as well as our own views, under the microscope in order to imagine new possibilities.

REFLECTIVE ACTIVITY 11.1

Pause here to consider these questions:

In what ways can active and critical thinking bring about change in global politics?

Is it convincing to claim that the ways we think are closely connected to the ways we act? Why or why not?

Discuss your answer with a friend or classmate.

11.2.2 COMMUNICATING DIFFERENTLY

One of Malik's proposed strategies for creating new stories is for us to learn to *argue better*. This stems from a now common view about social media and its perceived role in having supercharged political polarisation and the diffusion of toxic political ideas in recent years. One might think here of the countless instances of targeted (often negative) advertising deployed on Facebook and other social media platforms during election campaigns. It is also evident in the online comment feeds of most major daily newspapers, and the discounting of investigative journalism as 'fake news'. A hardening of discourse, a retrenchment within old ethnic, nationalist, or party-political echo chambers, an entrenchment of certain '-isms' in order to justify almost anything under the sun, and the dizzying proliferation of disinformation, have made even the most modest attempts at reasoned political debate online increasingly difficult. For example, in 2018, researchers at MIT decided to map out news story 'cascades' (i.e. unbroken retweet chains) on Twitter. The study found that it takes true stories about six times longer to reach 1,500 people than false ones; that untruths reach cascade depth of ten retweets twenty times faster than facts; and that false news stories are almost 70 per cent more likely to be forwarded than true stories are (Vosoughi, Roy, and Aral, 2018). Described by one of the researchers as the most shocking set of results he had seen in his career, the data highlight a real challenge to our attempts at problem-solving and collective political 'story-telling' in the 21st century.

But away from the fevered pitch of social media—and in contrast to either the routine elections and staid tools of democratic societies or the edicts and repressive tools of authoritarian ones—the last twenty years have also seen a slow and steady increase in the use of deliberative processes and settings to respond to various political challenges. At its most basic, deliberative democracy is an 'aspiration that places reasoned discussion at the centre of political life' (Curato, Hamond, and Min, 2019, 4). The goal is for reasoned (and not specifically 'rational') discussion, insofar as the aim is to consider (together) different sources of relevant information in order to arrive at solutions to political problem. There are many more permutations of deliberative models, but our aim here is to make present the fact that those variations do exist, and could be gleaned for inspiration.

For example, in 2004, the British Columbia government in Canada created a citizens' assembly of randomly selected participants to review the electoral system in the province (which, election after election, continued to return lopsided seat distribution of parties in the legislature, grossly inconsistent with the popular vote). The assembly's mandate was to consider the current voting system and all feasible alternatives, and to propose a preferred alternative which would be put to a referendum. Although the alternative system was rejected in the subsequent referenda in 2005 and 2009, this was a striking example of a deliberative process mandated to consider the redesign of a fundamental political institution. The method itself need not be reserved for matters of institutional reform. We have seen examples of citizens' assemblies which seek to arrive at a better understanding of contentious moral issues (such as on gay marriage or abortion in the Republic of Ireland in 2015 and 2018, respectively). It can be used to prioritise the political issues of most pressing concern to a society, such as California's deliberative assembly in 2011 (What Next California) tasked with setting the agenda for reform around 39 policy issues.

These experiments in agenda-setting and participatory budgeting are not limited to specific parts of the world. In 2015, the city government of Ulaanbaatar, Mongolia, convened a randomly selected assembly of 400 participants, tasked with suggesting the best allocation of budgetary resources to major infrastructure projects in the country's capital region. So successful was the exercise that the tool of participatory budgeting was enacted in law in 2017 for all future similar infrastructure goals. This method has also been famously used in Porto Alegre, Brazil, since 1989. More recently, the use of deliberative polling—involving questionnaires and a plenary meeting between over 200 randomly selected participants—was used to shape the Ugandan government's regional development policies in Bududa and Butaleja.

As James Fishkin argues in his *Democracy When the People Are Thinking* (2018), the point is not to design the perfect deliberative system (macrocosm) but to focus on the 'deliberative microcosm'—to, wherever feasible, employ deliberative tools in order to arrive at political outcomes reflective of inclusive, thoughtful, and reasoned discussion. Certainly, there are critiques of deliberative democracy, not least of which is scepticism about the possibility for democratic renewal in a world beset by deeply entrenched patterns of invested power and privilege. Some might suggest that these tools privilege the elite and the educated or well-spoken at the expense of others. However, as Fishkin (2018, 209) points out, the examples his study reviewed and evaluated come from all six inhabited continents on this planet, across developed and developing countries. To dismiss out of hand the possibility that 'people can rule, in a thoughtful and responsible manner, on at least some important issues some of the time, with the appropriate context and institutional design' is to ignore the disconnect from political power and outcomes, already felt by so many today. It is a disconnect which continues to fuel and amplify the polarisation and partisanship seen on social media and in contemporary public discourse.

REFLECTIVE ACTIVITY 11.2

Take a break here and think about your responses to these questions:

What techniques might we use to communicate better with one another?

What do we mean by 'active listening'? What examples can you think of?

Discuss your ideas with a friend or classmate.

Finally, while the values of broad inclusivity and discussion suggested above are important to these models and methods, our emphasis on *communicating* differently highlights another important element of deliberative democracy as a model for communicating differently. As theorist Mary Scudder reminds us, 'the concept of inclusion, typically understood, does not adequately capture the kind of harm that is done when one is allowed to speak, but is then ignored or not taken seriously' (Scudder, 2020, 33). Deliberation alone cannot guarantee fair consideration of often deeply opposed views and values. Making a comparison to the plumbing in a house, she suggests that while minimalist conceptions of democracy are slowly being replaced or supplemented with deliberative tools—bringing with them a focus on inclusion—the concept of inclusion itself also requires new fittings. A politics of *listening*, therefore, must be worked into deliberation, whereby all participants are assured of at least the *possibility* that their views might be swayed by what they hear (93). The aim of deliberative democracy, then, is not specifically to arrive at consensus, empathy, or friendship. In fact, decentring the aim of consensus in deliberation is likely to yield more space for a genuine exchange of views. Put simply, for Scudder it is specifically in the value and act of listening that democracy flourishes.

A key second step in bringing about change in global politics, then, involves learning to communicate differently and argue better. Doing this will allow us to express ourselves more clearly, evaluate information more rigorously, and learn to listen actively to others' arguments.

11.2.3 ACTING DIFFERENTLY

Malik's toolbox for critical engagement with the world around us is explicitly intended to enable us to act differently. Today, new kinds of political action are evolving all around us. Indeed, many of you will be involved with political action of various kinds. Some of you will have engaged in protests, demonstrations, or vigils. Others may belong to advocacy groups like Amnesty International or Greenpeace. Others might engage in online forms of political action through social media such as petitions or blogs. Still others might belong to a union through your university or employer. Many of us engage in forms of everyday resistance, often without thinking of it as such (Vinthagen and Johansson, 2013). This might include calling out a friend or family member for telling a racist joke, foot-dragging at work, or putting together a piece of art, music, or poetry which expresses something about your lived experiences. What unites these various activities is the desire to bring about change through acting differently in the world.

While we may not necessarily think about it this way, these actions are underpinned by a specific understanding of the world, and by an intention of conveying a message through our acts in a way that enables, or at least makes possible, political change. This is where the connections between thinking, communicating, and acting differently, and between this self-reflexive process and political change, become more immediately visible. Early in this book we mentioned that when we think theoretically we are already engaging in the process of theorising (Section 1.4). We then saw how engagement with different theories of politics raises different questions for political action and provides different answers to them (Section 2.3.2). We also saw how Wolin's distinction between 'politics' and 'the political' captures the dynamic relationship between political order and political action. More generally, any political activity, even within more traditional institutional channels afforded by elections, party membership, and the like, implies an understanding of agency and of the effect that such agency could have on politics. In fact, an understanding of agency exists even when our actions are geared towards keeping things as they are, so this is not the exclusive purview of those seeking political change but rather an inherent feature of political activity.

11.3 ACTING DIFFERENTLY IN PRACTICE: THREE EXAMPLES

This final section explores three recent examples of acting differently in global politics: BLM, Extinction Rebellion, and the Hong Kong protests. Through this book we have shown that we are all touched by global politics, that we possess the potential to be actors within it, and that active engagement with theory aids meaningful and purposeful political action, as discussed in Section 11.2.3. Various forms of protest and rebellion have in many instances been primary shapers of the world we inhabit, for example anticolonial movements bringing down empires (see Section 8.3.2). It is our hope that through these examples the connections between thinking, communicating, and acting differently will become clear, and that you can see how direct action from below matters in contemporary global politics.

11.3.1 BLM AND INTERSECTIONAL DIRECT ACTION

The origins of the BLM movement are in the everyday actions of ordinary people. The anger and frustration of three women—Alicia Garza, Opal Tometi, and Patrisse Cullors—at the murder by police of Trayvon Martin in 2012 (about which many people protested, as shown in photo 11.1) prompted them to create the Black Lives Matter hashtag and started using it on social media platforms in 2013.

Following the murder of Michael Brown in 2014, BLM went viral on Twitter and Facebook, with over thirty local chapters developing by 2016. Over the following years, huge numbers of people took to the streets across and beyond the US to protest police killings of Black people. In 2020, one article claimed that BLM may be the biggest grassroots movement in US history, with between 15 and 26 million people participating in demonstrations following the murder of George Floyd by police (Buchanan et al., 2020). You may already be familiar with these developments in the US, but parallel protests were held in Australia, the UK, Canada, Brazil, Denmark, Japan, New Zealand, Germany, France, and elsewhere. BLM's slogans of 'Hands Up, Don't Shoot', 'I'm Mike Brown', 'Say Her Name', and 'I Can't Breathe' are today known globally. As Ransby puts it, '[t]he breadth and impact of *Black Lives Matter* the term has been extraordinary. It has penetrated our consciousness and our lexicon, from professional sports to prime-time television, to corporate boardrooms, and to all sectors of the art world. The powerful phrase has resonated as a moral challenge, as a slap in the face, to the distorting and deceptive language of colorblindness and postracialism' (Ransby, 2018, 1–2).

Photo 11.1 **Protesters rally for justice for the murder of 17-year-old Trayvon Martin at the hands of the Sandford, Florida police.**

© Ira Bostic / Shutterstock.com

In addition to other forms of intervention, BLM uses direct action, including protests, demonstrations, vigils, rallies, and die-ins. In contrast to forms of political action that appeal to policymakers through lobbying or elections, direct action involves ordinary people engaging in acts of political contestation themselves. As IR scholar Chris Rossdale puts it, direct action involves 'a refusal to appeal to a "higher power" to achieve one's aims, and by replacing such appeals with interventions which seek to impact directly upon a situation' (Rossdale, 2019, 20). Used in different ways by the suffragettes, Martin Luther King, and Mahatma Gandhi, direct action uses spectacle and disruption to bring about change and involves both political and personal transformation.

REFLECTIVE ACTIVITY 11.3

Access and listen to the song 'B.L.M' by The Specials.

https://www.youtube.com/watch?v=7FyOjzUd57c

Pay attention to the story told in the lyrics. You can follow along with the words here:

https://genius.com/The-specials-blm-lyrics

Then consider this question:

What role can music play in learning to act differently in global politics?

Discuss your answers with a friend or classmate.

As this suggests, acting differently is closely connected to thinking differently. BLM is committed to a **black feminist intersectional** approach which takes seriously the power relations that affect poor and working-class people, disabled people, Indigenous people, LGBTQIA people, Latinx, and Afro-Asian people, Muslim and other religious minorities, and more. This inclusive approach is designed to emphasise the point that the movement seeks the liberation of all Black people rather than the relatively privileged members of the community like middle-class, straight, or cisgender people (Ransby, 2018, 2–4). As this suggests, part of acting differently involves rethinking standard or common-sense assumptions and ideas. For example, as media studies scholar and journalist Meredith D. Clark argues, new forms of allyship have been developed in online activism to allow white people to effectively support the BLM movement (Clark, 2019). This involves thinking differently about racial privilege by acknowledging and thinking critically about whiteness, taking part in anti-racist work particularly educating other white people about racism, and amplifying voices that are frequently silenced.

11.3.2 EXTINCTION REBELLION AND ENVIRONMENTAL DIRECT ACTION

A second example of a movement which tries to make change through acting differently is Extinction Rebellion (XR). Also using direct action, for example protests as shown in photo 11.2, XR seeks to change people's attitudes and behaviour when it comes to climate change. Like BLM, it began with a small group of people who decided to act to challenge

Photo 11.2 **Extinction Rebellion protestors on Waterloo Bridge, London in 2019.**

© Zefrog / Alamy Stock Photo

an urgent problem. Established by a group of 15 researchers in the UK in 2018, XR's goals include climate change mitigation, nature conservation, and environmental protection. Its actions to date have included demonstrations, occupations of government buildings, public transport links, and roads, sit-ins on bridges over the River Thames in London, and mock funeral processions. The movement has attracted support form high-profile figures including prominent politicians, journalists, and even religious leaders. Additionally, much like the BLM movement, it has extended far beyond its country of origin, with demonstrations and actions proliferating in places as different as US, Pakistan, Austria, Chile, Ghana, Australia, and more. Central to its mission is a 'regenerative culture' based on the principles of 'self-care, people care, and planet care' (Westwell and Bunting, 2020).

Declaring a rebellion against the UK government on the grounds of its inaction on climate change, the group devised a campaign of civil disobedience intended to transform the way we talk about climate change and compel action. In contrast to environmental groups that reject the possibility that the state will be a vehicle for change, as sociologists Brian Doherty, Joost de Moor, and Graeme Hayes argue, XR seeks to 'bring the (nation) state back in' by using direct action to force government action. In so doing, they argue, 'XR squarely puts the responsibility to act back with the government' (Doherty et al., 2018) by demanding that they 'tell the truth' about the climate emergency.

REFLECTIVE ACTIVITY 11.4

Take a pause here to reflect on this question:

How effective are XR's attempts to bring about change through direct action?

Why have some people criticised XR's actions, and how fair are these challenges?

Discuss your answers with a friend or classmate.

Just as it is connected to the ways we think about climate change, XR challenges us to communicate differently with one another too. As Berglund and Schmidt argue, in light of a loss of faith in electoral democracy, XR proposes a 'people's assembly' intended to reclaim decision-making and deliberation (Berglund and Schmidt, 2020, 59–61). This attempt to 'reimagine democracy' involves a commitment to radical inclusivity, active listening, and trust in order to generate ideas, gather feedback, and make decisions. As journalist John Harris reports, these assemblies are organised around 'the gloriously simple notion of bringing together groups of people representative of the population at large to try to plot a way through difficult issues, and thereby begin to reduce our susceptibility to division and rancour. In times as troubled as ours, that may sound almost absurd. The strange thing is, it actually appears to work' (Harris, 2020).

XR's goals and repertoires of political action echo those of many groups and organisations in the Global South fighting for environmental justice. We could in fact argue that the vanguard of the global environmental justice movement is to be found in Latin America and the Caribbean, and that any attempt at tackling climate collapse must build on 'the environmentalism of the poor' (Martínez Alier, 2003) underpinning political action in these regions. The centrality of Latin America and the Caribbean more specifically relates to their position right at the sharp edge of extractivism, a developmental model based on the large-scale exploitation of natural resources with little or no concern for the devastating environmental impact of these practices. The occupations of territories threatened by mining, but also the blockades, protests, and artistic manifestations of opposition organised by these movements are often framed in the context of forms of knowledge production usually deemed lacking in rigour or unscientific. For instance, the Inca goddess 'Pacha Mama', usually translated as 'Mother Earth', is invoked to justify political action in defence of the land in the name of the necessary symbiosis between all forms of life as well as nonliving beings that enable life on our planet (Villarreal and Echart Muñoz, 2020).

The retrieval of these forms of 'traditional' knowledge as inspiration for contemporary political action is important not only for praxis but also for how we study global politics, and for how we assess competing claims. In other words, which types of knowledge we deem analytically and practically relevant has methodological implications. In this regard, IR scholars Claudia Aradau and Jef Huysmans have argued that in 'validating' knowledge claims we should move away from variously defined standards of reliability, replicability, and objectivity (Aradau and Huysmans, 2019). We should instead accept that the world we study is messy and in constant flux, and that this means attempts to develop ahistorical scientific practices and standards will inevitability leave out key elements of the reality we are seeking to capture.

Additionally, and outlined by feminist scholars such as Sandra Harding, the emergence of dominant standards inevitably results in the marginalisation and exclusion of the views and perspectives of specific groups. Even though it does not necessarily conform to dominant standards of scientific rigour, Harding argues recuperating these views and perspectives does not result in weakening, let alone jettisoning, objectivity but rather results in 'strong objectivity' (Harding, 1992). We should thus always be alert to which perspectives and positions are privileged by specific practices of knowledge-making, and which ones are left out. In other words, methods are not neutral, and Aradau and Huysmans advise us against seeing them exclusively as techniques for representing the world we study, but rather also as devices and acts: 'Understood as devices, methods are seen to enact social and political worlds. Understood as acts, methods can become disruptive of social and political worlds' (Aradau and Huysmans 2014, 598).

11.3.3 HONG KONG AND MASS PROTESTS

To turn to our final example of acting differently, protestors in Hong Kong staged rallies of up to 1.7 million people in 2019 and 2020, objecting to a new national security law and extradition bill imposed by China. As with BLM and XR, the Hong Kong protests began with ordinary people asserting their views on a political issue, as shown in photo 11.3. People went out into the streets to protest about a change in the 'one country, two systems' approach which involved China tightening its control over Hong Kong by expanding laws to supress critics and eroding civil liberties. As journalist Verna Yu explains, 'what started off as a protest to stop a proposed extradition law intended to allow

Photo 11.3 **June 2019. Thousands of protesters in Hong Kong marched against a controversial extradition bill.**

© John YE / Shutterstock.com

people to be sent to China for trial exploded into a sweeping anti-government movement, unleashing unprecedented anger and frustration. Many people who did not care about politics became radicalised' (Yu, 2020).

As part of these protests, an attempt was made to hold unofficial election primaries to select opposition candidates ahead of the postponed 2020 election, in which 600,000 people voted. This was met with widespread arrests of pro-democracy leaders on the grounds that they were trying to overthrow the government. To date, over ten thousand arrests have been made and thousands of people have been injured. Because of this tight control of protest by security forces, the Hong Kong protestors had to be creative in the actions. One way they have done so is the 'be water' strategy, linked to the martial arts of Bruce Lee. As journalist Jamil Anderlini explains,

the protests have at times been placid and calm, with millions of citizens flowing peacefully through the streets and then melting away. At other times, including this past weekend, they have been whipped into a frenzy as clashes break out between riot police and demonstrators armed with petrol bombs, slingshots and spears. The protesters have extended the metaphor to describe their tactics. 'Be strong like ice' when confronted by police or violent vigilante groups; 'be fluid like water' in order to disrupt many parts of the city at once and stretch police resources; 'gather like dew' for 'flash-mob' protests that are hard to prepare for; 'scatter like mist' to avoid arrest and fight another day (Anderlini, 2019).

These tactics are an interesting example of using creative and adaptive methods to bring about change.

REFLECTIVE ACTIVITY 11.5

Pause here to link to the Hong Kong Human Rights Art Prize 2020:

https://eazel.net/exhibitions/613.

Spend some time looking at, and thinking about, the artworks submitted for the prize in the virtual gallery, then consider this question:

What role can visual art play in bringing about change in global politics?

Discuss your answers with a friend or classmate.

Protests in Hong Kong built on the return of mass protests, and indeed revolution, in the 2010s, perhaps nowhere more visible than in what you might know as the Arab Spring, a label heavily criticised for its **Orientalist** tones (Avery, 2021). The mass uprisings occurring in Arab-majority countries throughout the past decade, starting in Tunisia in 2010 and ending in Algeria, Sudan, and Iraq in 2019, called for an end to authoritarian rule. Demands for social and economic rights were central to this call for democracy and freedom, as perhaps best embodied by the main slogan of the Egyptian uprisings: 'bread, freedom, social justice' (Alexander and Bassiouny, 2014). This rallying cry communicated effectively how economic concerns related to living costs (and most notably the price of bread) combined by political and social demands (freedom and social justice respectively). It also showed how protestors throughout North Africa and the Middle East thought of democracy in much more expansive terms than the emphasis on free, fair, and competitive elections under universal suffrage promoted by international organisations and donors. The uprisings also provided an opportunity for enacting the prefiguration of an alternative society, once more most visible in its Egyptian manifestation through the occupation of Tahrir Square in Cairo (Van de Sande, 2013).

The examples of BLM, XR, and the Hong Kong protests show that thinking, communicating, and acting differently are deeply intertwined. This is because textual activism, deliberative agenda-setting, or organised street protest all equally require from us a different mode of engagement with the political world than what we might otherwise be accustomed to. Some of these movements have been criticised for reproducing various power relations. XR, for example, has been challenged for failing to pay enough attention to the racialised and colonial dimensions of climate change, and for relying on white privilege in their tactics such as deliberately getting arrested—something which is much safer for white people than people of colour (Slaven and Heydon, 2020, 60). Such criticisms themselves are formulated through the use of critical thinking. By using the same tool, groups like XR can change their practices so that they act differently and cease reproducing problematic power relations of this kind. It is through combining acting differently with communicating and thinking differently, we believe, that the reproduction of problematic power relations in groups seeking to make change in global politics might be guarded against.

11.4 **CONCLUSION**

We have argued throughout this book that learning to think critically is a vital tool in bringing about change in global politics. This is because the ways we *think* have a big impact on the ways we *act*. If, for example, we begin from the assumption that people are self-interested, or that violent conflict is inevitable this *leads us towards* inaction because it appears to us as though nothing can be done to change things. If, on the other hand, we think critically about these assumptions we can see that they are by no means watertight. In fact, such assumptions help to *bring about* the world they envisage by rendering it inevitable. What this means is that if we change our assumptions and leave room for multiple interpretations and possibilities of human behaviour, we can once again begin to work towards making change for the better.

Returning to Karen Armstrong's analysis of mythology, we are reminded that if a myth does not 'give us new insight into the deeper meaning of life, it has failed'. But, she continues, 'if it works, that is, if it forces us to change our minds and hearts, gives us new hope, and compels us to live more fully, it is a valid myth' (Armstrong, 2005, 10). From the many disciplinary myths we have explored in this book—and from the ongoing political crises and commitments which mark our individual interactions with the contemporary social world—it is clear that a need to find or engage with new and different stories about politics will always be with us. As Fishkin (2018, 209) reminds us, 'the reasoning citizen, who can engage with policy or politics, is not a unicorn [i.e. a mythical creature!], but a potential within all of us'. This is why theorising, understood as active critical thinking, is so important. The myths we are presented with can obstruct our capacity to believe that things could be other than they are. This undermines our capacity to make changes in global politics by denying the possibility in advance. If we are to make positive change for the future, then, a first vital step is learning to contest the myths that render the status quo inevitable or natural. In doing so, we can imagine new and different political ideas and arrangements that could benefit everyone.

 Access the online resources at www.oup.com/he/hirst1e for case studies to help contextualise your understanding of key concepts, further reading recommendations to guide you through your reading, and a library of web links to journal articles, blogs, and video content to help you take your learning further.

GLOSSARY

Ableism A form of power that privileges the able-bodied and explicitly or implicitly discriminates against people with disabilities. The concept suggests societies are unquestioningly organised around an assumption that to be able-bodied is the norm against which all bodies are measured.

Academic Disciplines Fields of study marked by delineated bodies of knowledge pursued by scholars.

Age of Empire A term denoting a period during the 19th century in which European powers, in particular France, Britain, and Germany, focused on imperial expansion and maintained colonial holdings across the world. The term indicates assumptions within Europe that imperialism, specifically European control over other peoples, was the natural state of affairs.

Agenda-Setting Power The power to set the public agenda, often through influencing or shaping public opinion in covert ways.

Alienation A condition of separation from one's surroundings, position, another subject or an object, which causes harm. In Karl Marx's work, the concept refers to the condition of being cut off from an aspect of one's humanity due to the dislocating effects of life in capitalist societies stratified by class hierarchy.

Anarchy A concept within Realism that emphasises the absence of an overarching governmental power in the international system that leads to the necessity of self-help behaviour among individual states. States are perpetually at risk from stronger powers and without a world government must look after their own security.

Apartheid A system of rule in South Africa, officially brought into being in 1948 though practised before then, that legislated for and legitimised racial segregation between White Afrikaans-speaking settlers and non-Whites and Indigenous people. Under apartheid, people were categorised according to 'White,' 'Black' or 'Mixed,' and assigned separate physical, social, and economic spheres of living.

Authority The power to make decisions over public affairs, including writing laws and policies.

Baader Meinhof Also called the 'Red Amy Faction', a German far-left militant organisation founded in the 1970s.

Balance of Power The idea within realist theories that states will attempt to mitigate the growing power of rival states by shoring up their own power or entering strategic alliances.

Berlin Conference A meeting from 1884 to 1885 during which European imperial powers discussed territorial claims in Africa, agreeing to formalise the partition of the Continent among colonising states.

Binary Oppositions A model of two related concepts or referents that constitute oppositional categories, each term containing the idea of its opposite, e.g. good and evil.

Black Feminist Intersectionality A term introduced by Kimberlé Crenshaw in 1989 to claim the significance of oppressions working at the axes of categorisations that marginalise people in multiple ways. As power operates at the intersection of identities to oppress, new categories are brought into being.

Bretton Woods An international system of monetary regulation established at a 1944 conference to plan the post-war economy, which established fixed currency exchange rates with all currencies defined against the dollar.

Buyer Firms Companies that buy up smaller companies within their industries identified as potentially profitable, based on assumptions that developing existing businesses is more effective than starting new ones.

Chicago School of Economics A school of economic thought associated with economists at Chicago University that upholds a theory of free market principles in contrast to Keynesian economics. The school's key claim is that society will most benefit from a market operating independently from government intervention.

Cisgender A term indicating a person whose gender identity and sex category are the same as those assigned at birth. The term can also imply the condition of heteronormativity, which privileges heterosexuality as the norm against which other gender and sexual identities are measured.

Citizenship The status of being assigned certain rights to reside and participate politically within a state. Individuals acknowledge the sovereignty of the state that grants them citizenship in return for protection, resources, and formal membership in the given political community.

Civil Disobedience A form of resistance that avoids direct militant or violent protest and involves refusal to comply with laws or policies instated by government control. The practice is associated with emancipatory social movements, such as the civil rights struggle in the US and the anti-colonial nationalist movement in India.

Civilising Mission A term used to justify colonising activities by imperial powers by portraying non-Europeans as backwards, barbaric, and irrational and therefore in need of the civilising influence of European forms of power and knowledge.

Coercion The use of physical threats or manipulation to force someone to do something they otherwise would not.

Collective Self-defence The right of states to use military force to protect other states from aggression, as inscribed in the 1945 UN Charter to define when war is just.

Colonial and Racial Aphasia Forms of dissociation from and ignorance about colonial histories within states that pursued imperial projects. Aphasia is not synonymous with forgetting, signifying a more active sense of producing obstacles to knowledge about colonialism and racialisations.

Coloniality A concept first used by Anibal Quijano to denote forms of power that reproduce discrimination against non-European and non-White peoples as an ongoing legacy of colonialism in the contemporary world. It refers to the privileging of Western forms of knowledge production against the implicit and assumed inferiority of other cultures considered to be at a lesser stage of modernity.

Colourism A form of discrimination against people with darker skin tones within a particular cultural group—associated with a racial category—in which lighter skin is privileged.

Conditionality Being contingent on specific conditions being met. For example, in finance, money may be loaned on condition the recipient follows certain rules.

Confucianism A system of political, social, and personal thought and behaviour which originated in ancient China with the teachings of the philosopher Confucius (551–479 BCE). More than simply a philosophy or religion, it is an all-encompassing worldview which is profoundly human-centred and focused on social harmony, family, and respect for ancestors.

Conspicuous Consumption Economic behaviour in which products are consumed in greater quantity than may be deemed practically required.

Constructivism A field of International Relations theory that posits ideational factors as shaping reality, diverging from material theorisations of international politics. The concern with ideas as historically and socially constructed, rather than being inherent and fixed, places Constructivism in opposition to Realism, which assumes a simpler and more ahistorical perspective on power as encapsulated by states' self-interest.

Contractualism A political theory based on the idea that a *social contract* exists between a ruler and her subjects. Doubling as an ethical theory, Contractualism is concerned with the rights enjoyed by citizens in a polity (i.e. good/right comes from upholding these individual rights and liberties; bad/wrong occurs when those rights are infringed upon). As a theory, Contractualism developed in order to justify why free individuals would leave a state of nature in order to form a society (Hobbes, Locke, Rousseau, Rawls).

Core/Periphery A framework to explain how political and economic power is distributed across core or dominant centres and peripheral or marginalised areas.

Creative Destruction A term introduced by Joseph Schumpeter to describe the intentional destruction of established procedures in order to facilitate more efficient means of production.

Critical Constructivism A theoretical approach that extends Constructivism by emphasising how knowledge production is always situated in a particular time, space, and context. Knowledge is constructed in a historical context shaped by social and cultural norms and one's perspective on the world is therefore shaped by their location within these norms.

Critical Race Theory A theory that approaches racial inequality as founded on race as a socially constructed category that is produced and maintained through particular power relations.

Critical Theory A theoretical approach associated with Frankfurt School scholars focusing on forms of domination produced in capitalist societies and on theorising means of emancipation from these structures.

Cultural Imperialism The process of a powerful state or institution imposing ideas and cultural norms on a less powerful group.

Currency War The practice of states devaluing their currencies to make exports more competitive in the global market. It involves a number of states aiming to devalue their currencies in order to stimulate their own economies.

Decision-Making Power A form of power exercised in the direct or indirect forcing of a group or individual to do something that, independently, they would not have done as it undermines them in some way.

Decolonial Theory A body of thinking that rejects the presumed authority and superiority of European and Western forms of knowledge.

Decolonisation The process through which colonial authorities leave a formerly colonised territory.

Deconstruction A form of analysis developed by Jacques Derrida that questions the integrity of binaries and dualisms at the centre of assumptions within Western traditions of thought and highlights their constructed dimensions.

Dehumanise To deny a group or individual the qualities and dignities associated with being human.

Democratic Peace Theory A theory that argues democracies are less likely to engage in violent conflict with other democracies.

Deontology An ethical theory concerned primarily with duties and rights, using rules in order to distinguish right from wrong. Most often associated with the philosophy of Immanuel Kant, Deontology is not concerned with the outcome of a particular action (i.e. its consequences) but rather with the correct application of universal rules (e.g. don't lie, don't cheat, don't steal, don't kill, etc.). To be ethical/moral/good, one must simply follow the rules.

Depoliticise To silence claims by denying the political legitimacy or intelligibility of the speaker.

Development A process of building and improving a state or group in social, economic, or political terms.

Direct Action A form of protest in which actors make direct contact or stage a direct confrontation with an object or institution identified as oppressive.

Discourse A system of language that is studied to gain insights into the production and maintenance of meanings and truths.

Disintermediation The process of removing an intermediary from a process, often a financial transaction or supply chain, in order to reduce cost or increase speed.

Dispossession The removal of land, property, or resources from a particular group. In the study of colonialism, this refers to land theft by which Indigenous peoples are removed from colonised space.

Distributive Justice In its most basic sense, this refers to the socially just allocation of goods or resources in a society, and to the principles by which that allocation occurs. The most well-known version of this theory comes from John Rawls's *Theory of Justice* (justice as fairness). More contemporary theorists (e.g. Martha Nussbaum or Amartya Sen) refer not to the allocation of material goods but to the fair promotion and flourishing of individual capabilities in any given society.

Double Consciousness Concept used by W. E. B. Du Bois to describe the condition of African Americans who lived segregated from, and to an extent invisible to, White Americans but who also entered White space. They therefore had access to knowledge about their own world and the White world, understanding how segregation shaped these societies in a way Whites did not.

El Requerimiento A written statement produced by Spanish monarchs in 1513 declaring their right to control Indigenous lands colonised in the Americas; according to the document, Spain had been divinely bequeathed the right to power over these lands and the people inhabiting them.

Empower To give a group or person the power to do something, or to support them to become stronger.

English School A tradition in the study of IR theory, which is often understood as a bridge between Liberal and Realist schools of thought. English School theorists argue that, despite the reality of anarchy at the international level, states can (and do) form an international society, bound by rules, norms, and institutions.

Enlightenment Intellectual movement in Europe in the 17th and 18th centuries defined by a pursuit of scientific knowledge and the privileging of reason.

Epistemic Violence Violence that is perpetrated through a system of knowledge claims.

Essentialism Assumption that subjects and objects are characterised by an essence, or fixed and unchanging marker that defines them.

Ethnicity The condition of membership in a particular group marked or defined by cultural, national, or linguistic characteristics.

Eugenics Scientific racism influenced by social Darwinism popular in the first part of the 20th century.

Eurocentrism The assumption that Europe is the central actor within world events and history, which eclipses the experiences and perspectives of non-Western histories and cultures.

Everyday Resistance A concept popularised by James Scott to describe less visible forms of resistance among oppressed groups through everyday forms of action.

Explanatory Theory A theory that provides an explanation for a problem and identifies solutions.

Exploitation The practice of mistreating a person or people to benefit from their labour.

Externalities A positive or negative effect that emerges when the production of a particular product has an impact on a group that is unrelated to the processing or consumption of that product.

Extraction of Surplus Value A Marxist concept in which capitalists pays workers less than the value their labour has given to a product. The remaining value is surplus and is the means by which workers are exploited.

Failed States States that have lost legitimacy among significant parts of the citizenry and therefore lost the sovereignty required to reproduce their authority.

False Consciousness The idea that, through capitalist economic structures, workers are invited to recognise themselves and their interests within capitalist ideology despite being oppressed by it.

Fatalism; Fatalistic A belief that phenomena and events have been predetermined and cannot be changed.

Foreign Direct Investment Practice of companies investing in or buying foreign businesses in order to expand economic activity outside national borders.

Feminism The belief in the social, political, and economic equality of all social groups, grounded in the struggle for women's rights.

Genocide The targeted and systematic killing of members of a group categorised by race, religion, language, or culture.

Gini Index This is one of the most common ways of measuring inequality within countries. Countries with a perfectly equal distribution of income (each member has the same income) would score 0 on the Gini index, whereas a country where all income is held by a single person would score 100. In sum, the higher the Gini index, the more unequal the country.

Global Commodity Chain The processes unfolding via global networks through which commodities are collected, processed and produced, distributed to consumers, and then disposed of.

Global Value Chain The actions that are part of economic agents' efforts to produce a product and put it on the market, comprising all stages of production.

Globalisation The process through which a huge growth in cultural and economic connections and interdependencies have come to define relations among states and peoples across the world.

Gold Standard A norm according to which states set their currencies in relation to the value of gold, so that gold determined the currency market.

Grassroots A form of organisation or action below the state or civil society, often appearing at community level.

Green Theory A body of Critical Theory that centres ecological life as primary and valuable independent of human society, rejecting the state-centred perspectives on the world within dominant theories of global politics.

Harmony of Interests A concept within IR theory based on the assumption states and individuals have some common interests and by identifying these can reach a position of peace and compromise.

Hegemonic Stability Theory A concept within realist theory that assumes the presence of one dominant state will maintain stability in the international order.

Hegemony; Hegemonic Dominance of a state, group, or region over others based on economic, military, or ideational power.

Heteronormativity The logic according to which societies are organised on the assumption that heterosexuality is the norm while other sexualities are aberrant.

Homophobia Discrimination against people identifying as homosexual, defined against heterosexuality as the norm.

Identity The condition and the process through which individuals and groups produce and reproduce ways of being, based on forms of cultural expression, that reflect a sense of self or collective selfhood.

Imaginary Also referred to as a social imaginary, this broadly refers to the values, laws, symbols, and institutions which are common to a particular social grouping, and through which that society is reflected. This stems from the idea that a society is not a 'given' but rather that it exists because it is imagined (and re-imagined) in different ways over time.

Immanent Violence Violence that operates through beliefs and thought systems, or ways of categorising people, that justifies their exclusion from safety, which are therefore oppressive.

Imperial; Imperialism The state practice of achieving domination over other states or areas through gaining control of land, economy, or political power.

Indigenous People who inhabit territories and have ancestral and family connections to their land.

Institutional Racism Racial prejudice that exists within practices, policies, and general functioning of institutions which strengthens individual racism while being reinforced by the latter in turn.

Inter-imperialist Rivalry Competition for resources and capital generation in the colonised world among different imperial powers that intensified in the period preceding the First World War.

International Criminal Court An international organisation designed as a forum for tribunals that prosecute individuals accused of breaking international law, such as committing war crimes or genocide.

International Criminal Law Legislation with international remit to prosecute and punish perpetrators of crimes such as war crimes and genocide.

International Human Rights Law Legislation created at the international level to protect human rights of groups and individuals, including treaties that bind states to certain practices as well as guidelines which act as standards of behaviour rather than having legal force.

Intersectionality Term developed in response to the marginalisation of Women of Colour according to gender as well as race. The concept highlights that people fixed in place by more than one category experience multiple oppressions together.

Invisible Hand A term coined by Adam Smith designating invisible economic forces, driven by the self-interest of individuals, that naturally produce positive economic effects for society.

IRA An Irish republican paramilitary organisation active during the Irish Troubles in the 1960s through to the 1990s.

Just War Theory A theoretical tradition that outlines when war is justified and when it is not.

League of Nations An international organisation of states established after the First World War intended as a bulwark against escalation of further conflict.

Legal tender That which is legally authorised to act as money in payment of a debt in a given state.

Legitimacy The widespread acceptance of a given government or political system as a beneficial or mainly positive one.

Liberalism An ideology that holds the freedom of the individual as a priority for political arrangements. Within Liberalism, limited government is deemed necessary to ensure this freedom, with the important caveat that measures must be in place to protect individuals from excessive government interference.

Liberation The process of breaking away from existing oppressive structures and norms.

Marginal Revolution A body of theory that marks a departure from classical thinking on economics. It assumes that decision-making in relation to purchasing an additional product is motivated by an individual's assessment of the added utility they stand to gain from it.

Marxism A school of thought influenced by the writing of Karl Marx that theorises economic structure and class hierarchy as the key determinant of social relations.

Misogyny The hatred of women.

Narrative The form in which stories are told, which involves representation of events, themes, and ideas reflecting a particular view of the world.

Nation-state A sovereign unit with territorial boundaries assumed to delineate a social and political community imagined as a nation, or a group naturally bound together through shared history, language, or traditions.

Natural Law A philosophical assumption of the existence of a form of justice defining human society that is naturally occurring rather than constructed by people.

Natural Rights Rights considered to originate from natural law, which are therefore universal rather than unique to particular societies.

Neo-colonialism Forms of indirect power over weaker states by powerful ones through economic, cultural, or political means.

New International Economic Order A 1974 UN declaration initiated by formerly colonised states to introduce greater equality into the international economic system based on the claim that, while colonialism had formerly ended, economic control by former imperial powers maintained the economic subjugation of developing states.

Norm Shared assumptions about what is and what is not appropriate and desirable within a given society or cultural group.

Normative Theory A theory that presents a vision of how society should function and critiques the way existing society is organised.

Nuremburg Trials A military tribunal held by the Allies to try Nazi leaders for war crimes, including the invasion of other states, during the Second World War.

Object of Study A topic defined as an object to be investigated that assumes some epistemological boundaries that guide knowledge production about the object in question.

Objectivity The concept that objective knowledge can be accessed by taking a neutral stance of describing facts about the world.

Offshoring The practice of relocating an aspect of a company's activities to a different country, usually moving from an economically developed to a developing state where labour costs are lower.

Ontology A branch of philosophical inquiry which concerns itself with the nature of being or of existence. This involves the study and articulation of basic categories of existence (reality, being, becoming), and in focusing on how these categories interact with one another.

Organisation for Economic Cooperation and Development An international organisation created for the purpose of promoting international trade and encouraging economic growth.

Orientalism A school of thought reproducing a binary between Orient as 'East' and Occident as 'West', portraying the former as mysterious, passive, and uncivilised and the latter as rational, progressive, and civilised. The term was popularised by Edward Said's critique of Orientalist knowledge production justifying European oppression of the 'Other'.

Othering The act of rendering a subject or place as different to and outside of Western history and norms.

Outsourcing The practice of companies transferring certain tasks, such as the production of goods, to be completed by an external company, usually to lower costs.

Pacifists; Pacifism A political position rejecting violent conflict as solutions to political disputes.

Pax Americana A period of relative security and peace following the Second World War in which international politics was shaped by US influence.

Positionality The concept, common within feminist thinking, that one's experiences and perceptions of the world are shaped by categories such as race, class, and gender.

Positive Law In contrast to natural law, this denotes the creation of particular laws by social groups to shape action and behaviour.

Postcolonial Theory A body of thinking on the ongoing effects of formal colonial rule by European states over much of the world. Despite the 'post', many Postcolonial theorists perceive the legacies of colonial power as continuing to shape the world.

Posthumanism A body of theory that decentres the human in its conceptualisation of agency. Rather than acting with autonomous intention, humans are imbricated in the context of their physical and social world and cannot be understood outside of or independent from these larger structures.

Poststructuralism; Poststructural Theory A theoretical approach that questions claims of universal truth and knowledge, treating narratives as produced in discourse rather than as objective.

Power Relations In international politics, this denotes the positioning of regions or states according to levels of power and therefore dominance compared to the relative lack of power.

Power/Knowledge Nexus A concept introduced by Michel Foucault based on the claim that power and knowledge constitute each other or emerge in an interconnected way.

Praxis The application or enactment of a theory in practice or action.

Preference-Shaping Power The location of power within social contexts, including cultural and political norms and institutions, that operates to shape the values, beliefs, and interests of groups, often in ways that undermine their actual interests.

Primitive Accumulation Idea within Marxian theory that theorises the origins of capital and of class distinction, highlighting the preconditions for capital to continue to accumulate. For Marx, the process was marked by violence and dispossession involving the expulsion of peasants from land to create an urban proletariat.

Private International Law Law that presides over conflicts or legal proceedings between citizens of more than one state to accommodate the difference in legal frameworks in which the parties to the dispute reside.

Privilege The condition in which a particular group or an individual is given rights and benefits, directly or indirectly, that are denied to others.

Public International Law Legislation, including laws and norms, that governs relations among, and sets standards of behaviour for, states and other actors such as international institutions.

Quantity Theory of Money The concept that a change in amount of money available will relate to a change in price. Over time, the supply of money will have the same rate of growth as price levels. For example, when taxes are lowered, consumers will be less aware of changes to price levels and spend more.

Queer A term appropriated by LBGTQ activists in the 1990s to claim symbolic space for and to celebrate nonheteronormative sexualities.

Queer Theory A body of knowledge that presents gender and sexualities as constructed and performed rather than essential. Strongly influenced by Judith Butler's *Gender Trouble*.

Racial Capitalism The theory that capitalism is already racial since the ideology of race encapsulates and ensures the inequality that capitalism needs to operate.

Racial Contract The idea that the fictional social contract imagined in the 17th century was already racialised. Writers like Hobbes and Rousseau viewed White people as rational and therefore capable of entering a contract, while non-Whites lacked such capacity for autonomy and reason.

Racialisation; Racialised The practice or process of defining people according to racial schemas, thereby creating race as an ontological category.

Realism A field within International Relations theory that theorises the international order as characterised by anarchy and the consequent need for states to prioritise self-defence and self-interest.

Realpolitik Also known as 'political realism', and associated with the first chancellor of Germany, Otto von Bismark, this is a concept which refers to national policy which is based on power (acquiring, maintaining, or wielding it) rather than on ideals. It is an approach to governing associated not with ethical considerations but rather with the constant pursuit of the perceived 'national interest'.

Reflexivity A way of thinking that poses questions about the person doing the thinking and the power relations that may affect their views and assumptions

Resistance The act of resisting power or refusing an action, and the capacity for this.

Responsibility to Protect A UN-devised mandate that obligates states to protect groups threatened by violence, intended to prevent genocide.

Rule of Law The norm or institution by which citizens are legally protected from arbitrary government interventions and forms of coercion deemed to be illegitimate.

Settler-colonialism A type of colonialism that operates by replacing Indigenous people with a settler population which claims sovereignty over Indigenous land and establishes a new society.

Sexism Discrimination on the basis of sex, usually disadvantaging women in patriarchal society.

Social Contract A hypothetical agreement in which individuals give up some sovereignty to the state in return for protection and the state's maintenance of the social order.

Social Darwinism A theory derived from Charles Darwin's theory of natural selection. It assumes the social world develops according to the natural growth in power and influence of the strongest groups while weaker groups come to be dominated by them.

Social Norms Implicit rules that shape actions and behaviours in a given society.

Social Technology The use of various forms of technological tools to shape processes that constitute social life.

Sovereignty Status under which the state as sovereign possesses the legitimate authority to police and maintain the status quo.

State of Nature An imagined condition in which people lived before the creation of the state to which people gave their sovereignty in exchange for the rule of law and protection.

State System System emerging from the Treaties of Westphalia in which European powers agreed to recognise each other's sovereignty over territory, resulting in a system of territorially bound political entities.

Structural Adjustment Programs A range of neoliberal economic policies to which states must agree in order to obtain financial support from the International Monetary Fund, such as opening economies to the global market and free trade and cutting government spending.

Structural Violence Violence that is produced through oppressive social structures and takes the form of inequality in access to resources and means of power.

Subaltern A term referring to working classes, peasants, or those denied access to dominant forms of social and political power.

Subjectification A concept associated with Michel Foucault's work referring to the production of a subject through a complex relationship to power—being both subjected to power and deriving agency from it.

Sumak Kawsay Roughly translated as 'good living' or *buen vivir* in Spanish, this is a worldview (or cosmology) of the Quechua peoples of the Andes region of South America. It is advocated as an ecologically balanced, community-centric, and culturally-sensitive approach to social and political organisation, most notable recently for the inclusion of the rights of Mother Nature (Pachamama) in the revised constitutions of Ecuador and Bolivia.

Supply Chain The processes involved in transforming materials into goods or services and delivering them from producer to consumer.

Surplus Population A concept within economics denoting how economic shifts created by the capitalist system, such as deindustrialisation and the growth of a service economy, lead to groups of unemployed and impoverished people displaced within the system.

Surplus Value A concept developed in Marxian theory referring to the difference between the wages a labourer receives and the value that their labour adds to the goods they produce.

Third World Term introduced during Cold War to designate regions not part of the economically developed states known as the First World, nor the Soviet states allied to the USSR as the Second World. It typically encapsulated formerly colonised, economically underdeveloped states and was abandoned by many for misnaming the hierarchy between oppressing and oppressed states.

Third World Feminism A field of Feminism to emerge in the Global South that maintains a distinct position from Feminism dominant in the Global North. The term Third World, while rejected by many as derogatory towards regions otherwise described as 'developing', has been reclaimed by inhabitants of these regions who uphold that the term highlights historical forms of inequality that continue to divide the world.

Thirty Years War A series of wars waged from 1618 to 1648 across Europe for power over territory and religious dominance, ending with the Treaties of Westphalia that transformed the map of Europe.

Trans; Transgender People whose gender identity is different to that assigned them at birth.

Transphobia Discrimination against and oppression of transgender people.

Transnational Corporation A company that has a base in a particular state but operates across a number of different countries.

Treaties of Westphalia Peace treaties that brought an end to the Thirty Years War, associated with the creation of the modern international order with its emphasis on territorial state sovereignty.

Ubuntu A collection of philosophical values and practices (or approach to life) associated with the Bantu-speaking peoples of Southern Africa, it suggests that connection, community, and relationship is what gives human beings their humanity ('Ubuntu'). Unlike Western traditions, which have focused on the primacy of rationality in ethical decision-making, Ubuntu is said to be present only with the combination of 'intelligence' (reason) and 'heart' (compassion, benevolence, empathy).

Ungrievable A concept referring to implicit assumptions that some lives deserve to be mourned while the lives of others are not worth grieving, as a means of separating the established community from outsiders.

United Nations The international body established in the aftermath of the Second World War with the aim of maintaining global security and preventing future wars.

United Nations General Assembly One of the most important policymaking bodies within the United Nations in which all member states are represented.

Upgrading A process through which, by mobilising updated technology and skills, firms or states transition from lower-value to higher-value economic activities within international networks of production.

Utilitarianism This ethical theory is the most well-known version of consequentialism, which suggests that in order to know if something is good or bad, right or wrong, one must first consider what the outcome of that action is likely to be. Associated with the philosophy of Jeremy Bentham or J. S. Mill, Utilitarianism states that the best action is always the one which brings the most advantages (e.g. happiness) to the most people (thus maximising utility).

Washington Consensus Neoliberal economic policies devised in the 1980s that heralded free market economics and limited state intervention as the cornerstone of Third World development.

Welfare State A state that maintains a range of institutions dedicated to promoting the social and economic welfare of its citizens.

White Supremacism A belief that White people are a distinctive racial group, superior to non-Whites, and that power ought to be concentrated in institutions and states that represent them.

Xenophobia The fear of foreigners and those perceived to be outside the established community or collective self.

REFERENCES

Abdelal, R. 2007. *Capital Rules: The Construction of Global Finance*. Cambridge, MA: Harvard University Press.

Abulafia, D. 2019. *The Boundless Sea: A Human History of the Oceans*. London: Allen Lane.

Akamatsu, K. 1962. A Historical Pattern of Economic Growth in Developing Countries. *Developing Economies*, 1, 3–25.

Al Jazeera. 2019. 'Cambodia's micro-loans: A form of predatory lending?'. 6 August: https://www.aljazeera.com/economy/2019/8/6/cambodias-micro-loans-a-form-of-predatory-lending.

Alexander, A., and Bassiouny, M. 2014. *Bread, Freedom, Social Justice: Workers and the Egyptian Revolution*, London: Bloomsbury.

Amnesty International. 2016. '"This is what we die for": Human rights abuses in the Democratic Republic of the Congo power the global trade in cobalt': https://www.amnesty.org/en/documents/afr62/3183/2016/en/.

Anderlini, J. 2019. 'Hong Kong's "water revolution" spins out of control'. *Financial Times*. 2 September: https://www.ft.com/content/d1f60a3a-cd58-11e9-b018-ca4456540ea6.

Andersen, E. 1990. *The Three Worlds of Welfare Capitalism*, Princeton, NJ: Princeton University Press.

Anghie, A. 2006. The Evolution of International Law: Colonial and Postcolonial Realities, *Third World Quarterly* 27(5): 739–753.

Anievas, A., Manchanda, N., and Shilliam, R. eds. 2015. *Race and Racism in International Relations: Confronting the Global Colour Line*. Interventions. London; New York: Routledge, Taylor & Francis Group.

Aradau, C., and Huysmans, J. 2014. Critical Methods in International Relations: The Politics of Techniques, Devices and Acts, *European Journal of International Relations* 20(3): 596–619.

Aradau, C., and Huysmans, J. 2019. Assembling Credibility: Knowledge, Method and Critique in Times of 'Post-Truth', *Security Dialogue*, 50(1): 40–58.

Arend, A. 1988. *Pursuing a Just and Durable Peace: John Foster Dulles and International Organization*. Westport, CT: Greenwood Press.

Arendt, H. 2005. *The Promise of Politics*. New York: Schocken Books.

Arendt, H. 1970. *On Violence*. New York: Harcourt Inc.

Armstrong, K. 2005. *A Short History of Myth*. Toronto: Alfred A. Knopf Canada Publishing.

Ashley, R. K. 1988. Untying the Sovereign State: A Double Reading of the Anarchy Problematique. *Millennium: Journal of International Studies* 17(2): 227–262.

Ashworth, L. 2014. *A History of International Thought: From the Origins of the Modern State to Academic International Relations*. London: Routledge.

Avery, I. 2021. Talkin' Bout A Revolution: Four Reasons Why the Term 'Arab Spring' Is Still Problematic, *Middle East Centre Blog*, London School of Economics: Middle East Centre, 20 January.

Aydin, B. N., Saka, N., Bas, F., Bas, E. K., Coban, A., Yildirim, S. K., Guran, T., and Darendeliler, F. 2019. Frequency of ambiguous genitalia in 14,177 newborns in Turkey. *Journal of the Endocrine Society* 3(6): 1185–1195.

Bachrach, P., and Baratz, M. 1962. Two Faces of Power. *The American Political Science Review*. 56(4): 947–952.

Bächtiger, A., Dryzek, J. S., Mansbridge, J., and Warren, M. E. eds. 2018. *The Oxford Handbook of Deliberative Democracy*. Oxford: Oxford University Press.

Bairoch, P. 1993. *Economics and World History: Myths and Paradoxes*, Chicago: University of Chicago Press.

Baldwin, R. 2016. *The Great Convergence: Information Technology and the New Globalization*, Cambridge, MA: Harvard University Press.

Bank of England 2014. Money creation in the modern economy, *Quarterly Bulletin*, 2014 Q1: 14–27.

Barkawi, T. 2017. Empire and Order in International Relations and Security Studies, in Denemark, R. and Marlin-Bennett, R. *The International Studies Encyclopedia*, Oxford: Oxford University Press: https://oxfordre.com/internationalstudies/internationalstudies/view/10.1093/acrefore/9780190846626.001.0001/acrefore-9780190846626-e-164.

Barthes, R. 2000. *Mythologies*. Translated by Annette Lavers. London: Vintage Books.

Bassiouni, M. 1999. Chairman, Drafting Comm., United Nations Diplomatic Conference of Plenipotentiaries on the Establishment of an Int'l Criminal Court, Address at the Ceremony for the Opening of Signature of the Treaty on the Establishment of an International Criminal Court, in *The Statute of The International Criminal Court: A Documentary History*. M. Cherif Bassiouni ed.

Beck, U. 2010. Re-mapping Social Inequalities in an Age of Climate Change: For a Cosmopolitan Renewal of Sociology, *Global Networks*, 10(2): 165–181.

Bell, D. 2011. Empire and Imperialism, in Stedman Jones, G. and Claeys, G. (eds) *The Cambridge History of Nineteenth-Century Political Thought*, Cambridge: Cambridge University Press: 864–892.

Benanav, A. 2020. *Automation and the Future of Work*. London: Verso.

Benedictus L. 2014. 'The artists who are giving a human face to the US's "bug splat" drone strikes'. *The Guardian*.

Berenskoetter, F. 2007. Thinking about power, in Berenskoetter, F. and Williams, M. J. (eds) *Power in World Politics*. London; New York: Routledge.

Berglund, O., and Schmidt, D. 2020. *Extinction Rebellion and Climate Change Activism: Breaking the Law to Change the World*. Cham: Palgrave Macmillan.

Berlin, I. 1980. *Against the Current: Essays in the History of Ideas*. New York: The Viking Press.

Bhambra, G., and Holmwood, J. 2018. Colonialism, Postcolonialism and the Liberal Welfare State, *New Political Economy*, 23(5): 574–587.

Bhambra, G. K. 2014. Postcolonial and decolonial dialogues, *Postcolonial Studies*, 17/2: 115–121. DOI: 10.1080/13688790.2014.966414.

Bhambra, G. K., Gebrial, D., and Nişancıoğlu, K. eds. 2018. *Decolonising the University*. Chicago: Pluto Press.

Bhambra, G. K., Bouka, Y., Persaud, R. B., Rutazibwa, O. U., Thakur, V., Bell, D., et al. 2020.'Why is mainstream international relations blind to racism?' *Foreign Policy* (blog): https://foreignpolicy.com/2020/07/03/why-is-mainstream-international-relations-ir-blind-to-racism-colonialism/.

Bhattacharya, T. ed. 2017. *Social Reproduction Theory: Remapping Class, Recentering Oppression*. London: Pluto Press.

Bliesemann de Guevara, B. 2016. Introduction: Myth and Narrative in International Politics, in Bliesemann de Guevara, B. (ed.) *From Myth and Narrative in International Relations: Interpretive Approaches to the Study of IR*. London: Palgrave Macmillan, 1–12.

Bliesemann de Guevara, B. ed. 2016. *From Myth and Narrative in International Relations: Interpretive Approaches to the Study of IR*. London: Palgrave Macmillan.

Boehmer, E., and Holland, T. The duel: Are empires always bad?, *Prospect Magazine*, 8 November 2020: https://www.prospectmagazine.co.uk/magazine/history-the-duel-are-empires-always-bad.

Bolton, J. 2000. Is There Really 'Law' in International Affairs, *Transnational Law and Contemporary Problems*, 10(1): 1–48.

Boucher, D. 2011. *The Limits of Ethics in International Relations: Natural Law, Natural Rights, and Human Rights in Transition*. Oxford: Oxford University Press.

Buchanan L., Bui Q., and Patel J. K. 'Black Lives Matter May Be the Largest Movement in U.S. History' *The New York Times*, 3 July 2020: https://www.nytimes.com/interactive/2020/07/03/us/george-floyd-protests-crowd-size.html.

Bufacchi V. 2005. Two Concepts of Violence. *Political Studies Review* 3: 193–204.

Bull, H. 1977 [3rd edn 2002; 4th edn 2012]. *The Anarchical Society: A Study in World Politics*. Basingstoke: Palgrave Macmillan.

Bush, B. 2006. *Imperialism and Postcolonialism*. History: concepts, theories and practice, 1st edn Harlow, England; New York, N.Y: Pearson Longman.

Butler J. 2006. *Precarious Life: The Powers of Mourning and Violence*. London; New York: Verso.

Butler J. 2010. *Frames of War: When Is Life Grievable?* London; New York: Verso.

Buzan, B., and Lawson, G. 2015. *The Global Transformation: History, Modernity and the Making of International Relations*. Cambridge: Cambridge University Press.

Bylander, M. 2015. Credit as Coping: Rethinking Microcredit in the Cambodian Context, *Oxford Development Studies*, 43(4): 533–553.

Campbell, D. 2013. Poststructuralism, in Dunne, T., Kurki, M., and Smith, S. *International Relations Theories: Discipline and Diversity*. Oxford: Oxford University Press.

Campbell D., and Dillon M. eds. 1993. *The Political Subject of Violence*. Manchester; New York: Manchester University Press.

Capan, Z. G. 2017. Decolonising International Relations?, *Third World Quarterly*, 38/1: 1–15. DOI: 10.1080/01436597.2016.1245100.

Carr, E. H. 2016. *The Twenty Years' Crisis, 1919–1939*. London: Palgrave Macmillan.

Chakrabarty, D. 2000. *Provincializing Europe: Postcolonial Thought and Historical Difference*. Princeton studies in culture/power/history. Princeton, N.J: Princeton University Press.

Chamayou, G. 2015. *Drone Theory*. Penguin.

Chan, J., Pun, N., and Selden, M. 2013. The Politics of Global Production: Apple, Foxconn and China's New Working Class, *New Technology, Work and Employment*, 28(2): 100–115.

Chancel, L., Piketty, T., Saez, E., and Zucman, G. 2021. *World Inequality Report 2022*. Nantes: World Inequality Lab: https://wid.world/document/world-inequality-report-2022/.

Chang, H.-J. 2003. *Kicking Away the Ladder: Development Strategy in Historical Perspective*, London: Anthem Books.

Chang, H.-J. 2007. *Bad Samaritans: The Myth of Free Trade and the Secret History of Capitalism*, New York: Bloomsbury.

Charlesworth, H. et al. 1991. Feminist Approaches to International Law. *The American Journal of International Law*, 8–(4): 613–645.

Clark, M. D. 2019. White folks' work: digital allyship praxis in the #BlackLivesMatter movement. *Social Movement Studies*. 18(5): 519–534.

Colás, A. 2007. *Empire*. Key concepts. Cambridge; Malden, MA: Polity.

Collins, P. H. 1998. It's All in the Family: Intersections of Gender, Race, and Nation. *Hypatia*. 13(3): 62–82.

Cook, S. 2012. *The Struggle for Egypt: From Nasser to Tahrir Square*, New York: Oxford University Press.

Cooper, A. J. 1892. *A Voice from the South*. Xenia, Aldine Printing House.

Crick, B. 2005. *In Defence of Politics*. London: Continuum.

Cudworth E., and Hobden S. 2013. *Posthuman International Relations: Complexity, Ecologism and Global Politics*. London; New York: Zed Books.

Curato, N., Hammond, M., and Min, J. B. 2019. *Power in Deliberative Democracy*. Cham, Switzerland: Palgrave Macmillan.

Dabla-Norris, E., Kochhar, K., Suphaphiphat, N., Ricka, F., and Tsounta, E. 2015. Causes and Consequences of Income Inequality: A Global Perspective. *IMF Staff Discussion Notes*, SDN/15/13, Washington, DC: The International Monetary Fund.

Dahl, R. 1957. The Concept of Power. *Behavioural Science*. 2(3): 201–215.

Davies, M. 2016. Everyday life as critique: Revisiting the everyday in IPE with Henri Lefebvre and postcolonialism. *International Political Sociology*, 10(1): 22–38.

de Carvalho, B., Leira, H., and Hobson, J. M. 2011. The Big Bangs of IR: The Myths That Your Teachers Still Tell You About 1648 and 1919. *Millennium: Journal of International Studies*, 39/3: 735–758.

Derrida, J. 1992. Force of Law: 'The Mystical Foundation of Authority', in Drucilla Cornell, Michael Rosenfeld, and David Gray Carlson (eds). *Deconstruction and the Possibility of Justice*. New York; London: Routledge.

Dewey, J. 2004 [1916]. *Democracy and Education*. Mineola: Dover Publications.

Dewey, J. 2012. *The Public and Its Problems: An Essay in Political Inquiry*. Edited by M. Rogers. University Park: Pennsylvania State University Press.

Digester, P. 1992. The Fourth Face of Power. *The Journal of Politics*, 54(4): 977–1007.

Diver, T. 2021. 'The Police, Crime, Sentencing and Courts Bill explained: how will it change protests?',

The Telegraph. 25 March 2021: https://www.telegraph.co.uk/politics/0/police-crime-sentencing-courts-what-bill-how-change-protests/.

Dodd, N. 2014. *The Social Life of Money*. Princeton: Princeton University Press.

Doherty, B., De Moor, J., and Hayes, G. 2018. 'The "new" climate politics of Extinction Rebellion?' *Open Democracy*, 27 November: https://www.opendemocracy.net/en/new-climate-politics-of-extinction-rebellion/.

Doty, R. L. 1993. The bounds of 'Race' in international relations. *Millennium*, 22(3): 443–461.

Doyle, M. 1983a. Kant, Liberal Legacies, and Foreign Affairs. *Philosophy and Public Affairs*, 12(3): 205–235.

Doyle, M. 1983b. Kant, Liberal Legacies, and Foreign Affairs, Part 2. *Philosophy and Public Affairs*, 12(4): 323–353.

Du Bois, W. E. B. 1903. *The Souls of Black Folk: Essays and Sketches*. Chicago: A. C. McClurg.

Du Bois, W. E. B. 2003. The Souls of White Folk, *Monthly Review*, 55/6: 44–58.

Duffield, C. 2020. 'Was Winston Churchill racist? Why some people accused the wartime PM of racism after his London statue was defaced'. Inews. 25 June: https://inews.co.uk/news/winston-churchill-racist-pm-racism-accusations-london-statue-protest-blm-explained-440668.

Edkins, J., Pin-Fat, V., and Shapiro, M. eds 2004. *Sovereign Lives: Power in Global Politics*. New York; Abingdon: Routledge.

Eichengreen, B. 2010. *Exorbitant Privilege: The Rise and Fall of the Dollar and the Future of the International Monetary System*. Oxford: Oxford University Press.

Enloe, C. 2014. *Bananas, Beaches and Bases: Making Feminist Sense of International Politics*. London: University of California Press.

Epstein, C. 2021. *Birth of the State: The Place of the Body in Crafting Modern Politics*. Oxford: Oxford University Press.

Extinction Rebellion, 'People's Assemblies': https://extinctionrebellion.uk/act-now/resources/peoples-assemblies/.

Extinction Rebellion, 2019. *This Is Not A Drill: An Extinction Rebellion Handbook*. Penguin, Random House.

Fanon, F. 2001. *The Wretched of the Earth*. London: Penguin Books.

Ferguson, Y., and Mansbach, R. 1996. *Polities: Authority, Identities, and Change*. Columbus: University of South Carolina Press.

Fishkin, J. S. 2018. *Democracy When the People Are Thinking*. Oxford: Oxford University Press.

Foley, D. 2006. *Adam's Fallacy: A Guide to Economic Theology*, Cambridge: Belknap Press.

Foucault, M. 1980. *Power/Knowledge: Selected Interviews and Other Writings 1972–1977*, New York: Pantheon Books.

Foucault, M. 2003. Truth and Power, in Rabinow, P. and Rose, N. *The Essential Foucault: Selections from the Essential Works of Foucault 1954–1984*. New York; London: The New Press.

Frank, A. G. 1966. The Development of Underdevelopment. *Monthly Review*, 18(4): 17–31.

Frazer E., and Hutchings K. 2019. *Can Political Violence Ever Be Justified?* Cambridge, UK; Medford, MA: Polity.

Freire, P. 1996. *Pedagogy of the Oppressed*. London: Penguin.

Fukuyama, F. 1989. The End of History? *The National Interest*, 16 (Summer), 3–18.

Galtung, J. 1969. Violence, Peace, and Peace Research. *Journal of Peace Research* 6: 167–191.

Garen, M, Carleton, M.-H., and Swaab, J. 2019. '"Zwarte Piet: Black Pete" is Dutch racism in full display': https://www.aljazeera.com/features/2019/11/27/zwarte-piet-black-pete-is-dutch-racism-in-full-display/.

Gereffi, G. 2014. 'Global Value Chains in a Post-Washington Consensus World', *Review of International Political Economy*, 21(1): 9–37.

Getachew, A. 2019. *Worldmaking After Empire: The Rise and Fall of Self-Determination*, Princeton, NJ: Princeton University Press.

Gilligan, C. 1982. *In a Different Voice: Psychological Theory and Women's Development*. Cambridge, MA: Harvard University Press.

Gilpin, R. 2001. *Global Political Economy: Understanding the International Economic Order*, Princeton, NJ: Princeton University Press.

Goldsmith, J., and Posner, E. 2006. *The Limits of International Law*. Oxford: Oxford University Press.

Graeber, D. 2011. *Debt: The First 5,000 Years*, New York: Melville House.

Gramsci, A. 1971. *Selections from the Prison Notebooks*. Edited and translated by Hoare, Q. and Nowell-Smith, G. London: Lawrence & Wishart.

Grosfoguel, R. 2011. Decolonizing Post-Colonial Studies and Paradigms of Political-Economy: Transmodernity, Decolonial Thinking, and Global Coloniality, *TRANSMODERNITY: Journal of Peripheral Cultural Production of the Luso-Hispanic World*.

Grovogui, S. 2011. Looking Beyond Spring for the Season: An African Perspective on the World Order after the Arab Revolt. *Globalizations*, 8(5): 567–572.

Grovogui, S. 2001. Come to Africa: A Hermeneutics of Race in International Theory. *Alternatives: Global, Local, Political*, 26: 425–448.

Grovogui, S. N. 2009. *Beyond Eurocentrism and Anarchy: Memories of International Order and Institutions*.

Gruffydd Jones, B. ed. 2006. *Decolonizing International Relations*. Lanham, Md: Rowman & Littlefield.

Hägglund, M. 2019. *This Life: Secular Faith and Spiritual Freedom*, New York: Penguin Random House.

Harding, S. 1992. Rethinking Standpoint Epistemology: What Is 'Strong Objectivity?', *The Centennial Review*, 36(2): 437–470.

Harris, J. 2020. 'If democracy looks doomed, Extinction Rebellion may have an answer'. *The Guardian*. 30 August: https://www.theguardian.com/commentisfree/2020/aug/30/extinction-rebellion-democracy-climate-emergency-bill-citizens-assembly.

Hay, C. 2002. *Political Analysis: A Critical Introduction*. Basingstoke; New York: Palgrave.

Hayek, F. A. 1945. 'The Use of Knowledge in Society', *American Economic Review*, 35(4): 519–530.

Hayek, F. A. 2008. *Prices and Production, and Other Works: F.A. Hayek on Money, the Business Cycle, and the Gold Standard*. Auburn: Ludwig von Mises Institute.

Hayward, C. R. 1998. De-Facing Power. *Polity*. 31(1): 1–22.

Held, D. 1989. *Political Theory and the Modern State: Essays on State, Power, and Democracy*. Cambridge, UK: Polity Press.

Helleiner, E. 1994. *States and the Reemergence of Global Finance: From Bretton Woods to the 1990s*, Ithaca: Cornell University Press.

Henderson, E. A. 1995. *Afrocentrism and World Politics: Towards a New Paradigm*. Westport, Conn: Praeger.

Hirst, A. 2022. Wargames Resurgent: The Hyperrealities of Military Gaming from Recruitment to Rehabilitation. *International Studies Quarterly*, 66(3). Online first.

Hirst, P., and Thompson, G. 1999. *Globalization in Question*. 2nd edn. Cambridge: Polity Press.

Hobbes, T. 1651 [2009]. *Leviathan*. Oxford World's Classics. Oxford: Oxford University Press.

Hobbes, T. 1996. *Leviathan*. Edited by R. Tuck. Rev. student edn. Cambridge: Cambridge University Press.

Hochschild, A. R. 2015. Global Care Chains and Emotional Surplus Value, in D. Engster and T. Metz (eds) *Justice, Politics, and the Family*, New York: Routledge, 249–261.

Hommon, Robert. 2013. *The Ancient Hawaiian State: Origins of a Political Society*. Oxford: Oxford University Press.

hooks, b. 1994. *Teaching to Transgress: Education as the Practice of Freedom*. New York; London: Routledge.

hooks, b. 2015. *Ain't I a Woman: Black Women and Feminism*. New York; London: Routledge.

Hoover, J. 2011. Egypt and the Failure of Realism. *Journal of Critical Globalisation Studies* 4, 127–137: https://blogs.lse.ac.uk/mec/2021/01/20/talkin-bout-a-revolution-four-reasons-why-the-term-arab-spring-is-still-problematic/#comments. https://www.bankofengland.co.uk/-/media/boe/files/quarterly-bulletin/2014/money-creation-in-the-modern-economy.pdf?la=en&hash=9A8788FD44A62D8BB927123544205CE476E01654. https://www.opendemocracy.net/en/democraciaabierta/luchas-resistencias-y-alternativas-al-extractivismo-en-am%C3%A9rica-latina-y-caribe-en/.

Hopkins, B. D. 2020. *Ruling the Savage Periphery: Frontier Governance and the Making of the Modern State*. Cambridge, MA: Harvard University Press.

Humphrey, C. 1985. Barter and Economic Disintegration. *Man, New Series*, 20(1): 48–72.

Huntington, S. 1993. The Clash of Civilizations? *Foreign Affairs*, 72(3): 22–49.

Husnain, M., and Parekh, R. 2013. 'Economics students demand an education that reflects post-crash world'. *The Guardian*. 13 November: https://www.theguardian.com/sustainable-business/economic-students-demand-education.

Hussain, N. 2013. The Sound of Terror: Phenomenology of a Drone Strike. *Boston Review*.

Hutchings, K. 2010. *Global Ethics: An Introduction*. Cambridge, UK: Polity Press.

Ibhawoh, B. 1999. Structural Adjustment, Authoritarianism and Human Rights in Africa. *Comparative Studies of South Asia, Africa and the Middle East*, Vol. XIX No. 1: 158–167.

Ingham, G. 2004. *The Nature of Money*, Cambridge: Polity.

Irving, H. 2016. *Citizenship, Alienage and the Modern Constitutional State: A Gendered History*. Cambridge, UK: Cambridge University Press.

Jackson, R. 1945. Second Day, Wednesday, 11/21/1945, Part 04, in Trial of the Major War Criminals before the International Military Tribunal. Volume II. Proceedings: 11/14/1945–11/30/1945. [Official text in the English language.] Nuremberg: IMT, 1947. 98–102.

Jahi, J. 2014. 'Why isn't my professor black?': https://blogs.ucl.ac.uk/events/2014/03/21/whyisntmyprofessorblack/.

Kant, I. 1998. *Kant: Political Writings*. Cambridge: Cambridge University Press.

Karim, L. 2008. Demystifying Micro-Credit: The Grameen Bank, NGOs, and Neoliberalism in Bangladesh, *Cultural Dynamics*, 20(5): 5–29.

Keene, E. 2005. *International Political Thought: A Historical Introduction*. Cambridge: Polity Press.

Kennedy, D. 2006. *Of Law and War*. Princeton and Oxford: Princeton University Press.

Keohane, R. O., and Nye, J. S. 1977. *Power and Interdependence: World Politics in Transition*. Boston: Little, Brown, and Company.

Keohane, R. O., and Nye, J. S. 2000. Globalization: What's New? What's Not? (And So What?). *Foreign Affairs*. 118 (Spring): 104–119.

Kerkvliet, B. J. T. 2009. Everyday politics in peasant societies (and ours). *The Journal of Peasant Studies*, 36(1): 227–243.

Khalili, L. 2020. *Sinews of War and Trade: Shipping and Capitalism in the Arabian Peninsula*, London: Verso.

Khanna, P. 2019. *The Future Is Asian: Global Order in the Twenty-First Century*, New York: Simon & Schuster.

Kipling, R. 1899. 'The White Man's Burden': http://www.kiplingsociety.co.uk/poems_burden.htm.

Kirby, P. 2022. Norman Angell's Defence of Empire, Paper presented at ISA 2022.

Kobie, N. 2019. The complicated truth about China's social credit system. *Wired* magazine, 7 June 2019.

Kohlberg, L. 1981. *Essays on Moral Development, Vol. 1: The Philosophy of Moral Development*. New York: Harper & Row.

Koskenniemi, M. 1990. The Politics of International Law. *European Journal of International Law*, 1(1): 4–32.

Koskennimi, M. Imagining the Rule of Law: Rereading the Grotian 'Tradition'. *European Journal of International Law*, 30 (1): 17–52.

Krasner, S. 1999. *Sovereignty: Organized Hypocrisy*. Princeton: Princeton University Press.

Krasner, S. 2002. Realist Views of International Law. *Proceedings of the Annual Meeting (American Society of International Law)* 96, 265–268.

Krenshaw, K. 1989. Demarginalizing the Intersection of Race and Sex: A Black Feminist Critique of Antidiscrimination Doctrine, Feminist Theory and Antiracist Politics. University of Chicago Legal Forum (1): 139–167.

Krishna, S. 1993. The importance of being ironic: A postcolonial view on critical international relations theory. *Alternatives: Global, Local, Political*, 18(3): 385–417.

Krishna, S. 2001. Race, Amnesia, and the Education of International Relations. *Alternatives* 26: 401–424.

Kronsell, A. Methods for studying silences: gender analysis in institutions of hegemonic masculinity, in Brooke A. Ackerly, Maria Stern, and Jacqui True (eds) *Feminist Methodologies for International Relations*. New York; Cambridge: Cambridge University Press.

Kuchay, B. 2019. 'Churchill's policies to blame for 1943 Bengal famine'. Al Jazeera. 1 April: https://www.aljazeera.com/news/2019/4/1/churchills-policies-to-blame-for-1943-bengal-famine-study.

Kvangraven, I. H. 2020. Beyond the Stereotype: Restating the Relevance of the Dependency Research Programme. *Development and Change*, 52(1): 76–112.

Lang Jr, A. 2007. The violence of rules? Rethinking the 2003 war against Iraq. *Contemporary Politics*, 13(3): 257–276.

Lasswell, H. D. 1936. *Politics: Who Gets What, When, How*. New York: Whittlesey House.

Lefebvre, H. 2005. *Critique of Everyday Life*. 3 Vols. London: Verso.

Lehr, D. 2015. 'The Racist Legacy of Woodrow Wilson'. *The Atlantic*. 27 November: https://www.theatlantic.com/politics/archive/2015/11/wilson-legacy-racism/417549/.

Leira, H., and de Carvalho, B. 2018. The Function of Myths in International Relations: Discipline and Identity, in Gofas, A., Hamati-Ataya, I., and Onuf, N. (eds) *The SAGE Handbook of the History, Philosophy and Sociology of International Relations*. London: SAGE Publications, 222–235.

Leonard, D. 2008. Young, Black (& Brown) and Don't Give a Fuck: Virtual Gangstas in the Era of State Violence, *Cultural Studies ↔ Critical Methodologies* 9(2): 248–272.

Lessnoff, M. ed. 1990. *Social Contract Theory*. New York: New York University Press.

Lévi-Strauss, C. 1955. The Structural Study of Myth. *The Journal of American Folklore* 68(270): 428–444.

Locke, John. 1689 [1988]. *Two Treatises of Government*. Cambridge Texts in the History of Political Thought (Peter Laslett, editor). Cambridge, UK: Cambridge University Press.

Lorde, A. 1984. *Sister Outsider: Essays and Speeches*. Trumansbury: Crossing Press.

Lukes, S. 2005. *Power: A Radical View*. Basingstoke; New York: Palgrave Macmillan.

Machiavelli, N. 1532 [2019]. *The Prince*. Cambridge Texts in the history of political thought, Q. Skinner and R. Price, eds. Cambridge, UK: Cambridge University Press.

MacIntyre, A. 1967 [2010]. *A Short History of Ethics*. Abingdon, UK: Routledge Classics.

MacKinnon, C. 1993. Crimes of War, Crimes of Peace. *UCLA Women's Law Journal*, 4: 59–86.

MacKinnon, C. 2006. Women's September 11th: Rethinking the International Law of Conflict. *Harvard International Law Journal*, 47(1): 1–32.

MacKinnon, C. 2008. The ICTR's Legacy on Sexual Violence. *New England Journal of International and Comparative Law*, 14(2): 101–110.

Malik, K. 2014. *The Quest for a Moral Compass: A Global History of Ethics*. London: Atlantic Books.

Malik, N. 2019. *We Need New Stories: Challenging the Toxic Myths Behind Our Age of Discontent*. London: Weidenfeld & Nicolson Publishing.

Mamdani, M. 2010. Responsibility to Protect or Right to Punish? *Journal of Intervention and Statebuilding*, 4(1): 53–67.

Marazzi, C. 1995. Money in the World Crisis: The New Basis of Capitalist Power, in W. Bonefeld and J. Holloway (eds) *Global Power, National State, and the Politics of Money*, Basingstoke: Macmillan, 69–91.

Marsh S., Mohdin A., and McIntyre, N. 2019. 'Homophobia and Transphobic Crimes Surge in England and Wales'. *The Guardian*.

Martínez Alier, J. 2003. *The Environmentalism of the Poor: A Study of Ecological Conflicts and Valuation*, Cheltenham: Edward Elgar.

Marx, K. 2000. *Marx: Selected Writings*. Edited by D. McLellan. Rev. edn. Oxford: Oxford University Press.

Marx, K. 2004 [1867]. *Capital: Volume I*, London: Penguin.

Marx, K. 2005. *Grundrisse: Foundations of the Critique of Political Economy*, London: Penguin.

Mauss, M. 1990 [1990]. *The Gift: Forms and Functions of Exchange in Archaic Societies*, Abingdon: Routledge.

Maxmen, A. 2018. 'Migrants and refugees are good for economies', *Nature*, 20 June: https://www.nature.com/articles/d41586-018-05507-0.

Mazzucato, M. 2013. *The Entrepreneurial State: Debunking Public vs. Private Sector Myths*, London: Anthem Books.

McNeill, J. R. 2014. *The Great Acceleration: An Environmental History of the Anthropocene since 1945*, Cambridge: Harvard University Press.

Meagher, K. 2019. Working in Chains: African Informal Workers and Global Value Chains. *Agrarian South: Journal of Political Economy*, 8(1–2): 64–92.

Micklethwait, J., and Wooldridge, A. 2014. *The Fourth Revolution: The Global Race to Reinvent the State*. New York: Penguin Books.

Milanovic, B. 2019. *Capitalism Alone: The Future of the System that Rules the World*, Cambridge, MA: Belknap Press.

Mills, C. W. 1997. *The Racial Contract*. Ithaca, NY: Cornell University Press.

Mills, C. W. 2011. *The Racial Contract*. Nachdr. Ithaca, NY: Cornell University Press.

Ming, Dong Gu. 2016. Confucian Ethics and the Spirit of World Order: A reconception of the Chinese way of tolerance. *Philosophy East and West*, 66(3): 787–804.

Misri D. 2014 *Beyond Partition: Gender, Violence, and Representation in Postcolonial India*. Urbana: University of Illinois Press.

Mitchell, T. 2011. *Carbon Democracy: Political Power in the Age of Oil*, London: Verso.

Mittelman, J. 2000. *The Globalization Syndrome: Transformation and Resistance*, Princeton: Princeton University Press.

Mohdin, A. 2020. 'RMT salutes worker who overturned racist recruitment at Euston station'. *The Guardian*. 15 August: https://www.theguardian.com/world/2020/aug/15/union-leaders-remember.

Moreno-Ocampo, L. 2010. 'Prosecutor, Int'l Criminal Court, Keynote Address at Council on Foreign Relations 6' (4 Feb. 2010) Transcript available at: http://i.cfr.org/content/publications/attachments/MorenoOcampo.CFR.2.4.2010.pdf.

Morgenthau, H. 1940. Positivism, Functionalism, and International Law. *The American Journal of International Law*, 34: 260–284.

Morgenthau, H. 1948. The Twilight of International Morality. *Ethics*. 58(2): 79–99.

Morgenthau, H. J. 1978 *Politics Among Nations: The Struggle for Power and Peace*, 5th edn, revised. New York: Alfred A. Knopf.

Morgenthau, H. 1985. *Politics Among Nations: The Struggle for Power and Peace*. New York: Alfred A. Knopf.

Morrissey, J. 2013. The Imperial Present: Geography, Imperialism, and its Continued Effects, in Johnson N. J., Schein R., and Winders J. (eds) *The Wiley-Blackwell Companion to Cultural Geography*: 591–606.

Muppidi, H. 2012 *The Colonial Signs of International Relations*. London: Hurst.

Murove, M. F. 2012. Ubuntu. *Diogenes*. 59(3–4): 36–47.

Murphy, H. 2018. '"Bitcoin whales" control third of market with $37.5bn holdings', *Financial Times*, 9 June 2018: https://www.ft.com/content/c4b68aec-6b26-11e8-8cf3-0c230fa67aec.

Nair, S. 1999. Colonial 'Others' and Nationalist Politics in Malaysia. Akademika, 54(1): 55–79.

Nisancioglu, K. 2019. Racial sovereignty. *European Journal of International Relations*, 135406611988299. DOI: 10.1177/1354066119882991.

Nkrumah, K. 1965. *Neo-Colonialism: The Last Stage of Imperialism*, New York: International.

Norton, A. 2017. 'Automation and Inequality: The Changing World of Work in the Global South', *Issue Paper*, August, London: International Institute for Environment and Development: https://pubs.iied.org/pdfs/11506IIED.pdf.

Ntibagirirwa, S. 2017. Ubuntu as a Metaphysical Concept. *The Journal of Value Inquiry*. 52: 113–133.

Nussbaum, M. 2011. *Creating Capabilities*. Cambridge, MA: The Belknap Press.

Nye, J. 2011. *The Future of Power*. New York: Public Affairs.

Oloka-Onyango J., and Tamale, S. 1995 'The Personal is Political', or Why Women's Rights are Indeed Human Rights: An African Perspective on International Feminism. *Human Rights Quarterly*. 17: 691–731.

Orford, A. 1999. Muscular Humanitarianism: Reading the Narratives of the New Interventionism. *European Journal of International Law*. 10(4): 679–711.

Ostry, J., Berg, A., and Tsangarides, C. 2014. Redistribution, Inequality and Growth, *IMF Staff Discussion Note*, SDN/14/02, Washington, DC: The International Monetary Fund.

Owen, J. 2016. 'British Empire: Students should be taught colonialism "not all good", say historians'. *The Independent*. 22 January: https://www.independent.co.uk/news/education/education-news/british-empire-students-should-be-taught-colonialism-not-all-good-say-historians-a6828266.html.

Pateman, C. 1988. *The Sexual Contract*. Cambridge, UK: Polity Press.

Patil, V. 2013. From Patriarchy to Intersectionality: A Transnational Feminist Assessment of How Far We've Really Come. *Signs: Journal of Women in Culture and Society*. 38(4): 847–867.

Patnaik, U. 2018. Revisiting the 'Drain', or Transfers from India to Britain in the Context of Global Diffusion of Capitalism, in S. Chakrabarty and U. Patnaik (eds) *Agrarian and Other Histories: Essays for Binay Bhushan Chaudhuri*, New Delhi: Tulika Books, 277–317.

Persaud, R. B., and Walker, R. B. J. 2001. Apertura: Race in international relations. *Alternatives*, October.

Piketty, T. 2014. *Capital in the Twenty-First Century*, Cambridge, MA: Harvard University Press.

Plato. 1991. *The Republic of Plato*. Translated by A. Bloom. 2nd edn. New York: Basic Books.

Polanyi, K. 2001 [1944]. *The Great Transformation: The Political and Economic Origins of Our Times*, Boston: Beacon Press.

Pomeranz, K. 2000. *The Great Divergence: China, Europe, and the Making of the Modern World Economy*, Princeton, NJ: Princeton University Press.

Popper, K. 2002. *The Open Society and Its Enemies, Volume 1: The Spell of Plato*. London and New York: Routledge.

Quijano, A. 2000. Coloniality of Power and Eurocentrism in Latin America. *International Sociology*. 15(2): 215–232.

Ransby, B. 2018. *Making All Black Lives Matter: Reimagining Freedom in the Twenty-First Century*, Oakland: University of California Press.

Rao, R. 2020. *Out of Time: The Queer Politics of Postcoloniality.* New York: Oxford University Press.

Rao, R. 2004. The Empire Writes Back (to Michael Ignatieff), *Millennium: Journal of International Studies,* 33(1): 145–166.

Rawls, J. 1971. A Theory of Justice. Cambridge, MA: Harvard University Press.

Reeskens, T., and Velasco Aguilar, R. 2020. Being white is a full time job? Explaining skin tone gradients in income in Mexico, *Journal of Ethnic and Migration Studies,* 1–23.

Robinson, J. 2006. *Economic Philosophy,* London: Aldine.

Robinson, N. 2016. Militarism and opposition in the living room: the case of military videogames. *Critical Studies on Security,* 4(3): 255–275.

Rodney, W. 1972. *How Europe Underdeveloped Africa.* London: Bolge-L'Ouverture Publications.

Roodman, D. 2012. 'Think Again: Microfinance', *Foreign Policy,* 1 February: https://foreignpolicy.com/2012/02/01/think-again-microfinance/.

Rossdale, C. 2019. *Resisting Militarism: Direct Action and the Politics of Subversion.* Edinburgh: Edinburgh University Press.

Rousseau, J.-J. 1755 [1999]. Political Economy (Économie politique), in *The Social Contract: A New Translation by Christopher Betts.* Oxford World's Classics. 1–41. Oxford: Oxford University Press.

Rousseau, J.-J. 1762 [1999]. The Social Contract (*Du Contrat Social*), in *The Social Contract: A New Translation by Christopher Betts.* Oxford World's Classics. 43–175. Oxford: Oxford University Press.

Rummel, R. J. 1994 *Death by Government: Genocide and Mass Murder Since 1900.* Abingdon; New York: Routledge.

Rutazibwa, O. U. 2016. From the Everyday to IR: In Defence of the Strategic Use of the R-word, *Postcolonial Studies,* 19(2): 191–200.

Sabaratnam, M. 2020. Is IR Theory White? Racialised Subject-Positioning in Three Canonical Texts. *Millennium: Journal of International Studies.* 49(1): 3–31.

Said, E. W. 1979. *Orientalism.,* 1st Vintage Books edn. New York: Vintage Books.

Said, E. W. 1994. *Culture and Imperialism.,* 1st Vintage Books edn. New York: Vintage Books.

Schmidt, B. 2005. Competing Realist Conceptions of Power. *Millennium: Journal of International Studies.* 33(3): 523–549.

Schumpeter, J. 2006 [1942]. *Capitalism, Socialism and Democracy,* Abingdon: Routledge.

Scott, J. 1985. *Weapons of the Weak: Everyday Forms of Peasant Resistance.* New Haven, CT: Yale University Press.

Scott, J. C. 1989. Everyday Forms of Resistance. *Copenhagen Papers.* 4: 33–62.

Scudder, M. F. 2020. *Beyond Empathy and Inclusion: The Challenge of Listening in Democratic Deliberation.* Oxford: Oxford University Press.

Segal, R. 1995. *The Black Diaspora: Five Centuries of the Black Experience Outside Africa.* New York: Farrar, Straus and Giroux.

Serhan, Y. 2018. 'When Even Legal Residents Face Deportation'. *The Atlantic,* 19 April: https://www.theatlantic.com/international/archive/2018/04/windrush-generation-uk-facing-deportation/558317/.

Shafik, M. 2021. *What We Owe Each Other: A New Social Contract.* London: The Bodley Head Publishing.

Sharman, J. C. 2019. *Empires of the Weak: The Real Story of European Expansion and the Creation of the New World Order.* Princeton, NJ: Princeton University Press.

Shilliam, R. ed. 2011. *International Relations and Non-Western Thought: Imperialism, Colonialism, and Investigations of Global Modernity.* Interventions. Abingdon, Oxon; New York: Routledge.

Shilliam, R. 2012. Civilization and the poetics of slavery. *Thesis Eleven* 108(1): 99–117.

Shilliam, R. 2014. 'Black Academia 1.2': https://robbieshilliam.wordpress.com/2016/07/10/black-academia-1-2/.

Shilliam, R. 2018. *Race and the Undeserving Poor: From Abolition to Brexit.* Newcastle: Agenda.

Shilliam, R. 2020. Race and racism in international relations: retrieving a scholarly inheritance. *International Politics Reviews,* 8: 152–195.

Simatei T. 2005. Colonial Violence, Postcolonial Violations: Violence, Landscape, and Memory in Kenyan Fiction. *Research in African Literatures,* 36: 85–94.

Singer, P. 2009. *The Life You Can Save: Acting Now to End World Poverty.* New York: Random House.

Skinner, Q. 2007. What is the State? The question that will not go away. Dr Lee See Inaugural Lecture, Cambridge UK, 24 October 2007. Full lecture available at: https://vimeo.com/14979551.

Slaughter, A. 2004. *A New World Order.* Princeton and Oxford: Princeton University Press.

Slaven, M., and Haydon, J. 2020. Crisis, deliberation, and Extinction Rebellion. *Critical Studies on Security* 8(1): 59–62.

Smith, A. 1982 [1776]. *The Wealth of Nations, Books I–III,* London: Penguin.

Smith, J. 2020. *Smart Machines and Service Work: Automation in an Age of Stagnation.* Chicago: University of Chicago Press.

SOAS, Decolonising Working Group 2018. Learning and Teaching Toolkit: https://blogs.soas.ac.uk/decolonisingsoas/files/2018/10/Decolonising-SOAS-Learning-and-Teaching-Toolkit-AB.pdf.

Solomon, T. 2012. Human Nature and the Limits of the Self: Hans Morgenthau on Love and Power. *International Studies Review*, 14: 201–224.

Srnicek, N. 2016. *Platform Capitalism*. Cambridge: Polity Press.

Srnicek, N., and Williams, A. 2015. *Inventing the Future: Postcapitalism and a World Without Work*. London: Verso.

Staton-Taiwo. 2004. The Effect of Cooper's *A Voice from the South* on W. E. B. Du Bois's *Souls* and *Black Flame* Trilogy. *Philosophia Africana*, 7(2): 59–80.

Stiglitz, J. 2012. *The Price of Inequality: How Today's Divided Society Endangers Our Future*, New York: W.W. Norton & Co.

Stone, D. 2017. *Concentration Camps: A Short History*. Oxford: Oxford University Press.

Strange, S. 1989. I never meant to be an academic, in J. Kruzel and J. N. Rosenau (eds) *Journeys through World Politics: Autobiographical Reflections of Thirty-four Academic Travelers*, New York: Lexington Books, 429–443.

Strange, S. 1996. *The Retreat of the State: The Diffusion of Power in the World Economy*, Cambridge: Cambridge University Press.

Taylor, J. 2012. 'Government admits Kenyans were tortured and sexually abused by colonial forces during Mau Mau uprising'. *The Independent*, 17 July: https://www.independent.co.uk/news/world/africa/government-admits-kenyans-were-tortured-and-sexually-abused-colonial-forces-during-mau-mau-uprising-7953300.html.

Teschke, B. 2003. *The Myth of 1648: Class, Geopolitics, and the Making of Modern International Relations*. London: Verso Books.

Teschke, B., and Wenten, F. 2016. Capitalism, in F. Berenskoetter (ed.) *Concepts in World Politics*, London: Sage, 157–179.

Thakur, V., Davis, A. E., and Vale, P. 2017. Imperial Mission, 'Scientific' Method: an Alternative Account of the Origins of IR, *Millennium: Journal of International Studies*, 46(1): 3–23.

The Week Staff, 2020. 'Winston Churchill: antifascist hero or racist warmonger – or both?' *The Week*, 9 June: https://www.theweek.co.uk/62209/winston-churchill-british-antifascist-hero-or-racist-warmongering-villain.

Thiong'o, N. W. 1986. *Decolonising the Mind: The Politics of Language in African Literature*. London: Portsmouth, N.H: J. Currey; Heinemann.

Thomas C. 2011. Why don't we talk about 'violence' in International Relations? *Review of International Studies* 37: 1815–1836.

Thompson, E. P. 1971. The Moral Economy of the English Crowd in the 18th Century, *Past & Present*, 50(1): 76–136.

Tricontinental: Institute for Social Research 2019. *The Rate of Exploitation: The Case of the iPhone*, Notebook No. 2: https://www.thetricontinental.org/wp-content/uploads/2019/09/190928_Notebook-2_EN_Final_Web.pdf.

Tronto, J. 2013. *Caring Democracy: Markets, Equality and Justice*. New York: New York University Press.

Trump, D. 2017. 'Inaugural Address', transcript, *The Miller Center*, 20 January, viewed 10 March 2021: https://millercenter.org/the-presidency/presidential-speeches/january-20-2017-inaugural-address.

Truth, S. 2015. 'Sojourner's Words and Music'. *Sojourner Truth Memorial*, viewed 21 June 2017: http://sojournertruthmemorial.org/sojourner-truth/her-words/.

Van de Sande, M. 2013. The Prefigurative Politics of Tahrir Square: An Alternative Perspective on the 2011 Revolutions, *Res Publica*, 19(3): 223–239.

Veblen, T. 1994 [1899]. *The Theory of the Leisure Class: An Economic Study in the Evolution of Institution*. London: Penguin.

Veracini, L. 2010. *Settler Colonialism: A Theoretical Overview*. Basingstoke; New York: Palgrave Macmillan.

Veracini, L. 2011. Introducing settler colonial studies. *Settler Colonial Studies* 1(1): 1–12.

Villalba, U. 2013. Buen Vivir vs. Development: A Paradigm Shift in the Andes? *Third World Quarterly* 34(8): 1427–1442.

Villarreal, M., and Echart Muñoz, E. 2020. Extractivism and Resistance in Latin America and the Caribbean, *Open Democracy*, 6 February.

Vincent, R. J. 1982. Race in International Relations, *International Affairs (Royal Institute of International Affairs 1944–)*, 58(4): 658–670.

Vinthagen, S., and Johansson, A. 2013. '"Everyday Resistance": Exploration of a Concept and its Theories'. *Resistance Studies Magazine*. 1: http://resistance-journal.org/wp-content/uploads/2016/04/Vinthagen-Johansson-2013-Everyday-resistance-Concept-Theory.pdf.

Vitalis, R. 2000. The graceful and generous Liberal Gesture: Making racism invisible in American International Relations. Millennium, 29(2): 331–356.

Vitalis, R. 2015. *White World Order, Black Power Politics: The Birth of American International Relations*. Ithaca; London: Cornell University Press).

Vosoughi, S., Roy, D., and Aral, S. 2018. The Spread of true and false news online. *Science* 356, 9 March 2018: 1146–1151.

Wada, Y. 2014. Relational Care Ethics from a Comparative Perspective: The Ethics of Care and Confucian Ethics. *Ethics and Social Welfare*. 8(4): 350–363.

Wade, Robert H. 2017. Global growth, inequality, and poverty: the globalization argument and the 'political' science of economics, in John Ravenhill (ed.) *Global Political Economy*, Oxford: Oxford University Press, 319–355.

Wallerstein, I. 1976. *The Modern World System: Capitalist Agriculture and the Origins of the European World-Economy in the Sixteenth Century*. New York: Academic Press.

Waltz. K. 1979. *Theory of International Politics*. Reading, Massachusetts: Addison-Wesley Publishing Company.

Warner, G. 2020. '"Rough Translation": The Controversial Dutch Character Black Pete'. NPR: https://www.npr.org/2020/06/30/885141871/rough-translation-the-controversial-dutch-character-black-pete?t=1647440306205.

Weber, C. 2020. *International Relations Theory: A Critical Introduction*. 5th edn. London and New York: Routledge.

Weber, M. 1978 [1922]. *Economy and Society: An Outline of Interpretive Sociology*. Ed. G. Roth and C. Wittich. Berkeley: University of California Press.

Weber M., Gerth H., and Mills C. W. 2015 *From Max Weber: Essays in Sociology*. Routledge.

Westwell, E., and Bunting, J. 2020. The regenerative culture of Extinction Rebellion: self-care, people care, planet care. *Environmental Politics*. 29(3): 546–551.

White, N. 2022 'Just 1% of UK professors are Black, new figures reveal', *The Independent*, 1 February: https://www.independent.co.uk/news/uk/home-news/uk-professors-black-government-figures-b2004891.html.

Wight, M. 1960. Why is there no international theory? *International Relations*. 2(1): 35–48.

Wilkinson, R., and Pickett, K. 2010. *The Spirit Level: Why Equality Is Better for Everyone*, London: Allen Lane.

Williams P., and Chrisman L. eds. 1994 *Colonial Discourse and Post-Colonial Theory: A Reader*. New York: Columbia University Press.

Wilson, P. 2003. *The International Theory of Leonard Woolf: A Study in Twentieth-Century Idealism*. New York: Palgrave Macmillan.

Wolin, S. 1994. Fugitive Democracy. *Constellations: An International Journal of Critical and Democratic Theory*. 1(1): 11–25.

Women's Budget Group 2018. 'The Impact of Austerity on Women', 3 December: https://wbg.org.uk/resources/the-impact-of-austerity-on-women/.

World Bank 2020. *World Development Report 2020: Trading for Development in the Age of Global Value Chains*, Washington, DC: The World Bank.

YouGov 2020. 'How Unique Are British Attitudes to Empire?': https://yougov.co.uk/topics/international/articles-reports/2020/03/11/how-unique-are-british-attitudes-empire.

Younis, M. 2018. Race, the World and Time: Haiti, Liberia and Ethiopia (1914–1945), *Millennium: Journal of International Studies*, 46(3): 352–370.

Yu, V. 2020. '"The anger is still there": Hong Kong defiant a year on from first protests'. 7 June: https://www.theguardian.com/world/2020/jun/07/anger-still-there-hong-kong-defiant-one-year-anniversary-first-protests-china.

Xi, Jinping. 2014. 'Xi Jinping's Speech in Commemoration of the 2,565th Anniversary of Confucius' Birth'. *Speech delivered to the 5th Congress of the International Confucian Association, 24th September, 2014*. Full text available at: http://library.chinausfocus.com/article-1534.html.

Zevin, A. 2019. *Liberalism at Large: The World According to the Economist*, London: Verso.

Zhang, Feng. 2015. Confucian Foreign Policy Traditions in Chinese History. *The Chinese Journal of International Politics*, 8(2): 197–218.

Zhu, Han, and Jun, Lu. 2021. The Crackdown on Rights-Advocacy in Xi's China: Politicizing the Law and Legalizing the Repression. *Journal of Contemporary China*, DOI: 10.1080/10670564.2021.1985829.

Žižek, S. 2009. *Violence: Six Sideways Reflections*. London: Profile Books.

Zucman, G. 2015. *The Hidden Wealth of Nations: The Scourge of Tax Havens*. Chicago: University of Chicago Press.

INDEX